SPURGEON *AND* *THE* GOSPELS

PRESENTED TO

BY

DATE

OCCASION

SPURGEON *AND* THE GOSPELS

SPURGEON *AND* *THE* GOSPELS

THOMAS NELSON
NKJV

THOMAS NELSON
Since 1798

www.ThomasNelson.com

NKJV Spurgeon and the Gospels

Library of Congress Control Number:

Published in Nashville, TN, by Thomas Nelson, a registered trademark of HarperCollins Christian Publishing, Inc.

Charles H. Spurgeon material compiled by Geoff Chang, PhD, and Matthew Warren, ThM.

Printed in India

25 26 27 28 29 30 31 32 /BPI/ 9 8 7 6 5 4 3 2 1

CONTENTS

Preface to the New King James Version® ix
Introduction xi

Matthew 1
Mark 111
Luke..177
John..283

Bibliography 367

PREFACE TO THE NEW KING JAMES VERSION®

To understand the heart behind the New King James Version, one need look no further than the stated intentions of the original King James scholars: "Not to make a new translation . . . but to make a good one better." The New King James Version is a continuation of the labors of the King James translators, unlocking for today's readers the spiritual treasures found especially in the Authorized Version of the Holy Bible.

While seeking to maintain the excellent *form* of the traditional English Bible, special care has also been taken to preserve the work of *precision* which is the legacy of the King James translators.

Where new translation has been necessary, the most complete representation of the original has been rendered by considering the definition and usage of the Hebrew words in their contexts. This translation principle, known as *complete equivalence*, seeks to preserve accurately all of the information in the text while presenting it in good literary form.

In addition to accuracy, the translators have also sought to maintain those lyrical and devotional qualities that are so highly regarded in the King James Version. The thought flow and selection of phrases from the King James Version have been preserved wherever possible without sacrificing clarity.

The format of the New King James Version is designed to enhance the vividness, devotional quality, and usefulness of the Bible. Words or phrases in italics indicate expressions in the original language that require clarification by additional English words, as was done in the King James Version. Poetry is structured as verse to reflect the form and beauty of the passage in the original language. The covenant name of God was usually translated from the Hebrew as LORD or GOD, using capital letters as shown, as in the King James Version. This convention is also maintained in the New King James Version when the Old Testament is quoted in the New.

The Hebrew text used for the Old Testament is the 1967/1977 Stuttgart edition of the *Biblia Hebraica*, with frequent comparisons to the Bomberg edition of 1524–1525. Ancient versions and the Dead Sea Scrolls were consulted, but the Hebrew is followed wherever possible.

The textual notes in the New King James Version make no evaluation, but objectively present the facts about variant readings.

INTRODUCTION

Charles Haddon Spurgeon (1834–1892) was the most famous preacher of the nineteenth century. Whenever people asked him the secret to his ministry, he had one answer: "We know that the greatest crowd in London has been held together these thirty years by nothing but the preaching of Christ crucified." Spurgeon was captivated by the Person and work of Jesus Christ and devoted his life to making Him known. It is no surprise that the Gospels were particularly dear to him. He preached and published hundreds of sermons from them throughout his life.

Underlying these sermons was a deep fellowship with Christ. In the last two years of Spurgeon's life, he worked on one last project: a commentary on Matthew. Though his wife urged him to rest, he would spend his final days communing with his Savior. She wrote,

> Much of the later portion of the work . . . was written on the very border-land of heaven, amid the nearing glories of the unseen world, and almost "within sight of the golden gates." Such words acquire a solemnity and pathos with which nothing else could invest them. We listen almost as to a voice "from the excellent glory."

This devotion presents a short passage from Spurgeon's sermons and writings for each chapter of the four Gospels to aid us in our meditation on Christ. As we listen to a voice "from the excellent glory," may we also be captivated by the Savior.

MATTHEW

MATTHEW 1

THE BIRTH OF JESUS CHRIST

The portion before us looks like a string of names, and we might fancy that it would yield us little spiritual food; but we may not think lightly of any line of the inspired volume. Here the Spirit sets before us the pedigree of Jesus and sketches the family tree of the "King of the Jews" (Matt. 2:2). Marvelous condescension that He should be a Man and have a genealogy, even He who was in the beginning with God (John 1:1) and "did not consider it robbery to be equal with God" (Phil. 2:6)! Let us read each line of "the book of the genealogy" with adoring gratitude that we have a King who is one with us in our nature.

Scriptural names, as a general rule, contain teaching, and especially is this the case in every name ascribed to the Lord Jesus. The Old Testament gave the coming Messiah the name Immanuel, translated into the Gentile tongue as "God with us," being interpreted that we may know that we are invited, that we are welcome, that God has seen our necessities and has provided for us and that now we may freely come, even we who were sinners of the Gentiles and far off from God. In the New Testament, He is named Jesus but not without a reason. By any other name Jesus would not be so sweet because no other name could fairly describe His great work of saving His people from their sins.

---

1 The book of the [a]genealogy of Jesus Christ, [b]the Son of Da-
vid, [c]the Son of Abraham:
2 [a]Abraham begot Isaac, [b]Isaac begot Jacob, and Jacob be-
got [c]Judah and his brothers.
3 [a]Judah begot Perez and Zerah by Tamar, [b]Perez begot Hez-
ron, and Hezron begot Ram.
4 Ram begot Amminadab, Amminadab begot Nahshon, and
Nahshon begot Salmon.
5 Salmon begot [a]Boaz by Rahab, Boaz begot Obed by Ruth,
Obed begot Jesse,
6 and [a]Jesse begot David the king.
[b]David the king begot Solomon by her *who had been the*
wife[1] of Uriah.
7 [a]Solomon begot Rehoboam, Rehoboam begot [b]Abijah,
and Abijah begot Asa.[1]
8 Asa begot [a]Jehoshaphat, Jehoshaphat begot Joram, and
Joram begot [b]Uzziah.

1:1[a]Luke 3:23 [b]John 7:42 [c]Gen. 12:3; 22:18 1:2[a]Gen. 21:2, 12 [b]Gen. 25:26; 28:14 [c]Gen. 29:35 1:3[a]Gen. 38:27; 49:10 [b]Ruth 4:18–22 1:5[a]Ruth 2:1; 4:1–13 1:6[a]1 Sam. 16:1 [b]2 Sam. 7:12; 12:24 [1]Words in italic type have been added for clarity. They are not found in the original Greek. 1:7[a]1 Chr. 3:10 [b]2 Chr. 11:20 [1]NU-Text reads *Asaph.* 1:8[a]1 Chr. 3:10 [b]2 Kin. 15:13

9 Uzziah begot Jotham, Jotham begot [a]Ahaz, and Ahaz be-
got Hezekiah.
10 [a]Hezekiah begot Manasseh, Manasseh begot Amon,[1] and
Amon begot [b]Josiah.
11 [a]Josiah begot Jeconiah and his brothers about the time
they were [b]carried away to Babylon.
12 And after they were brought to Babylon, [a]Jeconiah begot
Shealtiel, and Shealtiel begot [b]Zerubbabel.
13 Zerubbabel begot Abiud, Abiud begot Eliakim, and Elia-
kim begot Azor.
14 Azor begot Zadok, Zadok begot Achim, and Achim begot
Eliud.
15 Eliud begot Eleazar, Eleazar begot Matthan, and Matthan
begot Jacob.
16 And Jacob begot Joseph the husband of [a]Mary, of whom
was born Jesus who is called Christ.
17 So all the generations from Abraham to David *are* four-
teen generations, from David until the captivity in Babylon
are fourteen generations, and from the captivity in Babylon
until the Christ *are* fourteen generations.
18 Now the [a]birth of Jesus Christ was as follows: After His
mother Mary was betrothed to Joseph, before they came to-
gether, she was found with child [b]of the Holy Spirit.
19 Then Joseph her husband, being a just *man,* and not want-
ing [a]to make her a public example, was minded to put her
away secretly.
20 But while he thought about these things, behold, an an-
gel of the Lord appeared to him in a dream, saying, "Joseph,
son of David, do not be afraid to take to you Mary your wife,
[a]for that which is conceived in her is of the Holy Spirit.
21 [a]"And she will bring forth a Son, and you shall call His
name JESUS, [b]for He will save His people from their sins."
22 So all this was done that it might be fulfilled which was
spoken by the Lord through the prophet, saying:
23 [a]"Behold, the virgin shall be with child, and bear a Son,
and they shall call His name Immanuel,"[1] which is translat-
ed, "God with us."
24 Then Joseph, being aroused from sleep, did as the angel
of the Lord commanded him and took to him his wife,
25 and did not know her till she had brought forth [a]her first-
born Son.[1] And he called His name JESUS.

1:9 [a]2 Kin. 15:38 1:10 [a]2 Kin. 20:21 [b]1 Kin. 13:2 [1]NU-Text reads *Amos.* 1:11 [a]1 Chr. 3:15, 16 [b]2 Kin. 24:14–16 1:12 [a]1 Chr. 3:17 [b]Ezra 3:2 1:16 [a]Matt. 13:55 1:18 [a]Luke 1:27 [b]Luke 1:35 1:19 [a]Deut. 24:1 1:20 [a]Luke 1:35 1:21 [a]Luke 1:31; 2:21 [b]John 1:29 1:23 [a]Is. 7:14 [1]Isaiah 7:14 1:25 [a]Luke 2:7, 21 [1]NU-Text reads *a Son.*

MATTHEW 2

THE WISE MEN AND HEROD

The incarnation of the Son of God was one of the greatest events in the history of the universe. Its actual occurrence was not, however, known to all mankind but was specially revealed to the shepherds of Bethlehem and to certain wise men of the East. To shepherds—the illiterate men little versed in human learning—the angels in choral song made known the birth of the Savior, Christ the Lord, and they hastened to Bethlehem to see the great sight. The scribes, the writers of the law and expounders of it, knew nothing concerning the long-promised birth of the Messiah.

The glad tidings were made known also to wise men, magi, students of the stars and of old prophetic books from the far-off east. It would not be possible to tell how far off their native country lay; it may have been so distant that the journey occupied nearly the whole of the two years of which they spoke concerning the appearance of the star. Both in shepherds and in Eastern magi gathering around the young Child, I see God dispensing His favors as He wills.

Sovereignty in these cases clothed itself in the robes of mercy. It was great mercy that regarded the low estate of the shepherds, and it was far-reaching mercy that gathered from lands that lay in darkness a company of men made wise unto salvation.

1 Now after [a]Jesus was born in Bethlehem of Judea in the
days of Herod the king, behold, wise men [b]from the East came
to Jerusalem,
2 saying, [a]"Where is He who has been born King of the Jews?
For we have seen [b]His star in the East and have come to worship Him."
3 When Herod the king heard *this,* he was troubled, and all
Jerusalem with him.
4 And when he had gathered all [a]the chief priests and [b]scribes
of the people together, [c]he inquired of them where the Christ
was to be born.
5 So they said to him, "In Bethlehem of Judea, for thus it is
written by the prophet:

6 'But[a] you, Bethlehem, *in* the land of Judah,
Are not the least among the rulers of Judah;
For out of you shall come a Ruler
[b]Who will shepherd My people Israel.'"[1]

2:1[a]Mic. 5:2; Luke 2:4 [b]Gen. 25:6 2:2[a]Luke 2:11 [b][Num. 24:17] 2:4[a]2 Chr. 36:14 [b]2 Chr. 34:13 [c]Mal. 2:7 2:6[a]Mic. 5:2 [b][Rev. 2:27] [1]Micah 5:2

7 Then Herod, when he had secretly called the wise men,
determined from them what time the [a]star appeared.
8 And he sent them to Bethlehem and said, "Go and search
carefully for the young Child, and when you have found *Him,*
bring back word to me, that I may come and worship Him
also."
9 When they heard the king, they departed; and behold, the
star which they had seen in the East went before them, till it
came and stood over where the young Child was.
10 When they saw the star, they rejoiced with exceedingly
great joy.
11 And when they had come into the house, they saw the
young Child with Mary His mother, and fell down and wor-
shiped Him. And when they had opened their treasures, [a]they
presented gifts to Him: gold, frankincense, and myrrh.
12 Then, being divinely warned [a]in a dream that they should
not return to Herod, they departed for their own country an-
other way.
13 Now when they had departed, behold, an angel of the Lord
appeared to Joseph in a dream, saying, "Arise, take the young
Child and His mother, flee to Egypt, and stay there until I bring
you word; for Herod will seek the young Child to destroy Him."
14 When he arose, he took the young Child and His mother
by night and departed for Egypt,
15 and was there until the death of Herod, that it might be
fulfilled which was spoken by the Lord through the prophet,
saying, [a]"Out of Egypt I called My Son."[1]
16 Then Herod, when he saw that he was deceived by the
wise men, was exceedingly angry; and he sent forth and put
to death all the male children who were in Bethlehem and
in all its districts, from two years old and under, according
to the time which he had determined from the wise men.
17 Then was fulfilled what was spoken by Jeremiah the proph-
et, saying:

> 18 "A [a]voice was heard in Ramah,
> Lamentation, weeping, and great mourning,
> Rachel weeping *for* her children,
> Refusing to be comforted,
> Because they are no more."[1]

19 Now when Herod was dead, behold, an angel of the Lord
appeared in a dream to Joseph in Egypt,
20 [a]saying, "Arise, take the young Child and His mother,
and go to the land of Israel, for those who [b]sought the young
Child's life are dead."

2:7[a] Num. 24:17 2:11[a] Is. 60:6 2:12[a] Matt. 1:20 2:15[a] Hos. 11:1 [1] Hosea 11:1
2:18[a] Jer. 31:15 [1] Jeremiah 31:15 2:20[a] Luke 2:39 [b] Matt. 2:16

21 Then he arose, took the young Child and His mother, and
came into the land of Israel.
22 But when he heard that Archelaus was reigning over
Judea instead of his father Herod, he was afraid to go there.
And being warned by God in a [a]dream, he turned aside [b]into
the region of Galilee.
23 And he came and dwelt in a city called [a]Nazareth, that it
might be fulfilled [b]which was spoken by the prophets, "He
shall be called a Nazarene."

2:22 [a]Matt. 2:12, 13, 19 [b]Luke 2:39 2:23 [a]John 1:45, 46 [b]Judg. 13:5

MATTHEW 3

JOHN THE BAPTIST PREPARES THE WAY

Matthew keeps to his custom of quoting from the Old Testament. The prophets described not only the King but His forerunner also. They mention the character of this harbinger: he was a "voice"; his tone, "crying"; his place, "in the wilderness"; and his message, which was one of announcement in which he required preparation for the coming King: "Prepare the way of the LORD." Men's hearts were like a wilderness wherein there is no way, but as loyal subjects throw up roads for the approach of beloved princes, so were men to welcome the Lord with their hearts made right and ready to receive Him.

He will find a people in the slums if His gospel is rejected by the respectable. Let none of us, because we are orthodox or exceedingly scriptural in our religious observances, dream that we must therefore be in the favor of God and that we are under no necessity to repent. God can do without us, but we cannot do without repentance and the works that prove it true.

O Lord, I would welcome You if You would come to me. I have great need of Your royal presence, and therefore I would prepare a way for You. Into my heart my desires have made for You a path most short and smooth. Come, Lord, and tarry not! Come into my wilderness nature, and transform it into a garden of the Lord.

---

1 In those days [a]John the Baptist came preaching [b]in the
wilderness of Judea,
2 and saying, "Repent, for [a]the kingdom of heaven is at hand!"
3 For this is he who was spoken of by the prophet Isaiah,
saying:

> [a]"The voice of one crying in the wilderness:
> [b]'Prepare the way of the LORD;
> Make His paths straight.'"[1]

4 Now [a]John himself was clothed in camel's hair, with a
leather belt around his waist; and his food was [b]locusts and
[c]wild honey.
5 [a]Then Jerusalem, all Judea, and all the region around the
Jordan went out to him
6 [a]and were baptized by him in the Jordan, confessing their
sins.
7 But when he saw many of the Pharisees and Sadducees

3:1 [a]Mark 1:3–8 [b]Josh. 14:10 3:2 [a]Dan. 2:44 3:3 [a]Is. 40:3 [b]Luke 1:76 [1]Isaiah 40:3
3:4 [a]Mark 1:6 [b]Lev. 11:22 [c]1 Sam. 14:25, 26 3:5 [a]Mark 1:5 3:6 [a]Acts 19:4, 18

coming to his baptism, he said to them, [a]"Brood of vipers!
Who warned you to flee from [b]the wrath to come?
8 "Therefore bear fruits worthy of repentance,
9 "and do not think to say to yourselves, [a]'We have Abraham
as *our* father.' For I say to you that God is able to raise up chil-
dren to Abraham from these stones.
10 "And even now the ax is laid to the root of the trees. [a]There-
fore every tree which does not bear good fruit is cut down
and thrown into the fire.
11 [a]"I indeed baptize you with water unto repentance, but
He who is coming after me is mightier than I, whose sandals
I am not worthy to carry. [b]He will baptize you with the Holy
Spirit and fire.[1]
12 [a]"His winnowing fan *is* in His hand, and He will thorough-
ly clean out His threshing floor, and gather His wheat into
the barn; but He will [b]burn up the chaff with unquenchable
fire."
13 [a]Then Jesus came [b]from Galilee to John at the Jordan to
be baptized by him.
14 And John *tried to* prevent Him, saying, "I need to be bap-
tized by You, and are You coming to me?"
15 But Jesus answered and said to him, "Permit *it to be so*
now, for thus it is fitting for us to fulfill all righteousness."
Then he allowed Him.
16 [a]When He had been baptized, Jesus came up immediate-
ly from the water; and behold, the heavens were opened to
Him, and He[1] saw [b]the Spirit of God descending like a dove
and alighting upon Him.
17 [a]And suddenly a voice *came* from heaven, saying, [b]"This
is My beloved Son, in whom I am well pleased."

3:7[a]Matt. 12:34 [b][1 Thess. 1:10] 3:9[a]John 8:33 3:10[a]Matt. 7:19 3:11[a]Luke 3:16 [b][Acts 2:3, 4] [1]M-Text omits *and fire.* 3:12[a]Mal. 3:3 [b]Matt. 13:30 3:13[a]Mark 1:9–11 [b]Matt. 2:22 3:16[a]Mark 1:10 [b][Is. 11:2]; John 1:32 [1]Or *he* 3:17[a]John 12:28 [b]Ps. 2:7

MATTHEW 4

THE TEMPTATION OF JESUS

He now began to call one and another into His service. He was "walking by the Sea," and there and then He began His converting, calling, and ordaining work. Where He found Himself living, there He put forth His power. Our sphere is where we are.

Jesus had a special eye for fishers. He summoned to His side the fishing brothers whom He had chosen from of old. He had previously called them by grace, and now He calls them into the ministry. They were busy in a lawful occupation when He called them to be ministers: our Lord calls not idlers but fishers. His word was imperial—"Follow Me." His work was appropriate to their occupation as fishers; it was full of royal promise—"I will make you fishers of men"—and it was eminently instructive, for an evangelist and a fisher have many points of likeness. From this passage we learn that nobody can make a man-fisher but our Lord Himself, and those whom He calls can become successful only by following Him.

The call was effectual. No nets can entangle those whom Jesus calls to follow Him. They come straightway; they come at all costs; they come without question; they come to quit old haunts; they come to follow their Leader without stipulation or reserve. Lord, cause me ever to be Your faithful and unhesitating follower as long as I live! May no nets detain me when You call me!

---

1 Then [a]Jesus was led up by [b]the Spirit into the wilderness
to be tempted by the devil.
2 And when He had fasted forty days and forty nights, after-
ward He was hungry.
3 Now when the tempter came to Him, he said, "If You are
the Son of God, command that these stones become bread."
4 But He answered and said, "It is written, [a]'Man shall not
live by bread alone, but by every word that proceeds from
the mouth of God.'"[1]
5 Then the devil took Him up [a]into the holy city, set Him on
the pinnacle of the temple,
6 and said to Him, "If You are the Son of God, throw Yourself
down. For it is written:

> [a]'He shall give His angels charge over you,'

and,

4:1[a]Mark 1:12 [b]Ezek. 3:14 4:4[a]Deut. 8:3 [1]Deuteronomy 8:3
4:5[a]Neh. 11:1, 18 4:6[a]Ps. 91:11

[b]'In *their* hands they shall bear you up,
Lest you dash your foot against a stone.'"[1]

7 Jesus said to him, "It is written again, [a]'You shall not tempt
the LORD your God.'"[1]
8 Again, the devil took Him up on an exceedingly high moun-
tain, and [a]showed Him all the kingdoms of the world and
their glory.
9 And he said to Him, "All these things I will give You if You
will fall down and worship me."
10 Then Jesus said to him, "Away with you,[1] Satan! For it is
written, [a]'You shall worship the LORD your God, and Him
only you shall serve.'"[2]
11 Then the devil [a]left Him, and behold, [b]angels came and
ministered to Him.
12 [a]Now when Jesus heard that John had been put in prison,
He departed to Galilee.
13 And leaving Nazareth, He came and dwelt in Capernaum,
which is by the sea, in the regions of Zebulun and Naphtali,
14 that it might be fulfilled which was spoken by Isaiah the
prophet, saying:

15 "The[a] land of Zebulun and the land of Naphtali,
By the way of the sea, beyond the Jordan,
Galilee of the Gentiles:
16 [a]The people who sat in darkness
have seen a great light,
And upon those who sat in the region
and shadow of death
Light has dawned."[1]

17 [a]From that time Jesus began to preach and to say, [b]"Re-
pent, for the kingdom of heaven is at hand."
18 [a]And Jesus, walking by the Sea of Galilee, saw two brothers,
Simon [b]called Peter, and Andrew his brother, casting a net
into the sea; for they were fishermen.
19 Then He said to them, "Follow Me, and [a]I will make you
fishers of men."
20 [a]They immediately left *their* nets and followed Him.
21 [a]Going on from there, He saw two other brothers, James
the son of Zebedee, and John his brother, in the boat with
Zebedee their father, mending their nets. He called them,
22 and immediately they left the boat and their father, and
followed Him.

4:6[b]Ps. 91:12 [1]Psalm 91:11, 12 4:7[a]Deut. 6:16 [1]Deuteronomy 6:16 4:8[a][1 John 2:15–17] 4:10[a]Deut. 6:13; 10:20 [1]M-Text reads *Get behind Me.* [2]Deuteronomy 6:13 4:11[a][James 4:7] [b][Heb. 1:14] 4:12[a]John 4:43 4:15[a]Is. 9:1, 2 4:16[a]Luke 2:32 [1]Isaiah 9:1, 2 4:17[a]Mark 1:14, 15 [b]Matt. 3:2; 10:7 4:18[a]Mark 1:16–20 [b]John 1:40–42 4:19[a]Luke 5:10 4:20[a]Mark 10:28 4:21[a]Mark 1:19

23 And Jesus went about all Galilee, [a]teaching in their syn-
agogues, preaching [b]the gospel of the kingdom, [c]and heal-
ing all kinds of sickness and all kinds of disease among the
people.
24 Then His fame went throughout all Syria; and they
[a]brought to Him all sick people who were afflicted with var-
ious diseases and torments, and those who were demon-
possessed, epileptics, and paralytics; and He healed them.
25 [a]Great multitudes followed Him—from Galilee, and *from*
Decapolis, Jerusalem, Judea, and beyond the Jordan.

4:23 [a]Matt. 9:35 [b][Matt. 24:14] [c]Mark 1:34 4:24 [a]Luke 4:40 4:25 [a]Mark 3:7, 8

MATTHEW 5

THE BEATITUDES

Bearing in mind the object of our Savior's discourse, which was to describe the saved, we now come to consider the first of the Beatitudes: "Blessed are the poor in spirit, for theirs is the kingdom of heaven." A ladder, if it is to be of any use, must have its first step near the ground, or feeble climbers will never be able to mount. It would have been a grievous discouragement to struggling faith if the first blessing had been given to the pure in heart; to that excellence the young beginner makes no claim while to poverty of spirit he can reach without going beyond his line.

Had the Savior said "Blessed are the rich in grace," He would have spoken a great truth, but very few of us could have derived consolation therefrom. Our divine Instructor begins at the beginning, with the very ABC of experience, and so enables the babes in grace to learn of Him. Had He commenced with higher attainments, He must have left the little ones behind. A gigantic step at the bottom of these sacred stairs would have effectually prevented many from essaying to ascend; but tempted by the lowly step, which bears the inscription "Blessed are the poor in spirit," thousands are encouraged to attempt the heavenly way.

---

1 And seeing the multitudes, [a]He went up on a mountain,
and when He was seated His disciples came to Him.
2 Then He opened His mouth and [a]taught them, saying:

3 "Blessed[a] *are* the poor in spirit,
For theirs is the kingdom of heaven.
4 [a]Blessed *are* those who mourn,
For they shall be comforted.
5 [a]Blessed *are* the meek,
For [b]they shall inherit the earth.
6 Blessed *are* those who [a]hunger and thirst for righteousness,
[b]For they shall be filled.
7 Blessed *are* the merciful,
[a]For they shall obtain mercy.
8 [a]Blessed *are* the pure in heart,
For [b]they shall see God.
9 Blessed *are* the peacemakers,
For they shall be called sons of God.

5:1[a]Mark 3:13 5:2[a][Matt. 7:29] 5:3[a]Luke 6:20–23 5:4[a]Rev. 21:4 5:5[a]Ps. 37:11 [b][Rom. 4:13] 5:6[a]Luke 1:53 [b][Is. 55:1; 65:13] 5:7[a]Ps. 41:1 5:8[a]Ps. 15:2; 24:4 [b]1 Cor. 13:12

10 [a]Blessed *are* those who are persecuted
for righteousness' sake,
For theirs is the kingdom of heaven.

11 [a]Blessed are you when they revile and persecute you, and
say all kinds of [b]evil against you falsely for My sake.
12 [a]"Rejoice and be exceedingly glad, for great *is* your re-
ward in heaven, for [b]so they persecuted the prophets who
were before you.
13 "You are the salt of the earth; [a]but if the salt loses its fla-
vor, how shall it be seasoned? It is then good for nothing but
to be thrown out and trampled underfoot by men.
14 [a]"You are the light of the world. A city that is set on a hill
cannot be hidden.
15 "Nor do they [a]light a lamp and put it under a basket,
but on a lampstand, and it gives light to all *who are* in the
house.
16 "Let your light so shine before men, [a]that they may see
your good works and [b]glorify your Father in heaven.
17 [a]"Do not think that I came to destroy the Law or the Proph-
ets. I did not come to destroy but to fulfill.
18 "For assuredly, I say to you, [a]till heaven and earth pass
away, one jot or one tittle will by no means pass from the law
till all is fulfilled.
19 [a]"Whoever therefore breaks one of the least of these com-
mandments, and teaches men so, shall be called least in the
kingdom of heaven; but whoever does and teaches *them,* he
shall be called great in the kingdom of heaven.
20 "For I say to you, that unless your righteousness exceeds
[a]*the righteousness* of the scribes and Pharisees, you will by
no means enter the kingdom of heaven.
21 "You have heard that it was said to those of old, [a]'You shall
not murder,[1] and whoever murders will be in danger of the
judgment.'
22 "But I say to you that [a]whoever is angry with his brother
without a cause[1] shall be in danger of the judgment. And
whoever says to his brother, [b]'Raca!' shall be in danger of
the council. But whoever says, 'You fool!' shall be in danger
of hell fire.
23 "Therefore [a]if you bring your gift to the altar, and there
remember that your brother has something against you,
24 [a]"leave your gift there before the altar, and go your way.
First be reconciled to your brother, and then come and offer
your gift.

5:10 [a]1 Pet. 3:14 5:11 [a]Luke 6:22 [b]1 Pet. 4:14 5:12 [a]1 Pet. 4:13, 14 [b]Acts 7:52 5:13 [a]Luke 14:34 5:14 [a][John 8:12] 5:15 [a]Luke 8:16 5:16 [a]1 Pet. 2:12 [b][John 15:8] 5:17 [a]Rom. 10:4 5:18 [a]Luke 16:17 5:19 [a][James 2:10] 5:20 [a][Rom. 10:3] 5:21 [a]Ex. 20:13; Deut. 5:17 [1]Exodus 20:13; Deuteronomy 5:17 5:22 [a][1 John 3:15] [b][James 2:20; 3:6] [1]NU-Text omits *without a cause.* 5:23 [a]Matt. 8:4 5:24 [a][Job 42:8]

25 [a]"Agree with your adversary quickly, [b]while you are on the
way with him, lest your adversary deliver you to the judge,
the judge hand you over to the officer, and you be thrown
into prison.
26 "Assuredly, I say to you, you will by no means get out of
there till you have paid the last penny.
27 "You have heard that it was said to those of old,[1] [a]'You
shall not commit adultery.'[2]
28 "But I say to you that whoever [a]looks at a woman to lust
for her has already committed adultery with her in his heart.
29 [a]"If your right eye causes you to sin, [b]pluck it out and
cast *it* from you; for it is more profitable for you that one of
your members perish, than for your whole body to be cast
into hell.
30 "And if your right hand causes you to sin, cut it off and
cast *it* from you; for it is more profitable for you that one of
your members perish, than for your whole body to be cast
into hell.
31 "Furthermore it has been said, [a]'Whoever divorces his
wife, let him give her a certificate of divorce.'
32 "But I say to you that [a]whoever divorces his wife for any
reason except sexual immorality[1] causes her to commit adul-
tery; and whoever marries a woman who is divorced com-
mits adultery.
33 "Again you have heard that [a]it was said to those of old,
[b]'You shall not swear falsely, but [c]shall perform your oaths
to the Lord.'
34 "But I say to you, [a]do not swear at all: neither by heaven,
for it is [b]God's throne;
35 "nor by the earth, for it is His footstool; nor by Jerusalem,
for it is the city of [a]the great King.
36 "Nor shall you swear by your head, because you cannot
make one hair white or black.
37 [a]"But let your 'Yes' be 'Yes,' and your 'No,' 'No.' For what-
ever is more than these is from the evil one.
38 "You have heard that it was said, [a]'An eye for an eye and
a tooth for a tooth.'[1]
39 [a]"But I tell you not to resist an evil person. [b]But whoever
slaps you on your right cheek, turn the other to him also.
40 "If anyone wants to sue you and take away your tunic, let
him have *your* cloak also.
41 "And whoever [a]compels you to go one mile, go with
him two.

5:25[a] Luke 12:58, 59 [b][Is. 55:6] 5:27[a] Ex. 20:14; Deut. 5:18 [1]NU-Text and M-Text omit *to those of old.* [2]Exodus 20:14; Deuteronomy 5:18 5:28[a] Prov. 6:25 5:29[a] Mark 9:43 [b][Col. 3:5] 5:31[a] Deut. 24:1 5:32[a] [Luke 16:18] [1]Or *fornication* 5:33[a] Matt. 23:16 [b]Lev. 19:12 [c]Deut. 23:23 5:34[a] James 5:12 [b]Is. 66:1 5:35[a] Ps. 48:2 5:37[a] [Col. 4:6] 5:38[a] Ex. 21:24; Lev. 24:20; Deut. 19:21 [1]Exodus 21:24; Leviticus 24:20; Deuteronomy 19:21 5:39[a] Luke 6:29 [b]Is. 50:6 5:41[a] Matt. 27:32

42 "Give to him who asks you, and [a]from him who wants to
borrow from you do not turn away.
43 "You have heard that it was said, [a]'You shall love your
neighbor[1] [b]and hate your enemy.'
44 "But I say to you, [a]love your enemies, bless those who
curse you, [b]do good to those who hate you, and pray [c]for
those who spitefully use you and persecute you,[1]
45 "that you may be sons of your Father in heaven; for [a]He
makes His sun rise on the evil and on the good, and sends
rain on the just and on the unjust.
46 [a]"For if you love those who love you, what reward have
you? Do not even the tax collectors do the same?
47 "And if you greet your brethren[1] only, what do you do
more *than others?* Do not even the tax collectors[2] do so?
48 [a]"Therefore you shall be perfect, just [b]as your Father in
heaven is perfect.

5:42 [a]Luke 6:30–34 5:43 [a]Lev. 19:18 [b]Deut. 23:3–6 [1]Compare Leviticus 19:18 5:44 [a]Luke 6:27 [b][Rom. 12:20] [c]Acts 7:60 [1]NU-Text omits three clauses from this verse, leaving, *"But I say to you, love your enemies and pray for those who persecute you."* 5:45 [a]Job 25:3 5:46 [a]Luke 6:32 5:47 [1]M-Text reads *friends.* [2]NU-Text reads *Gentiles.* 5:48 [a][Col. 1:28; 4:12] [b]Eph. 5:1

MATTHEW 6

THE LORD'S PRAYER

The King contrasts the laws of His kingdom with the conduct of the outward religionists in the matters of alms and prayers. Those around our Lord knew what He meant when He alluded to the hypocrite: they had often seen the proud sectary standing in public places repeating his prayers, and very likely they had hitherto felt bound to hold such in repute for superior sanctity. By our Lord's words these hypocrites are unmasked and made to seem what they really are. Our King was wonderfully plainspoken and called both things and persons by their right names.

These religionists were not seekers of God but seekers after popularity—men who twisted even devotion into a means for self-aggrandizement. Repetitions we may have, but not "vain repetitions." Christians' prayers are measured by weight, not by length. This delightful prayer is short, devout, and full of meaning. Its first three petitions are for God and His glory. Our chief prayers to God are to be for His glory.

Do we thus begin with God in prayer? Does not the daily bread often come in before the kingdom? We shall best reach our end of being accepted by Him when we have no regard to the opinion of anyone else. It is the prayer of a lowly and contented mind, of one who is so sanctified that he waits upon God even about his daily food, and of one who lovingly links others with himself in his sympathy and prayer.

---

1 "Take heed that you do not do your charitable deeds before men, to be seen by them. Otherwise you have no reward from your Father in heaven.
2 "Therefore, [a]when you do a charitable deed, do not sound a trumpet before you as the hypocrites do in the synagogues and in the streets, that they may have glory from men. Assuredly, I say to you, they have their reward.
3 "But when you do a charitable deed, do not let your left hand know what your right hand is doing,
4 "that your charitable deed may be in secret; and your Father who sees in secret [a]will Himself reward you openly.[1]
5 "And when you pray, you shall not be like the hypocrites. For they love to pray standing in the synagogues and on the corners of the streets, that they may be seen by men. Assuredly, I say to you, they have their reward.
6 "But you, when you pray, [a]go into your room, and when you have shut your door, pray to your Father who *is* in the

6:2[a] Rom. 12:8 6:4[a] Luke 14:12–14 [1]NU-Text omits *openly*. 6:6[a] 2 Kin. 4:33

secret *place;* and your Father who sees in secret will reward
you openly.[1]
7 "And when you pray, [a]do not use vain repetitions as the
heathen *do.* [b]For they think that they will be heard for their
many words.
8 "Therefore do not be like them. For your Father [a]knows
the things you have need of before you ask Him.
9 "In this [a]manner, therefore, pray:

[b]Our Father in heaven,
Hallowed be Your [c]name.
10 Your kingdom come.
[a]Your will be done
On earth [b]as *it is* in heaven.
11 Give us this day our [a]daily bread.
12 And [a]forgive us our debts,
As we forgive our debtors.
13 [a]And do not lead us into temptation,
But [b]deliver us from the evil one.
For Yours is the kingdom and the power
and the glory forever. Amen.[1]

14 [a]"For if you forgive men their trespasses, your heavenly
Father will also forgive you.
15 "But [a]if you do not forgive men their trespasses, neither
will your Father forgive your trespasses.
16 "Moreover, [a]when you fast, do not be like the hypocrites,
with a sad countenance. For they disfigure their faces that
they may appear to men to be fasting. Assuredly, I say to you,
they have their reward.
17 "But you, when you fast, [a]anoint your head and wash your
face,
18 "so that you do not appear to men to be fasting, but to
your Father who *is* in the secret *place;* and your Father who
sees in secret will reward you openly.[1]
19 [a]"Do not lay up for yourselves treasures on earth, where
moth and rust destroy and where thieves break in and steal;
20 [a]"but lay up for yourselves treasures in heaven, where
neither moth nor rust destroys and where thieves do not
break in and steal.
21 "For where your treasure is, there your heart will be also.
22 [a]"The lamp of the body is the eye. If therefore your eye
is good, your whole body will be full of light.

6:6 [1]NU-Text omits *openly.* 6:7 [a]Eccl. 5:2 [b]1 Kin. 18:26 6:8 [a][Rom. 8:26, 27] 6:9 [a]Luke 11:2–4 [b][Matt. 5:9, 16] [c]Mal. 1:11 6:10 [a]Matt. 26:42 [b]Ps. 103:20 6:11 [a]Prov. 30:8 6:12 [a][Matt. 18:21, 22] 6:13 [a][2 Pet. 2:9] [b]John 17:15 [1]NU-Text omits *For Yours* through *Amen.* 6:14 [a]Mark 11:25 6:15 [a]Matt. 18:35 6:16 [a]Is. 58:3–7 6:17 [a]Ruth 3:3 6:18 [1]NU-Text and M-Text omit *openly.* 6:19 [a]Prov. 23:4 6:20 [a]Matt. 19:21 6:22 [a]Luke 11:34, 35

23 “But if your eye is bad, your whole body will be full of
darkness. If therefore the light that is in you is darkness, how
great *is* that darkness!
24 [a]“No one can serve two masters; for either he will hate
the one and love the other, or else he will be loyal to the one
and despise the other. [b]You cannot serve God and mammon.
25 “Therefore I say to you, [a]do not worry about your life,
what you will eat or what you will drink; nor about your body,
what you will put on. Is not life more than food and the body
more than clothing?
26 [a]“Look at the birds of the air, for they neither sow nor
reap nor gather into barns; yet your heavenly Father feeds
them. Are you not of more value than they?
27 “Which of you by worrying can add one cubit to his stat-
ure?
28 “So why do you worry about clothing? Consider the lilies
of the field, how they grow: they neither toil nor spin;
29 “and yet I say to you that even Solomon in all his glory
was not arrayed like one of these.
30 “Now if God so clothes the grass of the field, which today
is, and tomorrow is thrown into the oven, *will He* not much
more *clothe* you, O you of little faith?
31 “Therefore do not worry, saying, ‘What shall we eat?’ or
‘What shall we drink?’ or ‘What shall we wear?’
32 “For after all these things the Gentiles seek. For your heav-
enly Father knows that you need all these things.
33 “But [a]seek first the kingdom of God and His righteous-
ness, and all these things shall be added to you.
34 “Therefore do not worry about tomorrow, for tomorrow
will worry about its own things. Sufficient for the day *is* its
own trouble.

6:24 [a]Luke 16:9, 11, 13 [b][Gal. 1:10] 6:25 [a]Luke 12:22 6:26 [a]Luke 12:24
6:33 [a][1 Tim. 4:8]

MATTHEW 7

THINGS THAT COUNT WITH GOD

Jesus deals with matters in which we come into contact with our fellow men. Use your judgment, of course: the verse implies that you will *judge* in a right sense. But do not indulge the criticizing faculty upon others in a censorious manner or as if you were set in authority and had a right to dispense judgment among your fellows.

The judging faculty is best employed at home. Our tendency is to spy out splinters in other men's eyes and not to see the beam in our own. Instead of beholding, with gratified gaze, the small fault of another, we should act reasonably if we penitently considered the greater fault of ourselves. It is "the plank in [our] own eye" that blinds us to our own wrongdoing; but such blindness does not suffice to excuse us, since it evidently does not shut our eyes to the little error of our brother. Our reformations must begin with ourselves, or they are not true and do not spring from a right motive. Sin we may rebuke, but not if we indulge it. We may protest against evil but not if we willfully practice it.

The Pharisees were great at censuring but slow at amending. Our Lord will not have His kingdom made up of hypocritical theorists; He calls for practical obedience to the rules of holiness. After we are ourselves sanctified, we are bound to be eyes to the blind and correctors of unholy living—but not till then.

---

1 "Judge [a]not, that you be not judged.
2 "For with what judgment you judge, you will be judged; [a]and
with the measure you use, it will be measured back to you.
3 [a]"And why do you look at the speck in your brother's eye,
but do not consider the plank in your own eye?
4 "Or how can you say to your brother, 'Let me remove the
speck from your eye'; and look, a plank *is* in your own eye?
5 "Hypocrite! First remove the plank from your own eye,
and then you will see clearly to remove the speck from your
brother's eye.
6 [a]"Do not give what is holy to the dogs; nor cast your pearls
before swine, lest they trample them under their feet, and
turn and tear you in pieces.
7 [a]"Ask, and it will be given to you; seek, and you will find;
knock, and it will be opened to you.
8 "For [a]everyone who asks receives, and he who seeks finds,
and to him who knocks it will be opened.
9 [a]"Or what man is there among you who, if his son asks for
bread, will give him a stone?

7:1[a]Rom. 14:3 7:2[a]Luke 6:38 7:3[a]Luke 6:41 7:6[a]Prov. 9:7, 8 7:7[a][Mark 11:24] 7:8[a]Prov. 8:17 7:9[a]Luke 11:11

10 "Or if he asks for a fish, will he give him a serpent?

11 "If you then, [a]being evil, know how to give good gifts to your children, how much more will your Father who is in heaven give good things to those who ask Him!

12 "Therefore, [a]whatever you want men to do to you, do also to them, for [b]this is the Law and the Prophets.

13 [a]"Enter by the narrow gate; for wide *is* the gate and broad *is* the way that leads to destruction, and there are many who go in by it.

14 "Because[1] narrow *is* the gate and difficult *is* the way which leads to life, and there are few who find it.

15 [a]"Beware of false prophets, [b]who come to you in sheep's clothing, but inwardly they are ravenous wolves.

16 [a]"You will know them by their fruits. [b]Do men gather grapes from thornbushes or figs from thistles?

17 "Even so, [a]every good tree bears good fruit, but a bad tree bears bad fruit.

18 "A good tree cannot bear bad fruit, nor *can* a bad tree bear good fruit.

19 [a]"Every tree that does not bear good fruit is cut down and thrown into the fire.

20 "Therefore by their fruits you will know them.

21 "Not everyone who says to Me, [a]'Lord, Lord,' shall enter the kingdom of heaven, but he who [b]does the will of My Father in heaven.

22 "Many will say to Me in that day, 'Lord, Lord, have we [a]not prophesied in Your name, cast out demons in Your name, and done many wonders in Your name?'

23 "And [a]then I will declare to them, 'I never knew you; [b]depart from Me, you who practice lawlessness!'

24 "Therefore [a]whoever hears these sayings of Mine, and does them, I will liken him to a wise man who built his house on the rock:

25 "and the rain descended, the floods came, and the winds blew and beat on that house; and it did not fall, for it was founded on the rock.

26 "But everyone who hears these sayings of Mine, and does not do them, will be like a foolish man who built his house on the sand:

27 "and the rain descended, the floods came, and the winds blew and beat on that house; and it fell. And great was its fall."

28 And so it was, when Jesus had ended these sayings, that [a]the people were astonished at His teaching,

29 [a]for He taught them as one having authority, and not as the scribes.

7:11[a]Gen. 6:5; 8:21 7:12[a]Luke 6:31 [b]Gal. 5:14 7:13[a]Luke 13:24 7:14[1]NU-Text and M-Text read *How . . . !* 7:15[a]Jer. 23:16 [b]Mic. 3:5 7:16[a]Matt. 7:20; 12:33 [b]Luke 6:43 7:17[a]Matt. 12:33 7:19[a][John 15:2, 6] 7:21[a]Luke 6:46 [b]Rom. 2:13 7:22[a]Num. 24:4 7:23[a][2 Tim. 2:19] [b]Ps. 5:5; 6:8 7:24[a]Luke 6:47–49 7:28[a]Matt. 13:54 7:29[a][John 7:46]

MATTHEW 8

JESUS LORD OF ALL

After the Sermon on the Mount, we are given remarkable miracles as if to teach us that our Lord's words were confirmed by His works. Our Lord was mighty in both word and deed. His kingdom comes not only with truth but with power. He wrought miracles that men might see with their eyes that the power of God was upon Him and that He spoke with divine authority.

At this day, beloved, it is even so. Power goes forth with the preaching of the gospel. The words of the Lord Jesus are spirit and life; they are in themselves full of authority, and we ought to accept them with ready faith. Since we are slow to believe, the Lord continues to work as well as speak: the "accompanying signs" (Mark 16:20) are still to be perceived—blind eyes are opened, deaf ears are unstopped, hearts of stone are turned to flesh, and the dead in sin are quickened.

The words of the Lord Jesus came to a poor leper who dwelt alone outside a city wall. Though he feels the foul disease within him and fears that it has come to its worst, yet may he be emboldened to approach Him who can at once make him clean. If you feel yourself to be a mass of loathsomeness and corruption or, worse still, hardened and insensible in conscience, yet come to Jesus for healing. Come at once, saying, "Lord, if You are willing, You can make me clean."

1 When He had come down from the mountain, great multitudes followed Him.
2 [a]And behold, a leper came and [b]worshiped Him, saying, "Lord, if You are willing, You can make me clean."
3 Then Jesus put out *His* hand and touched him, saying, "I am willing; be cleansed." Immediately his leprosy [a]was cleansed.
4 And Jesus said to him, [a]"See that you tell no one; but go your way, show yourself to the priest, and offer the gift that [b]Moses [c]commanded, as a testimony to them."
5 [a]Now when Jesus had entered Capernaum, a [b]centurion came to Him, pleading with Him,
6 saying, "Lord, my servant is lying at home paralyzed, dreadfully tormented."
7 And Jesus said to him, "I will come and heal him."
8 The centurion answered and said, "Lord, [a]I am not worthy that You should come under my roof. But only [b]speak a word, and my servant will be healed.

8:2 [a]Mark 1:40–45 [b]John 9:38 8:3 [a]Luke 4:27 8:4 [a]Mark 5:43 [b]Luke 5:14 [c]Deut. 24:8 8:5 [a]Luke 7:1–3 [b]Matt. 27:54 8:8 [a]Luke 15:19, 21 [b]Ps. 107:20

9 "For I also am a man under authority, having soldiers un-
der me. And I say to this *one,* 'Go,' and he goes; and to anoth-
er, 'Come,' and he comes; and to my servant, 'Do this,' and he
does *it.*"
10 When Jesus heard *it,* He marveled, and said to those who
followed, "Assuredly, I say to you, I have not found such great
faith, not even in Israel!
11 "And I say to you that [a]many will come from east and west,
and sit down with Abraham, Isaac, and Jacob in the kingdom
of heaven.
12 "But [a]the sons of the kingdom [b]will be cast out into outer
darkness. There will be weeping and gnashing of teeth."
13 Then Jesus said to the centurion, "Go your way; and as
you have believed, *so* let it be done for you." And his servant
was healed that same hour.
14 [a]Now when Jesus had come into Peter's house, He saw
[b]his wife's mother lying sick with a fever.
15 So He touched her hand, and the fever left her. And she
arose and served them.[1]
16 [a]When evening had come, they brought to Him many
who were demon-possessed. And He cast out the spirits with
a word, and healed all who were sick,
17 that it might be fulfilled which was spoken by Isaiah the
prophet, saying:

> [a]"He Himself took our infirmities
> And bore *our* sicknesses."[1]

18 And when Jesus saw great multitudes about Him, He gave
a command to depart to the other side.
19 [a]Then a certain scribe came and said to Him, "Teacher, I
will follow You wherever You go."
20 And Jesus said to him, "Foxes have holes and birds of
the air *have* nests, but the Son of Man has nowhere to lay *His*
head."
21 [a]Then another of His disciples said to Him, "Lord, [b]let
me first go and bury my father."
22 But Jesus said to him, "Follow Me, and let the dead bury
their own dead."
23 Now when He got into a boat, His disciples followed Him.
24 [a]And suddenly a great tempest arose on the sea, so that
the boat was covered with the waves. But He was asleep.
25 Then His disciples came to *Him* and awoke Him, saying,
"Lord, save us! We are perishing!"
26 But He said to them, "Why are you fearful, O you of little

8:11[a]Is. 2:2, 3; Mal. 1:11 8:12[a][Matt. 21:43] [b]Luke 13:28 8:14[a]Mark 1:29–31 [b]1 Cor. 9:5
8:15[1]NU-Text and M-Text read *Him.* 8:16[a]Luke 4:40, 41 8:17[a]Is. 53:4 [1]Isaiah 53:4
8:19[a]Luke 9:57, 58 8:21[a]Luke 9:59, 60 [b]1 Kin. 19:20 8:24[a]Mark 4:37

faith?" Then [a]He arose and rebuked the winds and the sea,
and there was a great calm.
27 So the men marveled, saying, "Who can this be, that even
the winds and the sea obey Him?"
28 [a]When He had come to the other side, to the country of
the Gergesenes,[1] there met Him two demon-possessed *men,*
coming out of the tombs, exceedingly fierce, so that no one
could pass that way.
29 And suddenly they cried out, saying, "What have we to
do with You, Jesus, You Son of God? Have You come here to
torment us before the time?"
30 Now a good way off from them there was a herd of many
swine feeding.
31 So the demons begged Him, saying, "If You cast us out,
permit us to go away[1] into the herd of swine."
32 And He said to them, "Go." So when they had come out,
they went into the herd of swine. And suddenly the whole
herd of swine ran violently down the steep place into the
sea, and perished in the water.
33 Then those who kept *them* fled; and they went away into
the city and told everything, including what *had happened*
to the demon-possessed *men.*
34 And behold, the whole city came out to meet Jesus. And
when they saw Him, [a]they begged *Him* to depart from their
region.

8:26[a]Ps. 65:7; 89:9; 107:29 8:28[a]Mark 5:1–4 [1]NU-Text reads *Gadarenes.* 8:31[1]NU-Text reads *send us.* 8:34[a]Luke 5:8; Acts 16:39

MATTHEW 9

JESUS' MINISTRY AT NAZARETH

Verse 9 is a little bit of autobiography. Matthew wrote this verse about himself. I can fancy him, with his pen in his hand, writing all the rest of this Gospel, but I can imagine that when he came to this very personal passage, he laid the pen down a minute and wiped his eyes. He was coming to a most memorable and pathetic incident in his own life, and he recorded it with tremulous emotion. I do not think there is any part of Matthew's Gospel that touched him more than this portion in which he was writing down the story of divine love to himself, of how he himself was called to be a disciple of Christ.

Please notice whereabouts Matthew has put this story: it is placed immediately after a miracle. *There,* said he, *I will tell them one miracle about the Savior having made the palsied man take up his bed and walk, and then I will tell them of another miracle—a greater miracle still—how there was another man who was more than palsied, chained to his gains and to an injurious traffic.*

Whenever you think about your own conversion, dear friend, regard it as a miracle, and always say within yourself, *It was a wonder of grace. If the conversion of anybody was ever a miracle of mercy, it was my conversion; it was extraordinary condescension on Christ's part to look on such a sinner as I was, and nothing but a miracle of grace could have saved me.*

---

1 So He got into a boat, crossed over, [a]and came to His own
city.
2 [a]Then behold, they brought to Him a paralytic lying on
a bed. [b]When Jesus saw their faith, He said to the paralytic,
"Son, be of good cheer; your sins are forgiven you."
3 And at once some of the scribes said within themselves,
"This Man blasphemes!"
4 But Jesus, [a]knowing their thoughts, said, "Why do you
think evil in your hearts?
5 "For which is easier, to say, '*Your* sins are forgiven you,' or
to say, 'Arise and walk'?
6 "But that you may know that the Son of Man has power on
earth to forgive sins"—then He said to the paralytic, "Arise,
take up your bed, and go to your house."
7 And he arose and departed to his house.
8 Now when the multitudes saw *it,* they [a]marveled[1] and glo-
rified God, who had given such power to men.

9:1[a]Matt. 4:13; 11:23 9:2[a]Luke 5:18–26 [b]Matt. 8:10 9:4[a]Matt. 12:25 9:8[a]John 7:15
[1]NU-Text reads *were afraid.*

9 [a]As Jesus passed on from there, He saw a man named Mat-
thew sitting at the tax office. And He said to him, "Follow Me."
So he arose and followed Him.
10 [a]Now it happened, as Jesus sat at the table in the house,
that behold, many tax collectors and sinners came and sat
down with Him and His disciples.
11 And when the Pharisees saw *it,* they said to His disciples,
"Why does your Teacher eat with [a]tax collectors and [b]sin-
ners?"
12 When Jesus heard *that,* He said to them, "Those who are
well have no need of a physician, but those who are sick.
13 "But go and learn what *this* means: [a]'I desire mercy and
not sacrifice.'[1] For I did not come to call the righteous, [b]but
sinners, to repentance."[2]
14 Then the disciples of John came to Him, saying, [a]"Why
do we and the Pharisees fast often,[1] but Your disciples do not
fast?"
15 And Jesus said to them, "Can [a]the friends of the bride-
groom mourn as long as the bridegroom is with them? But
the days will come when the bridegroom will be taken away
from them, and [b]then they will fast.
16 "No one puts a piece of unshrunk cloth on an old garment;
for the patch pulls away from the garment, and the tear is
made worse.
17 "Nor do they put new wine into old wineskins, or else the
wineskins break, the wine is spilled, and the wineskins are
ruined. But they put new wine into new wineskins, and both
are preserved."
18 [a]While He spoke these things to them, behold, a ruler came
and worshiped Him, saying, "My daughter has just died, but
come and lay Your hand on her and she will live."
19 So Jesus arose and followed him, and so *did* His [a]disciples.
20 [a]And suddenly, a woman who had a flow of blood for
twelve years came from behind and [b]touched the hem of His
garment.
21 For she said to herself, "If only I may touch His garment,
I shall be made well."
22 But Jesus turned around, and when He saw her He said,
"Be of good cheer, daughter; [a]your faith has made you well."
And the woman was made well from that hour.
23 [a]When Jesus came into the ruler's house, and saw [b]the
flute players and the noisy crowd wailing,
24 He said to them, [a]"Make room, for the girl is not dead,
but sleeping." And they ridiculed Him.

9:9 [a]Luke 5:27 9:10 [a]Mark 2:15 9:11 [a]Matt. 11:19 [b][Gal. 2:15] 9:13 [a]Hos. 6:6 [b]1 Tim. 1:15 [1]Hosea 6:6 [2]NU-Text omits *to repentance.* 9:14 [a]Luke 5:33–35; 18:12 [1]NU-Text brackets *often* as disputed. 9:15 [a]John 3:29 [b]Acts 13:2, 3; 14:23 9:18 [a]Luke 8:41–56 9:19 [a]Matt. 10:2–4 9:20 [a]Luke 8:43 [b]Matt. 14:36; 23:5 9:22 [a]Luke 7:50; 8:48; 17:19; 18:42 9:23 [a]Mark 5:38 [b]2 Chr. 35:25 9:24 [a]Acts 20:10

25 But when the crowd was put outside, He went in and [a]took
her by the hand, and the girl arose.
26 And the [a]report of this went out into all that land.
27 When Jesus departed from there, [a]two blind men fol-
lowed Him, crying out and saying, [b]"Son of David, have mercy
on us!"
28 And when He had come into the house, the blind men
came to Him. And Jesus said to them, "Do you believe that I
am able to do this?" They said to Him, "Yes, Lord."
29 Then He touched their eyes, saying, "According to your
faith let it be to you."
30 And their eyes were opened. And Jesus sternly warned
them, saying, [a]"See *that* no one knows *it*."
31 [a]But when they had departed, they spread the news about
Him in all that country.
32 [a]As they went out, behold, they brought to Him a man,
mute and demon-possessed.
33 And when the demon was cast out, the mute spoke. And
the multitudes marveled, saying, "It was never seen like this
in Israel!"
34 But the Pharisees said, [a]"He casts out demons by the rul-
er of the demons."
35 Then Jesus went about all the cities and villages, [a]teach-
ing in their synagogues, preaching the gospel of the king-
dom, and healing every sickness and every disease among
the people.[1]
36 [a]But when He saw the multitudes, He was moved with
compassion for them, because they were weary[1] and scat-
tered, [b]like sheep having no shepherd.
37 Then He said to His disciples, [a]"The harvest truly *is* plen-
tiful, but the laborers *are* few.
38 [a]"Therefore pray the Lord of the harvest to send out la-
borers into His harvest."

9:25 [a]Mark 1:31 9:26 [a]Matt. 4:24 9:27 [a]Matt. 20:29–34 [b]Luke 18:38, 39 9:30 [a]Matt. 8:4 9:31 [a]Mark 7:36 9:32 [a]Matt. 12:22, 24 9:34 [a]Luke 11:15 9:35 [a]Matt. 4:23 [1]NU-Text omits *among the people*. 9:36 [a]Mark 6:34 [b]Num. 27:17 [1]NU-Text and M-Text read *harassed*. 9:37 [a]Luke 10:2 9:38 [a]2 Thess. 3:1

MATTHEW 10

DISCIPLESHIP AND ITS COST

Now, I am persuaded that there are in this professing Christian England hundreds and thousands of persons who have some kind of faith in Christ, and I trust also a sincere faith, who, nevertheless, pass over in silence the plain command of Christ about professing Him before men. "Whoever confesses Me before men, him I will also confess." Observe the word. It is not *profess*. It means that, but it means more.

To *profess* Christ may be work that anyone would do, especially in soft and silken times when a profession may even be remunerative, when it may even add respectability to a man's character and make his path smooth. But the confession has this difference in it—it is a kind of thing that comes out when a sort of accusation is brought. A man professes Christ before his brethren because they will all be pleased with him for it. Another man, in the midst of enemies who will revile and persecute him, pleads guilty to the blessed impeachment of being a Christian, confesses that what they count a crime he counts a virtue.

To *profess* Christ is but an easy thing; to "confess" Him implies that the circumstances make that confession a deed of courage that exposes the confessing soul to peril and penalty. But he gladly accepts the suffering or the shame and confesses that what may seem to be a foolish thing to others is a wise thing to him. He confesses Christ.

---

1 And [a]when He had called His twelve disciples to *Him,* He
gave them power *over* unclean spirits, to cast them out, and
to heal all kinds of sickness and all kinds of disease.
2 Now the names of the twelve apostles are these: first,
Simon, [a]who is called Peter, and Andrew his brother; James
the *son* of Zebedee, and John his brother;
3 Philip and Bartholomew; Thomas and Matthew the tax
collector; James the *son* of Alphaeus, and Lebbaeus, whose
surname was[1] Thaddaeus;
4 [a]Simon the Cananite,[1] and Judas [b]Iscariot, who also be-
trayed Him.
5 These twelve Jesus sent out and commanded them, say-
ing: [a]"Do not go into the way of the Gentiles, and do not en-
ter a city of [b]the Samaritans.
6 [a]"But go rather to the [b]lost sheep of the house of Israel.

10:1[a]Luke 6:13 10:2[a]John 1:42 10:3[1]NU-Text omits *Lebbaeus, whose surname was.* 10:4[a]Acts 1:13 [b]John 13:2, 26 [1]NU-Text reads *Cananaean.* 10:5[a]Matt. 4:15 [b]John 4:9 10:6[a]Matt. 15:24 [b]Jer. 50:6

7 [a]"And as you go, preach, saying, [b]'The kingdom of heaven
is at hand.'
8 "Heal the sick, cleanse the lepers, raise the dead,[1] cast out
demons. [a]Freely you have received, freely give.
9 [a]"Provide neither gold nor silver nor [b]copper in your money
belts,
10 "nor bag for *your* journey, nor two tunics, nor sandals, nor
staffs; [a]for a worker is worthy of his food.
11 [a]"Now whatever city or town you enter, inquire who in it
is worthy, and stay there till you go out.
12 "And when you go into a household, greet it.
13 [a]"If the household is worthy, let your peace come upon
it. [b]But if it is not worthy, let your peace return to you.
14 [a]"And whoever will not receive you nor hear your words,
when you depart from that house or city, [b]shake off the dust
from your feet.
15 "Assuredly, I say to you, [a]it will be more tolerable for the
land of Sodom and Gomorrah in the day of judgment than
for that city!
16 [a]"Behold, I send you out as sheep in the midst of wolves.
[b]Therefore be wise as serpents and [c]harmless as doves.
17 "But beware of men, for [a]they will deliver you up to coun-
cils and [b]scourge you in their synagogues.
18 [a]"You will be brought before governors and kings for My
sake, as a testimony to them and to the Gentiles.
19 [a]"But when they deliver you up, do not worry about how
or what you should speak. For [b]it will be given to you in that
hour what you should speak;
20 [a]"for it is not you who speak, but the Spirit of your Father
who speaks in you.
21 [a]"Now brother will deliver up brother to death, and a fa-
ther *his* child; and children will rise up against parents and
cause them to be put to death.
22 "And [a]you will be hated by all for My name's sake. [b]But he
who endures to the end will be saved.
23 [a]"When they persecute you in this city, flee to another.
For assuredly, I say to you, you will not have [b]gone through
the cities of Israel [c]before the Son of Man comes.
24 [a]"A disciple is not above *his* teacher, nor a servant above
his master.
25 "It is enough for a disciple that he be like his teacher, and
a servant like his master. If [a]they have called the master of

10:7[a]Luke 9:2 [b]Matt. 3:2 10:8[a][Acts 8:18] [1]NU-Text reads *raise the dead, cleanse the lepers;* M-Text omits *raise the dead.* 10:9[a]1 Sam. 9:7 [b]Mark 6:8 10:10[a]1 Tim. 5:18 10:11[a]Luke 10:8 10:13[a]Luke 10:5 [b]Ps. 35:13 10:14[a]Mark 6:11 [b]Acts 13:51 10:15[a]Matt. 11:22, 24 10:16[a]Luke 10:3 [b]Eph. 5:15 [c][Phil. 2:14–16] 10:17[a]Mark 13:9 [b]Acts 5:40; 22:19; 26:11 10:18[a]2 Tim. 4:16 10:19[a]Luke 12:11, 12; 21:14, 15 [b]Ex. 4:12 10:20[a]2 Sam. 23:2 10:21[a]Mic. 7:6 10:22[a]Luke 21:17 [b]Mark 13:13 10:23[a]Acts 8:1 [b][Mark 13:10] [c]Matt. 16:28 10:24[a]John 15:20 10:25[a]John 8:48, 52

the house Beelzebub,[1] how much more *will they call* those
of his household!
26 "Therefore do not fear them. [a]For there is nothing cov-
ered that will not be revealed, and hidden that will not be
known.
27 "Whatever I tell you in the dark, [a]speak in the light; and
what you hear in the ear, preach on the housetops.
28 [a]"And do not fear those who kill the body but cannot kill
the soul. But rather [b]fear Him who is able to destroy both
soul and body in hell.
29 "Are not two [a]sparrows sold for a copper coin? And not
one of them falls to the ground apart from your Father's will.
30 [a]"But the very hairs of your head are all numbered.
31 "Do not fear therefore; you are of more value than many
sparrows.
32 [a]"Therefore whoever confesses Me before men, [b]him I
will also confess before My Father who is in heaven.
33 [a]"But whoever denies Me before men, him I will also deny
before My Father who is in heaven.
34 [a]"Do not think that I came to bring peace on earth. I did
not come to bring peace but a sword.
35 "For I have come to [a]'set a man against his father, a daugh-
ter against her mother, and a daughter-in-law against her
mother-in-law';
36 "and [a]'a man's enemies will be those of his *own* house-
hold.'[1]
37 [a]"He who loves father or mother more than Me is not
worthy of Me. And he who loves son or daughter more than
Me is not worthy of Me.
38 [a]"And he who does not take his cross and follow after Me
is not worthy of Me.
39 [a]"He who finds his life will lose it, and he who loses his
life for My sake will find it.
40 [a]"He who receives you receives Me, and he who receives
Me receives Him who sent Me.
41 [a]"He who receives a prophet in the name of a prophet
shall receive a prophet's reward. And he who receives a righ-
teous man in the name of a righteous man shall receive a
righteous man's reward.
42 [a]"And whoever gives one of these little ones only a cup of
cold *water* in the name of a disciple, assuredly, I say to you,
he shall by no means lose his reward."

10:25 [1]NU-Text and M-Text read *Beelzebul.* 10:26 [a]Mark 4:22 10:27 [a]Acts 5:20 10:28 [a]Luke 12:4 [b]Luke 12:5 10:29 [a]Luke 12:6, 7 10:30 [a]Luke 21:18 10:32 [a]Luke 12:8 [b][Rev. 3:5] 10:33 [a]2 Tim. 2:12 10:34 [a][Luke 12:49] 10:35 [a]Mic. 7:6 10:36 [a]John 13:18 [1]Micah 7:6 10:37 [a]Luke 14:26 10:38 [a][Mark 8:34] 10:39 [a]John 12:25 10:40 [a]Luke 9:48 10:41 [a]1 Kin. 17:10 10:42 [a]Mark 9:41

MATTHEW 11

JESUS EXPLAINS HIS MINISTRY

Perhaps no verse in the whole of Scripture has been handled in the pulpit more frequently than Matthew 11:28, and yet it has not been exhausted, and never can it be. It is a great soul-saving text. There are some words of Scripture that seem to be like special stars in the sky.

Men bear great burdens, some of them burdens of care, some burdens of grief, some burdens of foolish hope; but if they come to Him, being heavy-laden or heavily loaded, He will take off the load from them and give them rest.

Do I not address some who are laboring hard to establish a righteousness of their own? Oh! Sinful attempt, since God has forbidden it, and He declares the effort to be futile! If you are ever to get rest, you must cease from your own doings, and you must come to Christ. Oh! You who are heavily laden with your sins and feel them like a burden depressing your heart, bowing you to the ground, and crushing you, as it were, down to the lowest hell—that burden can never be lifted from off your weary back except by one hand, and that the pierced hand that has felt the weight of the burden before. To you who toil, to you who are bowed down and crushed with the load, Jesus speaks tonight as He did of old, and He says, "Come to Me . . . and I will give you rest."

---

1 Now it came to pass, when Jesus finished commanding
His twelve disciples, that He departed from there to [a]teach
and to preach in their cities.
2 [a]And when John had heard [b]in prison about the works of
Christ, he sent two of[1] his disciples
3 and said to Him, "Are You [a]the Coming One, or do we look
for another?"
4 Jesus answered and said to them, "Go and tell John the
things which you hear and see:
5 [a]"*The* blind see and *the* lame walk; *the* lepers are cleansed
and *the* deaf hear; *the* dead are raised up and [b]*the* poor have
the gospel preached to them.
6 "And blessed is he who is not [a]offended because of Me."
7 [a]As they departed, Jesus began to say to the multitudes
concerning John: "What did you go out into the wilderness
to see? [b]A reed shaken by the wind?
8 "But what did you go out to see? A man clothed in soft

11:1 [a]Luke 23:5 11:2 [a]Luke 7:18–35 [b]Matt. 4:12; 14:3 [1]NU-Text reads *by* for *two of.*
11:3 [a]John 6:14 11:5 [a]Is. 29:18; 35:4–6 [b]Ps. 22:26; Is. 61:1
11:6 [a][Rom. 9:32] 11:7 [a]Luke 7:24 [b][Eph. 4:14]

garments? Indeed, those who wear soft *clothing* are in kings'
houses.
9 "But what did you go out to see? A prophet? Yes, I say to
you, [a]and more than a prophet.
10 "For this is *he* of whom it is written:

> [a]'Behold, I send My messenger before Your face,
> Who will prepare Your way before You.'[1]

11 "Assuredly, I say to you, among those born of women there
has not risen one greater than John the Baptist; but he who
is least in the kingdom of heaven is greater than he.
12 [a]"And from the days of John the Baptist until now the
kingdom of heaven suffers violence, and the violent take it
by force.
13 [a]"For all the prophets and the law prophesied until John.
14 "And if you are willing to receive *it,* he is [a]Elijah who is to
come.
15 [a]"He who has ears to hear, let him hear!
16 [a]"But to what shall I liken this generation? It is like children
sitting in the marketplaces and calling to their companions,
17 "and saying:

> 'We played the flute for you,
> And you did not dance;
> We mourned to you,
> And you did not lament.'

18 "For John came neither eating nor drinking, and they say,
'He has a demon.'
19 "The Son of Man came eating and drinking, and they say,
'Look, a glutton and a winebibber, [a]a friend of tax collectors
and sinners!' [b]But wisdom is justified by her children."[1]
20 [a]Then He began to rebuke the cities in which most of His
mighty works had been done, because they did not repent:
21 "Woe to you, Chorazin! Woe to you, Bethsaida! For if the
mighty works which were done in you had been done in Tyre
and Sidon, they would have repented long ago [a]in sackcloth
and ashes.
22 "But I say to you, [a]it will be more tolerable for Tyre and
Sidon in the day of judgment than for you.
23 "And you, Capernaum, [a]who are exalted to heaven, will
be[1] brought down to Hades; for if the mighty works which
were done in you had been done in Sodom, it would have re-
mained until this day.

11:9 [a]Luke 1:76; 20:6 11:10 [a]Mal. 3:1 [1]Malachi 3:1 11:12 [a]Luke 16:16 11:13 [a]Mal. 4:4–6 11:14 [a]Luke 1:17 11:15 [a]Luke 8:8 11:16 [a]Luke 7:31 11:19 [a]Matt. 9:10 [b]Luke 7:35 [1]NU-Text reads *works*. 11:20 [a]Luke 10:13–15, 18 11:21 [a]Jon. 3:6–8 11:22 [a]Matt. 10:15; 11:24 11:23 [a]Is. 14:13 [1]NU-Text reads *will you be exalted to heaven? No, you will be.*

24 "But I say to you [a]that it shall be more tolerable for the
land of Sodom in the day of judgment than for you."
25 [a]At that time Jesus answered and said, "I thank You, Fa-
ther, Lord of heaven and earth, that [b]You have hidden these
things from *the* wise and prudent [c]and have revealed them
to babes.
26 "Even so, Father, for so it seemed good in Your sight.
27 [a]"All things have been delivered to Me by My Father, and
no one knows the Son except the Father. [b]Nor does anyone
know the Father except the Son, and *the one* to whom the Son
wills to reveal *Him*.
28 "Come to [a]Me, all *you* who labor and are heavy laden, and
I will give you rest.
29 "Take My yoke upon you [a]and learn from Me, for I am
gentle and [b]lowly in heart, [c]and you will find rest for your
souls.
30 [a]"For My yoke *is* easy and My burden is light."

11:24 [a]Matt. 10:15 11:25 [a]Luke 10:21, 22 [b]Ps. 8:2 [c]Matt. 16:17 11:27 [a]Matt. 28:18 [b]John 1:18; 6:46; 10:15 11:28 [a][John 6:35–37] 11:29 [a][Phil. 2:5] [b]Zech. 9:9 [c]Jer. 6:16 11:30 [a][1 John 5:3]

MATTHEW 12

SABBATH WORKS, GOOD FRUIT, AND JESUS' TRUE FAMILY

Sermons and books are well enough, but streams that run for a long distance aboveground gradually gather for themselves somewhat of the soil through which they flow, and they lose the cool freshness with which they started from the springhead. Truth is sweetest where it breaks from the smitten Rock, for at its first gush it has lost none of its heavenliness and vitality.

It is always best to drink at the well and not from the tank. You shall find that reading the Word of God for yourselves, reading *it* rather than notes upon it, is the surest way of growing in grace. Drink of the unadulterated milk of the Word of God and not of the skim milk or the milk and water of man's word.

Many of the veils that are cast over Scripture are meant not to hide the meaning from the diligent but to compel the mind to be active, for oftentimes the diligence of the heart in seeking to know the divine mind does the heart more good than the knowledge itself. Meditation and careful thought exercise us and strengthen the soul for the reception of the yet more lofty truths.

---

1 At that time [a]Jesus went through the grainfields on the
Sabbath. And His disciples were hungry, and began to [b]pluck
heads of grain and to eat.
2 And when the Pharisees saw *it,* they said to Him, "Look,
Your disciples are doing what is not lawful to do on the Sab-
bath!"
3 But He said to them, "Have you not read [a]what David did
when he was hungry, he and those who were with him:
4 "how he entered the house of God and ate [a]the showbread
which was not lawful for him to eat, nor for those who were
with him, [b]but only for the priests?
5 "Or have you not read in the [a]law that on the Sabbath the
priests in the temple profane the Sabbath, and are blame-
less?
6 "Yet I say to you that in this place there is [a]*One* greater than
the temple.
7 "But if you had known what *this* means, [a]'I desire mercy
and not sacrifice,'[1] you would not have condemned the guilt-
less.
8 "For the Son of Man is Lord even[1] of the Sabbath."

12:1 [a]Luke 6:1–5 [b]Deut. 23:25 12:3 [a]1 Sam. 21:6 12:4 [a]Lev. 24:5 [b]Ex. 29:32
12:5 [a]Num. 28:9 12:6 [a][Is. 66:1, 2] 12:7 [a][Hos. 6:6] [1]Hosea 6:6
12:8 [1]NU-Text and M-Text omit *even.*

9 [a]Now when He had departed from there, He went into their
synagogue.
10 And behold, there was a man who had a withered hand.
And they asked Him, saying, [a]"Is it lawful to heal on the
Sabbath?"—that they might accuse Him.
11 Then He said to them, "What man is there among you
who has one sheep, and if it falls into a pit on the Sabbath,
will not lay hold of it and lift *it* out?
12 "Of how much more value then is a man than a sheep?
Therefore it is lawful to do good on the Sabbath."
13 Then He said to the man, "Stretch out your hand." And he
stretched *it* out, and it was restored as whole as the other.
14 Then [a]the Pharisees went out and plotted against Him,
how they might destroy Him.
15 But when Jesus knew *it,* [a]He withdrew from there. [b]And
great multitudes[1] followed Him, and He healed them all.
16 Yet He [a]warned them not to make Him known,
17 that it might be fulfilled which was spoken by Isaiah the
prophet, saying:

18 "Behold![a] My Servant whom I have chosen,
My Beloved [b]in whom My soul is well pleased!
I will put My Spirit upon Him,
And He will declare justice to the Gentiles.
19 He will not quarrel nor cry out,
Nor will anyone hear His voice in the streets.
20 A bruised reed He will not break,
And smoking flax He will not quench,
Till He sends forth justice to victory;
21 And in His name Gentiles will trust."[1]

22 [a]Then one was brought to Him who was demon-possessed,
blind and mute; and He healed him, so that the blind and[1]
mute man both spoke and saw.
23 And all the multitudes were amazed and said, "Could this
be the [a]Son of David?"
24 [a]Now when the Pharisees heard *it* they said, "This *fellow*
does not cast out demons except by Beelzebub,[1] the ruler of
the demons."
25 But Jesus [a]knew their thoughts, and said to them: "Every
kingdom divided against itself is brought to desolation, and
every city or house divided against itself will not stand.
26 "If Satan casts out Satan, he is divided against himself.
How then will his kingdom stand?

12:9[a]Mark 3:1–6 12:10[a]John 9:16 12:14[a]Mark 3:6 12:15[a]Mark 3:7 [b]Matt. 19:2 [1]NU-Text brackets *multitudes* as disputed. 12:16[a]Matt. 8:4; 9:30; 17:9 12:18[a]Is. 42:1–4; 49:3 [b]Matt. 3:17; 17:5 12:21[1]Isaiah 42:1–4 12:22[a]Luke 11:14, 15 [1]NU-Text omits *blind and.* 12:23[a]Matt. 9:27; 21:9 12:24[a]Matt. 9:34 [1]NU-Text and M-Text read *Beelzebul.* 12:25[a]Matt. 9:4

27 "And if I cast out demons by Beelzebub, by whom do your
sons cast *them* out? Therefore they shall be your judges.
28 "But if I cast out demons by the Spirit of God, [a]surely the
kingdom of God has come upon you.
29 [a]"Or how can one enter a strong man's house and plunder
his goods, unless he first binds the strong man? And then he
will plunder his house.
30 "He who is not with Me is against Me, and he who does
not gather with Me scatters abroad.
31 "Therefore I say to you, [a]every sin and blasphemy will be
forgiven men, [b]but the blasphemy *against* the Spirit will not
be forgiven men.
32 "Anyone who [a]speaks a word against the Son of Man, [b]it
will be forgiven him; but whoever speaks against the Holy
Spirit, it will not be forgiven him, either in this age or in the
age to come.
33 "Either make the tree good and [a]its fruit good, or else
make the tree bad and its fruit bad; for a tree is known by *its*
fruit.
34 [a]"Brood of vipers! How can you, being evil, speak good
things? [b]For out of the abundance of the heart the mouth
speaks.
35 "A good man out of the good treasure of his heart[1] brings
forth good things, and an evil man out of the evil treasure
brings forth evil things.
36 "But I say to you that for every idle word men may speak,
they will give account of it in the day of judgment.
37 "For by your words you will be justified, and by your words
you will be condemned."
38 [a]Then some of the scribes and Pharisees answered, say-
ing, "Teacher, we want to see a sign from You."
39 But He answered and said to them, "An evil and [a]adulter-
ous generation seeks after a sign, and no sign will be given
to it except the sign of the prophet Jonah.
40 [a]"For as Jonah was three days and three nights in the
belly of the great fish, so will the Son of Man be three days
and three nights in the heart of the earth.
41 [a]"The men of Nineveh will rise up in the judgment with
this generation and [b]condemn it, [c]because they repented at
the preaching of Jonah; and indeed a greater than Jonah *is*
here.
42 [a]"The queen of the South will rise up in the judgment with
this generation and condemn it, for she came from the ends
of the earth to hear the wisdom of Solomon; and indeed a
greater than Solomon *is* here.

12:28 [a][Dan. 2:44; 7:14] 12:29 [a]Is. 49:24 12:31 [a]Mark 3:28–30 [b]Acts 7:51 12:32 [a]John 7:12, 52 [b]1 Tim. 1:13 12:33 [a]Matt. 7:16–18 12:34 [a]Matt. 3:7; 23:33 [b]Luke 6:45 12:35 [1]NU-Text and M-Text omit *of his heart*. 12:38 [a]Mark 8:11 12:39 [a]Matt. 16:4 12:40 [a]Jon. 1:17 12:41 [a]Luke 11:32 [b]Jer. 3:11 [c]Jon. 3:5 12:42 [a]1 Kin. 10:1–13

43 [a]"When an unclean spirit goes out of a man, [b]he goes
through dry places, seeking rest, and finds none.
44 "Then he says, 'I will return to my house from which I
came.' And when he comes, he finds *it* empty, swept, and put
in order.
45 "Then he goes and takes with him seven other spirits
more wicked than himself, and they enter and dwell there;
[a]and the last *state* of that man is worse than the first. So shall
it also be with this wicked generation."
46 While He was still talking to the multitudes, [a]behold,
His mother and [b]brothers stood outside, seeking to speak
with Him.
47 Then one said to Him, "Look, [a]Your mother and Your
brothers are standing outside, seeking to speak with You."
48 But He answered and said to the one who told Him, "Who
is My mother and who are My brothers?"
49 And He stretched out His hand toward His disciples and
said, "Here are My mother and My [a]brothers!
50 "For [a]whoever does the will of My Father in heaven is My
brother and sister and mother."

12:43[a]Luke 11:24–26 [b][1 Pet. 5:8] 12:45[a][2 Pet. 2:20–22] 12:46[a]Luke 8:19–21 [b]John 2:12; 7:3, 5 12:47[a]Matt. 13:55, 56 12:49[a]John 20:17 12:50[a]John 15:14

MATTHEW 13

PARABLES ABOUT THE KINGDOM OF HEAVEN

There is a remnant, according to the election of grace, among every nation and people, but the angels will gather all the good grain to the same granary. The saints will be found in all ranks of society. Many will be collected from the lowly cottages of our villages and hamlets, and others will be upraised from the back slums of our great cities to the metropolis of God. From the darkest places angels will bring those children of sweetness and light who seldom beheld the sun, and yet they were pure in heart and saw their God. The hidden and obscure shall be brought into the light, for "the Lord knows those who are His" (2 Tim. 2:19), and his harvest-men will not miss them.

No matter when or where the wheat grew, it shall be gathered into the one barn—gathered never to be scattered, gathered out of all divisions of the visible church and never to be divided again. They grew in different fields. Some flourished on the hillside where Episcopalians grow in all their glory, and others in the lowlier soil where Baptists multiply and Methodists flourish; but once the wheat is in the barn none can tell in which field the ears grew. Then indeed shall the Master's prayer have a glorious answer—"that they all may be one" (John 17:21).

---

1 On the same day Jesus went out of the house [a]and sat by
the sea.
2 [a]And great multitudes were gathered together to Him,
so that [b]He got into a boat and sat; and the whole multitude
stood on the shore.
3 Then He spoke many things to them in parables, saying:
[a]"Behold, a sower went out to sow.
4 "And as he sowed, some *seed* fell by the wayside; and the
birds came and devoured them.
5 "Some fell on stony places, where they did not have much
earth; and they immediately sprang up because they had no
depth of earth.
6 "But when the sun was up they were scorched, and because
they had no root they withered away.
7 "And some fell among thorns, and the thorns sprang up
and choked them.
8 "But others fell on good ground and yielded a crop: some
[a]a hundredfold, some sixty, some thirty.
9 [a]"He who has ears to hear, let him hear!"

13:1[a]Mark 4:1–12 13:2[a]Luke 8:4 [b]Luke 5:3 13:3[a]Luke 8:5 13:8[a]Gen. 26:12 13:9[a]Matt. 11:15

10 And the disciples came and said to Him, "Why do You
speak to them in parables?"
11 He answered and said to them, "Because [a]it has been given
to you to know the mysteries of the kingdom of heaven, but
to them it has not been given.
12 [a]"For whoever has, to him more will be given, and he will
have abundance; but whoever does not have, even what he
has will be taken away from him.
13 "Therefore I speak to them in parables, because seeing
they do not see, and hearing they do not hear, nor do they
understand.
14 "And in them the prophecy of Isaiah is fulfilled, which
says:

> [a]'Hearing you will hear and shall not understand,
> And seeing you will see and not [b]perceive;
> 15 For the hearts of this people have grown dull.
> *Their* ears [a]are hard of hearing,
> And their eyes they have [b]closed,
> Lest they should see with *their* eyes
> and hear with *their* ears,
> Lest they should understand with
> *their* hearts and turn,
> So that I should[1] [c]heal them.'[2]

16 "But [a]blessed *are* your eyes for they see, and your ears for
they hear;
17 "for assuredly, I say to you [a]that many prophets and righ-
teous *men* desired to see what you see, and did not see *it*, and
to hear what you hear, and did not hear *it*.
18 [a]"Therefore hear the parable of the sower:
19 "When anyone hears the word [a]of the kingdom, and does
not understand *it*, then the wicked *one* comes and snatch-
es away what was sown in his heart. This is he who received
seed by the wayside.
20 "But he who received the seed on stony places, this is he
who hears the word and immediately [a]receives it with joy;
21 "yet he has no root in himself, but endures only for a
while. For when [a]tribulation or persecution arises because
of the word, immediately [b]he stumbles.
22 "Now [a]he who received seed [b]among the thorns is he who
hears the word, and the cares of this world and the deceitful-
ness of riches choke the word, and he becomes unfruitful.
23 "But he who received seed on the good ground is he who
hears the word and understands *it*, who indeed bears [a]fruit

13:11[a]Mark 4:10, 11 13:12[a]Matt. 25:29 13:14[a]Is. 6:9, 10; Ezek. 12:2 [b][John 3:36]
13:15[a]Heb. 5:11 [b]Luke 19:42 [c]Acts 28:26, 27 [1]NU-Text and M-Text read *would*.
[2]Isaiah 6:9, 10 13:16[a]Luke 10:23, 24 13:17[a]Heb. 11:13 13:18[a]Mark 4:13–20
13:19[a]Matt. 4:23 13:20[a]Is. 58:2 13:21[a][Acts 14:22] [b]Matt. 11:6
13:22[a]1 Tim. 6:9 [b]Jer. 4:3 13:23[a]Col. 1:6

and produces: some a hundredfold, some sixty, some thirty."
24 Another parable He put forth to them, saying: "The king-
dom of heaven is like a man who sowed good seed in his field;
25 "but while men slept, his enemy came and sowed tares
among the wheat and went his way.
26 "But when the grain had sprouted and produced a crop,
then the tares also appeared.
27 "So the servants of the owner came and said to him, 'Sir,
did you not sow good seed in your field? How then does it
have tares?'
28 "He said to them, 'An enemy has done this.' The servants
said to him, 'Do you want us then to go and gather them up?'
29 "But he said, 'No, lest while you gather up the tares you
also uproot the wheat with them.
30 'Let both grow together until the harvest, and at the time
of harvest I will say to the reapers, "First gather together the
tares and bind them in bundles to burn them, but [a]gather
the wheat into my barn." ' "
31 Another parable He put forth to them, saying: [a]"The king-
dom of heaven is like a mustard seed, which a man took and
sowed in his field,
32 "which indeed is the least of all the seeds; but when it is
grown it is greater than the herbs and becomes a [a]tree, so
that the birds of the air come and nest in its branches."
33 [a]Another parable He spoke to them: "The kingdom of
heaven is like leaven, which a woman took and hid in three
measures[1] of meal till [b]it was all leavened."
34 [a]All these things Jesus spoke to the multitude in para-
bles; and without a parable He did not speak to them,
35 that it might be fulfilled which was spoken by the proph-
et, saying:

> [a]"I will open My mouth in parables;
> [b]I will utter things kept secret from the
> foundation of the world."[1]

36 Then Jesus sent the multitude away and went into the
house. And His disciples came to Him, saying, "Explain to
us the parable of the tares of the field."
37 He answered and said to them: "He who sows the good
seed is the Son of Man.
38 [a]"The field is the world, the good seeds are the sons of
the kingdom, but the tares are [b]the sons of the wicked *one*.
39 "The enemy who sowed them is the devil, [a]the harvest is
the end of the age, and the reapers are the angels.

13:30[a]Matt. 3:12 13:31[a]Luke 13:18, 19 13:32[a]Ezek. 17:22–24; 31:3–9 13:33[a]Luke 13:20, 21 [b][1 Cor. 5:6] [1]Greek *sata,* approximately two pecks in all 13:34[a]Ps. 78:2; Mark 4:33, 34 13:35[a]Ps. 78:2 [b]Eph. 3:9 [1]Psalm 78:2 13:38[a]Rom. 10:18 [b]John 8:44 13:39[a]Rev. 14:15

40 "Therefore as the tares are gathered and burned in the
fire, so it will be at the end of this age.
41 "The Son of Man will send out His angels, [a]and they will
gather out of His kingdom all things that offend, and those
who practice lawlessness,
42 [a]"and will cast them into the furnace of fire. [b]There will
be wailing and gnashing of teeth.
43 [a]"Then the righteous will shine forth as the sun in the king-
dom of their Father. [b]He who has ears to hear, let him hear!
44 "Again, the kingdom of heaven is like treasure hidden
in a field, which a man found and hid; and for joy over it he
goes and [a]sells all that he has and [b]buys that field.
45 "Again, the kingdom of heaven is like a merchant seek-
ing beautiful pearls,
46 "who, when he had found [a]one pearl of great price, went
and sold all that he had and bought it.
47 "Again, the kingdom of heaven is like a dragnet that was
cast into the sea and [a]gathered some of every kind,
48 "which, when it was full, they drew to shore; and they sat
down and gathered the good into vessels, but threw the bad
away.
49 "So it will be at the end of the age. The angels will come
forth, [a]separate the wicked from among the just,
50 "and cast them into the furnace of fire. There will be wail-
ing and gnashing of teeth."
51 Jesus said to them,[1] "Have you understood all these
things?" They said to Him, "Yes, Lord."[2]
52 Then He said to them, "Therefore every scribe instruct-
ed concerning[1] the kingdom of heaven is like a householder
who brings out of his treasure [a]*things* new and old."
53 Now it came to pass, when Jesus had finished these par-
ables, that He departed from there.
54 [a]When He had come to His own country, He taught them
in their synagogue, so that they were astonished and said,
"Where did this *Man* get this wisdom and *these* mighty works?
55 [a]"Is this not the carpenter's son? Is not His mother called
Mary? And [b]His brothers [c]James, Joses,[1] Simon, and Judas?
56 "And His sisters, are they not all with us? Where then did
this *Man* get all these things?"
57 So they [a]were offended at Him. But Jesus said to them,
[b]"A prophet is not without honor except in his own country
and in his own house."
58 Now [a]He did not do many mighty works there because
of their unbelief.

13:41 [a]Matt. 18:7 13:42 [a]Rev. 19:20; 20:10 [b]Matt. 8:12; 13:50 13:43 [a][Dan. 12:3] [b]Matt. 13:9 13:44 [a]Phil. 3:7, 8 [b][Is. 55:1] 13:46 [a]Prov. 2:4; 3:14, 15; 8:10, 19 13:47 [a]Matt. 22:9, 10 13:49 [a]Matt. 25:32 13:51 [1]NU-Text omits *Jesus said to them.* [2]NU-Text omits *Lord.* 13:52 [a]Song 7:13 [1]Or *for* 13:54 [a]Luke 4:16 13:55 [a]John 6:42 [b]Matt. 12:46 [c]Mark 15:40 [1]NU-Text reads *Joseph.* 13:57 [a]Matt. 11:6 [b]Luke 4:24 13:58 [a]Mark 6:5, 6

MATTHEW 14

FIVE THOUSAND FED

Our Lord did not begin His dealings with Peter on this emergency by asking him a question. He first stretched out His hand and saved him from his peril, and then He said to him, "O you of little faith, why did you doubt?"

I am probably addressing some brothers and sisters—perhaps a great many who have been through a season of profound gloom, and in the midst of that gloom there has been the element of spiritual evil. To be gloomy and depressed is not sinful at all, but there may have been in the midst of that the sin of unbelief: there may have been a doubting of God—a distrust of His providence—a questioning of His love. Now I come at this time to such a brother or sister and say, "O you of little faith, why did you doubt?"

Now, do you believe for a single moment that God is changed in His love or in the objects of it? Do you think that He has cast away His people whom He did foreknow, that Christ will lose that which He bought with His precious blood? Do you not remember reading the words "Having loved His own who were in the world, He loved them to the end" (John 13:1)? Well, brothers, since those things are so, I shall have to come back to my old question and say, "O you of little faith, with an unchanged God to trust to, why did you doubt?"

---

1 At that time [a]Herod the tetrarch heard the report about
Jesus
2 and said to his servants, "This is John the Baptist; he is
risen from the dead, and therefore these powers are at work
in him."
3 [a]For Herod had laid hold of John and bound him, and put
him in prison for the sake of Herodias, his brother Philip's
wife.
4 Because John had said to him, [a]"It is not lawful for you to
have her."
5 And although he wanted to put him to death, he feared
the multitude, [a]because they counted him as a prophet.
6 But when Herod's birthday was celebrated, the daughter
of Herodias danced before them and pleased Herod.
7 Therefore he promised with an oath to give her whatever
she might ask.
8 So she, having been prompted by her mother, said, "Give
me John the Baptist's head here on a platter."

14:1[a]Mark 6:14–29 14:3[a]Luke 3:19, 20 14:4[a]Lev. 18:16; 20:21 14:5[a]Luke 20:6

9 And the king was sorry; nevertheless, because of the oaths
and because of those who sat with him, he commanded *it* to
be given to *her*.
10 So he sent and had John beheaded in prison.
11 And his head was brought on a platter and given to the
girl, and she brought *it* to her mother.
12 Then his disciples came and took away the body and bur-
ied it, and went and told Jesus.
13 [a]When Jesus heard *it,* He departed from there by boat to
a deserted place by Himself. But when the multitudes heard
it, they followed Him on foot from the cities.
14 And when Jesus went out He saw a great multitude; and
He [a]was moved with compassion for them, and healed their
sick.
15 [a]When it was evening, His disciples came to Him, saying,
"This is a deserted place, and the hour is already late. Send
the multitudes away, that they may go into the villages and
buy themselves food."
16 But Jesus said to them, "They do not need to go away. You
give them something to eat."
17 And they said to Him, "We have here only five loaves and
two fish."
18 He said, "Bring them here to Me."
19 Then He commanded the multitudes to sit down on the
grass. And He took the five loaves and the two fish, and look-
ing up to heaven, [a]He blessed and broke and gave the loaves
to the disciples; and the disciples gave to the multitudes.
20 So they all ate and were filled, and they took up twelve
baskets full of the fragments that remained.
21 Now those who had eaten were about five thousand men,
besides women and children.
22 Immediately Jesus made His disciples get into the boat
and go before Him to the other side, while He sent the mul-
titudes away.
23 [a]And when He had sent the multitudes away, He went
up on the mountain by Himself to pray. [b]Now when evening
came, He was alone there.
24 But the boat was now in the middle of the sea,[1] tossed by
the waves, for the wind was contrary.
25 Now in the fourth watch of the night Jesus went to them,
walking on the sea.
26 And when the disciples saw Him [a]walking on the sea, they
were troubled, saying, "It is a ghost!" And they cried out for
fear.
27 But immediately Jesus spoke to them, saying, "Be of good
[a]cheer! It is I; do not be afraid."

14:13[a]John 6:1, 2 14:14[a]Mark 6:34 14:15[a]Luke 9:12 14:19[a]Matt. 15:36; 26:26 14:23[a]Mark 6:46 [b]John 6:16 14:24[1]NU-Text reads *many furlongs away from the land.* 14:26[a]Job 9:8 14:27[a]Acts 23:11; 27:22, 25, 36

28 And Peter answered Him and said, "Lord, if it is You, com-
mand me to come to You on the water."
29 So He said, "Come." And when Peter had come down out
of the boat, he walked on the water to go to Jesus.
30 But when he saw that the wind *was* boisterous,[1] he was
afraid; and beginning to sink he cried out, saying, "Lord,
save me!"
31 And immediately Jesus stretched out *His* hand and caught
him, and said to him, "O you of [a]little faith, why did you
doubt?"
32 And when they got into the boat, the wind ceased.
33 Then those who were in the boat came and[1] worshiped
Him, saying, "Truly [a]You are the Son of God."
34 [a]When they had crossed over, they came to the land of[1]
Gennesaret.
35 And when the men of that place recognized Him, they
sent out into all that surrounding region, brought to Him all
who were sick,
36 and begged Him that they might only [a]touch the hem of
His garment. And [b]as many as touched *it* were made perfect-
ly well.

14:30 [1]NU-Text brackets *that* and *boisterous* as disputed. 14:31 [a]Matt. 6:30; 8:26 14:33 [a]Ps. 2:7 [1]NU-Text omits *came and*. 14:34 [a]Mark 6:53 [1]NU-Text reads *came to land at*. 14:36 [a][Mark 5:24–34] [b][Luke 6:19]

MATTHEW 15

GOD'S COMMANDMENTS AND MEN'S TRADITIONS

The Gentile woman heard that Christ was not sent to that country, but she seemed to say, *If You are not sent, Lord, yet still I am here. If you were not sent to me, perhaps I was sent to You.* She felt that there must be some way of getting over the difficulty. She believed that, by some kind of ingenuity, even if she could not tell how, the difficulty could be removed. This glorious, loving Savior, into whose radiant face she looked, could not repulse her—she felt that He could not.

And, dear friends, I can no more believe that Christ will repulse a sinner than I can look up to the sun and believe that it will ever freeze me. It cannot be: it is too bright, too full of warmth to turn me into ice, and I cannot look into the Savior's face and believe that He will ever cast away a poor soul who comes to Him. So, somehow or other, this poor woman seemed to feel, *I cannot get over the difficulty, but I will go around it.*

My friend, when you come hard and fast against something you cannot get over, do not try to get over it, but just pull up there and say, "If it be so, let it be so; but anyhow, God is gracious, Christ is merciful, and I am going to cast myself at the crucified Savior's feet and trust in Him."

---

1 Then [a]the scribes and Pharisees who were from Jerusa-
lem came to Jesus, saying,
2 [a]"Why do Your disciples transgress the tradition of the el-
ders? For they do not wash their hands when they eat bread."
3 He answered and said to them, "Why do you also trans-
gress the commandment of God because of your tradition?
4 "For God commanded, saying, [a]'Honor your father and
your mother';[1] and, [b]'He who curses father or mother, let
him be put to death.'[2]
5 "But you say, 'Whoever says to his father or mother,
[a]"Whatever profit you might have received from me *is* a gift
to God"—
6 'then he need not honor his father or mother.'[1] Thus you
have made the commandment[2] of God of no effect by your
tradition.
7 [a]"Hypocrites! Well did Isaiah prophesy about you, saying:

15:1 [a]Mark 7:1 15:2 [a]Mark 7:5 15:4 [a][Deut. 5:16] [b]Ex. 21:17 [1]Exodus 20:12; Deuteronomy 5:16 [2]Exodus 21:17 15:5 [a]Mark 7:11, 12 15:6 [1]NU-Text omits *or mother.* [2]NU-Text reads *word.* 15:7 [a]Mark 7:6

8 'These[a] people draw near to
Me with their mouth,
And[1] honor Me with *their* lips,
But their heart is far from Me.
9 And in vain they worship Me,
[a]Teaching *as* doctrines the
commandments of men.'"[1]

10 [a]When He had called the multitude to *Himself,* He said to
them, "Hear and understand:
11 [a]"Not what goes into the mouth defiles a man; but what
comes out of the mouth, this defiles a man."
12 Then His disciples came and said to Him, "Do You know
that the Pharisees were offended when they heard this say-
ing?"
13 But He answered and said, [a]"Every plant which My heav-
enly Father has not planted will be uprooted.
14 "Let them alone. [a]They are blind leaders of the blind. And
if the blind leads the blind, both will fall into a ditch."
15 [a]Then Peter answered and said to Him, "Explain this par-
able to us."
16 So Jesus said, [a]"Are you also still without understanding?
17 "Do you not yet understand that [a]whatever enters the
mouth goes into the stomach and is eliminated?
18 "But [a]those things which proceed out of the mouth come
from the heart, and they defile a man.
19 [a]"For out of the heart proceed evil thoughts, murders,
adulteries, fornications, thefts, false witness, blasphemies.
20 "These are *the things* which defile a man, but to eat with
unwashed hands does not defile a man."
21 [a]Then Jesus went out from there and departed to the re-
gion of Tyre and Sidon.
22 And behold, a woman of Canaan came from that region
and cried out to Him, saying, "Have mercy on me, O Lord,
[a]Son of David! My daughter is severely demon-possessed."
23 But He answered her not a word. And His disciples came
and urged Him, saying, "Send her away, for she cries out af-
ter us."
24 But He answered and said, [a]"I was not sent except to the
lost sheep of the house of Israel."
25 Then she came and worshiped Him, saying, "Lord,
help me!"
26 But He answered and said, "It is not good to take the chil-
dren's bread and throw *it* to the little [a]dogs."

15:8[a]Ps. 78:36; Is. 29:13 [1]NU-Text omits *draw near to Me with their mouth, And.* 15:9[a][Col. 2:18–22] [1]Isaiah 29:13 15:10[a]Mark 7:14 15:11[a][Acts 10:15] 15:13[a][John 15:2] 15:14[a]Luke 6:39 15:15[a]Mark 7:17 15:16[a]Matt. 16:9 15:17[a][1 Cor. 6:13] 15:18[a][James 3:6] 15:19[a]Prov. 6:14 15:21[a]Mark 7:24–30 15:22[a]Matt. 1:1; 22:41, 42 15:24[a]Matt. 10:5, 6 15:26[a]Matt. 7:6

27 And she said, "Yes, Lord, yet even the little dogs eat the
crumbs which fall from their masters' table."
28 Then Jesus answered and said to her, "O woman, [a]great
is your faith! Let it be to you as you desire." And her daugh-
ter was healed from that very hour.
29 [a]Jesus departed from there, [b]skirted the Sea of Galilee,
and went up on the mountain and sat down there.
30 [a]Then great multitudes came to Him, having with them
the lame, blind, mute, maimed, and many others; and they
laid them down at Jesus' [b]feet, and He healed them.
31 So the multitude marveled when they saw *the* mute speak-
ing, *the* maimed made whole, *the* lame walking, and *the* blind
seeing; and they [a]glorified the God of Israel.
32 [a]Now Jesus called His disciples to *Himself* and said, "I
have compassion on the multitude, because they have now
continued with Me three days and have nothing to eat. And
I do not want to send them away hungry, lest they faint on
the way."
33 [a]Then His disciples said to Him, "Where could we get
enough bread in the wilderness to fill such a great multi-
tude?"
34 Jesus said to them, "How many loaves do you have?" And
they said, "Seven, and a few little fish."
35 So He commanded the multitude to sit down on the
ground.
36 And [a]He took the seven loaves and the fish and [b]gave
thanks, broke *them* and gave *them* to His disciples; and the
disciples *gave* to the multitude.
37 So they all ate and were filled, and they took up seven
large baskets full of the fragments that were left.
38 Now those who ate were four thousand men, besides
women and children.
39 [a]And He sent away the multitude, got into the boat, and
came to the region of Magdala.[1]

15:28 [a]Luke 7:9 15:29 [a]Mark 7:31–37 [b]Matt. 4:18 15:30 [a]Is. 35:5, 6 [b]Luke 7:38; 8:41; 10:39 15:31 [a]Luke 5:25, 26; 19:37, 38 15:32 [a]Mark 8:1–10 15:33 [a]2 Kin. 4:43 15:36 [a]Matt. 14:19; 26:27 [b]Luke 22:19 15:39 [a]Mark 8:10 [1]NU-Text reads *Magadan.*

MATTHEW 16

PETER'S CONFESSION OF FAITH

The Pharisees could prognosticate the weather by certain signs, yet they could not read the plainer and more plentiful warnings of the near future. Each country has its own sky warnings, but the signs of the times are the same in all lands. Our Lord singled out an instance of their supposed weather wisdom: the same sign that, in the evening, was a token of fair weather was, in the morning, a mark of foul weather. They were able to draw nice distinctions on the variable condition of "the face of the sky": Why could they not "discern the signs of the times"? They could have seen, if they had chosen to do so, that all the prophecies were one in declaring that the date of Messiah's appearing had arrived, and they could also have observed that every event was fulfilling those prophecies. But they were false at heart, would not see, and yet cried out for a sign. Signs were all around them, and yet they repeated the parrot cry, *Show us a sign.*

Lord, do not allow any of us to be blind to the heavenly signs—Your cross, Your resurrection, Your Word, Your Spirit, and Your work of grace. Teach us carefully to discern these things as being in very deed the abiding "signs of the times." Even in the growing coldness of the church and the abounding iniquity of the world, let us see the tokens of Your Advent and stand waiting and watching for Your long-promised appearing.

---

1 Then the [a]Pharisees and Sadducees came, and testing Him
asked that He would show them a sign from heaven.
2 He answered and said to them, "When it is evening you
say, '*It will be* fair weather, for the sky is red';
3 "and in the morning, '*It will be* foul weather today, for the
sky is red and threatening.' Hypocrites![1] You know how to
discern the face of the sky, but you cannot *discern* the signs
of the times.
4 [a]"A wicked and adulterous generation seeks after a sign,
and no sign shall be given to it except the sign of the proph-
et[1] Jonah." And He left them and departed.
5 Now [a]when His disciples had come to the other side, they
had forgotten to take bread.
6 Then Jesus said to them, [a]"Take heed and beware of the
leaven of the Pharisees and the Sadducees."
7 And they reasoned among themselves, saying, "*It is* be-
cause we have taken no bread."

16:1 [a]Mark 8:11 16:3 [1]NU-Text omits *Hypocrites.* 16:4 [a]Matt. 12:39 [1]NU-Text omits *the prophet.* 16:5 [a]Mark 8:14 16:6 [a]Luke 12:1

8 But Jesus, being aware of *it,* said to them, "O you of little faith, why do you reason among yourselves because you have brought no bread?[1]
9 [a]"Do you not yet understand, or remember the five loaves of the five thousand and how many baskets you took up?
10 [a]"Nor the seven loaves of the four thousand and how many large baskets you took up?
11 "How is it you do not understand that I did not speak to you concerning bread?—*but* to beware of the leaven of the Pharisees and Sadducees."
12 Then they understood that He did not tell *them* to beware of the leaven of bread, but of the doctrine of the Pharisees and Sadducees.
13 When Jesus came into the region of Caesarea Philippi, He asked His disciples, saying, [a]"Who do men say that I, the Son of Man, am?"
14 So they said, [a]"Some *say* John the Baptist, some Elijah, and others Jeremiah or [b]one of the prophets."
15 He said to them, "But who do [a]you say that I am?"
16 Simon Peter answered and said, [a]"You are the Christ, the Son of the living God."
17 Jesus answered and said to him, "Blessed are you, Simon Bar-Jonah, [a]for flesh and blood has not revealed *this* to you, but [b]My Father who is in heaven.
18 "And I also say to you that [a]you are Peter, and [b]on this rock I will build My church, and [c]the gates of Hades shall not prevail against it.
19 [a]"And I will give you the keys of the kingdom of heaven, and whatever you bind on earth will be bound in heaven, and whatever you loose on earth will be loosed[1] in heaven."
20 [a]Then He commanded His disciples that they should tell no one that He was Jesus the Christ.
21 From that time Jesus began [a]to show to His disciples that He must go to Jerusalem, and suffer many things from the elders and chief priests and scribes, and be killed, and be raised the third day.
22 Then Peter took Him aside and began to rebuke Him, saying, "Far be it from You, Lord; this shall not happen to You!"
23 But He turned and said to Peter, "Get behind Me, [a]Satan! [b]You are an offense to Me, for you are not mindful of the things of God, but the things of men."
24 [a]Then Jesus said to His disciples, "If anyone desires to come after Me, let him deny himself, and take up his cross, and [b]follow Me.

16:8 [1]NU-Text reads *you have no bread.* 16:9 [a]Matt. 14:15–21 16:10 [a]Matt. 15:32–38 16:13 [a]Luke 9:18 16:14 [a]Matt. 14:2 [b]Matt. 21:11 16:15 [a]John 6:67 16:16 [a]Acts 8:37; 9:20 16:17 [a][Eph. 2:8] [b]Gal. 1:16 16:18 [a]John 1:42 [b][Eph. 2:20] [c]Is. 38:10 16:19 [a]Matt. 18:18 [1]Or *will have been bound . . . will have been loosed* 16:20 [a]Luke 9:21 16:21 [a]Luke 9:22; 18:31; 24:46 16:23 [a]Matt. 4:10 [b][Rom. 8:7] 16:24 [a][2 Tim. 3:12] [b][1 Pet. 2:21]

25 "For [a]whoever desires to save his life will lose it, but who-
ever loses his life for My sake will find it.
26 "For what [a]profit is it to a man if he gains the whole world,
and loses his own soul? Or [b]what will a man give in exchange
for his soul?
27 "For [a]the Son of Man will come in the glory of His Father
[b]with His angels, [c]and then He will reward each according to
his works.
28 "Assuredly, I say to you, [a]there are some standing here
who shall not taste death till they see the Son of Man com-
ing in His kingdom."

16:25[a]John 12:25 16:26[a]Luke 12:20, 21 [b]Ps. 49:7, 8 16:27[a]Mark 8:38 [b][Dan. 7:10] [c]Rom. 2:6 16:28[a]Luke 9:27

MATTHEW 17

THE TRANSFIGURATION OF CHRIST

When our Lord Jesus Christ was transfigured, there came a voice that said, "This is My beloved Son, in whom I am well pleased. Hear Him!" It was the voice of the Father concerning His Son: a testimony to His Person, a notification of His office, an announcement of His authority to teach and to legislate. You can understand how imperative it then was for those who heard it to heed Him.

But now He is gone up from us. He has entered into the excellent glory; He no longer teaches in our streets, yet still, as though present with us, He speaks to us. By the written Word, His sayings are handed down to us infallibly. Oftentimes, when the Holy Spirit rests upon God's servants, they become as the voice of Christ to us, and when that same blessed Spirit, the Comforter, brings to our remembrance the things of Christ, seems it not as though Jesus Himself spoke to our souls? The admonition is not out of date; it has not lost its telling point or its vital force. Still does the Father say to us concerning His well-beloved Son, "Hear Him."

Does not our Lord Jesus Christ Himself deserve to be heard? Peerless among the princes of heaven, is He not very God of very God? And immaculate among the children of men, is He not Man of the substance of His mother? Here is a double claim upon our attention.

---

1 Now [a]after six days Jesus took Peter, James, and John his
brother, led them up on a high mountain by themselves;
2 and He was transfigured before them. His face shone like
the sun, and His clothes became as white as the light.
3 And behold, Moses and Elijah appeared to them, talking
with Him.
4 Then Peter answered and said to Jesus, "Lord, it is good
for us to be here; if You wish, let us[1] make here three tabernacles: one for You, one for Moses, and one for Elijah."
5 [a]While he was still speaking, behold, a bright cloud overshadowed them; and suddenly a voice came out of the cloud,
saying, [b]"This is My beloved Son, [c]in whom I am well pleased.
[d]Hear Him!"
6 [a]And when the disciples heard *it,* they fell on their faces
and were greatly afraid.
7 But Jesus came and [a]touched them and said, "Arise, and
do not be afraid."

17:1[a]Mark 9:2–8 17:4[1]NU-Text reads *I will.* 17:5[a]2 Pet. 1:17 [b]Mark 1:11 [c]Matt. 3:17; 12:18 [d][Deut. 18:15, 19] 17:6[a]2 Pet. 1:18 17:7[a]Dan. 8:18

8 When they had lifted up their eyes, they saw no one but
Jesus only.
9 Now as they came down from the mountain, Jesus com-
manded them, saying, "Tell the vision to no one until the Son
of Man is risen from the dead."
10 And His disciples asked Him, saying, [a]"Why then do the
scribes say that Elijah must come first?"
11 Jesus answered and said to them, "Indeed, Elijah is com-
ing first[1] and will [a]restore all things.
12 [a]"But I say to you that Elijah has come already, and they
[b]did not know him but did to him whatever they wished. Like-
wise [c]the Son of Man is also about to suffer at their hands."
13 [a]Then the disciples understood that He spoke to them of
John the Baptist.
14 [a]And when they had come to the multitude, a man came
to Him, kneeling down to Him and saying,
15 "Lord, have mercy on my son, for he is an epileptic[1] and
suffers severely; for he often falls into the fire and often into
the water.
16 "So I brought him to Your disciples, but they could not
cure him."
17 Then Jesus answered and said, "O faithless and [a]perverse
generation, how long shall I be with you? How long shall I
bear with you? Bring him here to Me."
18 And Jesus [a]rebuked the demon, and it came out of him;
and the child was cured from that very hour.
19 Then the disciples came to Jesus privately and said, "Why
could we not cast it out?"
20 So Jesus said to them, "Because of your unbelief;[1] for as-
suredly, I say to you, [a]if you have faith as a mustard seed, you
will say to this mountain, 'Move from here to there,' and it
will move; and nothing will be impossible for you.
21 "However, this kind does not go out except by prayer and
fasting."[1]
22 [a]Now while they were staying[1] in Galilee, Jesus said to
them, "The Son of Man is about to be betrayed into the hands
of men,
23 "and they will kill Him, and the third day He will be raised
up." And they were exceedingly [a]sorrowful.
24 [a]When they had come to Capernaum,[1] those who received
the *temple* tax came to Peter and said, "Does your Teacher
not pay the *temple* tax?"
25 He said, "Yes." And when he had come into the house,

17:10[a]Mal. 4:5 17:11[a][Mal. 4:6] [1]NU-Text omits *first.* 17:12[a]Mark 9:12, 13 [b]Matt. 14:3, 10 [c]Matt. 16:21 17:13[a]Matt. 11:14 17:14[a]Mark 9:14–28 17:15[1]Literally *moonstruck* 17:17[a]Phil. 2:15 17:18[a]Luke 4:41 17:20[a]Luke 17:6 [1]NU-Text reads *little faith.* 17:21[1]NU-Text omits this verse. 17:22[a]Mark 8:31 [1]NU-Text reads *gathering together.* 17:23[a]John 16:6; 19:30 17:24[a]Mark 9:33 [1]NU-Text reads *Capharnaum* (here and elsewhere).

Jesus anticipated him, saying, "What do you think, Simon?
From whom do the kings of the earth take customs or taxes,
from their sons or from [a]strangers?"
26 Peter said to Him, "From strangers." Jesus said to him,
"Then the sons are free.
27 "Nevertheless, lest we offend them, go to the sea, cast in
a hook, and take the fish that comes up first. And when you
have opened its mouth, you will find a piece of money;[1] take
that and give it to them for Me and you."

17:25[a] [Is. 60:10–17] 17:27[1] Greek *stater,* the exact amount to pay the temple tax (didrachma) for two

MATTHEW 18

OFFENSES AND FORGIVENESS

Thus the Savior sets His seal upon assemblies of the faithful, even of the smallest kind, not only in their acts of discipline but in their intercessions. Note how tenderly Jesus speaks of His followers: *Poor as you are, if two of you agree in prayer on earth,* "My Father in heaven" *will hearken to your pleading.* Prayer should be matter for previous consideration, and persons about to join in prayer should "agree . . . concerning anything that they ask." Then they come together with an intelligent design, seeking a known blessing and agreeing to combine their desires and their faith in reference to the one chosen object. Two believers united in holy desire and solemn prayer will have great power with God. Instead of despising the verdict of so small a gathering, we ought to respect it since the Father does so.

The presence of Jesus is the fixed center of the assembly, the warrant for its coming together, and the power with which it acts. The church, however small, is gathered in His name. Jesus arrives first: "I am there in the midst of them." We are gathered together by the holy impulses of Christian brotherhood, and our meeting is in the name of Jesus; therefore He is near not only to the leader or to the minister but in the midst and therefore to each worshiper. We meet to do Him honor, to hear His Word, to stir each other up to obey His will, and He is there to aid us.

---

1 At [a]that time the disciples came to Jesus, saying, "Who
then is greatest in the kingdom of heaven?"
2 Then Jesus called a little [a]child to Him, set him in the midst
of them,
3 and said, "Assuredly, I say to you, [a]unless you are converted and become as little children, you will by no means enter
the kingdom of heaven.
4 [a]"Therefore whoever humbles himself as this little child
is the greatest in the kingdom of heaven.
5 [a]"Whoever receives one little child like this in My name
receives Me.
6 [a]"But whoever causes one of these little ones who believe
in Me to sin, it would be better for him if a millstone were
hung around his neck, and he were drowned in the depth of
the sea.
7 "Woe to the world because of offenses! For [a]offenses must
come, but [b]woe to that man by whom the offense comes!

18:1[a]Luke 9:46–48; 22:24–27 18:2[a]Matt. 19:14 18:3[a]Luke 18:16 18:4[a][Matt. 20:27; 23:11] 18:5[a][Matt. 10:42] 18:6[a]Mark 9:42 18:7[a][1 Cor. 11:19] [b]Matt. 26:24; 27:4, 5

8 [a]"If your hand or foot causes you to sin, cut it off and cast *it*
from you. It is better for you to enter into life lame or maimed,
rather than having two hands or two feet, to be cast into the
everlasting fire.
9 "And if your eye causes you to sin, pluck it out and cast *it*
from you. It is better for you to enter into life with one eye,
rather than having two eyes, to be cast into hell fire.
10 "Take heed that you do not despise one of these little ones,
for I say to you that in heaven [a]their angels always [b]see the
face of My Father who is in heaven.
11 [a]"For the Son of Man has come to save that which was
lost.[1]
12 [a]"What do you think? If a man has a hundred sheep, and
one of them goes astray, does he not leave the ninety-nine
and go to the mountains to seek the one that is straying?
13 "And if he should find it, assuredly, I say to you, he rejoic-
es more over that *sheep* than over the ninety-nine that did
not go astray.
14 "Even so it is not the [a]will of your Father who is in heaven
that one of these little ones should perish.
15 "Moreover [a]if your brother sins against you, go and tell
him his fault between you and him alone. If he hears you,
[b]you have gained your brother.
16 "But if he will not hear, take with you one or two more,
that [a]'by the mouth of two or three witnesses every word may
be established.'[1]
17 "And if he refuses to hear them, tell *it* to the church. But
if he refuses even to hear the church, let him be to you like a
[a]heathen and a tax collector.
18 "Assuredly, I say to you, [a]whatever you bind on earth will
be bound in heaven, and whatever you loose on earth will be
loosed in heaven.
19 [a]"Again I say[1] to you that if two of you agree on earth con-
cerning anything that they ask, [b]it will be done for them by
My Father in heaven.
20 "For where two or three are gathered [a]together in My
name, I am there in the midst of them."
21 Then Peter came to Him and said, "Lord, how often shall
my brother sin against me, and I forgive him? [a]Up to seven
times?"
22 Jesus said to him, "I do not say to you, [a]up to seven times,
but up to seventy times seven.
23 "Therefore the kingdom of heaven is like a certain king
who wanted to settle accounts with his servants.

18:8[a] Matt. 5:29, 30 18:10[a] [Heb. 1:14] [b] Luke 1:19 18:11[a] Luke 9:56 [1] NU-Text omits this verse. 18:12[a] Luke 15:4–7 18:14[a] [1 Tim. 2:4] 18:15[a] Lev. 19:17 [b] [James 5:20] 18:16[a] Deut. 17:6; 19:15 [1] Deuteronomy 19:15 18:17[a] [2 Thess. 3:6, 14] 18:18[a] [John 20:22, 23] 18:19[a] [1 Cor. 1:10] [b] [1 John 3:22; 5:14] [1] NU-Text and M-Text read *Again, assuredly, I say.* 18:20[a] Acts 20:7 18:21[a] Luke 17:4 18:22[a] Col. 3:13

24 "And when he had begun to settle accounts, one was
brought to him who owed him ten thousand talents.
25 "But as he was not able to pay, his master commanded
[a]that he be sold, with his wife and children and all that he
had, and that payment be made.
26 "The servant therefore fell down before him, saying, 'Mas-
ter, have patience with me, and I will pay you all.'
27 "Then the master of that servant was moved with com-
passion, released him, and forgave him the debt.
28 "But that servant went out and found one of his fellow
servants who owed him a hundred denarii; and he laid hands
on him and took *him* by the throat, saying, 'Pay me what
you owe!'
29 "So his fellow servant fell down at his feet[1] and begged
him, saying, 'Have patience with me, and I will pay you all.'[2]
30 "And he would not, but went and threw him into prison
till he should pay the debt.
31 "So when his fellow servants saw what had been done,
they were very grieved, and came and told their master all
that had been done.
32 "Then his master, after he had called him, said to him,
'You wicked servant! I forgave you [a]all that debt because you
begged me.
33 'Should you not also have had compassion on your fel-
low servant, just as I had pity on you?'
34 "And his master was angry, and delivered him to the tor-
turers until he should pay all that was due to him.
35 [a]"So My heavenly Father also will do to you if each of you,
from his heart, does not forgive his brother his trespasses."[1]

18:25[a] 2 Kin. 4:1 18:29[1] NU-Text omits *at his feet.* [2] NU-Text and M-Text omit *all.* 18:32[a] Luke 7:41–43 18:35[a] James 2:13 [1] NU-Text omits *his trespasses.*

MATTHEW 19

CHRIST'S TEACHING ON DIVORCE

Our Savior very often preached upon the moral precepts of the law. Many of the sermons of Christ—and what sermons shall compare with them—have not what is now currently called "the gospel" in them at all. Our Savior did not, every time He stood up to preach, declare the doctrine of election, atonement, effectual calling, or final perseverance. No, He just as frequently spoke upon the duties of human life and upon those precious fruits of the Spirit that are begotten in us by the grace of God.

"You shall love your neighbor as yourself." We can split the command into three parts. Whom am I to love? My neighbor. What am I to do? I am to love him. How am I to do it? I am to love him as myself.

Your neighbor thinks differently. His religion is unsound and untrue: love him for all that. Let not your differences separate him from you. Perhaps he may be right, or he may be wrong— he shall be the rightest in practice who loves the most. Possibly he has no religion at all. He disregards your God; he breaks the Sabbath; he is confessedly an atheist. Love him still. And if you make any distinction, make it this: *Because you are not of my religion, I will serve you the more that you may be converted to the right.*

---

1 Now it came to pass, [a]when Jesus had finished these say-
ings, *that* He departed from Galilee and came to the region
of Judea beyond the Jordan.
2 [a]And great multitudes followed Him, and He healed them
there.
3 The Pharisees also came to Him, testing Him, and saying
to Him, "Is it lawful for a man to divorce his wife for *just* any
reason?"
4 And He answered and said to them, "Have you not read
that He who made[1] *them* at the beginning [a]'made them male
and female,'[2]
5 "and said, [a]'For this reason a man shall leave his father and
mother and be joined to his wife, and [b]the two shall become
one flesh'?[1]
6 "So then, they are no longer two but one flesh. Therefore
what God has joined together, let not man separate."
7 They said to Him, [a]"Why then did Moses command to give
a certificate of divorce, and to put her away?"
8 He said to them, "Moses, because of the [a]hardness of your

19:1 [a]Mark 10:1–12 19:2 [a]Matt. 12:15 19:4 [a]Gen. 1:27; 5:2 [1]NU-Text reads *created.* [2]Genesis 1:27; 5:2 19:5 [a]Gen. 2:24 [b][1 Cor. 6:16; 7:2] [1]Genesis 2:24 19:7 [a]Deut. 24:1–4 19:8 [a]Heb. 3:15

hearts, permitted you to divorce your [b]wives, but from the
beginning it was not so.
9 [a]"And I say to you, whoever divorces his wife, except for
sexual immorality,[1] and marries another, commits adultery;
and whoever marries her who is divorced commits adultery."
10 His disciples said to Him, [a]"If such is the case of the man
with *his* wife, it is better not to marry."
11 But He said to them, [a]"All cannot accept this saying, but
only *those* to whom it has been given:
12 "For there are eunuchs who were born thus from *their*
mother's womb, and [a]there are eunuchs who were made eu-
nuchs by men, and there are eunuchs who have made them-
selves eunuchs for the kingdom of heaven's sake. He who is
able to accept *it,* let him accept *it.*"
13 [a]Then little children were brought to Him that He might
put *His* hands on them and pray, but the disciples rebuked
them.
14 But Jesus said, "Let the little children come to Me, and do
not forbid them; for [a]of such is the kingdom of heaven."
15 And He laid *His* hands on them and departed from there.
16 [a]Now behold, one came and said to Him, [b]"Good[1] Teach-
er, what good thing shall I do that I may have eternal life?"
17 So He said to him, "Why do you call Me good?[1] No one *is*
[a]good but One, *that is,* God.[2] But if you want to enter into life,
[b]keep the commandments."
18 He said to Him, "Which ones?" Jesus said, [a]" 'You shall
not murder,' 'You shall not commit adultery,' 'You shall not
steal,' 'You shall not bear false witness,'
19 [a]'Honor your father and *your* mother,'[1] and, [b]'You shall
love your neighbor as yourself.' "[2]
20 The young man said to Him, "All these things I have [a]kept
from my youth.[1] What do I still lack?"
21 Jesus said to him, "If you want to be perfect, [a]go, sell what
you have and give to the poor, and you will have treasure in
heaven; and come, follow Me."
22 But when the young man heard that saying, he went away
sorrowful, for he had great possessions.
23 Then Jesus said to His disciples, "Assuredly, I say to you
that [a]it is hard for a rich man to enter the kingdom of heav-
en.
24 "And again I say to you, it is easier for a camel to go
through the eye of a needle than for a rich man to enter the
kingdom of God."

19:8[b]Mal. 2:16 19:9[a][Matt. 5:32] [1]Or *fornication* 19:10[a][Prov. 21:19] 19:11[a][1 Cor. 7:2, 7, 9, 17] 19:12[a][1 Cor. 7:32] 19:13[a]Luke 18:15 19:14[a]Matt. 18:3, 4 19:16[a]Mark 10:17–30 [b]Luke 10:25 [1]NU-Text omits *Good.* 19:17[a]Nah. 1:7 [b]Lev. 18:5 [1]NU-Text reads *Why do you ask Me about what is good?* [2]NU-Text reads *There is One who is good.* 19:18[a]Ex. 20:13–16 19:19[a]Ex. 20:12–16; Deut. 5:16–20 [b]Lev. 19:18 [1]Exodus 20:12–16; Deuteronomy 5:16–20 [2]Leviticus 19:18 19:20[a][Phil. 3:6, 7] [1]NU-Text omits *from my youth.* 19:21[a]Acts 2:45; 4:34, 35 19:23[a][1 Tim. 6:9]

25 When His disciples heard *it,* they were greatly astonished,
saying, "Who then can be saved?"
26 But Jesus looked at *them* and said to them, "With men
this is impossible, but [a]with God all things are possible."
27 Then Peter answered and said to Him, "See, [a]we have left
all and followed You. Therefore what shall we have?"
28 So Jesus said to them, "Assuredly I say to you, that in
the regeneration, when the Son of Man sits on the throne of
His glory, [a]you who have followed Me will also sit on twelve
thrones, judging the twelve tribes of Israel.
29 [a]"And everyone who has left houses or brothers or sis-
ters or father or mother or wife[1] or children or lands, for My
name's sake, shall receive a hundredfold, and inherit eternal
life.
30 [a]"But many *who are* first will be last, and the last first.

19:26[a] Jer. 32:17 19:27[a] Deut. 33:9 19:28[a] Luke 22:28–30 19:29[a] Mark 10:29, 30
[1] NU-Text omits *or wife.* 19:30[a] Luke 13:30

MATTHEW 20

CHRIST FORETELLS HIS SUFFERINGS

The householder says, "Is it not lawful for me to do what I will with mine own?" and even so does the God of heaven and earth ask, "Is it not lawful for Me to do what I wish with My own things?" There is no attribute of God more comforting to His children than the doctrine of divine sovereignty. Under the most adverse circumstances, in the most severe troubles, they believe that sovereignty has ordained their afflictions, that sovereignty overrules them, and that sovereignty will sanctify them all. There is nothing for which the children of God ought more earnestly to contend than the dominion of their Master over all creation—the kingship of God over all the works of His own hands—the throne of God, and His right to sit upon that throne.

On the other hand, there is no doctrine more hated by worldlings. Men will allow God to be everywhere except on His throne. But when God ascends His throne, His creatures then gnash their teeth; and when we proclaim an enthroned God and His right to do as He wills with His own, to dispose of His creatures as He thinks well without consulting them in the matter, then it is that we are hissed and execrated, and then it is that men turn a deaf ear to us, for God on His throne is not the God they love. But it is God upon the throne that we love to preach. It is God upon His throne whom we trust.

---

1 "For the kingdom of heaven is like a landowner who went
out early in the morning to hire laborers for his vineyard.
2 "Now when he had agreed with the laborers for a denarius
a day, he sent them into his vineyard.
3 "And he went out about the third hour and saw others
standing idle in the marketplace,
4 "and said to them, 'You also go into the vineyard, and whatever is right I will give you.' So they went.
5 "Again he went out about the sixth and the ninth hour, and
did likewise.
6 "And about the eleventh hour he went out and found others
standing idle,[1] and said to them, 'Why have you been standing here idle all day?'
7 "They said to him, 'Because no one hired us.' He said to
them, 'You also go into the vineyard, and whatever is right you will receive.'[1]
8 "So when evening had come, the owner of the vineyard said

20:6 [1]NU-Text omits *idle*. 20:7 [1]NU-Text omits the last clause of this verse.

to his steward, 'Call the laborers and give them *their* wages,
beginning with the last to the first.'
9 "And when those came who *were hired* about the eleventh
hour, they each received a denarius.
10 "But when the first came, they supposed that they would
receive more; and they likewise received each a denarius.
11 "And when they had received *it*, they complained against
the landowner,
12 "saying, 'These last *men* have worked *only* one hour, and
you made them equal to us who have borne the burden and
the heat of the day.'
13 "But he answered one of them and said, 'Friend, I am do-
ing you no wrong. Did you not agree with me for a denarius?
14 'Take *what is* yours and go your way. I wish to give to this
last man *the same* as to you.
15 [a]'Is it not lawful for me to do what I wish with my own
things? Or [b]is your eye evil because I am good?'
16 [a]"So the last will be first, and the first last. [b]For many are
called, but few chosen."[1]
17 [a]Now Jesus, going up to Jerusalem, took the twelve dis-
ciples aside on the road and said to them,
18 [a]"Behold, we are going up to Jerusalem, and the Son of
Man will be betrayed to the chief priests and to the scribes;
and they will condemn Him to death,
19 [a]"and deliver Him to the Gentiles to [b]mock and to [c]scourge
and to [d]crucify. And the third day He will [e]rise again."
20 [a]Then the mother of [b]Zebedee's sons came to Him with
her sons, kneeling down and asking something from Him.
21 And He said to her, "What do you wish?" She said to Him,
"Grant that these two sons of mine [a]may sit, one on Your right
hand and the other on the left, in Your kingdom."
22 But Jesus answered and said, "You do not know what you
ask. Are you able to drink [a]the cup that I am about to drink,
and be baptized with [b]the baptism that I am baptized with?"[1]
They said to Him, "We are able."
23 So He said to them, [a]"You will indeed drink My cup, and
be baptized with the baptism that I am baptized with;[1] but to
sit on My right hand and on My left is not Mine to give, but
it is for those for whom it is prepared by My Father."
24 [a]And when the ten heard *it*, they were greatly displeased
with the two brothers.
25 But Jesus called them to *Himself* and said, "You know that

20:15[a][Rom. 9:20, 21] [b]Deut. 15:9 20:16[a]Matt. 19:30 [b]Matt. 22:14 [1]NU-Text omits the last sentence of this verse. 20:17[a]Mark 10:32–34 20:18[a]Matt. 16:21; 26:47–57 20:19[a]Matt. 27:2 [b]Matt. 26:67, 68; 27:29, 41 [c]Matt. 27:26 [d]Acts 3:13–15 [e]Matt. 28:5, 6 20:20[a]Mark 10:35–45 [b]Matt. 4:21; 10:2 20:21[a][Matt. 19:28] 20:22[a]Luke 22:42 [b]Luke 12:50 [1]NU-Text omits *and be baptized with the baptism that I am baptized with.* 20:23[a][Acts 12:2] [1]NU-Text omits *and be baptized with the baptism that I am baptized with.* 20:24[a]Mark 10:41

the rulers of the Gentiles lord it over them, and those who
are great exercise authority over them.
26 "Yet [a]it shall not be so among you; but [b]whoever desires
to become great among you, let him be your servant.
27 [a]"And whoever desires to be first among you, let him be
your slave—
28 [a]"just as the [b]Son of Man did not come to be served, [c]but
to serve, and [d]to give His life a ransom [e]for many."
29 [a]Now as they went out of Jericho, a great multitude fol-
lowed Him.
30 And behold, [a]two blind men sitting by the road, when
they heard that Jesus was passing by, cried out, saying, "Have
mercy on us, O Lord, [b]Son of David!"
31 Then the multitude [a]warned them that they should be
quiet; but they cried out all the more, saying, "Have mercy
on us, O Lord, Son of David!"
32 So Jesus stood still and called them, and said, "What do
you want Me to do for you?"
33 They said to Him, "Lord, that our eyes may be opened."
34 So Jesus had [a]compassion and touched their eyes. And
immediately their eyes received sight, and they followed Him.

20:26[a][1 Pet. 5:3] [b]Matt. 23:11 20:27[a][Matt. 18:4] 20:28[a]John 13:4 [b][Phil. 2:6, 7] [c]Luke 22:27 [d][Is. 53:10, 11] [e][Rom. 5:15, 19] 20:29[a]Mark 10:46–52 20:30[a]Matt. 9:27 [b][Ezek. 37:21–25] 20:31[a]Matt. 19:13 20:34[a]Matt. 9:36; 14:14; 15:32; 18:27

MATTHEW 21

JESUS RIDES INTO JERUSALEM

There is space left you for repentance; though you may have been a drunkard, a swearer, or unchaste, the die is not yet cast; a change is yet possible. The son in the parable said to himself, *I will consider the matter—second thoughts are often best. I growled at my good father and gave him a sharp answer, and I saw the tear standing in the good man's eye. I am sorry I grieved him. I said no to him,* said he, *but I did not think about it. I forgot that if I go and work in my father's vineyard, I shall be working for myself, for I am his eldest son and all that he has will belong to me. I am very foolish to refuse to work to my own advantage. Ah! Now I see my father had my advantage at heart. I will even go as he bade me.*

See, he shoulders his tools, and away he marches to labor with all his might. He said, "I will not," but he repented and went, and it is admitted by all that he did the will of his father. Oh, I hope that many a man and woman will this day cry, "I do retract what I have said. I will go to my Father and say to Him, 'I will do Your bidding. I will not grieve Your love. I will not lose the opportunity of advancing my soul's best interest; I obey the gospel command.'"

---

1 Now [a]when they drew near Jerusalem, and came to Beth-
phage,[1] at [b]the Mount of Olives, then Jesus sent two disciples,
2 saying to them, "Go into the village opposite you, and im-
mediately you will find a donkey tied, and a colt with her.
Loose *them* and bring *them* to Me.
3 "And if anyone says anything to you, you shall say, 'The
Lord has need of them,' and immediately he will send them."
4 All[1] this was done that it might be fulfilled which was spo-
ken by the prophet, saying:

5 "Tell[a] the daughter of Zion,
'Behold, your King is coming to you,
Lowly, and sitting on a donkey,
A colt, the foal of a donkey.'"[1]

6 [a]So the disciples went and did as Jesus commanded them.
7 They brought the donkey and the colt, [a]laid their clothes
on them, and set *Him*[1] on them.
8 And a very great multitude spread their clothes on the
road; [a]others cut down branches from the trees and spread
them on the road.

21:1[a]Luke 19:29–38 [b][Zech. 14:4] [1]M-Text reads *Bethsphage.* 21:4[1]NU-Text omits *All.* 21:5[a]Zech. 9:9 [1]Zechariah 9:9 21:6[a]Mark 11:4 21:7[a]2 Kin. 9:13 [1]NU-Text reads *and He sat.* 21:8[a]Lev. 23:40

9 Then the multitudes who went before and those who followed cried out, saying:

> "Hosanna to the Son of David!
> [a]'Blessed *is* He who comes in the name of the LORD!'[1]
> Hosanna in the highest!"

10 [a]And when He had come into Jerusalem, all the city was
moved, saying, "Who is this?"
11 So the multitudes said, "This is Jesus, [a]the prophet from
Nazareth of Galilee."
12 [a]Then Jesus went into the temple of God[1] and drove out
all those who bought and sold in the temple, and overturned
the tables of the [b]money changers and the seats of those who
sold doves.
13 And He said to them, "It is written, [a]'My house shall be
called a house of prayer,'[1] but you have made it a [b]'den of
thieves.'"[2]
14 Then *the* blind and *the* lame came to Him in the temple,
and He healed them.
15 But when the chief priests and scribes saw the wonderful
things that He did, and the children crying out in the temple
and saying, "Hosanna to the [a]Son of David!" they were indignant
16 and said to Him, "Do You hear what these are saying?"
And Jesus said to them, "Yes. Have you never read,

> [a]'Out of the mouth of babes and nursing infants
> You have perfected praise'?"[1]

17 Then He left them and [a]went out of the city to Bethany,
and He lodged there.
18 [a]Now in the morning, as He returned to the city, He was
hungry.
19 [a]And seeing a fig tree by the road, He came to it and found
nothing on it but leaves, and said to it, "Let no fruit grow on
you ever again." Immediately the fig tree withered away.
20 [a]And when the disciples saw *it*, they marveled, saying,
"How did the fig tree wither away so soon?"
21 So Jesus answered and said to them, "Assuredly, I say to
you, [a]if you have faith and [b]do not doubt, you will not only
do what was done to the fig tree, [c]but also if you say to this
mountain, 'Be removed and be cast into the sea,' it will be
done.

21:9 [a]Ps. 118:26; Matt. 23:39 [1]Psalm 118:26 21:10 [a]John 2:13, 15 21:11 [a]John 6:14; 7:40; 9:17 21:12 [a]Mark 11:15–18 [b]Deut. 14:25 [1]NU-Text omits *of God*. 21:13 [a]Is. 56:7 [b]Jer. 7:11 [1]Isaiah 56:7 [2]Jeremiah 7:11 21:15 [a]John 7:42 21:16 [a]Ps. 8:2 [1]Psalm 8:2 21:17 [a]John 11:1, 18; 12:1 21:18 [a]Mark 11:12–14, 20–24 21:19 [a]Mark 11:13 21:20 [a]Mark 11:20 21:21 [a]Matt. 17:20 [b]James 1:6 [c]1 Cor. 13:2

22 "And [a]whatever things you ask in prayer, believing, you
will receive."
23 [a]Now when He came into the temple, the chief priests and
the elders of the people confronted Him as He was teaching,
and [b]said, "By what authority are You doing these things?
And who gave You this authority?"
24 But Jesus answered and said to them, "I also will ask you
one thing, which if you tell Me, I likewise will tell you by what
authority I do these things:
25 "The [a]baptism of [b]John—where was it from? From heaven
or from men?" And they reasoned among themselves, say-
ing, "If we say, 'From heaven,' He will say to us, 'Why then did
you not believe him?'
26 "But if we say, 'From men,' we [a]fear the multitude, [b]for all
count John as a prophet."
27 So they answered Jesus and said, "We do not know." And
He said to them, "Neither will I tell you by what authority I
do these things.
28 "But what do you think? A man had two sons, and he came
to the first and said, 'Son, go, work today in my [a]vineyard.'
29 "He answered and said, 'I will not,' but afterward he re-
gretted it and went.
30 "Then he came to the second and said likewise. And he
answered and said, 'I *go,* sir,' but he did not go.
31 "Which of the two did the will of *his* father?" They said to
Him, "The first." Jesus said to them, [a]"Assuredly, I say to you
that tax collectors and harlots enter the kingdom of God be-
fore you.
32 "For [a]John came to you in the way of righteousness, and
you did not believe him; [b]but tax collectors and harlots be-
lieved him; and when you saw *it,* you did not afterward relent
and believe him.
33 "Hear another parable: There was a certain landowner
[a]who planted a vineyard and set a hedge around it, dug a
winepress in it and built a tower. And he leased it to vine-
dressers and [b]went into a far country.
34 "Now when vintage-time drew near, he sent his servants
to the vinedressers, that they might receive its fruit.
35 [a]"And the vinedressers took his servants, beat one, killed
one, and stoned another.
36 "Again he sent other servants, more than the first, and
they did likewise to them.
37 "Then last of all he sent his [a]son to them, saying, 'They
will respect my son.'
38 "But when the vinedressers saw the son, they said among

21:22[a]Matt. 7:7–11 21:23[a]Luke 20:1–8 [b]Ex. 2:14 21:25[a][John 1:29–34] [b]John 1:15–28 21:26[a]Matt. 14:5; 21:46 [b]Mark 6:20 21:28[a]Matt. 20:1; 21:33 21:31[a]Luke 7:29, 37–50 21:32[a]Luke 3:1–12; 7:29 [b]Luke 3:12, 13 21:33[a]Luke 20:9–19 [b]Matt. 25:14 21:35[a][1 Thess. 2:15] 21:37[a][John 3:16]

themselves, [a]'This is the heir. [b]Come, let us kill him and seize
his inheritance.'
39 [a]"So they took him and cast *him* out of the vineyard and
killed *him*.
40 "Therefore, when the owner of the vineyard comes, what
will he do to those vinedressers?"
41 [a]They said to Him, [b]"He will destroy those wicked men
miserably, [c]and lease *his* vineyard to other vinedressers who
will render to him the fruits in their seasons."
42 Jesus said to them, "Have you never read in the Scrip-
tures:

> [a]'The stone which the builders rejected
> Has become the chief cornerstone.
> This was the LORD's doing,
> And it is marvelous in our eyes'?[1]

43 "Therefore I say to you, [a]the kingdom of God will be taken
from you and given to a nation bearing the fruits of it.
44 "And [a]whoever falls on this stone will be broken; but on
whomever it falls, [b]it will grind him to powder."
45 Now when the chief priests and Pharisees heard His par-
ables, they perceived that He was speaking of them.
46 But when they sought to lay hands on Him, they [a]feared
the multitudes, because [b]they took Him for a prophet.

21:38 [a][Heb. 1:2] [b]John 11:53 21:39 [a][Acts 2:23] 21:41 [a]Luke 20:16 [b][Luke 21:24] [c][Acts 13:46] 21:42 [a]Ps. 118:22, 23 [1]Psalm 118:22, 23 21:43 [a][Matt. 8:12] 21:44 [a]Is. 8:14, 15 [b][Dan. 2:44] 21:46 [a]Matt. 21:26 [b]Matt. 21:11

MATTHEW 22

THE MARRIAGE OF THE KING'S SON

To understand the parable before us, we must first direct our attention to the design of the "certain king" here spoken of. He had a grand object in view: he desired to do honor to his son upon the occasion of his marriage. We shall then notice the very generous method by which he proposed to accomplish his purpose: he made a dinner and bade many. This mode would best display his bounty.

It is even so with the gospel. It is for love; in the gospel, sinner, you are invited to be reconciled to God—you are assured that God forgives your sins, ceases to be angry, and would have you reconciled to Him through His Son. Thus love is established between God and the soul. Then it is for laughter, for happiness, for joy. Those who come to God in Christ Jesus and believe in Him have their hearts filled with overflowing peace.

A feast, moreover, is for fullness. The hungry, famished soul of man is satisfied with the blessings of grace. There is not a faculty of our nature that is not made to feel its need supplied when the soul accepts the provisions of mercy; our whole person is satisfied with good things, and our youth is renewed like the eagle's. To crown all, the gospel brings us into fellowship with the Father and His Son, Jesus Christ. In Christ Jesus, we commune with the sacred Trinity. God becomes our Father and reveals His paternal heart.

---

1 And Jesus answered [a]and spoke to them again by parables and said:
2 "The kingdom of heaven is like a certain king who arranged a marriage for his son,
3 "and sent out his servants to call those who were invited to the wedding; and they were not willing to come.
4 "Again, he sent out other servants, saying, 'Tell those who are invited, "See, I have prepared my dinner; [a]my oxen and fatted cattle *are* killed, and all things *are* ready. Come to the wedding."'
5 "But they made light of it and went their ways, one to his own farm, another to his business.
6 "And the rest seized his servants, treated *them* spitefully, and killed *them*.
7 "But when the king heard *about it,* he was furious. And he sent out [a]his armies, destroyed those murderers, and burned up their city.

22:1[a] [Rev. 19:7–9] 22:4[a] Prov. 9:2 22:7[a] [Dan. 9:26]

8 "Then he said to his servants, 'The wedding is ready, but
those who were invited were not [a]worthy.
9 'Therefore go into the highways, and as many as you find,
invite to the wedding.'
10 "So those servants went out into the highways and [a]gath-
ered together all whom they found, both bad and good. And
the wedding *hall* was filled with guests.
11 "But when the king came in to see the guests, he saw a
man there [a]who did not have on a wedding garment.
12 "So he said to him, 'Friend, how did you come in here
without a wedding garment?' And he was [a]speechless.
13 "Then the king said to the servants, 'Bind him hand and
foot, take him away, and[1] cast *him* [a]into outer darkness; there
will be weeping and gnashing of teeth.'
14 [a]"For many are called, but few *are* chosen."
15 [a]Then the Pharisees went and plotted how they might en-
tangle Him in *His* talk.
16 And they sent to Him their disciples with the [a]Herodians,
saying, "Teacher, we know that You are true, and teach the
way of God in truth; nor do You care about anyone, for You
do not regard the person of men.
17 "Tell us, therefore, what do You think? Is it lawful to pay
taxes to Caesar, or not?"
18 But Jesus perceived their wickedness, and said, "Why do
you test Me, *you* hypocrites?
19 "Show Me the tax money." So they brought Him a denar-
ius.
20 And He said to them, "Whose image and inscription *is*
this?"
21 They said to Him, "Caesar's." And He said to them, [a]"Ren-
der therefore to Caesar the things that are [b]Caesar's, and to
God the things that are [c]God's."
22 When they had heard *these words,* they marveled, and
left Him and went their way.
23 [a]The same day the Sadducees, [b]who say there is no res-
urrection, came to Him and asked Him,
24 saying: "Teacher, [a]Moses said that if a man dies, having
no children, his brother shall marry his wife and raise up
offspring for his brother.
25 "Now there were with us seven brothers. The first died
after he had married, and having no offspring, left his wife
to his brother.
26 "Likewise the second also, and the third, even to the sev-
enth.
27 "Last of all the woman died also.

22:8[a]Matt. 10:11 22:10[a]Matt. 13:38, 47, 48 22:11[a][Col. 3:10, 12] 22:12[a][Rom. 3:19] 22:13[a]Matt. 8:12; 25:30 [1]NU-Text omits *take him away, and.* 22:14[a]Matt. 20:16 22:15[a]Mark 12:13–17 22:16[a]Mark 3:6; 8:15; 12:13 22:21[a]Matt. 17:25 [b][Rom. 13:1–7] [c][1 Cor. 3:23; 6:19, 20; 12:27] 22:23[a]Luke 20:27–40 [b]Acts 23:8 22:24[a]Deut. 25:5

28 "Therefore, in the resurrection, whose wife of the seven
will she be? For they all had her."
29 Jesus answered and said to them, "You are mistaken, [a]not
knowing the Scriptures nor the power of God.
30 "For in the resurrection they neither marry nor are given
in marriage, but [a]are like angels of God[1] in heaven.
31 "But concerning the resurrection of the dead, have you
not read what was spoken to you by God, saying,
32 [a]'I am the God of Abraham, the God of Isaac, and the God
of Jacob'?[1] God is not the God of the dead, but of the living."
33 And when the multitudes heard *this,* [a]they were aston-
ished at His teaching.
34 [a]But when the Pharisees heard that He had silenced the
Sadducees, they gathered together.
35 Then one of them, [a]a lawyer, asked *Him a question,* test-
ing Him, and saying,
36 "Teacher, which *is* the great commandment in the law?"
37 Jesus said to him, [a]" 'You shall love the LORD your God
with all your heart, with all your soul, and with all your mind.'[1]
38 "This is *the* first and great commandment.
39 "And *the* second *is* like it: [a]'You shall love your neighbor
as yourself.'[1]
40 [a]"On these two commandments hang all the Law and the
Prophets."
41 [a]While the Pharisees were gathered together, Jesus asked
them,
42 saying, "What do you think about the Christ? Whose Son
is He?" They said to Him, "*The* [a]*Son* of David."
43 He said to them, "How then does David in the Spirit call
Him 'Lord,' saying:

44 'The[a] LORD said to my Lord,
"Sit at My right hand,
Till I make Your enemies Your footstool" '?[1]

45 "If David then calls Him 'Lord,' how is He his Son?"
46 [a]And no one was able to answer Him a word, [b]nor from
that day on did anyone dare question Him anymore.

22:29[a] John 20:9 22:30[a] [1 John 3:2] [1]NU-Text omits *of God.* 22:32[a] Ex. 3:6, 15 [1]Exodus 3:6, 15 22:33[a] Matt. 7:28 22:34[a] Mark 12:28–31 22:35[a] Luke 7:30; 10:25; 11:45, 46, 52; 14:3 22:37[a] Deut. 6:5; 10:12; 30:6 [1]Deuteronomy 6:5 22:39[a] Lev. 19[illegible] [1]Leviticus 19:18 22:40[a] [Matt. 7:12] 22:41[a] Luke 20:41–44 22:42[a] Matt. 1:1; [illegible] 22:44[a] Ps. 110:1 [1]Psalm 110:1 22:46[a] Luke 14:6 [b]Mark 12:34

MATTHEW 23

JESUS REBUKES THE SCRIBES AND PHARISEES

The text seems to say to me that if Jerusalem was not saved—if her children were not gathered together in safety as a brood of chickens is gathered beneath the hen—if Christ did not gather and protect them, it was not because there was any unwillingness on His part. There was always a willingness in His heart to bless Jerusalem, and therefore He could truly say, "How often I wanted to gather your children together, as a hen gathers her chicks under her wings." From this utterance of our Lord I learn that if any man be not saved, the cause of his nonsalvation does not lie in any want of graciousness or willingness on God's part. They who dare to say that it does venture are very audacious in their assertions. This text says the very opposite, and so far as it is applicable to the sons of men in general, it declares that God wills not the death of any but desires that they should turn unto Him and live.

The next truth that I learn from this passage is that if Jerusalem perished, as it did perish in a most awful manner, it was because it would not be saved. It was often invited, persuaded, exhorted, warned, and threatened. And even when Christ Himself came, the loveliest and the lowliest, the tenderest and the truest, bringing to them love and mercy without stint, and when He spoke as never man spoke in notes of warning yet wooing love, still they would not receive His rebukes.

---

1 Then Jesus spoke to the multitudes and to His disciples,
2 saying: [a]"The scribes and the Pharisees sit in Moses' seat.
3 "Therefore whatever they tell you to observe,[1] *that* observe
and do, but do not do according to their works; for [a]they say,
and do not do.
4 [a]"For they bind heavy burdens, hard to bear, and lay *them*
on men's shoulders; but they *themselves* will not move them
with one of their fingers.
5 "But all their works they do to [a]be seen by men. They make
their phylacteries broad and enlarge the borders of their gar-
ments.
6 [a]"They love the best places at feasts, the best seats in the
synagogues,
7 "greetings in the marketplaces, and to be called by men,
'Rabbi, Rabbi.'
8 [a]"But you, do not be called 'Rabbi'; for One is your Teach-
er, the Christ,[1] and you are all brethren.

23:2 [a]Neh. 8:4, 8 23:3 [a][Rom. 2:19] [1]NU-Text omits *to observe.* 23:4 [a]Luke 11:46 23:5 [a][Matt. 6:1–6, 16–18] 23:6 [a]Luke 11:43; 20:46 23:8 [a][James 3:1] [1]NU-Text omits *the Christ.*

9 "Do not call anyone on earth your father; [a]for One is your
Father, He who is in heaven.
10 "And do not be called teachers; for One is your Teacher,
the Christ.
11 "But [a]he who is greatest among you shall be your servant.
12 [a]"And whoever exalts himself will be humbled, and he
who humbles himself will be exalted.
13 "But [a]woe to you, scribes and Pharisees, hypocrites! For
you shut up the kingdom of heaven against men; for you
neither go in *yourselves,* nor do you allow those who are en-
tering to go in.
14 "Woe to you, scribes and Pharisees, hypocrites! [a]For you
devour widows' houses, and for a pretense make long prayers.
Therefore you will receive greater condemnation.[1]
15 "Woe to you, scribes and Pharisees, hypocrites! For you
travel land and sea to win one proselyte, and when he is won,
you make him twice as much a son of hell as yourselves.
16 "Woe to you, [a]blind guides, who say, [b]'Whoever swears by
the temple, it is nothing; but whoever swears by the gold of
the temple, he is obliged *to perform it.*'
17 "Fools and blind! For which is greater, the gold [a]or the
temple that sanctifies[1] the gold?
18 "And, 'Whoever swears by the altar, it is nothing; but who-
ever swears by the gift that is on it, he is obliged *to perform it.*'
19 "Fools and blind! For which is greater, the gift [a]or the al-
tar that sanctifies the gift?
20 "Therefore he who swears by the altar, swears by it and
by all things on it.
21 "He who swears by the temple, swears by it and by [a]Him
who dwells[1] in it.
22 "And he who swears by heaven, swears by [a]the throne of
God and by Him who sits on it.
23 "Woe to you, scribes and Pharisees, hypocrites! [a]For you
pay tithe of mint and anise and cummin, and [b]have neglect-
ed the weightier *matters* of the law: justice and mercy and
faith. These you ought to have done, without leaving the oth-
ers undone.
24 "Blind guides, who strain out a gnat and swallow a camel!
25 "Woe to you, scribes and Pharisees, hypocrites! [a]For you
cleanse the outside of the cup and dish, but inside they are
full of extortion and self-indulgence.[1]
26 "Blind Pharisee, first cleanse the inside of the cup and
dish, that the outside of them may be clean also.
27 "Woe to you, scribes and Pharisees, hypocrites! [a]For you

23:9[a][Mal. 1:6] 23:11[a]Matt. 20:26, 27 23:12[a]Luke 14:11; 18:14 23:13[a]Luke 11:52 23:14[a]Mark 12:40 [1]NU-Text omits this verse. 23:16[a]Matt. 15:14; 23:24 [b][Matt. 5:33, 34] 23:17[a]Ex. 30:29 [1]NU-Text reads *sanctified.* 23:19[a]Ex. 29:37 23:21[a]1 Kin. 8:13 [1]M-Text reads *dwelt.* 23:22[a]Matt. 5:34 23:23[a]Luke 11:42; 18:12 [b][Hos. 6:6] 23:25[a]Luke 11:39 [1]M-Text reads *unrighteousness.* 23:27[a]Acts 23:3

are like whitewashed tombs which indeed appear beautiful
outwardly, but inside are full of dead *men's* bones and all un-
cleanness.
28 "Even so you also outwardly appear righteous to men,
but inside you are full of hypocrisy and lawlessness.
29 [a]"Woe to you, scribes and Pharisees, hypocrites! Because
you build the tombs of the prophets and adorn the monu-
ments of the righteous,
30 "and say, 'If we had lived in the days of our fathers, we
would not have been partakers with them in the blood of the
prophets.'
31 "Therefore you are witnesses against yourselves that [a]you
are sons of those who murdered the prophets.
32 [a]"Fill up, then, the measure of your fathers' *guilt*.
33 "Serpents, [a]brood of vipers! How can you escape the con-
demnation of hell?
34 [a]"Therefore, indeed, I send you prophets, wise men, and
scribes: [b]*some* of them you will kill and crucify, and [c]*some*
of them you will scourge in your synagogues and persecute
from city to city,
35 [a]"that on you may come all the righteous blood shed on
the earth, [b]from the blood of righteous Abel to [c]the blood of
Zechariah, son of Berechiah, whom you murdered between
the temple and the altar.
36 "Assuredly, I say to you, all these things will come upon
this generation.
37 [a]"O Jerusalem, Jerusalem, the one who kills the prophets
[b]and stones those who are sent to her! How often [c]I wanted
to gather your children together, as a hen gathers her chicks
[d]under *her* wings, but you were not willing!
38 "See! Your house is left to you desolate;
39 "for I say to you, you shall see Me no more till you say,
[a]'Blessed *is* He who comes in the name of the LORD!'"[1]

23:29 [a]Luke 11:47, 48 23:31 [a][Acts 7:51, 52] 23:32 [a][1 Thess. 2:16] 23:33 [a]Matt. 3:7; 12:34 23:34 [a]Luke 11:49 [b]Acts 7:54–60; 22:19 [c]2 Cor. 11:24, 25 23:35 [a]Rev. 18:24 [b]Gen. 4:8 [c]2 Chr. 24:20, 21 23:37 [a]Luke 13:34, 35 [b]2 Chr. 24:20, 21; 36:15, 16 [c]Deut. 32:11, 12 [d]Ps. 17:8; 91:4 23:39 [a]Ps. 118:26 [1]Psalm 118:26

MATTHEW 24

DESTRUCTION OF THE TEMPLE FORETOLD

The King, having finished His first discourse in the temple, left it, never to return. As His disciples moved away with Him toward the Mount of Olives, they called His attention to the great stones of which the temple was constructed and the costly adornments of the beautiful building. To them the appearance was glorious, but to their Lord it was a sad sight. His Father's house, which ought to have been "a house of prayer for all nations" (Is. 56:7), had become a "den of thieves" (Matt. 21:13) and soon would be utterly destroyed. Jesus said unto them, "Do you not see all these things? Assuredly, I say to you, not one stone shall be left here upon another, that shall not be thrown down."

Josephus tells us that Titus at first tried to save the temple, even after it was set on fire, but his efforts were of no avail, and at last he gave orders that the whole city and temple should be leveled. This was so thoroughly done that the historian says that there was left nothing to make those who came there believe it had ever been inhabited.

We sometimes delight in the temporal prosperity of the church as if it were something that must certainly endure, but all that is external will pass away or be destroyed. Let us reckon only that to be substantial comes from God and is God's work. The things that are seen are temporal.

---

1 Then [a]Jesus went out and departed from the temple, and
His disciples came up to show Him the buildings of the
temple.
2 And Jesus said to them, "Do you not see all these things?
Assuredly, I say to you, [a]not *one* stone shall be left here upon
another, that shall not be thrown down."
3 Now as He sat on the Mount of Olives, [a]the disciples came
to Him privately, saying, [b]"Tell us, when will these things be?
And what *will be* the sign of Your coming, and of the end of
the age?"
4 And Jesus answered and said to them: [a]"Take heed that
no one deceives you.
5 "For [a]many will come in My name, saying, 'I am the Christ,'
[b]and will deceive many.
6 "And you will hear of [a]wars and rumors of wars. See that
you are not troubled; for all[1] *these things* must come to pass,
but the end is not yet.

24:1 [a]Mark 13:1 24:2 [a]Luke 19:44 24:3 [a]Mark 13:3 [b][1 Thess. 5:1–3] 24:4 [a][Col. 2:8, 18] 24:5 [a]John 5:43 [b]Matt. 24:11 24:6 [a][Rev. 6:2–4] [1]NU-Text omits *all*.

7 “For [a]nation will rise against nation, and kingdom against
kingdom. And there will be [b]famines, pestilences,[1] and earth-
quakes in various places.
8 “All these *are* the beginning of sorrows.
9 [a]“Then they will deliver you up to tribulation and kill you,
and you will be hated by all nations for My name’s sake.
10 “And then many will be offended, will betray one anoth-
er, and will hate one another.
11 “Then [a]many false prophets will rise up and [b]deceive
many.
12 “And because lawlessness will abound, the love of many
will grow [a]cold.
13 [a]“But he who endures to the end shall be saved.
14 “And this [a]gospel of the kingdom [b]will be preached in all
the world as a witness to all the nations, and then the end
will come.
15 [a]“Therefore when you see the [b]‘abomination of desola-
tion,’[1] spoken of by Daniel the prophet, standing in the holy
place” [c](whoever reads, let him understand),
16 “then let those who are in Judea flee to the mountains.
17 “Let him who is on the housetop not go down to take any-
thing out of his house.
18 “And let him who is in the field not go back to get his
clothes.
19 “But [a]woe to those who are pregnant and to those who
are nursing babies in those days!
20 “And pray that your flight may not be in winter or on the
Sabbath.
21 “For [a]then there will be great tribulation, such as has not
been since the beginning of the world until this time, no, nor
ever shall be.
22 “And unless those days were shortened, no flesh would be
saved; [a]but for the elect’s sake those days will be shortened.
23 [a]“Then if anyone says to you, ‘Look, here *is* the Christ!’ or
‘There!’ do not believe *it*.
24 “For [a]false christs and false prophets will rise and show
great signs and wonders to deceive, [b]if possible, even the
elect.
25 “See, I have told you beforehand.
26 “Therefore if they say to you, ‘Look, He is in the desert!’
do not go out; *or* ‘Look, *He is* in the inner rooms!’ do not be-
lieve *it*.
27 [a]“For as the lightning comes from the east and flashes to
the west, so also will the coming of the Son of Man be.

24:7 [a]Hag. 2:22 [b]Rev. 6:5, 6 [1]NU-Text omits *pestilences*. 24:9 [a]Matt. 10:17 24:11 [a]2 Pet. 2:1 [b][1 Tim. 4:1] 24:12 [a][2 Thess. 2:3] 24:13 [a]Matt. 10:22 24:14 [a]Matt. 4:23 [b]Rom. 10:18 24:15 [a]Mark 13:14 [b]Dan. 9:27; 11:31; 12:11 [c]Dan. 9:23 [1]Daniel 11:31; 12:11 24:19 [a]Luke 23:29 24:21 [a]Dan. 9:26 24:22 [a]Is. 65:8, 9 24:23 [a]Luke 17:23 24:24 [a][2 Thess. 2:9] [b][2 Tim. 2:19] 24:27 [a]Luke 17:24

28 [a]"For wherever the carcass is, there the eagles will be gathered together.

29 [a]"Immediately after the tribulation of those days [b]the sun will be darkened, and the moon will not give its light; the stars will fall from heaven, and the powers of the heavens will be shaken.

30 [a]"Then the sign of the Son of Man will appear in heaven, [b]and then all the tribes of the earth will mourn, and they will see the Son of Man coming on the clouds of heaven with power and great glory.

31 [a]"And He will send His angels with a great sound of a trumpet, and they will gather together His elect from the four winds, from one end of heaven to the other.

32 "Now learn [a]this parable from the fig tree: When its branch has already become tender and puts forth leaves, you know that summer *is* near.

33 "So you also, when you see all these things, know [a]that it[1] is near—at the doors!

34 "Assuredly, I say to you, [a]this generation will by no means pass away till all these things take place.

35 [a]"Heaven and earth will pass away, but My words will by no means pass away.

36 [a]"But of that day and hour no one knows, not even the angels of heaven,[1] [b]but My Father only.

37 "But as the days of Noah *were,* so also will the coming of the Son of Man be.

38 [a]"For as in the days before the flood, they were eating and drinking, marrying and giving in marriage, until the day that Noah entered the ark,

39 "and did not know until the flood came and took them all away, so also will the coming of the Son of Man be.

40 [a]"Then two *men* will be in the field: one will be taken and the other left.

41 "Two *women will be* grinding at the mill: one will be taken and the other left.

42 [a]"Watch therefore, for you do not know what hour[1] your Lord is coming.

43 [a]"But know this, that if the master of the house had known what hour the thief would come, he would have watched and not allowed his house to be broken into.

44 [a]"Therefore you also be ready, for the Son of Man is coming at an hour you do not expect.

45 [a]"Who then is a faithful and wise servant, whom his master made ruler over his household, to give them food in due season?

24:28[a]Luke 17:37 24:29[a][Dan. 7:11] [b]Ezek. 32:7 24:30[a][Dan. 7:13, 14] [b]Zech. 12:12 24:31[a][1 Cor. 15:52] 24:32[a]Luke 21:29 24:33[a][James 5:9] [1]Or *He* 24:34[a][Matt. 10:23; 16:28; 23:36] 24:35[a]Luke 21:33 24:36[a]Acts 1:7 [b]Zech. 14:7 [1]NU-Text adds *nor the Son.* 24:38[a][Gen. 6:3–5] 24:40[a]Luke 17:34 24:42[a]Matt. 25:13 [1]NU-Text reads *day.* 24:43[a]Luke 12:39 24:44[a][1 Thess. 5:6] 24:45[a]Luke 12:42–46

46 [a]"Blessed *is* that servant whom his master, when he comes,
will find so doing.
47 "Assuredly, I say to you that [a]he will make him ruler over
all his goods.
48 "But if that evil servant says in his heart, 'My master [a]is
delaying his coming,'[1]
49 "and begins to beat *his* fellow servants, and to eat and
drink with the drunkards,
50 "the master of that servant will come on a day when he is
not looking for *him* and at an hour that he is [a]not aware of,
51 "and will cut him in two and appoint *him* his portion
with the hypocrites. [a]There shall be weeping and gnashing
of teeth.

24:46[a] Rev. 16:15 24:47[a] Matt. 25:21, 23 24:48[a] [2 Pet. 3:4–9] [1]NU-Text omits *his coming.* 24:50[a] Mark 13:32 24:51[a] Matt. 8:12; 25:30

MATTHEW 25

THE RETURN OF CHRIST IN JUDGMENT

All that men have they must trace to the Giver of all good. Have you talents? They were given to you by the God of talents. Have you time? Have you wealth, influence, power? Have you powers of tongue? Have you powers of thought? Are you a poet, statesman, or philosopher? Whatever your position and whatever your gifts, remember that they are not yours; they are lent to you from on high.

No man has anything of his own except his sins. We are but tenants at will. God has put us into His estates, and He has said, *Occupy till I come*. All the honor of our ability and the use of it must be unto God because He is the Giver.

The parable tells us this very pointedly, for it makes every person acknowledge that his talents come from the Lord. Even the man who dug in the earth and hid his lord's money did not deny that his talent belonged to his master; for though his reply, "Look, there you have what is yours," was exceedingly impertinent, it was not a denial of this fact. So even this man was ahead of those who deny their obligations to God, who superciliously toss their heads at the very mention of obedience to their Creator. Oh, that we were all wise to believe and to act upon this most evident of all truths, that everything we have the Most High has given us.

---

1 "Then the kingdom of heaven shall be likened to ten vir-
gins who took their lamps and went out to meet [a]the bride-
groom.
2 [a]"Now five of them were wise, and five *were* foolish.
3 "Those who *were* foolish took their lamps and took no oil
with them,
4 "but the wise took oil in their vessels with their lamps.
5 "But while the bridegroom was delayed, [a]they all slum-
bered and slept.
6 "And at midnight [a]a cry was *heard:* 'Behold, the bridegroom
is coming;[1] go out to meet him!'
7 "Then all those virgins arose and [a]trimmed their lamps.
8 "And the foolish said to the wise, 'Give us *some* of your oil,
for our lamps are going out.'
9 "But the wise answered, saying, '*No,* lest there should not
be enough for us and you; but go rather to those who sell,
and buy for yourselves.'
10 "And while they went to buy, the bridegroom came, and

25:1[a][Eph. 5:29, 30] 25:2[a]Matt. 13:47; 22:10 25:5[a]1 Thess. 5:6 25:6[a][1 Thess. 4:16] [1]NU-Text omits *is coming.* 25:7[a]Luke 12:35

those who were ready went in with him to the wedding; and
[a]the door was shut.
11 "Afterward the other virgins came also, saying, [a]'Lord,
Lord, open to us!'
12 "But he answered and said, 'Assuredly, I say to you, [a]I do
not know you.'
13 [a]"Watch therefore, for you [b]know neither the day nor the
hour[1] in which the Son of Man is coming.
14 [a]"For *the kingdom of heaven is* [b]like a man traveling to a
far country, *who* called his own servants and delivered his
goods to them.
15 "And to one he gave five talents, to another two, and to
another one, [a]to each according to his own ability; and im-
mediately he went on a journey.
16 "Then he who had received the five talents went and trad-
ed with them, and made another five talents.
17 "And likewise he who *had received* two gained two more
also.
18 "But he who had received one went and dug in the ground,
and hid his lord's money.
19 "After a long time the lord of those servants came and
settled accounts with them.
20 "So he who had received five talents came and brought
five other talents, saying, 'Lord, you delivered to me five tal-
ents; look, I have gained five more talents besides them.'
21 "His lord said to him, 'Well *done,* good and faithful ser-
vant; you were [a]faithful over a few things, [b]I will make you
ruler over many things. Enter into [c]the joy of your lord.'
22 "He also who had received two talents came and said,
'Lord, you delivered to me two talents; look, I have gained
two more talents besides them.'
23 "His lord said to him, [a]'Well *done,* good and faithful ser-
vant; you have been faithful over a few things, I will make
you ruler over many things. Enter into [b]the joy of your lord.'
24 "Then he who had received the one talent came and said,
'Lord, I knew you to be a hard man, reaping where you have
not sown, and gathering where you have not scattered seed.
25 'And I was afraid, and went and hid your talent in the
ground. Look, *there* you have *what is* yours.'
26 "But his lord answered and said to him, 'You [a]wicked and
lazy servant, you knew that I reap where I have not sown, and
gather where I have not scattered seed.
27 'So you ought to have deposited my money with the bank-
ers, and at my coming I would have received back my own
with interest.

25:10[a]Luke 13:25 25:11[a][Matt. 7:21–23] 25:12[a][Hab. 1:13] 25:13[a]Mark 13:35 [b]Matt. 24:36, 42 [1]NU-Text omits the rest of this verse. 25:14[a]Luke 19:12–27 [b]Matt. 21:33 25:15[a][Rom. 12:6] 25:21[a][1 Cor. 4:2] [b][Luke 12:44; 22:29, 30] [c][Heb. 12:2] 25:23[a]Matt. 24:45, 47; 25:21 [b][Ps. 16:11] 25:26[a]Matt. 18:32

28 'So take the talent from him, and give *it* to him who has
ten talents.
29 [a]'For to everyone who has, more will be given, and he will
have abundance; but from him who does not have, even what
he has will be taken away.
30 'And cast the unprofitable servant [a]into the outer dark-
ness. [b]There will be weeping and [c]gnashing of teeth.'
31 [a]"When the Son of Man comes in His glory, and all the
holy[1] angels with Him, then He will sit on the throne of His
glory.
32 [a]"All the nations will be gathered before Him, and [b]He
will separate them one from another, as a shepherd divides
his sheep from the goats.
33 "And He will set the [a]sheep on His right hand, but the
goats on the left.
34 "Then the King will say to those on His right hand, 'Come,
you blessed of My Father, [a]inherit the kingdom [b]prepared for
you from the foundation of the world:
35 [a]'for I was hungry and you gave Me food; I was thirsty and
you gave Me drink; [b]I was a stranger and you took Me in;
36 'I *was* [a]naked and you clothed Me; I was sick and you vis-
ited Me; [b]I was in prison and you came to Me.'
37 "Then the righteous will answer Him, saying, 'Lord, when
did we see You hungry and feed *You,* or thirsty and give *You*
drink?
38 'When did we see You a stranger and take *You* in, or na-
ked and clothe *You?*
39 'Or when did we see You sick, or in prison, and come
to You?'
40 "And the King will answer and say to them, 'Assuredly, I
say to you, [a]inasmuch as you did *it* to one of the least of these
My brethren, you did *it* to Me.'
41 "Then He will also say to those on the left hand, [a]'Depart
from Me, you cursed, [b]into the everlasting fire prepared for
[c]the devil and his angels:
42 'for I was hungry and you gave Me no food; I was thirsty
and you gave Me no drink;
43 'I was a stranger and you did not take Me in, naked and
you did not clothe Me, sick and in prison and you did not
visit Me.'
44 "Then they also will answer Him,[1] saying, 'Lord, when did
we see You hungry or thirsty or a stranger or naked or sick
or in prison, and did not minister to You?'
45 "Then He will answer them, saying, 'Assuredly, I say to

25:29 [a]Matt. 13:12 25:30 [a]Matt. 8:12; 22:13 [b]Matt. 7:23; 8:12; 24:51 [c]Ps. 112:10
25:31 [a][1 Thess. 4:16] [1]NU-Text omits *holy.* 25:32 [a][2 Cor. 5:10] [b]Ezek. 20:38
25:33 [a][John 10:11, 27, 28] 25:34 [a][Rom. 8:17] [b]Mark 10:40 25:35 [a]Is. 58:7 [b][Heb.
13:2] 25:36 [a][James 2:15, 16] [b]2 Tim. 1:16 25:40 [a]Mark 9:41 25:41 [a]Matt. 7:23
[b]Matt. 13:40, 42 [c][2 Pet. 2:4] 25:44 [1]NU-Text and M-Text omit *Him.*

you, [a]inasmuch as you did not do *it* to one of the least of
these, you did not do *it* to Me.'
46 "And [a]these will go away into everlasting punishment,
but the righteous into eternal life."

25:45 [a]Prov. 14:31 25:46 [a][Dan. 12:2]

MATTHEW 26

THE BEGINNING OF THE LORD'S SUPPER

He who, as God, knew all things had to learn obedience in the time of His humiliation. He who is in Himself Wisdom Incarnate did Himself condescend to enter the school of suffering. There we learn that important lesson of the Christian life: obedience to the will of God. And here, in Gethsemane's garden, you can see the divine Scholar going forth to practice His lesson. He had been all His lifetime learning it, and now He has to learn it for the last time in His agony and bloody sweat and in His terrible death upon the cross. Now is He to discover the utmost depths of suffering and to attain the height of the knowledge of obedience.

See how well He has learned His lesson; note how complete and ripe a Scholar He is. He has attained to the very highest class in that school and, in the immediate respect of death, can say to His Father, "Not as I will, but as You will."

The object of this discourse is to commend to you the blessed example of our Lord Jesus Christ and to urge you to be made like unto your glorious Head, and yourself to learn, by all the daily providences with which God is pleased to surround you, this lesson of resignation to the will of God and of making an entire surrender to Him.

---

1 Now it came to pass, when Jesus had finished all these say-
ings, *that* He said to His disciples,
2 [a]"You know that after two days is the Passover, and the Son
of Man will be delivered up to be crucified."
3 [a]Then the chief priests, the scribes,[1] and the elders of the
people assembled at the palace of the high priest, who was
called Caiaphas,
4 and [a]plotted to take Jesus by trickery and kill *Him.*
5 But they said, "Not during the feast, lest there be an uproar
among the [a]people."
6 And when Jesus was in [a]Bethany at the house of Simon
the leper,
7 a woman came to Him having an alabaster flask of very
costly fragrant oil, and she poured *it* on His head as He sat
at the table.
8 [a]But when His disciples saw *it,* they were indignant, say-
ing, "Why this waste?
9 "For this fragrant oil might have been sold for much and
given to *the* poor."

26:2[a]Luke 22:1, 2 26:3[a]John 11:47 [1]NU-Text omits *the scribes.* 26:4[a]Acts 4:25–28 26:5[a]Matt. 21:26 26:6[a]Mark 14:3–9 26:8[a]John 12:4

10 But when Jesus was aware of *it,* He said to them, "Why
do you trouble the woman? For she has done a good work
for Me.
11 [a]"For you have the poor with you always, but [b]Me you do
not have always.
12 "For in pouring this fragrant oil on My body, she did *it* for
My [a]burial.
13 "Assuredly, I say to you, wherever this gospel is preached
in the whole world, what this woman has done will also be
told as a memorial to her."
14 [a]Then one of the twelve, called [b]Judas Iscariot, went to
the chief priests
15 and said, [a]"What are you willing to give me if I deliver Him
to you?" And they counted out to him thirty pieces of silver.
16 So from that time he sought opportunity to betray Him.
17 [a]Now on the first *day of the Feast* of the Unleavened Bread
the disciples came to Jesus, saying to Him, "Where do You
want us to prepare for You to eat the Passover?"
18 And He said, "Go into the city to a certain man, and say to
him, 'The Teacher says, [a]"My time is at hand; I will keep the
Passover at your house with My disciples."'"
19 So the disciples did as Jesus had directed them; and they
prepared the Passover.
20 [a]When evening had come, He sat down with the twelve.
21 Now as they were eating, He said, "Assuredly, I say to you,
one of you will [a]betray Me."
22 And they were exceedingly sorrowful, and each of them
began to say to Him, "Lord, is it I?"
23 He answered and said, [a]"He who dipped *his* hand with
Me in the dish will betray Me.
24 "The Son of Man indeed goes just [a]as it is written of Him,
but [b]woe to that man by whom the Son of Man is betrayed! [c]It
would have been good for that man if he had not been born."
25 Then Judas, who was betraying Him, answered and said,
"Rabbi, is it I?" He said to him, "You have said it."
26 [a]And as they were eating, [b]Jesus took bread, blessed[1] and
broke *it,* and gave *it* to the disciples and said, "Take, eat; [c]this
is My body."
27 Then He took the cup, and gave thanks, and gave *it* to
them, saying, [a]"Drink from it, all of you.
28 "For [a]this is My blood [b]of the new[1] covenant, which is
shed [c]for many for the remission of sins.
29 "But [a]I say to you, I will not drink of this fruit of the vine

26:11[a][Deut. 15:11] [b][John 13:33; 14:19; 16:5, 28; 17:11] 26:12[a]John 19:38–42 26:14[a]Mark 14:10, 11; Luke 22:3–6 [b]Matt. 10:4 26:15[a]Zech. 11:12 26:17[a]Ex. 12:6, 18–20 26:18[a]Luke 9:51 26:20[a]Mark 14:17–21 26:21[a]John 6:70, 71; 13:21 26:23[a]Ps. 41:9 26:24[a]1 Cor. 15:3 [b]Luke 17:1 [c]John 17:12 26:26[a]Mark 14:22–25 [b]1 Cor. 11:23–25 [c][1 Pet. 2:24] [1]M-Text reads *gave thanks for.* 26:27[a]Mark 14:23 26:28[a][Ex. 24:8] [b]Jer. 31:31 [c]Matt. 20:28 [1]NU-Text omits *new.* 26:29[a]Mark 14:25

from now on [b]until that day when I drink it new with you in
My Father's kingdom."
30 [a]And when they had sung a hymn, they went out to the
Mount of Olives.
31 Then Jesus said to them, [a]"All of you will [b]be made to
stumble because of Me this night, for it is written:

> [c]'I will strike the Shepherd,
> And the sheep of the flock will be scattered.'[1]

32 "But after I have been raised, [a]I will go before you to Gal-
ilee."
33 Peter answered and said to Him, "Even if all are made to
stumble because of You, I will never be made to stumble."
34 Jesus said to him, [a]"Assuredly, I say to you that this night,
before the rooster crows, you will deny Me three times."
35 Peter said to Him, "Even if I have to die with You, I will
not deny You!" And so said all the disciples.
36 [a]Then Jesus came with them to a place called Gethsem-
ane, and said to the disciples, "Sit here while I go and pray
over there."
37 And He took with Him Peter and [a]the two sons of Zebe-
dee, and He began to be sorrowful and deeply distressed.
38 Then He said to them, [a]"My soul is exceedingly sorrow-
ful, even to death. Stay here and watch with Me."
39 He went a little farther and fell on His face, and [a]prayed,
saying, [b]"O My Father, if it is possible, [c]let this cup pass from
Me; nevertheless, [d]not as I will, but as You *will*."
40 Then He came to the disciples and found them sleeping,
and said to Peter, "What? Could you not watch with Me one
hour?
41 [a]"Watch and pray, lest you enter into temptation. [b]The
spirit indeed *is* willing, but the flesh *is* weak."
42 Again, a second time, He went away and prayed, saying,
"O My Father, if this cup cannot pass away from Me unless[1]
I drink it, Your will be done."
43 And He came and found them asleep again, for their eyes
were heavy.
44 So He left them, went away again, and prayed the third
time, saying the same words.
45 Then He came to His disciples and said to them, "Are *you*
still sleeping and resting? Behold, the hour is at hand, and
the Son of Man is being [a]betrayed into the hands of sinners.
46 "Rise, let us be going. See, My betrayer is at hand."

26:29 [b]Acts 10:41 26:30 [a]Mark 14:26–31 26:31 [a]John 16:32 [b][Matt. 11:6] [c]Zech. 13:7 [1]Zechariah 13:7 26:32 [a]Matt. 28:7, 10, 16 26:34 [a]John 13:38 26:36 [a]Mark 14:32–35 26:37 [a]Matt. 4:21; 17:1 26:38 [a]John 12:27 26:39 [a][Heb. 5:7–9] [b]John 12:27 [c]Matt. 20:22 [d]John 5:30; 6:38 26:41 [a]Luke 22:40, 46 [b][Gal. 5:17] 26:42 [1]NU-Text reads *if this may not pass away unless.* 26:45 [a]Matt. 17:22, 23; 20:18, 19

47 And [a]while He was still speaking, behold, Judas, one of
the twelve, with a great multitude with swords and clubs,
came from the chief priests and elders of the people.
48 Now His betrayer had given them a sign, saying, "Whom-
ever I kiss, He is the One; seize Him."
49 Immediately he went up to Jesus and said, "Greetings,
Rabbi!" [a]and kissed Him.
50 But Jesus said to him, [a]"Friend, why have you come?"
Then they came and laid hands on Jesus and took Him.
51 And suddenly, [a]one of those *who were* with Jesus stretched
out *his* hand and drew his sword, struck the servant of the
high priest, and cut off his ear.
52 But Jesus said to him, "Put your sword in its place, [a]for
all who take the sword will perish[1] by the sword.
53 "Or do you think that I cannot now pray to My Father, and
He will provide Me with [a]more than twelve legions of angels?
54 "How then could the Scriptures be fulfilled, [a]that it must
happen thus?"
55 In that hour Jesus said to the multitudes, "Have you come
out, as against a robber, with swords and clubs to take Me?
I sat daily with you, teaching in the temple, and you did not
seize Me.
56 "But all this was done that the [a]Scriptures of the proph-
ets might be fulfilled." Then [b]all the disciples forsook Him
and fled.
57 [a]And those who had laid hold of Jesus led *Him* away to
Caiaphas the high priest, where the scribes and the elders
were assembled.
58 But [a]Peter followed Him at a distance to the high priest's
courtyard. And he went in and sat with the servants to see
the end.
59 Now the chief priests, the elders,[1] and all the council
sought [a]false testimony against Jesus to put Him to death,
60 but found none. Even though [a]many false witnesses came
forward, they found none.[1] But at last [b]two false witnesses[2]
came forward
61 and said, "This *fellow* said, [a]'I am able to destroy the tem-
ple of God and to build it in three days.'"
62 [a]And the high priest arose and said to Him, "Do You an-
swer nothing? What *is it* these men testify against You?"
63 But [a]Jesus kept silent. And the high priest answered and
said to Him, [b]"I put You under oath by the living God: Tell us
if You are the Christ, the Son of God!"

26:47 [a]Acts 1:16 26:49 [a]2 Sam. 20:9 26:50 [a]Ps. 41:9; 55:13 26:51 [a]John 18:10 26:52 [a]Rev. 13:10 [1]M-Text reads *die.* 26:53 [a]Dan. 7:10 26:54 [a]Is. 50:6; 53:2–11 26:56 [a]Lam. 4:20 [b]John 18:15 26:57 [a]John 18:12, 19–24 26:58 [a]John 18:15, 16 26:59 [a]Ps. 35:11 [1]NU-Text omits *the elders.* 26:60 [a]Mark 14:55 [b]Deut. 19:15 [1]NU-Text puts a comma after *but found none,* does not capitalize *Even,* and omits *they found none.* [2]NU-Text omits *false witnesses.* 26:61 [a]John 2:19 26:62 [a]Mark 14:60 26:63 [a]Is. 53:7 [b]Lev. 5:1

64 Jesus said to him, "*It is as* you said. Nevertheless, I say to
you, [a]hereafter you will see the Son of Man [b]sitting at the right
hand of the Power, and coming on the clouds of heaven."
65 [a]Then the high priest tore his clothes, saying, "He has
spoken blasphemy! What further need do we have of wit-
nesses? Look, now you have heard His [b]blasphemy!
66 "What do you think?" They answered and said, [a]"He is
deserving of death."
67 [a]Then they spat in His face and beat Him; and [b]others
struck *Him* with the palms of their hands,
68 saying, [a]"Prophesy to us, Christ! Who is the one who
struck You?"
69 [a]Now Peter sat outside in the courtyard. And a servant
girl came to him, saying, "You also were with Jesus of Gali-
lee."
70 But he denied it before *them* all, saying, "I do not know
what you are saying."
71 And when he had gone out to the gateway, another *girl*
saw him and said to those *who were* there, "This *fellow* also
was with Jesus of Nazareth."
72 But again he denied with an oath, "I do not know the Man!"
73 And a little later those who stood by came up and said to
Peter, "Surely you also are *one* of them, for your [a]speech be-
trays you."
74 Then [a]he began to curse and swear, *saying,* "I do not know
the Man!" Immediately a rooster crowed.
75 And Peter remembered the word of Jesus who had said
to him, [a]"Before the rooster crows, you will deny Me three
times." So he went out and wept bitterly.

26:64 [a]Dan. 7:13 [b][Acts 7:55] 26:65 [a]2 Kin. 18:37 [b]John 10:30–36 26:66 [a]Lev. 24:16 26:67 [a]Is. 50:6; 53:3 [b]Luke 22:63–65 26:68 [a]Mark 14:65 26:69 [a]John 18:16–18, 25–27 26:73 [a]Luke 22:59 26:74 [a]Mark 14:71 26:75 [a]Matt. 26:34

MATTHEW 27

JESUS IS TRIED AND CRUCIFIED

What an enthronement was accorded to Him! See that scarlet robe—it is a contemptuous imitation of the imperial purple that a king wears. See that old chair into which the soldiers have thrust Him so that He may be seated upon a mockery of a throne. See, above all, that crown upon His head. It has rubies in it, but the rubies are composed of His own blood forced from His blessed temples by the cruel thorns. See, they pay Him homage, but the homage is their own filthy spittle that runs down His cheeks. They bow the knee before Him, but it is only in mockery. They salute Him with the cry "Hail, King of the Jews!" but it is done in scorn.

Was there ever grief like his? It amazes us that such superlative goodness should have been treated with such fiendish malice, that such mercy should have been in such misery, that such majesty should have been reduced to such despising.

Remember that Jesus Christ stood in the sinner's place. This is an old truth with which you are very familiar but of which you are never tired of hearing. He was made "in the likeness of men" and "found in appearance as a man" (Phil. 2:7–8) and had agreed to stand in the place of sinners as if He had been Himself a sinner: you see in Jesus Christ the full result of sin epitomized. Ah, foolish man, see what kind of royalty it is that sin can bring you!

---

1 When morning came, [a]all the chief priests and elders of
the people plotted against Jesus to put Him to death.
2 And when they had bound Him, they led Him away and
[a]delivered Him to Pontius[1] Pilate the governor.
3 [a]Then Judas, His betrayer, seeing that He had been con-
demned, was remorseful and brought back the thirty [b]pieces
of silver to the chief priests and elders,
4 saying, "I have sinned by betraying innocent blood." And
they said, "What *is that* to us? You see *to it!*"
5 Then he threw down the pieces of silver in the temple and
[a]departed, and went and hanged himself.
6 But the chief priests took the silver pieces and said, "It is
not lawful to put them into the treasury, because they are the
price of blood."
7 And they consulted together and bought with them the
potter's field, to bury strangers in.
8 Therefore that field has been called [a]the Field of Blood to
this day.

27:1[a]John 18:28 27:2[a]Acts 3:13 [1]NU-Text omits *Pontius*. 27:3[a]Matt. 26:14 [b]Matt. 26:15 27:5[a]Acts 1:18 27:8[a]Acts 1:19

9 Then was fulfilled what was spoken by Jeremiah the proph-
et, saying, [a]"And they took the thirty pieces of silver, the value of Him who was priced, whom they of the children of Israel priced,
10 "and [a]gave them for the potter's field, as the LORD direct-
ed me."[1]
11 Now Jesus stood before the governor. [a]And the governor
asked Him, saying, "Are You the King of the Jews?" Jesus said to him, [b]"*It is as* you say."
12 And while He was being accused by the chief priests and
elders, [a]He answered nothing.
13 Then Pilate said to Him, [a]"Do You not hear how many
things they testify against You?"
14 But He answered him not one word, so that the governor
marveled greatly.
15 [a]Now at the feast the governor was accustomed to releas-
ing to the multitude one prisoner whom they wished.
16 And at that time they had a notorious prisoner called Bar-
abbas.[1]
17 Therefore, when they had gathered together, Pilate said
to them, "Whom do you want me to release to you? Barabbas, or Jesus who is called Christ?"
18 For he knew that they had handed Him over because of
[a]envy.
19 While he was sitting on the judgment seat, his wife sent
to him, saying, "Have nothing to do with that just Man, for I have suffered many things today in a dream because of Him."
20 [a]But the chief priests and elders persuaded the multi-
tudes that they should ask for Barabbas and destroy Jesus.
21 The governor answered and said to them, "Which of the
two do you want me to release to you?" They said, [a]"Barabbas!"
22 Pilate said to them, "What then shall I do with Jesus who
is called Christ?" *They* all said to him, "Let Him be crucified!"
23 Then the governor said, [a]"Why, what evil has He done?"
But they cried out all the more, saying, "Let Him be crucified!"
24 When Pilate saw that he could not prevail at all, but rather
that a tumult was rising, he [a]took water and washed *his* hands before the multitude, saying, "I am innocent of the blood of this just Person.[1] You see *to it*."
25 And all the people answered and said, [a]"His blood *be* on
us and on our children."

27:9[a] Zech. 11:12 27:10[a] Jer. 32:6–9; Zech. 11:12, 13 [1] Jeremiah 32:6–9 27:11[a] Mark 15:2–5 [b] John 18:37 27:12[a] John 19:9 27:13[a] Matt. 26:62 27:15[a] Luke 23:17–25 27:16[1] NU-Text reads *Jesus Barabbas.* 27:18[a] Matt. 21:38 27:20[a] Acts 3:14 27:21[a] Acts 3:14 27:23[a] Acts 3:13 27:24[a] Deut. 21:6–8 [1] NU-Text omits *just.* 27:25[a] Josh. 2:19

26 Then he released Barabbas to them; and when [a]he had
scourged Jesus, he delivered *Him* to be crucified.
27 [a]Then the soldiers of the governor took Jesus into the
Praetorium and gathered the whole garrison around Him.
28 And they [a]stripped Him and [b]put a scarlet robe on Him.
29 [a]When they had twisted a crown of thorns, they put *it* on
His head, and a reed in His right hand. And they bowed the
knee before Him and mocked Him, saying, "Hail, King of the
Jews!"
30 Then [a]they spat on Him, and took the reed and struck
Him on the head.
31 And when they had mocked Him, they took the robe off
Him, put His *own* clothes on Him, [a]and led Him away to be
crucified.
32 [a]Now as they came out, [b]they found a man of Cyrene,
Simon by name. Him they compelled to bear His cross.
33 [a]And when they had come to a place called Golgotha, that
is to say, Place of a Skull,
34 [a]they gave Him sour[1] wine mingled with gall to drink.
But when He had tasted *it,* He would not drink.
35 [a]Then they crucified Him, and divided His garments,
casting lots,[1] that it might be fulfilled which was spoken by
the prophet:

> [b]"They divided My garments among them,
> And for My clothing they cast lots."[2]

36 [a]Sitting down, they kept watch over Him there.
37 And they [a]put up over His head the accusation written
against Him:

THIS IS JESUS THE KING OF THE JEWS.

38 [a]Then two robbers were crucified with Him, one on the
right and another on the left.
39 And [a]those who passed by blasphemed Him, wagging
their heads
40 and saying, [a]"You who destroy the temple and build *it* in
three days, save Yourself! [b]If You are the Son of God, come
down from the cross."
41 Likewise the chief priests also, mocking with the scribes
and elders,[1] said,
42 "He [a]saved others; Himself He cannot save. If He is the

27:26 [a][Is. 50:6; 53:5] 27:27 [a]Mark 15:16–20 27:28 [a]John 19:2 [b]Luke 23:11 27:29 [a]Is. 53:3 27:30 [a]Matt. 26:67 27:31 [a]Is. 53:7 27:32 [a]Heb. 13:12 [b]Mark 15:21 27:33 [a]John 19:17 27:34 [a]Ps. 69:21 [1]NU-Text omits *sour.* 27:35 [a]Luke 23:34 [b]Ps. 22:18 [1]NU-Text and M-Text omit the rest of this verse. [2]Psalm 22:18 27:36 [a]Matt. 27:54 27:37 [a]John 19:19 27:38 [a]Is. 53:9, 12 27:39 [a]Mark 15:29 27:40 [a]John 2:19 [b]Matt. 26:63 27:41 [1]M-Text reads *with the scribes, the Pharisees, and the elders.* 27:42 [a][John 3:14, 15]

King of Israel,[1] let Him now come down from the cross, and
we will believe Him.[2]
43 [a]"He trusted in God; let Him deliver Him now if He will
have Him; for He said, 'I am the Son of God.'"
44 [a]Even the robbers who were crucified with Him reviled
Him with the same thing.
45 [a]Now from the sixth hour until the ninth hour there was
darkness over all the land.
46 And about the ninth hour [a]Jesus cried out with a loud
voice, saying, "Eli, Eli, lama sabachthani?" that is, [b]"My God,
My God, why have You forsaken Me?"[1]
47 Some of those who stood there, when they heard *that,*
said, "This Man is calling for Elijah!"
48 Immediately one of them ran and took a sponge, [a]filled
it with sour wine and put *it* on a reed, and offered it to Him
to drink.
49 The rest said, "Let Him alone; let us see if Elijah will come
to save Him."
50 And Jesus [a]cried out again with a loud voice, and [b]yield-
ed up His spirit.
51 Then, behold, [a]the veil of the temple was torn in two from
top to bottom; and the earth quaked, and the rocks were split,
52 and the graves were opened; and many bodies of the
saints who had fallen asleep were raised;
53 and coming out of the graves after His resurrection, they
went into the holy city and appeared to many.
54 [a]So when the centurion and those with him, who were
guarding Jesus, saw the earthquake and the things that had
happened, they feared greatly, saying, [b]"Truly this was the
Son of God!"
55 And many women [a]who followed Jesus from Galilee,
ministering to Him, were there looking on from afar,
56 [a]among whom were Mary Magdalene, Mary the mother
of James and Joses,[1] and the mother of Zebedee's sons.
57 Now [a]when evening had come, there came a rich man
from Arimathea, named Joseph, who himself had also be-
come a disciple of Jesus.
58 This man went to Pilate and asked for the body of Jesus.
Then Pilate commanded the body to be given to him.
59 When Joseph had taken the body, he wrapped it in a clean
linen cloth,
60 and [a]laid it in his new tomb which he had hewn out of
the rock; and he rolled a large stone against the door of the
tomb, and departed.

27:42[1]NU-Text reads *He is the King of Israel!* [2]NU-Text and M-Text read *we will believe in Him.* 27:43[a]Ps. 22:8 27:44[a]Luke 23:39–43 27:45[a]Mark 15:33–41 27:46[a][Heb. 5:7] [b]Ps. 22:1 [1]Psalm 22:1 27:48[a]Ps. 69:21 27:50[a]Luke 23:46 [b][John 10:18] 27:51[a]Ex. 26:31 27:54[a]Mark 15:39 [b]Matt. 14:33 27:55[a]Luke 8:2, 3 27:56[a]Mark 15:40, 47; 16:9 [1]NU-Text reads *Joseph.* 27:57[a]John 19:38–42 27:60[a]Is. 53:9

61 And Mary Magdalene was there, and the other Mary, sit-
ting opposite the tomb.
62 On the next day, which followed the Day of Preparation,
the chief priests and Pharisees gathered together to Pilate,
63 saying, "Sir, we remember, while He was still alive, how
that deceiver said, [a]'After three days I will rise.'
64 "Therefore command that the tomb be made secure until
the third day, lest His disciples come by night[1] and steal Him
away, and say to the people, 'He has risen from the dead.' So
the last deception will be worse than the first."
65 Pilate said to them, "You have a guard; go your way, make
it as secure as you know how."
66 So they went and made the tomb secure, [a]sealing the
stone and setting the guard.

27:63[a] Mark 8:31; 10:34 27:64[1] NU-Text omits *by night.* 27:66[a] Dan. 6:17

MATTHEW 28

THE RISEN CHRIST

By virtue of His kingly authority, Jesus issued this last great command to His disciples: *Go ye therefore and teach* or "Make disciples of all the nations, baptizing them in the name of the Father and of the Son and of the Holy Spirit, teaching them to observe all things that I have commanded you." This is our commission as well as theirs. From it we learn that our first business is to make disciples, and we can do that only by teaching them the truth as it is revealed in the Scriptures and seeking the power of the Holy Spirit to make our teaching effective.

Next, those who by faith in Christ become His disciples are to be baptized into the name of the triune Jehovah, and after baptism they are still to be taught all that Christ commanded. We are not to invent anything new or to change anything to suit the current age but to teach the baptized believers to observe "all things" our divine King has commanded.

This is the perpetual commission of the church of Christ. The great seal of the kingdom attached to it that gives the power to execute it and guarantees its success is the King's assurance of His continual presence with His faithful followers: "Lo, I am with you always, even to the end of the age." May all of us realize His presence with us until He calls us to "always be with the Lord" (1 Thess. 4:17). Amen.

---

1 Now [a]after the Sabbath, as the first *day* of the week began
to dawn, Mary Magdalene [b]and the other Mary came to see
the tomb.
2 And behold, there was a great earthquake; for [a]an angel of
the Lord descended from heaven, and came and rolled back
the stone from the door,[1] and sat on it.
3 [a]His countenance was like lightning, and his clothing as
white as snow.
4 And the guards shook for fear of him, and became like
[a]dead *men*.
5 But the angel answered and said to the women, "Do not
be afraid, for I know that you seek Jesus who was crucified.
6 "He is not here; for He is risen, [a]as He said. Come, see the
place where the Lord lay.
7 "And go quickly and tell His disciples that He is risen from
the dead, and indeed [a]He is going before you into Galilee;
there you will see Him. Behold, I have told you."

28:1[a]Luke 24:1–10 [b]Matt. 27:56, 61 28:2[a]Mark 16:5 [1]NU-Text omits *from the door.* 28:3[a]Dan. 7:9; 10:6 28:4[a]Rev. 1:17 28:6[a]Matt. 12:40; 16:21; 17:23; 20:19 28:7[a]Mark 16:7

8 So they went out quickly from the tomb with fear and great
joy, and ran to bring His disciples word.
9 And as they went to tell His disciples,[1] behold, [a]Jesus met
them, saying, "Rejoice!" So they came and held Him by the
feet and worshiped Him.
10 Then Jesus said to them, "Do not be afraid. Go *and* tell
[a]My brethren to go to Galilee, and there they will see Me."
11 Now while they were going, behold, some of the guard
came into the city and reported to the chief priests all the
things that had happened.
12 When they had assembled with the elders and consulted
together, they gave a large sum of money to the soldiers,
13 saying, "Tell them, 'His disciples came at night and stole
Him *away* while we slept.'
14 "And if this comes to the governor's ears, we will appease
him and make you secure."
15 So they took the money and did as they were instructed;
and this saying is commonly reported among the Jews until
this day.
16 Then the eleven disciples went away into Galilee, to the
mountain [a]which Jesus had appointed for them.
17 When they saw Him, they worshiped Him; but some
[a]doubted.
18 And Jesus came and spoke to them, saying, [a]"All author-
ity has been given to Me in heaven and on earth.
19 [a]"Go therefore[1] and [b]make disciples of all the nations, bap-
tizing them in the name of the Father and of the Son and of
the Holy Spirit,
20 [a]"teaching them to observe all things that I have com-
manded you; and lo, I am [b]with you always, *even* to the end
of the age." Amen.[1]

28:9[a]John 20:14 [1]NU-Text omits the first clause of this verse. 28:10[a]John 20:17 28:16[a]Matt. 26:32; 28:7, 10 28:17[a]John 20:24–29 28:18[a][Dan. 7:13, 14] 28:19[a]Mark 16:15 [b]Luke 24:47 [1]M-Text omits *therefore.* 28:20[a][Acts 2:42] [b][Acts 4:31; 18:10; 23:11] [1]NU-Text omits *Amen.*

MARK

MARK 1

JOHN AND JESUS BEGIN THEIR MINISTRY

"They were astonished at His teaching, for He taught them as one having authority." Why did the Savior's teaching have such a remarkable power about it? Was it not first because He preached the truth? There is no power in falsehood except so far as men choose to yield to it because it flatters them. But there is great force in truth—it makes its own way into the soul.

Moreover, the Savior spoke the truth in a very natural, unaffected manner: the truth was in Him, and it flowed freely from Him. His manner was truthful as well as His matter. He spoke truth as truth should be spoken, as one who preached not professionally but out of the fullness of His heart. Moreover, our great Exemplar delivered His teaching as one who most heartily believed what He was speaking. Jesus had no doubts, no hesitancy, no questions, and His style was as calmly forcible as His faith. Truth seemed to be reflected from His face just as it shone forth from God in all its native purity and splendor. He could not speak otherwise than He did, for He spoke as He was, as He felt, and as He knew.

Consequently, for all these reasons and many besides, Jesus spoke as one who had authority: His tone was commanding, and His teaching was convincing.

---

1 The [a]beginning of the gospel of Jesus Christ, [b]the Son
of God.
2 As it is written in the Prophets:[1]

> [a]"Behold, I send My messenger before Your face,
> Who will prepare Your way before You."[2]
> 3 "The[a] voice of one crying in the wilderness:
> 'Prepare the way of the LORD;
> Make His paths straight.'"[1]

4 [a]John came baptizing in the wilderness and preaching a
baptism of repentance for the remission of sins.
5 [a]Then all the land of Judea, and those from Jerusalem,
went out to him and were all baptized by him in the Jordan
River, confessing their sins.
6 Now John was [a]clothed with camel's hair and with a leath-
er belt around his waist, and he ate locusts and wild honey.
7 And he preached, saying, [a]"There comes One after me

1:1[a]Luke 3:22 [b]Matt. 14:33 1:2[a]Mal. 3:1 [1]NU-Text reads *Isaiah the prophet.* [2]Malachi 3:1 1:3[a]Is. 40:3 [1]Isaiah 40:3 1:4[a]Matt. 3:1 1:5[a]Matt. 3:5 1:6[a]Matt. 3:4 1:7[a]John 1:27

who is mightier than I, whose sandal strap I am not worthy
to stoop down and loose.
8 [a]"I indeed baptized you with water, but He will baptize you
[b]with the Holy Spirit."
9 [a]It came to pass in those days *that* Jesus came from Naz-
areth of Galilee, and was baptized by John in the Jordan.
10 [a]And immediately, coming up from[1] the water, He saw the
heavens parting and the Spirit [b]descending upon Him like a
dove.
11 Then a voice came from heaven, [a]"You are My beloved
Son, in whom I am well pleased."
12 [a]Immediately the Spirit drove Him into the wilderness.
13 And He was there in the wilderness forty days, tempted
by Satan, and was with the wild beasts; [a]and the angels min-
istered to Him.
14 [a]Now after John was put in prison, Jesus came to Galilee,
[b]preaching the gospel of the kingdom[1] of God,
15 and saying, [a]"The time is fulfilled, and [b]the kingdom of
God is at hand. Repent, and believe in the gospel."
16 [a]And as He walked by the Sea of Galilee, He saw Simon
and Andrew his brother casting a net into the sea; for they
were fishermen.
17 Then Jesus said to them, "Follow Me, and I will make you
become [a]fishers of men."
18 [a]They immediately left their nets and followed Him.
19 When He had gone a little farther from there, He saw
James the *son* of Zebedee, and John his brother, who also
were in the boat mending their nets.
20 And immediately He called them, and they left their fa-
ther Zebedee in the boat with the hired servants, and went
after Him.
21 [a]Then they went into Capernaum, and immediately on
the Sabbath He entered the [b]synagogue and taught.
22 [a]And they were astonished at His teaching, for He taught
them as one having authority, and not as the scribes.
23 Now there was a man in their synagogue with an [a]unclean
spirit. And he cried out,
24 saying, "Let *us* alone! [a]What have we to do with You, Jesus
of Nazareth? Did You come to destroy us? I [b]know who You
are—the [c]Holy One of God!"
25 But Jesus [a]rebuked him, saying, "Be quiet, and come out
of him!"
26 And when the unclean spirit [a]had convulsed him and
cried out with a loud voice, he came out of him.

1:8 [a]Acts 1:5; 11:16 [b]Is. 44:3 1:9 [a]Matt. 3:13–17 1:10 [a]Matt. 3:16 [b]Acts 10:38 [1]NU-Text reads *out of.* 1:11 [a]Matt. 3:17; 12:18 1:12 [a]Matt. 4:1–11 1:13 [a]Matt. 4:10, 11 1:14 [a]Matt. 4:12 [b]Matt. 4:23 [1]NU-Text omits *of the kingdom.* 1:15 [a][Gal. 4:4] [b]Matt. 3:2; 4:17 1:16 [a]Luke 5:2–11 1:17 [a]Matt. 13:47, 48 1:18 [a][Luke 14:26] 1:21 [a]Luke 4:31–37 [b]Matt. 4:23 1:22 [a]Matt. 7:28, 29; 13:54 1:23 [a][Matt. 12:43] 1:24 [a]Matt. 8:28, 29 [b]James 2:19 [c]Ps. 16:10 1:25 [a][Luke 4:39] 1:26 [a]Mark 9:20

27 Then they were all amazed, so that they questioned among
themselves, saying, "What is this? What new doctrine *is* this?
For with authority[1] He commands even the unclean spirits,
and they obey Him."
28 And immediately His [a]fame spread throughout all the
region around Galilee.
29 [a]Now as soon as they had come out of the synagogue,
they entered the house of Simon and Andrew, with James
and John.
30 But Simon's wife's mother lay sick with a fever, and they
told Him about her at once.
31 So He came and took her by the hand and lifted her up,
and immediately the fever left her. And she served them.
32 [a]At evening, when the sun had set, they brought to Him
all who were sick and those who were demon-possessed.
33 And the whole city was gathered together at the door.
34 Then He healed many who were sick with various diseas-
es, and [a]cast out many demons; and He [b]did not allow the
demons to speak, because they knew Him.
35 Now [a]in the morning, having risen a long while before
daylight, He went out and departed to a solitary place; and
there He [b]prayed.
36 And Simon and those *who were* with Him searched
for Him.
37 When they found Him, they said to Him, [a]"Everyone [b]is
looking for You."
38 But He said to them, [a]"Let us go into the next towns, that
I may preach there also, because [b]for this purpose I have
come forth."
39 [a]And He was preaching in their synagogues throughout
all Galilee, and [b]casting out demons.
40 [a]Now a leper came to Him, imploring Him, kneeling down
to Him and saying to Him, "If You are willing, You can make
me clean."
41 Then Jesus, moved with [a]compassion, stretched out *His*
hand and touched him, and said to him, "I am willing; be
cleansed."
42 As soon as He had spoken, [a]immediately the leprosy left
him, and he was cleansed.
43 And He strictly warned him and sent him away at once,
44 and said to him, "See that you say nothing to anyone; but
go your way, show yourself to the priest, and offer for your
cleansing those things [a]which Moses commanded, as a tes-
timony to them."

1:27[1] NU-Text reads *What is this? A new doctrine with authority.* 1:28[a] Matt. 4:24; 9:31 1:29[a] Luke 4:38, 39 1:32[a] Matt. 8:16, 17 1:34[a] Luke 13:32 [b] Acts 16:17, 18 1:35[a] Luke 4:42, 43 [b] Luke 5:16; 6:12; 9:28, 29 1:37[a] John 3:26; 12:19 [b] [Heb. 11:6] 1:38[a] Luke 4:43 [b] [Is. 61:1, 2] 1:39[a] Matt. 4:23; 9:35 [b] Mark 5:8, 13; 7:29, 30 1:40[a] Luke 5:12–14 1:41[a] Luke 7:13 1:42[a] Matt. 15:28 1:44[a] Lev. 14:1–32

45 [a]However, he went out and began to proclaim *it* freely,
and to spread the matter, so that Jesus could no longer openly
enter the city, but was outside in deserted places; [b]and they
came to Him from every direction.

1:45 [a]Luke 5:15 [b]Mark 2:2, 13; 3:7

MARK 2

JESUS IS LORD OF HEALING AND THE SABBATH

What did Christ come into the world for? For whom did He come? These are questions of the greatest importance, and they are clearly answered in Scripture. On the principle of *good for the good*, they infer that grace is for the excellent and Christ for the virtuous.

Hence it is a most useful thing for us continually to be reminding men what the gospel is and for whom it is sent into the world. Though you know full well, yet there are multitudes around us who persist in grave mistakes and need to be instructed over and over again in the very simplest of the doctrines of grace. Our business is to show that the gospel is intended for sinners; that it has an eye to guilty persons; that it is not sent into the world as a reward for the good and for the excellent or for those who think they have any measure of fitness or preparation for the divine favor. It is intended for lawbreakers, for the undeserving, for the ungodly, for those who have gone astray like lost sheep or left their father's house like the prodigal.

Christ died to save sinners, and He justifies the ungodly. The truth is plain enough in the Word, but since the human heart kicks against it we will the more earnestly insist upon it.

---

1 And again [a]He entered Capernaum after *some* days, and
it was heard that He was in the house.
2 Immediately[1] many gathered together, so that there was
no longer room to receive *them*, not even near the door. And
He preached the word to them.
3 Then they came to Him, bringing a [a]paralytic who was car-
ried by four *men*.
4 And when they could not come near Him because of the
crowd, they uncovered the roof where He was. So when they
had broken through, they let down the bed on which the par-
alytic was lying.
5 When Jesus saw their faith, He said to the paralytic, "Son,
your sins are forgiven you."
6 And some of the scribes were sitting there and reasoning
in their hearts,
7 "Why does this *Man* speak blasphemies like this? [a]Who
can forgive sins but God alone?"
8 But immediately, when Jesus perceived in His spirit that

2:1[a]Matt. 9:1 2:2[1]NU-Text omits *Immediately*. 2:3[a]Matt. 4:24; 8:6 2:7[a]Is. 43:25

they reasoned thus within themselves, He said to them, "Why
do you reason about these things in your hearts?
9 [a]"Which is easier, to say to the paralytic, '*Your* sins are for-
given you,' or to say, 'Arise, take up your bed and walk'?
10 "But that you may know that the Son of Man has power
on earth to forgive sins"—He said to the paralytic,
11 "I say to you, arise, take up your bed, and go to your house."
12 Immediately he arose, took up the bed, and went out in
the presence of them all, so that all were amazed and [a]glori-
fied God, saying, "We never saw *anything* like this!"
13 [a]Then He went out again by the sea; and all the multitude
came to Him, and He taught them.
14 [a]As He passed by, He saw Levi the *son* of Alphaeus sitting
at the tax office. And He said to him, [b]"Follow Me." So he arose
and [c]followed Him.
15 [a]Now it happened, as He was dining in *Levi's* house,
that many tax collectors and sinners also sat together with
Jesus and His disciples; for there were many, and they fol-
lowed Him.
16 And when the scribes and[1] Pharisees saw Him eating with
the tax collectors and sinners, they said to His disciples, "How
is it that He eats and drinks with tax collectors and sinners?"
17 When Jesus heard *it,* He said to them, [a]"Those who are
well have no need of a physician, but those who are sick. I did
not come to call *the* righteous, but sinners, to repentance."[1]
18 [a]The disciples of John and of the Pharisees were fasting.
Then they came and said to Him, "Why do the disciples of
John and of the Pharisees fast, but Your disciples do not fast?"
19 And Jesus said to them, "Can the friends of the bridegroom
fast while the bridegroom is with them? As long as they have
the bridegroom with them they cannot fast.
20 "But the days will come when the bridegroom will be
[a]taken away from them, and then they will fast in those days.
21 "No one sews a piece of unshrunk cloth on an old gar-
ment; or else the new piece pulls away from the old, and the
tear is made worse.
22 "And no one puts new wine into old wineskins; or else
the new wine bursts the wineskins, the wine is spilled, and
the wineskins are ruined. But new wine must be put into new
wineskins."
23 [a]Now it happened that He went through the grainfields on
the Sabbath; and as they went His disciples began [b]to pluck
the heads of grain.
24 And the Pharisees said to Him, "Look, why do they do
what is [a]not lawful on the Sabbath?"

2:9[a]Matt. 9:5 2:12[a][Phil. 2:11] 2:13[a]Matt. 9:9 2:14[a]Luke 5:27–32 [b]John 1:43; 12:26; 21:22 [c]Luke 18:28 2:15[a]Matt. 9:10 2:16[1]NU-Text reads *of the.* 2:17[a]Matt. 9:12, 13; 18:11 [1]NU-Text omits *to repentance.* 2:18[a]Luke 5:33–38 2:20[a]Acts 1:9; 13:2, 3; 14:23 2:23[a]Luke 6:1–5 [b]Deut. 23:25 2:24[a]Ex. 20:10; 31:15

25 But He said to them, "Have you never read [a]what David
did when he was in need and hungry, he and those with him:
26 "how he went into the house of God *in the days* of Abi-
athar the high priest, and ate the showbread, [a]which is not
lawful to eat except for the priests, and also gave some to
those who were with him?"
27 And He said to them, "The Sabbath was made for man,
and not man for the [a]Sabbath.
28 "Therefore [a]the Son of Man is also Lord of the Sabbath."

2:25[a]1 Sam. 21:1–6 2:26[a]Lev. 24:5–9 2:27[a]Deut. 5:14 2:28[a]Matt. 12:8

MARK 3

JESUS' APOSTLES AND HIS TRUE FAMILY

The opposition of the great ones of the earth did not, after all, hinder the cause of Christ. So let us not, dear friends, be at all dismayed if great men and learned men and nominally religious men oppose the simple gospel of Christ. All the world is not bound up in a Pharisee's phylactery or held in chains by a philosopher's new fancy. If some will not have our Savior, others will.

God's eternal purpose will stand, and the kingdom of His Anointed shall come. If our Lord Jesus be rejected by the great, nevertheless the common people hear Him gladly. To the poor the gospel is preached, and it is His joy and His delight that out of them He still gathers a company who, though poor in this world, are rich in faith and give glory to God. I would have you, beloved, count upon opposition and regard it as a token of coming blessing. Dread not the black cloud—it does but prognosticate a shower.

March may howl and bluster, and April may damp all things with its rains, but the May flowers and the autumn's harvest of varied fruits will come and by this very means. Go on and serve your God in the serenity of holy confidence, and you shall live to see that the hand of the Lord is not to be turned back though the kings of the earth set themselves and the rulers take counsel together.

---

1 And [a]He entered the synagogue again, and a man was there
who had a withered hand.
2 So they [a]watched Him closely, whether He would [b]heal
him on the Sabbath, so that they might accuse Him.
3 And He said to the man who had the withered hand, "Step
forward."
4 Then He said to them, "Is it lawful on the Sabbath to do
good or to do evil, to save life or to kill?" But they kept silent.
5 And when He had looked around at them with anger, being grieved by the [a]hardness of their hearts, He said to the man, "Stretch out your hand." And he stretched *it* out, and his hand was restored as whole as the other.[1]
6 [a]Then the Pharisees went out and immediately plotted with
[b]the Herodians against Him, how they might destroy Him.
7 But Jesus withdrew with His disciples to the sea. And a
great multitude from Galilee followed Him, [a]and from Judea
8 and Jerusalem and Idumea and beyond the Jordan; and

3:1 [a]Luke 6:6–11 3:2 [a]Luke 14:1; 20:20 [b]Luke 13:14 3:5 [a]Zech. 7:12 [1]NU-Text omits *as whole as the other.* 3:6 [a]Mark 12:13 [b]Matt. 22:16 3:7 [a]Luke 6:17

those from Tyre and Sidon, a great multitude, when they
heard how [a]many things He was doing, came to Him.
9 So He told His disciples that a small boat should be kept
ready for Him because of the multitude, lest they should
crush Him.
10 For He healed [a]many, so that as many as had afflictions
pressed about Him to [b]touch Him.
11 [a]And the unclean spirits, whenever they saw Him, fell
down before Him and cried out, saying, [b]"You are the Son
of God."
12 But [a]He sternly warned them that they should not make
Him known.
13 [a]And He went up on the mountain and called to *Him* those
He Himself wanted. And they came to Him.
14 Then He appointed twelve,[1] that they might be with Him
and that He might send them out to preach,
15 and to have power to heal sicknesses and[1] to cast out de-
mons:
16 Simon,[1] [a]to whom He gave the name Peter;
17 James the *son* of Zebedee and John the brother of James,
to whom He gave the name Boanerges, that is, "Sons of Thun-
der";
18 Andrew, Philip, Bartholomew, Matthew, Thomas, James
the *son* of Alphaeus, Thaddaeus, Simon the Cananite;
19 and Judas Iscariot, who also betrayed Him. And they went
into a house.
20 Then the multitude came together again, [a]so that they
could not so much as eat bread.
21 But when His [a]own people heard *about this,* they went out
to lay hold of Him, [b]for they said, "He is out of His mind."
22 And the scribes who came down from Jerusalem said,
[a]"He has Beelzebub," and, "By the [b]ruler of the demons He
casts out demons."
23 [a]So He called them to *Himself* and said to them in para-
bles: "How can Satan cast out Satan?
24 "If a kingdom is divided against itself, that kingdom can-
not stand.
25 "And if a house is divided against itself, that house can-
not stand.
26 "And if Satan has risen up against himself, and is divid-
ed, he cannot stand, but has an end.
27 [a]"No one can enter a strong man's house and plunder his
goods, unless he first binds the strong man. And then he will
plunder his house.

3:8 [a]Mark 5:19 3:10 [a]Luke 7:21 [b]Matt. 9:21; 14:36 3:11 [a]Luke 4:41 [b]Matt. 8:29; 14:33 3:12 [a]Mark 1:25, 34 3:13 [a]Luke 9:1 3:14 [1]NU-Text adds *whom He also named apostles.* 3:15 [1]NU-Text omits *to heal sicknesses and.* 3:16 [a]John 1:42 [1]NU-Text reads *and He appointed the twelve: Simon . . . .* 3:20 [a]Mark 6:31 3:21 [a]Mark 6:3 [b]John 7:5; 10:20 3:22 [a]Matt. 9:34; 10:25 [b][John 12:31; 14:30; 16:11] 3:23 [a]Matt. 12:25–29 3:27 [a][Is. 49:24, 25]

28 [a]"Assuredly, I say to you, all sins will be forgiven the sons
of men, and whatever blasphemies they may utter;
29 "but he who blasphemes against the Holy Spirit never
has forgiveness, but is subject to eternal condemnation"—
30 because they [a]said, "He has an unclean spirit."
31 [a]Then His brothers and His mother came, and standing
outside they sent to Him, calling Him.
32 And a multitude was sitting around Him; and they said
to Him, "Look, Your mother and Your brothers[1] are outside
seeking You."
33 But He answered them, saying, "Who is My mother, or
My brothers?"
34 And He looked around in a circle at those who sat about
Him, and said, "Here are My mother and My brothers!
35 "For whoever does the [a]will of God is My brother and My
sister and mother."

3:28[a] Luke 12:10 3:30[a] Matt. 9:34 3:31[a] Matt. 12:46–50 3:32[1] NU-Text and M-Text add *and Your sisters.* 3:35[a] Eph. 6:6

MARK 4

PARABLES OF THE KINGDOM OF GOD

Here is a lesson for sowers, for the laborers upon the farm of God who are concerned in the kingdom of God. All who are loyal subjects to King Jesus, all who are commissioned to scatter seed for the royal Farmer will be glad to know how the kingdom advances, how the harvest is preparing for Him whom they serve.

"The kingdom of God is as if a man should scatter seed on the ground": this the gracious worker can do. "And the seed should sprout and grow, he himself does not know how": this is what he cannot do, for it belongs to a higher power. Man can neither make the seed spring nor grow up; he is out of the field in that respect and may go home to "sleep by night and rise by day."

Seed once sown is beyond human jurisdiction and is under divine care. Yet ere long the worker comes in again—"When the grain ripens, immediately he puts in the sickle." We can reap in due season, and it is both our duty and our privilege so to do. You see, then, that there is a place for the worker at the beginning, and though there is no room for him in the middle passage, yet another opportunity is given him further on when that which he sowed has actually yielded fruit.

---

1 And [a]again He began to teach by the sea. And a great multitude was gathered to Him, so that He got into a boat and sat *in it* on the sea; and the whole multitude was on the land facing the sea.
2 Then He taught them many things by parables, [a]and said to them in His teaching:
3 "Listen! Behold, a sower went out to sow.
4 "And it happened, as he sowed, *that* some *seed* fell by the wayside; and the birds of the air[1] came and devoured it.
5 "Some fell on stony ground, where it did not have much earth; and immediately it sprang up because it had no depth of earth.
6 "But when the sun was up it was scorched, and because it had no root it withered away.
7 "And some *seed* fell among thorns; and the thorns grew up and choked it, and it yielded no crop.
8 "But other *seed* fell on good ground and yielded a crop that sprang up, increased and produced: some thirtyfold, some sixty, and some a hundred."
9 And He said to them,[1] "He who has ears to hear, let him hear!"

4:1[a] Luke 8:4–10 4:2[a] Mark 12:38 4:4[1] NU-Text and M-Text omit *of the air.* 4:9[1] NU-Text and M-Text omit *to them.*

10 [a]But when He was alone, those around Him with the twelve
asked Him about the parable.
11 And He said to them, "To you it has been given to [a]know
the mystery of the kingdom of God; but to [b]those who are
outside, all things come in parables,
12 "so that

> [a]'Seeing they may see and not perceive,
> And hearing they may hear and not understand;
> Lest they should turn,
> And *their* sins be forgiven them.'"[1]

13 And He said to them, "Do you not understand this para-
ble? How then will you understand all the parables?
14 [a]"The sower sows the word.
15 "And these are the ones by the wayside where the word is
sown. When they hear, Satan comes immediately and takes
away the word that was sown in their hearts.
16 "These likewise are the ones sown on stony ground who,
when they hear the word, immediately receive it with glad-
ness;
17 "and they have no root in themselves, and so endure only
for a time. Afterward, when tribulation or persecution arises
for the word's sake, immediately they stumble.
18 "Now these are the ones sown among thorns; *they are* the
ones who hear the word,
19 "and the [a]cares of this world, [b]the deceitfulness of riches,
and the desires for other things entering in choke the word,
and it becomes unfruitful.
20 "But these are the ones sown on good ground, those who
hear the word, accept *it,* and bear [a]fruit: some thirtyfold, some
sixty, and some a hundred."
21 [a]Also He said to them, "Is a lamp brought to be put under
a basket or under a bed? Is it not to be set on a lampstand?
22 [a]"For there is nothing hidden which will not be revealed,
nor has anything been kept secret but that it should come to
light.
23 [a]"If anyone has ears to hear, let him hear."
24 Then He said to them, "Take heed what you hear. [a]With
the same measure you use, it will be measured to you; and
to you who hear, more will be given.
25 [a]"For whoever has, to him more will be given; but whoever
does not have, even what he has will be taken away from him."
26 And He said, [a]"The kingdom of God is as if a man should
scatter seed on the ground,

4:10[a]Luke 8:9 4:11[a][1 Cor. 2:10–16] [b][Col. 4:5] 4:12[a]Is. 6:9, 10; 43:8 [1]Isaiah 6:9, 10 4:14[a]Matt. 13:18–23 4:19[a]Luke 21:34 [b]1 Tim. 6:9, 10, 17 4:20[a][Rom. 7:4] 4:21[a]Matt. 5:15 4:22[a]Matt. 10:26, 27 4:23[a]Matt. 11:15; 13:9, 43 4:24[a]Matt. 7:2 4:25[a]Luke 8:18; 19:26 4:26[a][Matt. 13:24–30, 36–43]

27 "and should sleep by night and rise by day, and the seed
should sprout and [a]grow, he himself does not know how.
28 "For the earth [a]yields crops by itself: first the blade, then
the head, after that the full grain in the head.
29 "But when the grain ripens, immediately [a]he puts in the
sickle, because the harvest has come."
30 Then He said, [a]"To what shall we liken the kingdom of
God? Or with what parable shall we picture it?
31 "*It is* like a mustard seed which, when it is sown on the
ground, is smaller than all the seeds on earth;
32 "but when it is sown, it grows up and becomes greater
than all herbs, and shoots out large branches, so that the
birds of the air may nest under its shade."
33 [a]And with many such parables He spoke the word to them
as they were able to hear *it*.
34 But without a parable He did not speak to them. And when
they were alone, [a]He explained all things to His disciples.
35 [a]On the same day, when evening had come, He said to
them, "Let us cross over to the other side."
36 Now when they had left the multitude, they took Him
along in the boat as He was. And other little boats were also
with Him.
37 And a great windstorm arose, and the waves beat into the
boat, so that it was already filling.
38 But He was in the stern, asleep on a pillow. And they awoke
Him and said to Him, [a]"Teacher, [b]do You not care that we are
perishing?"
39 Then He arose and [a]rebuked the wind, and said to the
sea, [b]"Peace, be still!" And the wind ceased and there was a
great calm.
40 But He said to them, "Why are you so fearful? [a]How *is it*
that you have no faith?"[1]
41 And they feared exceedingly, and said to one another,
"Who can this be, that even the wind and the sea obey Him!"

4:27[a][2 Pet. 3:18] 4:28[a][John 12:24] 4:29[a]Rev. 14:15 4:30[a]Matt. 13:31, 32 4:33[a]Matt. 13:34, 35 4:34[a]Luke 24:27, 45 4:35[a]Luke 8:22, 25 4:38[a][Matt. 23:8–10] [b]Ps. 44:23 4:39[a]Luke 4:39 [b]Ps. 65:7; 89:9; 93:4; 104:6, 7 4:40[a]Matt. 14:31, 32 [1]NU-Text reads *Have you still no faith?*

MARK 5

JESUS COMMANDS DEMONS, DEATH, AND DISEASE

"He ran and worshiped Him." I do not know that he did intelligently, and after the right manner, worship Christ as the disciples worshiped Him. Perhaps at first, when the man was up a hill, howling and cutting himself with stones, he espied a boat come near the shore, and he saw a single stranger coming up from the boat, and his horrible instinct moved him to fly down at once to the beach, perhaps to attack the Man who dared in open daylight to intrude on the wild man's domain. But as he approached this mysterious stranger, quite a new feeling came over him. His step grew slower, his fierce eye beamed with a duller fire, and the beastlike instinct became calm; the ravening wolf, the roaring lion within him began to tremble, for it perceived its Master. And when he had come near enough to get a fuller view of Christ, who stood there in simple majesty, calm and serene, the very opposite of the poor creature's mad fury, the man fell down at Jesus' feet and worshiped Him.

O soul, I am not telling you to do any great thing now, am I? I am not urging you to exercise any unreasonable confidence, but I do advise you to fall down and worship at my Lord's dear feet. Mad though you are, and your mad worship so poor and imperfect, nevertheless He will accept you and do great things for you.

---

1 Then [a]they came to the other side of the sea, to the coun-
try of the Gadarenes.[1]
2 And when He had come out of the boat, immediately there
met Him out of the tombs a man with an [a]unclean spirit,
3 who had *his* dwelling among the tombs; and no one could
bind him,[1] not even with chains,
4 because he had often been bound with shackles and chains.
And the chains had been pulled apart by him, and the shack-
les broken in pieces; neither could anyone tame him.
5 And always, night and day, he was in the mountains and
in the tombs, crying out and cutting himself with stones.
6 When he saw Jesus from afar, he ran and worshiped Him.
7 And he cried out with a loud voice and said, "What have I
to do with You, Jesus, Son of the Most High God? I [a]implore
You by God that You do not torment me."
8 For He said to him, [a]"Come out of the man, unclean spirit!"
9 Then He asked him, "What *is* your name?" And he answered,
saying, "My name *is* Legion; for we are many."

5:1[a] Matt. 8:28–34 [1] NU-Text reads *Gerasenes.* 5:2[a] Mark 1:23; 7:25 5:3[1] NU-Text adds *anymore.* 5:7[a] Acts 19:13 5:8[a] Mark 1:25; 9:25

10 Also he begged Him earnestly that He would not send
them out of the country.
11 Now a large herd of [a]swine was feeding there near the
mountains.
12 So all the demons begged Him, saying, “Send us to the
swine, that we may enter them.”
13 And at once Jesus[1] gave them permission. Then the un-
clean spirits went out and entered the swine (there were
about two thousand); and the herd ran violently down the
steep place into the sea, and drowned in the sea.
14 So those who fed the swine fled, and they told *it* in the city
and in the country. And they went out to see what it was that
had happened.
15 Then they came to Jesus, and saw the one *who had been*
[a]demon-possessed and had the legion, [b]sitting and [c]clothed
and in his right mind. And they were afraid.
16 And those who saw it told them how it happened to him
who had been demon-possessed, and about the swine.
17 Then [a]they began to plead with Him to depart from their
region.
18 And when He got into the boat, [a]he who had been demon-
possessed begged Him that he might be with Him.
19 However, Jesus did not permit him, but said to him, “Go
home to your friends, and tell them what great things the Lord
has done for you, and how He has had compassion on you.”
20 And he departed and began to [a]proclaim in Decapolis all
that Jesus had done for him; and all [b]marveled.
21 [a]Now when Jesus had crossed over again by boat to the
other side, a great multitude gathered to Him; and He was
by the sea.
22 [a]And behold, one of the rulers of the synagogue came,
Jairus by name. And when he saw Him, he fell at His feet
23 and begged Him earnestly, saying, “My little daughter
lies at the point of death. Come and [a]lay Your hands on her,
that she may be healed, and she will live.”
24 So *Jesus* went with him, and a great multitude followed
Him and thronged Him.
25 Now a certain woman [a]had a flow of blood for twelve
years,
26 and had suffered many things from many physicians.
She had spent all that she had and was no better, but rather
grew worse.
27 When she heard about Jesus, she came behind *Him* in
the crowd and [a]touched His garment.

5:11[a]Deut. 14:8 5:13[1]NU-Text reads *And He gave.* 5:15[a]Matt. 4:24; 8:16 [b]Luke 10:39 [c][Is. 61:10] 5:17[a]Acts 16:39 5:18[a]Luke 8:38, 39 5:20[a]Ps. 66:16 [b]Matt. 9:8, 33 5:21[a]Luke 8:40 5:22[a]Matt. 9:18–26 5:23[a]Acts 9:17; 28:8 5:25[a]Lev. 15:19, 25 5:27[a]Matt. 14:35, 36

28 For she said, "If only I may touch His clothes, I shall be
made well."
29 Immediately the fountain of her blood was dried up, and
she felt in *her* body that she was healed of the affliction.
30 And Jesus, immediately knowing in Himself that [a]power
had gone out of Him, turned around in the crowd and said,
"Who touched My clothes?"
31 But His disciples said to Him, "You see the multitude
thronging You, and You say, 'Who touched Me?'"
32 And He looked around to see her who had done this thing.
33 But the woman, [a]fearing and trembling, knowing what
had happened to her, came and fell down before Him and
told Him the whole truth.
34 And He said to her, "Daughter, [a]your faith has made you
well. [b]Go in peace, and be healed of your affliction."
35 [a]While He was still speaking, *some* came from the ruler
of the synagogue's *house* who said, "Your daughter is dead.
Why trouble the Teacher any further?"
36 As soon as Jesus heard the word that was spoken, He
said to the ruler of the synagogue, "Do not be afraid; only
[a]believe."
37 And He permitted no one to follow Him except Peter,
James, and John the brother of James.
38 Then He came to the house of the ruler of the synagogue,
and saw a tumult and those who [a]wept and wailed loudly.
39 When He came in, He said to them, "Why make this com-
motion and weep? The child is not dead, but [a]sleeping."
40 And they ridiculed Him. [a]But when He had put them all
outside, He took the father and the mother of the child, and
those *who were* with Him, and entered where the child was
lying.
41 Then He took the child by the hand, and said to her, "Tali-
tha, cumi," which is translated, "Little girl, I say to you, arise."
42 Immediately the girl arose and walked, for she was twelve
years *of age*. And they were [a]overcome with great amazement.
43 But [a]He commanded them strictly that no one should
know it, and said that *something* should be given her to eat.

5:30[a]Luke 6:19; 8:46 5:33[a][Ps. 89:7] 5:34[a]Matt. 9:22 [b]Luke 7:50; 8:48
5:35[a]Luke 8:49 5:36[a][John 11:40] 5:38[a]Acts 9:39 5:39[a]John 11:4, 11
5:40[a]Acts 9:40 5:42[a]Mark 1:27; 7:37 5:43[a][Matt. 8:4; 12:16–19; 17:9]

MARK 6

THE DEATH OF JOHN THE BAPTIST

That Jesus marveled was in itself a marvel. We never read that either science or art, nature or providence excited His wonder. There were but two occasions when our Lord Jesus is recorded to have marveled at all, and both of these were concerning faith. First, He marveled at the centurion: "I have not found such great faith, not even in Israel!" (Matt. 8:10). And on the second occasion, He marveled at the absence of faith where it might have been expected to be found, namely in His own fellow townsmen: "And He marveled because of their unbelief." In both instances it was faith or the absence of it that caused Christ to wonder.

See the importance of faith! Never place that precious grace in a secondary position. That which can make Jesus marvel, that which seems to Him to be both in its presence and in its absence a thing to be marveled at, ought to be a very great point of consideration with us; it should be frequently thought upon and always estimated at the highest rate. Have you believed? No man ever asked you a weightier question. Are you still in unbelief? No tongue can ever suggest a more solemn enquiry.

---

1 Then [a]He went out from there and came to His own coun-
try, and His disciples followed Him.
2 And when the Sabbath had come, He began to teach in the
synagogue. And many hearing *Him* were [a]astonished, saying,
[b]"Where *did* this Man *get* these things? And what wisdom *is*
this which is given to Him, that such mighty works are per-
formed by His hands!
3 "Is this not the carpenter, the Son of Mary, and [a]brother
of James, Joses, Judas, and Simon? And are not His sisters
here with us?" So they [b]were offended at Him.
4 But Jesus said to them, [a]"A prophet is not without honor
except in his own country, among his own relatives, and in
his own house."
5 [a]Now He could do no mighty work there, except that He
laid His hands on a few sick people and healed *them*.
6 And [a]He marveled because of their unbelief. [b]Then He
went about the villages in a circuit, teaching.
7 [a]And He called the twelve to *Himself*, and began to send
them out [b]two *by* two, and gave them power over unclean
spirits.
8 He commanded them to take nothing for the journey

6:1[a]Matt. 13:54 6:2[a]Matt. 7:28 [b]John 6:42 6:3[a]Matt. 12:46 [b][Matt. 11:6]
6:4[a]John 4:44 6:5[a]Gen. 19:22; 32:25 6:6[a]Is. 59:16 [b]Matt. 9:35
6:7[a]Mark 3:13, 14 [b][Eccl. 4:9, 10]

except a staff—no bag, no bread, no copper in *their* money
belts—
9 but [a]to wear sandals, and not to put on two tunics.
10 [a]Also He said to them, "In whatever place you enter a
house, stay there till you depart from that place.
11 [a]"And whoever[1] will not receive you nor hear you, when
you depart from there, [b]shake off the dust under your feet
as a testimony against them.[2] Assuredly, I say to you, it will
be more tolerable for Sodom and Gomorrah in the day of
judgment than for that city!"
12 So they went out and preached that *people* should repent.
13 And they cast out many demons, [a]and anointed with oil
many who were sick, and healed *them*.
14 [a]Now King Herod heard *of Him,* for His name had become
well known. And he said, "John the Baptist is risen from the
dead, and therefore [b]these powers are at work in him."
15 [a]Others said, "It is Elijah." And others said, "It is the Proph-
et, [b]or[1] like one of the prophets."
16 [a]But when Herod heard, he said, "This is John, whom I
beheaded; he has been raised from the dead!"
17 For Herod himself had sent and laid hold of John, and
bound him in prison for the sake of Herodias, his brother
Philip's wife; for he had married her.
18 Because John had said to Herod, [a]"It is not lawful for you
to have your brother's wife."
19 Therefore Herodias held it against him and wanted to kill
him, but she could not;
20 for Herod [a]feared John, knowing that he *was* a just and
holy man, and he protected him. And when he heard him,
he did many things, and heard him gladly.
21 [a]Then an opportune day came when Herod [b]on his birth-
day gave a feast for his nobles, the high officers, and the chief
men of Galilee.
22 And when Herodias' daughter herself came in and danced,
and pleased Herod and those who sat with him, the king
said to the girl, "Ask me whatever you want, and I will give *it*
to you."
23 He also swore to her, [a]"Whatever you ask me, I will give
you, up to half my kingdom."
24 So she went out and said to her mother, "What shall I
ask?" And she said, "The head of John the Baptist!"
25 Immediately she came in with haste to the king and asked,
saying, "I want you to give me at once the head of John the
Baptist on a platter."

6:9[a][Eph. 6:15] 6:10[a]Matt. 10:11 6:11[a]Matt. 10:14 [b]Acts 13:51; 18:6 [1]NU-Text reads *whatever place*. [2]NU-Text omits the rest of this verse. 6:13[a][James 5:14] 6:14[a]Luke 9:7–9 [b]Luke 19:37 6:15[a]Mark 8:28 [b]Matt. 21:11 [1]NU-Text and M-Text omit *or*. 6:16[a]Luke 3:19 6:18[a]Lev. 18:16; 20:21 6:20[a]Matt. 14:5; 21:26 6:21[a]Matt. 14:6 [b]Gen. 40:20 6:23[a]Esth. 5:3, 6; 7:2

26 [a]And the king was exceedingly sorry; *yet,* because of the
oaths and because of those who sat with him, he did not want
to refuse her.
27 Immediately the king sent an executioner and command-
ed his head to be brought. And he went and beheaded him
in prison,
28 brought his head on a platter, and gave it to the girl; and
the girl gave it to her mother.
29 When his disciples heard *of it,* they came and [a]took away
his corpse and laid it in a tomb.
30 [a]Then the apostles gathered to Jesus and told Him all
things, both what they had done and what they had taught.
31 [a]And He said to them, "Come aside by yourselves to a de-
serted place and rest a while." For [b]there were many coming
and going, and they did not even have time to eat.
32 [a]So they departed to a deserted place in the boat by them-
selves.
33 But the multitudes[1] saw them departing, and many [a]knew
Him and ran there on foot from all the cities. They arrived
before them and came together to Him.
34 [a]And Jesus, when He came out, saw a great multitude and
was moved with compassion for them, because they were like
[b]sheep not having a shepherd. So [c]He began to teach them
many things.
35 [a]When the day was now far spent, His disciples came to
Him and said, "This is a deserted place, and already the hour
is late.
36 "Send them away, that they may go into the surround-
ing country and villages and buy themselves bread;[1] for they
have nothing to eat."
37 But He answered and said to them, "You give them some-
thing to eat." And they said to Him, [a]"Shall we go and buy two
hundred denarii worth of bread and give them *something*
to eat?"
38 But He said to them, "How many loaves do you have? Go
and see." And when they found out they said, [a]"Five, and two
fish."
39 Then He [a]commanded them to make them all sit down
in groups on the green grass.
40 So they sat down in ranks, in hundreds and in fifties.
41 And when He had taken the five loaves and the two fish,
He [a]looked up to heaven, [b]blessed and broke the loaves, and
gave *them* to His disciples to set before them; and the two
fish He divided among *them* all.

6:26[a]Matt. 14:9 6:29[a]1 Kin. 13:29, 30 6:30[a]Luke 9:10 6:31[a]Matt. 14:13 [b]Mark 3:20 6:32[a]Matt. 14:13–21 6:33[a][Col. 1:6] [1]NU-Text and M-Text read *they.* 6:34[a]Matt. 9:36; 14:14 [b]Num. 27:17 [c]Luke 9:11 6:35[a]Matt. 14:15 6:36[1]NU-Text reads *something to eat* and omits the rest of this verse. 6:37[a]2 Kin. 4:43 6:38[a]John 6:9 6:39[a]Matt. 15:35 6:41[a]John 11:41, 42 [b]Matt. 15:36; 26:26

42 So they all ate and were filled.
43 And they took up twelve baskets full of fragments and of
the fish.
44 Now those who had eaten the loaves were about[1] five
thousand men.
45 [a]Immediately He made His disciples get into the boat
and go before Him to the other side, to Bethsaida, while He
sent the multitude away.
46 And when He had sent them away, He [a]departed to the
mountain to pray.
47 Now when evening came, the boat was in the middle of
the sea; and He *was* alone on the land.
48 Then He saw them straining at rowing, for the wind was
against them. Now about the fourth watch of the night He
came to them, walking on the sea, and [a]would have passed
them by.
49 And when they saw Him walking on the sea, they sup-
posed it was a [a]ghost, and cried out;
50 for they all saw Him and were troubled. But immediately
He talked with them and said to them, [a]"Be of good cheer! It
is I; do not be [b]afraid."
51 Then He went up into the boat to them, and the wind
[a]ceased. And they were greatly [b]amazed in themselves be-
yond measure, and marveled.
52 For [a]they had not understood about the loaves, because
their [b]heart was hardened.
53 [a]When they had crossed over, they came to the land of
Gennesaret and anchored there.
54 And when they came out of the boat, immediately the
people recognized Him,
55 ran through that whole surrounding region, and began
to carry about on beds those who were sick to wherever they
heard He was.
56 Wherever He entered, into villages, cities, or the coun-
try, they laid the sick in the marketplaces, and begged Him
that [a]they might just touch the [b]hem of His garment. And as
many as touched Him were made well.

6:44[1] NU-Text and M-Text omit *about.* 6:45[a] John 6:15–21 6:46[a] Luke 5:16 6:48[a] Luke 24:28 6:49[a] Matt. 14:26 6:50[a] Matt. 9:2 [b] Is. 41:10 6:51[a] Ps. 107:29 [b] Mark 1:27; 2:12; 5:42; 7:37 6:52[a] Mark 8:17, 18 [b] Mark 3:5; 16:14 6:53[a] Matt. 14:34–36 6:56[a] Matt. 9:20 [b] Num. 15:38, 39

MARK 7

JESUS REBUKES THE PHARISEES' TRADITIONS

Observe in our text that faith assents to all the Lord says. She said, "Yes, Lord." What had He said? *You are comparable to a dog! Yes, Lord, so I am.* "It is not good to take the children's bread and throw it to the little dogs." *Yes, Lord, it would not be fitting.* She virtually replies, *I know it, Lord, and agree thereto.*

She does not raise a question or dispute the justice of the Lord's dispensing His own grace according to His sovereign good pleasure. She fails not, as some do who criticize divine sovereignty. It would have proved that she had little or no faith if she had done that. She disputes not as to the Lord's set time and order. She assents to all the Lord's appointments. That is the faith that saves the soul: it agrees with the mind of God even if it seems adverse. It believes the revealed declarations of God whether they appear to be pleasant or terrible and assents to God's word whether it be like a balm to its wound or like a sword to cut and slay.

If the word of God be true, do not fight against it; bow before it. It is not the way to a living faith in Jesus Christ or to obtain peace with God, to take up arms against anything God declares. In yielding lies safety. Say "Yes, Lord," and you shall find salvation.

---

1 Then [a]the Pharisees and some of the scribes came together to Him, having come from Jerusalem.
2 Now when[1] they saw some of His disciples eat bread with defiled, that is, with [a]unwashed hands, they found fault.
3 For the Pharisees and all the Jews do not eat unless they wash *their* hands in a special way, holding the [a]tradition of the elders.
4 *When they come* from the marketplace, they do not eat unless they wash. And there are many other things which they have received and hold, *like* the washing of cups, pitchers, copper vessels, and couches.
5 [a]Then the Pharisees and scribes asked Him, "Why do Your disciples not walk according to the tradition of the elders, but eat bread with unwashed hands?"
6 He answered and said to them, "Well did Isaiah prophesy of you [a]hypocrites, as it is written:

> [b]'This people honors Me with *their* lips,
> But their heart is far from Me.

7:1 [a]Matt. 15:1–20 7:2 [a]Matt. 15:20 [1]NU-Text omits *when* and *they found fault.* 7:3 [a]Gal. 1:14 7:5 [a]Matt. 15:2 7:6 [a]Matt. 23:13–29 [b]Is. 29:13

7 And in vain they worship Me,
Teaching *as* doctrines the commandments of men.'[1]

8 "For laying aside the commandment of God, you hold
the tradition of men[1]—the washing of pitchers and cups,
and many other such things you do."
9 He said to them, "*All too* well [a]you reject the command-
ment of God, that you may keep your tradition.
10 "For Moses said, [a]'Honor your father and your mother';[1]
and, [b]'He who curses father or mother, let him be put to
death.'[2]
11 "But you say, 'If a man says to his father or mother, [a]"What-
ever profit you might have received from me *is* Corban"—'
(that is, a gift *to God*),
12 "then you no longer let him do anything for his father or
his mother,
13 "making the word of God of no effect through your tra-
dition which you have handed down. And many such things
you do."
14 [a]When He had called all the multitude to *Himself,* He said
to them, "Hear Me, everyone, and [b]understand:
15 "There is nothing that enters a man from outside which
can defile him; but the things which come out of him, those
are the things that [a]defile a man.
16 [a]"If anyone has ears to hear, let him hear!"[1]
17 [a]When He had entered a house away from the crowd, His
disciples asked Him concerning the parable.
18 So He said to them, [a]"Are you thus without understanding
also? Do you not perceive that whatever enters a man from
outside cannot defile him,
19 "because it does not enter his heart but his stomach, and
is eliminated, *thus* purifying all foods?"[1]
20 And He said, [a]"What comes out of a man, that defiles
a man.
21 [a]"For from within, out of the heart of men, [b]proceed evil
thoughts, [c]adulteries, [d]fornications, murders,
22 "thefts, [a]covetousness, wickedness, [b]deceit, [c]lewdness,
an evil eye, [d]blasphemy, [e]pride, foolishness.
23 "All these evil things come from within and defile a man."
24 [a]From there He arose and went to the region of Tyre and
Sidon.[1] And He entered a house and wanted no one to know
it, but He could not be [b]hidden.

7:7 [1]Isaiah 29:13 7:8 [1]NU-Text omits the rest of this verse. 7:9 [a]Prov. 1:25 7:10 [a]Ex. 20:12; Deut. 5:16 [b]Ex. 21:17 [1]Exodus 20:12; Deuteronomy 5:16 [2]Exodus 21:17 7:11 [a]Matt. 15:5; 23:18 7:14 [a]Matt. 15:10 [b]Matt. 16:9, 11, 12 7:15 [a]Is. 59:3 7:16 [a]Matt. 11:15 [1]NU-Text omits this verse. 7:17 [a]Matt. 15:15 7:18 [a][Heb. 5:11–14] 7:19 [1]NU-Text ends quotation with *eliminated,* setting off the final clause as Mark's comment that Jesus has declared all foods clean. 7:20 [a]Ps. 39:1 7:21 [a]Gen. 6:5; 8:21 [b][Gal. 5:19–21] [c]2 Pet. 2:14 [d]1 Thess. 4:3 7:22 [a]Luke 12:15 [b]Rom. 1:28, 29 [c]1 Pet. 4:3 [d]Rev. 2:9 [e]1 John 2:16 7:24 [a]Matt. 15:21 [b]Mark 2:1, 2 [1]NU-Text omits *and Sidon.*

25 For a woman whose young daughter had an unclean spir-
it heard about Him, and she came and [a]fell at His feet.
26 The woman was a Greek, a Syro-Phoenician by birth, and
she kept asking Him to cast the demon out of her daughter.
27 But Jesus said to her, "Let the children be filled first, for
it is not good to take the children's bread and throw *it* to the
little dogs."
28 And she answered and said to Him, "Yes, Lord, yet even
the little dogs under the table eat from the children's crumbs."
29 Then He said to her, "For this saying go your way; the de-
mon has gone out of your daughter."
30 And when she had come to her house, she found the de-
mon gone out, and her daughter lying on the bed.
31 [a]Again, departing from the region of Tyre and Sidon, He
came through the midst of the region of Decapolis to the Sea
of Galilee.
32 Then [a]they brought to Him one who was deaf and had an
impediment in his speech, and they begged Him to put His
hand on him.
33 And He took him aside from the multitude, and put His
fingers in his ears, and [a]He spat and touched his tongue.
34 Then, [a]looking up to heaven, [b]He sighed, and said to him,
"Ephphatha," that is, "Be opened."
35 [a]Immediately his ears were opened, and the impediment
of his tongue was loosed, and he spoke plainly.
36 Then [a]He commanded them that they should tell no one;
but the more He commanded them, the more widely they
proclaimed *it*.
37 And they were [a]astonished beyond measure, saying, "He
has done all things well. He [b]makes both the deaf to hear and
the mute to speak."

7:25 [a]John 11:32 7:31 [a]Matt. 15:29 7:32 [a]Luke 11:14 7:33 [a]Mark 8:23 7:34 [a]Mark 6:41 [b]John 11:33, 38 7:35 [a]Is. 35:5, 6 7:36 [a]Mark 5:43 7:37 [a]Mark 6:51; 10:26 [b]Matt. 12:22

MARK 8

THE FOUR THOUSAND FED

It is a common weakness of faith to expect grace to come in a certain fixed way. Just as these people expected the healing of the blind man to come by the touch of Christ's hand, so many expect deliverance from trouble to come in a specific way. You know it is so. You have taken your troubles to the Lord—you have told Him all about your case, you have entrusted it to Him, but you have laid down the plan by which God is to work on your behalf. You remember how He delivered you on a former occasion, and you expect Him to deliver you in exactly the same way again. Or you have been reading the biography of some worthy man who cast his care upon the Lord, and he was helped in a certain manner, so you think you will be helped in the same manner.

It's very likely God will do nothing of the kind; He is not bound to give you any blessing in the particular way you choose to select. He has His own method of giving a blessing and His own plan of warding off evil, so you must leave the *how* and the *when* entirely with Him. It is useless for you to think of mapping out the route for Him to whom the psalmist said, "Your way was in the sea, Your path in the great waters, and Your footsteps were not known" (Ps. 77:19).

---

1 In those days, [a]the multitude being very great and having
nothing to eat, Jesus called His disciples *to Him* and said to
them,
2 "I have [a]compassion on the multitude, because they have
now continued with Me three days and have nothing to eat.
3 "And if I send them away hungry to their own houses, they
will faint on the way; for some of them have come from afar."
4 Then His disciples answered Him, "How can one satisfy
these people with bread here in the wilderness?"
5 [a]He asked them, "How many loaves do you have?" And
they said, "Seven."
6 So He commanded the multitude to sit down on the ground.
And He took the seven loaves and gave thanks, broke *them*
and gave *them* to His disciples to set before *them;* and they
set *them* before the multitude.
7 They also had a few small fish; and [a]having blessed them,
He said to set them also before *them.*
8 So they ate and were filled, and they took up seven large
baskets of leftover fragments.

8:1[a] Matt. 15:32–39 8:2[a] Mark 1:41; 6:34 8:5[a] Mark 6:38 8:7[a] Matt. 14:19

9 Now those who had eaten were about four thousand. And
He sent them away,
10 [a]immediately got into the boat with His disciples, and
came to the region of Dalmanutha.
11 [a]Then the Pharisees came out and began to dispute with
Him, seeking from Him a sign from heaven, testing Him.
12 But He [a]sighed deeply in His spirit, and said, "Why does
this generation seek a sign? Assuredly, I say to you, [b]no sign
shall be given to this generation."
13 And He left them, and getting into the boat again, de-
parted to the other side.
14 [a]Now the disciples[1] had forgotten to take bread, and they
did not have more than one loaf with them in the boat.
15 [a]Then He charged them, saying, "Take heed, beware of
the leaven of the Pharisees and the leaven of Herod."
16 And they reasoned among themselves, saying, "*It is* be-
cause we have no bread."
17 But Jesus, being aware of *it,* said to them, "Why do you
reason because you have no bread? [a]Do you not yet perceive
nor understand? Is your heart still[1] hardened?
18 "Having eyes, do you not see? And having ears, do you
not hear? And do you not remember?
19 [a]"When I broke the five loaves for the five thousand, how
many baskets full of fragments did you take up?" They said
to Him, "Twelve."
20 "Also, [a]when I broke the seven for the four thousand, how
many large baskets full of fragments did you take up?" And
they said, "Seven."
21 So He said to them, "How *is it* [a]you do not understand?"
22 Then He came to Bethsaida; and they brought a [a]blind
man to Him, and begged Him to [b]touch him.
23 So He took the blind man by the hand and led him out
of the town. And when [a]He had spit on his eyes and put His
hands on him, He asked him if he saw anything.
24 And he looked up and said, "I see men like trees, walking."
25 Then He put *His* hands on his eyes again and made him
look up. And he was restored and saw everyone clearly.
26 Then He sent him away to his house, saying, "Neither go
into the town, [a]nor tell anyone in the town."[1]
27 [a]Now Jesus and His disciples went out to the towns of
Caesarea Philippi; and on the road He asked His disciples,
saying to them, "Who do men say that I am?"
28 So they answered, [a]"John the Baptist; but some *say,* [b]Eli-
jah; and others, one of the prophets."

8:10[a]Matt. 15:39 8:11[a]Matt. 12:38; 16:1 8:12[a]Mark 7:34 [b]Matt. 12:39 8:14[a]Matt. 16:5 [1]NU-Text and M-Text read *they.* 8:15[a]Luke 12:1 8:17[a]Mark 6:52; 16:14 [1]NU-Text omits *still.* 8:19[a]Matt. 14:20 8:20[a]Matt. 15:37 8:21[a][Mark 6:52] 8:22[a]John 9:1 [b]Luke 18:15 8:23[a]Mark 7:33 8:26[a]Mark 5:43; 7:36 [1]NU-Text reads *"Do not even go into the town."* 8:27[a]Luke 9:18–20 8:28[a]Matt. 14:2 [b]Luke 9:7, 8

29 He said to them, "But who do you say that I am?" Peter
answered and said to Him, [a]"You are the Christ."
30 [a]Then He strictly warned them that they should tell no
one about Him.
31 And [a]He began to teach them that the Son of Man must
suffer many things, and be [b]rejected by the elders and chief
priests and scribes, and be [c]killed, and after three days rise
again.
32 He spoke this word openly. Then Peter took Him aside
and began to rebuke Him.
33 But when He had turned around and looked at His dis-
ciples, He [a]rebuked Peter, saying, "Get behind Me, Satan!
For you are not mindful of the things of God, but the things
of men."
34 When He had called the people to *Himself,* with His dis-
ciples also, He said to them, [a]"Whoever desires to come after
Me, let him deny himself, and take up his cross, and follow Me.
35 "For [a]whoever desires to save his life will lose it, but who-
ever loses his life for My sake and the gospel's will save it.
36 "For what will it profit a man if he gains the whole world,
and loses his own soul?
37 "Or what will a man give in exchange for his soul?
38 [a]"For whoever [b]is ashamed of Me and My words in this
adulterous and sinful generation, of him the Son of Man also
will be ashamed when He comes in the glory of His Father
with the holy angels."

8:29 [a]John 1:41; 4:42; 6:69; 11:27 8:30 [a]Matt. 8:4; 16:20 8:31 [a]Matt. 16:21; 20:19 [b]Mark 10:33 [c]Mark 9:31; 10:34 8:33 [a][Rev. 3:19] 8:34 [a]Luke 14:27 8:35 [a]John 12:25 8:38 [a]Matt. 10:33 [b]2 Tim. 1:8, 9; 2:12

MARK 9

THE TRANSFIGURATION OF CHRIST

If you go to Jesus Christ for anything, either for yourself or someone else, the Savior will earnestly desire that you should know what you are asking of Him. You know there is much asking for mercies because such and such words are proper without your having a clear and vivid idea of the blessing that is intended by those words. Christ would have you know why and wherefore you are pleading with Him.

Hence, when this man came with his sick child, the Savior permitted him to give a statement of the case and with the eagerness of love, the father entered into full particulars of the evil that had befallen his son. This was not needed by the Savior for His own information, but the heartrending account was given in order that the father might distinctly recollect the evil from which he desired his child to be saved; and then that those who were standing round might know what kind of miracle it was that Jesus Christ was about to work. Sometimes it will be a very healthy thing for seekers to stop a while and say to themselves, *What is it we are seeking?* Christ may say to you, *What do you want Me to do for you? What are you really asking for?* There are many who cry, "Lord, save me!" who perhaps have no distinct idea from what they are to be saved or to what they are to be saved.

---

1 And He said to them, [a]"Assuredly, I say to you that there
are some standing here who will not taste death till they see
[b]the kingdom of God present with power."
2 [a]Now after six days Jesus took Peter, James, and John, and
led them up on a high mountain apart by themselves; and
He was transfigured before them.
3 His clothes became shining, exceedingly [a]white, like snow,
such as no launderer on earth can whiten them.
4 And Elijah appeared to them with Moses, and they were
talking with Jesus.
5 Then Peter answered and said to Jesus, "Rabbi, it is good
for us to be here; and let us make three tabernacles: one for
You, one for Moses, and one for Elijah"—
6 because he did not know what to say, for they were greatly
afraid.
7 And a [a]cloud came and overshadowed them; and a voice
came out of the cloud, saying, "This is [b]My beloved Son.
[c]Hear Him!"

9:1[a]Luke 9:27 [b][Matt. 24:30] 9:2[a]Matt. 17:1–8 9:3[a]Dan. 7:9 9:7[a]Ex. 40:34 [b]Mark 1:11 [c]Acts 3:22

8 Suddenly, when they had looked around, they saw no one
anymore, but only Jesus with themselves.
9 [a]Now as they came down from the mountain, He com-
manded them that they should tell no one the things they
had seen, till the Son of Man had risen from the dead.
10 So they kept this word to themselves, questioning [a]what
the rising from the dead meant.
11 And they asked Him, saying, "Why do the scribes say [a]that
Elijah must come first?"
12 Then He answered and told them, "Indeed, Elijah is com-
ing first and restores all things. And [a]how is it written con-
cerning the Son of Man, that He must suffer many things
and [b]be treated with contempt?
13 "But I say to you that [a]Elijah has also come, and they did
to him whatever they wished, as it is written of him."
14 [a]And when He came to the disciples, He saw a great mul-
titude around them, and scribes disputing with them.
15 Immediately, when they saw Him, all the people were
greatly amazed, and running to *Him,* greeted Him.
16 And He asked the scribes, "What are you discussing with
them?"
17 Then [a]one of the crowd answered and said, "Teacher, I
brought You my son, who has a mute spirit.
18 "And wherever it seizes him, it throws him down; he foams
at the mouth, gnashes his teeth, and becomes rigid. So I
spoke to Your disciples, that they should cast it out, but they
could not."
19 He answered him and said, "O [a]faithless generation, how
long shall I be with you? How long shall I bear with you? Bring
him to Me."
20 Then they brought him to Him. And [a]when he saw Him,
immediately the spirit convulsed him, and he fell on the
ground and wallowed, foaming at the mouth.
21 So He asked his father, "How long has this been happen-
ing to him?" And he said, "From childhood.
22 "And often he has thrown him both into the fire and into
the water to destroy him. But if You can do anything, have
compassion on us and help us."
23 Jesus said to him, [a]"If you can believe,[1] all things *are* pos-
sible to him who believes."
24 Immediately the father of the child cried out and said
with tears, "Lord, I believe; [a]help my unbelief!"
25 When Jesus saw that the people came running together, He
[a]rebuked the unclean spirit, saying to it, "Deaf and dumb spir-
it, I command you, come out of him and enter him no more!"

9:9[a]Matt. 17:9–13 9:10[a]John 2:19–22 9:11[a]Mal. 4:5 9:12[a]Is. 53:3 [b]Phil. 2:7 9:13[a]Luke 1:17 9:14[a]Matt. 17:14–19 9:17[a]Luke 9:38 9:19[a]John 4:48 9:20[a]Mark 1:26 9:23[a]John 11:40 [1]NU-Text reads "*'If You can!' All things . . . .*" 9:24[a]Luke 17:5 9:25[a]Mark 1:25

26 Then *the spirit* cried out, convulsed him greatly, and came
out of him. And he became as one dead, so that many said,
"He is dead."
27 But Jesus took him by the hand and lifted him up, and
he arose.
28 [a]And when He had come into the house, His disciples
asked Him privately, "Why could we not cast it out?"
29 So He said to them, "This kind can come out by nothing
but [a]prayer and fasting."[1]
30 Then they departed from there and passed through Gal-
ilee, and He did not want anyone to know *it.*
31 [a]For He taught His disciples and said to them, "The Son
of Man is being betrayed into the hands of men, and they will
[b]kill Him. And after He is killed, He will [c]rise the third day."
32 But they [a]did not understand this saying, and were afraid
to ask Him.
33 [a]Then He came to Capernaum. And when He was in the
house He asked them, "What was it you disputed among
yourselves on the road?"
34 But they kept silent, for on the road they had [a]disputed
among themselves who *would be the* [b]greatest.
35 And He sat down, called the twelve, and said to them, [a]"If
anyone desires to be first, he shall be last of all and servant
of all."
36 Then [a]He took a little child and set him in the midst of
them. And when He had taken him in His arms, He said to
them,
37 "Whoever receives one of these little children in My name
receives Me; and [a]whoever receives Me, receives not Me but
Him who sent Me."
38 [a]Now John answered Him, saying, "Teacher, we saw some-
one who does not follow us casting out demons in Your name,
and we forbade him because he does not follow us."
39 But Jesus said, "Do not forbid him, [a]for no one who works
a miracle in My name can soon afterward speak evil of Me.
40 "For [a]he who is not against us is on our[1] side.
41 [a]"For whoever gives you a cup of water to drink in My
name, because you belong to Christ, assuredly, I say to you,
he will by no means lose his reward.
42 [a]"But whoever causes one of these little ones who believe
in Me to stumble, it would be better for him if a millstone were
hung around his neck, and he were thrown into the sea.
43 [a]"If your hand causes you to sin, cut it off. It is better for

9:28[a]Matt. 17:19 9:29[a][James 5:16] [1]NU-Text omits *and fasting.* 9:31[a]Luke 9:44 [b]Matt. 16:21; 27:50 [c]1 Cor. 15:4 9:32[a]Luke 2:50; 18:34 9:33[a]Matt. 18:1–5 9:34[a][Prov. 13:10] [b]Luke 22:24; 23:46; 24:46 9:35[a]Luke 22:26, 27 9:36[a]Mark 10:13–16 9:37[a]Matt. 10:40 9:38[a]Num. 11:27–29 9:39[a]1 Cor. 12:3 9:40[a][Matt. 12:30] [1]M-Text reads *against you is on your side.* 9:41[a]Matt. 10:42 9:42[a]Luke 17:1, 2 9:43[a]Matt. 5:29, 30; 18:8, 9

you to enter into life maimed, rather than having two hands,
to go to hell, into the fire that shall never be quenched—
44 "where

> [a]'Their worm does not die,
> And the fire is not quenched.'[1]

45 "And if your foot causes you to sin, cut it off. It is better
for you to enter life lame, rather than having two feet, to be
cast into hell, into the fire that shall never be quenched—
46 "where

> [a]'Their worm does not die,
> And the fire is not quenched.'[1]

47 And if your eye causes you to sin, pluck it out. It is bet-
ter for you to enter the kingdom of God with one eye, rather
than having two eyes, to be cast into hell fire—
48 "where

> [a]'Their worm does not die,
> And the [b]fire is not quenched.'[1]

49 "For everyone will be [a]seasoned with fire,[1] [b]and every
sacrifice will be seasoned with salt.
50 [a]"Salt *is* good, but if the salt loses its flavor, how will you
season it? [b]Have salt in yourselves, and [c]have peace with one
another."

9:44[a]Is. 66:24 [1]NU-Text omits this verse. 9:46[a]Is. 66:24 [1]NU-Text omits the last clause of verse 45 and all of verse 46. 9:48[a]Is. 66:24 [b]Jer. 7:20 [1]Isaiah 66:24 9:49[a][Matt. 3:11] [b]Lev. 2:13 [1]NU-Text omits the rest of this verse. 9:50[a]Matt. 5:13 [b]Col. 4:6 [c]Rom. 12:18; 14:19

MARK 10

DIVORCE AND THE DANGER OF RICHES

"Jesus, Son of David, have mercy on me!" We have here a picture of the power of faith. In every case, if you would be saved, your faith must exercise itself in crying. The gate of heaven is to be opened only in one way: by the very earnest use of the knocker of prayer.

You cannot have your eyes opened until your mouth is opened. Open your mouth in prayer, and He shall open your eyes to see: so you shall find joy and gladness. Mark you, when a man has faith in the soul and earnestness combined with it, he will pray indeed. When a poor soul in some weighty trouble, fainting and athirst, lifts up its streaming eyes and wrings its hands and beats its bosom, then cries, "Jesus, Son of David, have mercy on me!"—that is prayer.

It is the soul that has a furnace within—a very volcano of grief and sorrow—and that burning lava of prayer that finds its way to God. No prayer ever reaches God's heart that does not come from our hearts.

My dear hearers, are you now seeking Christ in earnest prayer? Be not afraid of being too earnest or too persevering. Go to Christ this day, agonize and wrestle with Him; beg Him to have mercy on you, and if He hears you not, go to Him again, again, and again.

---

1 Then [a]He arose from there and came to the region of Judea
by the other side of the Jordan. And multitudes gathered to
Him again, and as He was accustomed, He taught them again.
2 [a]The Pharisees came and asked Him, "Is it lawful for a man
to divorce *his* wife?" testing Him.
3 And He answered and said to them, "What did Moses com-
mand you?"
4 They said, [a]"Moses permitted *a man* to write a certificate
of divorce, and to dismiss *her*."
5 And Jesus answered and said to them, "Because of the
hardness of your heart he wrote you this precept.
6 "But from the beginning of the creation, God [a]'made them
male and female.'[1]
7 [a]'For this reason a man shall leave his father and mother
and be joined to his wife,
8 'and the two shall become one flesh';[1] so then they are no
longer two, but one flesh.
9 "Therefore what God has joined together, let not man sep-
arate."

10:1[a]Matt. 19:1–9 10:2[a]Matt. 19:3 10:4[a]Deut. 24:1–4 10:6[a]Gen. 1:27; 5:2 [1]Genesis 1:27; 5:2 10:7[a]Gen. 2:24 10:8[1]Genesis 2:24

10 In the house His disciples also asked Him again about
the same *matter.*
11 So He said to them, [a]"Whoever divorces his wife and mar-
ries another commits adultery against her.
12 "And if a woman divorces her husband and marries an-
other, she commits adultery."
13 [a]Then they brought little children to Him, that He might
touch them; but the disciples rebuked those who brought
them.
14 But when Jesus saw *it,* He was greatly displeased and said
to them, "Let the little children come to Me, and do not for-
bid them; for [a]of such is the kingdom of God.
15 "Assuredly, I say to you, [a]whoever does not receive the
kingdom of God as a little child will [b]by no means enter it."
16 And He took them up in His arms, laid *His* hands on them,
and blessed them.
17 [a]Now as He was going out on the road, one came running,
knelt before Him, and asked Him, "Good Teacher, what shall
I [b]do that I may inherit eternal life?"
18 So Jesus said to him, "Why do you call Me good? No one
is good but One, *that is,* [a]God.
19 "You know the commandments: [a]'Do not commit adul-
tery,' 'Do not murder,' 'Do not steal,' 'Do not bear false
witness,' 'Do not defraud,' 'Honor your father and your
mother.'"[1]
20 And he answered and said to Him, "Teacher, all these
things I have [a]kept from my youth."
21 Then Jesus, looking at him, loved him, and said to him,
"One thing you lack: Go your way, [a]sell whatever you have
and give to the poor, and you will have [b]treasure in heaven;
and come, [c]take up the cross, and follow Me."
22 But he was sad at this word, and went away sorrowful, for
he had great possessions.
23 [a]Then Jesus looked around and said to His disciples,
"How hard it is for those who have riches to enter the king-
dom of God!"
24 And the disciples were astonished at His words. But Jesus
answered again and said to them, "Children, how hard it is
for those [a]who trust in riches[1] to enter the kingdom of God!
25 "It is easier for a camel to go through the eye of a needle
than for a [a]rich man to enter the kingdom of God."
26 And they were greatly astonished, saying among them-
selves, "Who then can be saved?"

10:11[a] [Matt. 5:32; 19:9] 10:13[a] Luke 18:15–17 10:14[a] [1 Pet. 2:2] 10:15[a] Matt. 18:3, 4; 19:14 [b] Luke 13:28 10:17[a] Matt. 19:16–30 [b] John 6:28 10:18[a] 1 Sam. 2:2 10:19[a] Ex. 20:12–16; Deut. 5:16–20 [1] Exodus 20:12–16; Deuteronomy 5:16–20 10:20[a] Phil. 3:6 10:21[a] [Luke 12:33; 16:9] [b] Matt. 6:19, 20; 19:21 [c] [Mark 8:34] 10:23[a] Matt. 19:23 10:24[a] [1 Tim. 6:17] [1] NU-Text omits *for those who trust in riches.* 10:25[a] [Matt. 13:22; 19:24]

27 But Jesus looked at them and said, "With men *it is* impos-
sible, but not [a]with God; for with God all things are possible."
28 [a]Then Peter began to say to Him, "See, we have left all
and followed You."
29 So Jesus answered and said, "Assuredly, I say to you, there
is no one who has left house or brothers or sisters or father
or mother or wife[1] or children or lands, for My sake and the
gospel's,
30 [a]"who shall not receive a hundredfold now in this time—
houses and brothers and sisters and mothers and children
and lands, with [b]persecutions—and in the age to come, eter-
nal life.
31 [a]"But many *who are* first will be last, and the last first."
32 [a]Now they were on the road, going up to Jerusalem, and
Jesus was going before them; and they were amazed. And as
they followed they were afraid. [b]Then He took the twelve aside
again and began to tell them the things that would happen
to Him:
33 "Behold, we are going up to Jerusalem, and the Son of
Man will be betrayed to the chief priests and to the scribes;
and they will condemn Him to death and deliver Him to the
Gentiles;
34 "and they will mock Him, and scourge Him, and spit on
Him, and kill Him. And the third day He will rise again."
35 [a]Then James and John, the sons of Zebedee, came to Him,
saying, "Teacher, we want You to do for us whatever we ask."
36 And He said to them, "What do you want Me to do for you?"
37 They said to Him, "Grant us that we may sit, one on Your
right hand and the other on Your left, in Your glory."
38 But Jesus said to them, "You do not know what you ask.
Are you able to drink the [a]cup that I drink, and be baptized
with the [b]baptism that I am baptized with?"
39 They said to Him, "We are able." So Jesus said to them,
[a]"You will indeed drink the cup that I drink, and with the
baptism I am baptized with you will be baptized;
40 "but to sit on My right hand and on My left is not Mine to
give, but *it is for those* [a]for whom it is prepared."
41 [a]And when the ten heard *it*, they began to be greatly dis-
pleased with James and John.
42 But Jesus called them to *Himself* and said to them, [a]"You
know that those who are considered rulers over the Gentiles
lord it over them, and their great ones exercise authority over
them.
43 [a]"Yet it shall not be so among you; but whoever desires
to become great among you shall be your servant.

10:27 [a]Jer. 32:17 10:28 [a]Luke 18:28 10:29 [1]NU-Text omits *or wife*. 10:30 [a]Luke 18:29, 30 [b][1 Pet. 4:12, 13] 10:31 [a]Luke 13:30 10:32 [a]Matt. 20:17–19 [b]Mark 8:31; 9:31 10:35 [a][James 4:3] 10:38 [a]John 18:11 [b]Luke 12:50 10:39 [a]Acts 12:2 10:40 [a][Heb. 11:16] 10:41 [a]Matt. 20:24 10:42 [a]Luke 22:25 10:43 [a]Mark 9:35

44 "And whoever of you desires to be first shall be slave of all.
45 "For even [a]the Son of Man did not come to be served, but
to serve, and [b]to give His life a ransom for many."
46 [a]Now they came to Jericho. As He went out of Jericho
with His disciples and a great multitude, blind Bartimaeus,
the son of Timaeus, sat by the road begging.
47 And when he heard that it was Jesus of Nazareth, he be-
gan to cry out and say, "Jesus, [a]Son of David, [b]have mercy
on me!"
48 Then many warned him to be quiet; but he cried out all
the more, "Son of David, have mercy on me!"
49 So Jesus stood still and commanded him to be called.
Then they called the blind man, saying to him, "Be of good
cheer. Rise, He is calling you."
50 And throwing aside his garment, he rose and came to
Jesus.
51 So Jesus answered and said to him, "What do you want
Me to do for you?" The blind man said to Him, "Rabboni, that
I may receive my sight."
52 Then Jesus said to him, "Go your way; [a]your faith has
made you well." And immediately he received his sight and
followed Jesus on the road.

10:45[a][Phil. 2:7, 8] [b][Titus 2:14] 10:46[a]Luke 18:35–43 10:47[a]Rev. 22:16 [b]Matt. 15:22 10:52[a]Matt. 9:22

MARK 11

JESUS RIDES INTO JERUSALEM

With the exception of the miracle before us, and perhaps a part of another, all the miracles of Jesus were entirely benevolent in their character; indeed this one is no exception in reality but only in appearance. The raising of the dead, the feeding of the multitude, the stilling of the tempest, the healing of diseases: What were all these but displays of the lovingkindness of God? Yet, as if to show that Jesus the Savior is also Jesus the Judge, one gleam of justice must dart forth. Where shall mercy direct its fall? See, my brethren, it glances not upon a man but lights upon an unconscious, unsuffering thing—a tree. It bore upon itself the signs of barrenness and perhaps was no one's property; little, therefore, was the loss that any man sustained by the withering of that verdant mockery while instruction more precious than a thousand acres of fig trees has been left for the benefit of all ages.

Observe, then, with attention this solitary instance of stern judgment wrought by the Savior's hand, the lesson so unique it must be very full of meaning. The curse, you at once perceive, falls in its metaphorical and spiritual meaning upon those high professors who are destitute of true holiness—upon those who manifest a great show of leaves but who bring forth no fruit unto God. Only one thunderbolt, and that for boasting pretenders; only one curse, and that for hypocrites. O blessed Spirit, write this heart-searching truth upon our hearts!

---

1 Now [a]when they drew near Jerusalem, to Bethphage[1] and Bethany, at the Mount of Olives, He sent two of His disciples;
2 and He said to them, "Go into the village opposite you; and as soon as you have entered it you will find a colt tied, on which no one has sat. Loose it and bring *it*.
3 "And if anyone says to you, 'Why are you doing this?' say, 'The Lord has need of it,' and immediately he will send it here."
4 So they went their way, and found the[1] colt tied by the door outside on the street, and they loosed it.
5 But some of those who stood there said to them, "What are you doing, loosing the colt?"
6 And they spoke to them just as Jesus had commanded. So they let them go.
7 Then they brought the colt to Jesus and threw their clothes on it, and He sat on it.

11:1 [a]Matt. 21:1–9 [1]M-Text reads *Bethsphage.* 11:4 [1]NU-Text and M-Text read *a.*

8 [a]And many spread their clothes on the road, and others
cut down leafy branches from the trees and spread *them* on
the road.
9 Then those who went before and those who followed cried
out, saying:

> "Hosanna!
> [a]'Blessed *is* He who comes in the name of the LORD!'[1]
> 10 Blessed *is* the kingdom of our father David
> That comes in the name of the Lord![1]
> [a]Hosanna in the highest!"

11 [a]And Jesus went into Jerusalem and into the temple. So
when He had looked around at all things, as the hour was al-
ready late, He went out to Bethany with the twelve.
12 [a]Now the next day, when they had come out from Betha-
ny, He was hungry.
13 [a]And seeing from afar a fig tree having leaves, He went
to see if perhaps He would find something on it. When He
came to it, He found nothing but leaves, for it was not the
season for figs.
14 In response Jesus said to it, "Let no one eat fruit from you
ever again." And His disciples heard *it*.
15 [a]So they came to Jerusalem. Then Jesus went into the
temple and began to drive out those who bought and sold in
the temple, and overturned the tables of the money chang-
ers and the seats of those who sold [b]doves.
16 And He would not allow anyone to carry wares through
the temple.
17 Then He taught, saying to them, "Is it not written, [a]'My
house shall be called a house of prayer for all nations'?[1] But
you have made it a [b]'den of thieves.'"[2]
18 And [a]the scribes and chief priests heard it and sought
how they might destroy Him; for they feared Him, because
[b]all the people were astonished at His teaching.
19 When evening had come, He went out of the city.
20 [a]Now in the morning, as they passed by, they saw the fig
tree dried up from the roots.
21 And Peter, remembering, said to Him, "Rabbi, look! The
fig tree which You cursed has withered away."
22 So Jesus answered and said to them, "Have faith in God.
23 "For [a]assuredly, I say to you, whoever says to this moun-
tain, 'Be removed and be cast into the sea,' and does not
doubt in his heart, but believes that those things he says will
be done, he will have whatever he says.

11:8[a]Matt. 21:8 11:9[a]Ps. 118:25, 26 [1]Psalm 118:26 11:10[a]Ps. 148:1 [1]NU-Text omits *in the name of the Lord.* 11:11[a]Matt. 21:12 11:12[a]Matt. 21:18–22 11:13[a]Matt. 21:19 11:15[a]John 2:13–16 [b]Lev. 14:22 11:17[a]Is. 56:7 [b]Jer. 7:11 [1]Isaiah 56:7 [2]Jeremiah 7:11 11:18[a]Matt. 21:45, 46 [b]Matt. 7:28 11:20[a]Matt. 21:19–22 11:23[a]Matt. 17:20; 21:21

24 "Therefore I say to you, [a]whatever things you ask when
you pray, believe that you receive *them,* and you will have
them.
25 "And whenever you stand praying, [a]if you have anything
against anyone, forgive him, that your Father in heaven may
also forgive you your trespasses.
26 "But [a]if you do not forgive, neither will your Father in
heaven forgive your trespasses."[1]
27 Then they came again to Jerusalem. [a]And as He was walk-
ing in the temple, the chief priests, the scribes, and the elders
came to Him.
28 And they said to Him, "By what [a]authority are You doing
these things? And who gave You this authority to do these
things?"
29 But Jesus answered and said to them, "I also will ask you
one question; then answer Me, and I will tell you by what au-
thority I do these things:
30 "The [a]baptism of John—was it from heaven or from men?
Answer Me."
31 And they reasoned among themselves, saying, "If we say,
'From heaven,' He will say, 'Why then did you not believe him?'
32 "But if we say, 'From men' "—they feared the people, for
[a]all counted John to have been a prophet indeed.
33 So they answered and said to Jesus, "We do not know."
And Jesus answered and said to them, "Neither will I tell you
by what authority I do these things."

11:24[a]Matt. 7:7 11:25[a][Col. 3:13] 11:26[a]Matt. 6:15; 18:35 [1]NU-Text omits this verse. 11:27[a]Luke 20:1–8 11:28[a]John 5:27 11:30[a]Luke 7:29, 30 11:32[a]Matt. 3:5; 14:5

MARK 12

WICKED VINEDRESSERS

Unless changed by divine grace, we have all refused to pay to our great God the service due to Him. He has put us here and given us this life, like a vineyard, for us to cultivate; but many have cultivated that vineyard entirely for themselves—themselves or their families and friends and not for their God, their Maker: "God is in none of his thoughts" (Ps. 10:4).

Now, the Lord has sent to such many messengers. We have had no prophets in these days living among us, but we have the Word of God and the record of the testimonies of His inspired messengers, and these virtually speak to us. Many are the voices around us and within us that persuade us to render unto the great Householder His due, but in many cases none of these have been successful. Last of all God has sent to each one of us His Son, that He in His own Person may lovingly repeat with greater emphasis the requirements of the Lord of love.

The incarnate Wisdom now cries to us, *My child, give Me your heart*. Jesus warns us, "Unless you repent you will all likewise perish" (Luke 13:3). He sets before us the way of reconciliation and bids us to believe in Him and live. The very coming of the Son of God in human form is love's great plea for reconciliation. It is in the Person of Jesus Christ that God makes His last and strongest appeal to the human conscience.

---

1 Then [a]He began to speak to them in parables: "A man plant-
ed a vineyard and set a hedge around *it*, dug *a place for* the
wine vat and built a tower. And he leased it to vinedressers
and went into a far country.
2 "Now at vintage-time he sent a servant to the vinedressers,
that he might receive some of the fruit of the vineyard from
the vinedressers.
3 "And they took *him* and beat him and sent *him* away empty-
handed.
4 "Again he sent them another servant, and at him they
threw stones,[1] wounded *him* in the head, and sent *him* away
shamefully treated.
5 "And again he sent another, and him they killed; and many
others, [a]beating some and killing some.
6 "Therefore still having one son, his beloved, he also sent
him to them last, saying, 'They will respect my son.'
7 "But those vinedressers said among themselves, 'This is

12:1[a]Luke 20:9–19 12:4[1]NU-Text omits *and at him they threw stones.* 12:5[a]2 Chr. 36:16

the heir. Come, let us kill him, and the inheritance will be
ours.'
8 "So they took him and [a]killed *him* and cast *him* out of the
vineyard.
9 "Therefore what will the owner of the vineyard do? He will
come and destroy the vinedressers, and give the vineyard to
others.
10 "Have you not even read this Scripture:

> [a]'The stone which the builders rejected
> Has become the chief cornerstone.
> 11 This was the LORD's doing,
> And it is marvelous in our eyes'?"[1]

12 [a]And they sought to lay hands on Him, but feared the
multitude, for they knew He had spoken the parable against
them. So they left Him and went away.
13 [a]Then they sent to Him some of the Pharisees and the
Herodians, to catch Him in *His* words.
14 When they had come, they said to Him, "Teacher, we know
that You are true, and care about no one; for You do not re-
gard the person of men, but teach the [a]way of God in truth.
Is it lawful to pay taxes to Caesar, or not?
15 "Shall we pay, or shall we not pay?" But He, knowing their
[a]hypocrisy, said to them, "Why do you test Me? Bring Me a
denarius that I may see *it*."
16 So they brought *it*. And He said to them, "Whose image
and inscription *is* this?" They said to Him, "Caesar's."
17 And Jesus answered and said to them, "Render to Caesar
the things that are Caesar's, and to [a]God the things that are
God's." And they marveled at Him.
18 [a]Then *some* Sadducees, [b]who say there is no resurrection,
came to Him; and they asked Him, saying:
19 "Teacher, [a]Moses wrote to us that if a man's brother
dies, and leaves *his* wife behind, and leaves no children,
his brother should take his wife and raise up offspring for
his brother.
20 "Now there were seven brothers. The first took a wife; and
dying, he left no offspring.
21 "And the second took her, and he died; nor did he leave
any offspring. And the third likewise.
22 "So the seven had her and left no offspring. Last of all the
woman died also.
23 "Therefore, in the resurrection, when they rise, whose
wife will she be? For all seven had her as wife."
24 Jesus answered and said to them, "Are you not therefore

12:8[a] [Acts 2:23] 12:10[a] Ps. 118:22, 23 12:11[1] Psalm 118:22, 23 12:12[a] John 7:25, 30, 44 12:13[a] Luke 20:20–26 12:14[a] Acts 18:26 12:15[a] Luke 12:1 12:17[a] [Eccl. 5:4, 5] 12:18[a] Luke 20:27–38 [b] Acts 23:8 12:19[a] Deut. 25:5

mistaken, because you do not know the Scriptures nor the
power of God?
25 "For when they rise from the dead, they neither marry
nor are given in marriage, but [a]are like angels in heaven.
26 "But concerning the dead, that they [a]rise, have you not
read in the book of Moses, in the *burning* bush *passage,* how
God spoke to him, saying, [b]'I *am* the God of Abraham, the
God of Isaac, and the God of Jacob'?[1]
27 "He is not the God of the dead, but the God of the living.
You are therefore greatly mistaken."
28 [a]Then one of the scribes came, and having heard them
reasoning together, perceiving[1] that He had answered them
well, asked Him, "Which is the first commandment of all?"
29 Jesus answered him, "The first of all the commandments
is: [a]'Hear, O Israel, the LORD our God, the LORD is one.
30 'And you shall [a]love the LORD your God with all your
heart, with all your soul, with all your mind, and with all your
strength.'[1] This *is* the first commandment.[2]
31 "And the second, like *it, is* this: [a]'You shall love your neigh-
bor as yourself.'[1] There is no other commandment greater
than [b]these."
32 So the scribe said to Him, "Well *said,* Teacher. You have
spoken the truth, for there is one God, [a]and there is no other
but He.
33 "And to love Him with all the heart, with all the under-
standing, with all the soul,[1] and with all the strength, and to
love one's neighbor as oneself, [a]is more than all the whole
burnt offerings and sacrifices."
34 Now when Jesus saw that he answered wisely, He said to
him, "You are not far from the kingdom of God." [a]But after
that no one dared question Him.
35 [a]Then Jesus answered and said, while He taught in the
temple, "How *is it* that the scribes say that the Christ is the
Son of David?
36 "For David himself said [a]by the Holy Spirit:

> [b]'The LORD said to my Lord,
> "Sit at My right hand,
> Till I make Your enemies Your
> footstool."'[1]

37 "Therefore David himself calls Him 'Lord'; how is He *then*
his [a]Son?" And the common people heard Him gladly.

12:25 [a][1 Cor. 15:42, 49, 52] 12:26 [a][Rev. 20:12, 13] [b]Ex. 3:6, 15 [1]Exodus 3:6, 15 12:28 [a]Matt. 22:34–40 [1]NU-Text reads *seeing.* 12:29 [a]Deut. 6:4, 5 12:30 [a][Deut. 10:12; 30:6] [1]Deuteronomy 6:4, 5 [2]NU-Text omits this sentence. 12:31 [a]Lev. 19:18 [b][Rom. 13:9] [1]Leviticus 19:18 12:32 [a]Deut. 4:39 12:33 [a][Hos. 6:6] [1]NU-Text omits *with all the soul.* 12:34 [a]Matt. 22:46 12:35 [a]Luke 20:41–44 12:36 [a]2 Sam. 23:2 [b]Ps. 110:1 [1]Psalm 110:1 12:37 [a][Acts 2:29–31]

38 Then [a]He said to them in His teaching, [b]"Beware of the
scribes, who desire to go around in long robes, [c]*love* greet-
ings in the marketplaces,
39 "the [a]best seats in the synagogues, and the best places at
feasts,
40 [a]"who devour widows' houses, and for a pretense make
long prayers. These will receive greater condemnation."
41 [a]Now Jesus sat opposite the treasury and saw how the
people put money [b]into the treasury. And many *who were*
rich put in much.
42 Then one poor widow came and threw in two mites,[1]
which make a quadrans.
43 So He called His disciples to *Himself* and said to them,
"Assuredly, I say to you that [a]this poor widow has put in more
than all those who have given to the treasury;
44 "for they all put in out of their abundance, but she out of
her poverty put in all that she had, [a]her whole livelihood."

12:38 [a]Mark 4:2 [b]Matt. 23:1–7 [c]Matt. 23:7 12:39 [a]Luke 14:7 12:40 [a]Matt. 23:14 12:41 [a]Luke 21:1–4 [b]2 Kin. 12:9 12:42 [1]Greek *lepta,* very small copper coins worth a fraction of a penny 12:43 [a][2 Cor. 8:12] 12:44 [a]Deut. 24:6

MARK 13

JESUS FORETELLS THE DESTRUCTION OF THE TEMPLE

We observe in this text that it is very certain there is an elect, and that these elect are a special people. It is equally clear that these elect ones cannot be deceived. The text informs us that if it were possible, those deceivers who had gone to the full stretch of great signs and wonders, doubtless adding thereto all kinds of eloquence and persuasion, were not able to deceive the elect. The elect could not possibly be turned from the steadfastness of their faith.

In the dealings of God's providence and surely also in the dealings of His grace, God has a special regard for His chosen and justified ones. For the elect's sake, He does many things that otherwise would not enter into the plan of His government. If our Bibles were read by us in the original, we should be exceedingly struck with the prominence given to the doctrine of election; and if you were at all acquainted with the manners and letters of the early Christian church, you would be astonished to find how conspicuously this great doctrine appears, so much so that Christians were accustomed to address each other as *elect ones*. The word "elect" recurred so frequently in conversation and was so mixed up with all their preaching, with all their assembling together, and with all their church acts that it is impossible to conceive that its meaning could be obscured or held in low esteem.

---

1 Then [a]as He went out of the temple, one of His disciples
said to Him, "Teacher, see what manner of stones and what
buildings *are here!*"
2 And Jesus answered and said to him, "Do you see these
great buildings? [a]Not *one* stone shall be left upon another,
that shall not be thrown down."
3 Now as He sat on the Mount of Olives opposite the temple,
[a]Peter, [b]James, [c]John, and [d]Andrew asked Him privately,
4 [a]"Tell us, when will these things be? And what *will be* the
sign when all these things will be fulfilled?"
5 And Jesus, answering them, began to say: [a]"Take heed that
no one deceives you.
6 "For many will come in My name, saying, 'I am *He*,' and
will deceive many.
7 "But when you hear of wars and rumors of wars, do not be
troubled; for *such things* must happen, but the end *is* not yet.

13:1[a]Luke 21:5–36 13:2[a]Luke 19:44 13:3[a]Matt. 16:18 [b]Mark 1:19 [c]Mark 1:19 [d]John 1:40 13:4[a]Matt. 24:3 13:5[a]Eph. 5:6

8 "For nation will rise against nation, and [a]kingdom against
kingdom. And there will be earthquakes in various places,
and there will be famines and troubles.[1] [b]These *are* the be-
ginnings of sorrows.
9 "But [a]watch out for yourselves, for they will deliver you up
to councils, and you will be beaten in the synagogues. You
will be brought[1] before rulers and kings for My sake, for a
testimony to them.
10 "And [a]the gospel must first be preached to all the nations.
11 [a]"But when they arrest *you* and deliver you up, do not
worry beforehand, or premeditate[1] what you will speak. But
whatever is given you in that hour, speak that; for it is not
you who speak, [b]but the Holy Spirit.
12 "Now [a]brother will betray brother to death, and a father
his child; and children will rise up against parents and cause
them to be put to death.
13 [a]"And you will be hated by all for My name's sake. But [b]he
who endures to the end shall be saved.
14 [a]"So when you see the [b]'abomination of desolation,'[1] spo-
ken of by Daniel the prophet,[2] standing where it ought not"
(let the reader understand), "then [c]let those who are in Judea
flee to the mountains.
15 "Let him who is on the housetop not go down into the
house, nor enter to take anything out of his house.
16 "And let him who is in the field not go back to get his
clothes.
17 [a]"But woe to those who are pregnant and to those who
are nursing babies in those days!
18 "And pray that your flight may not be in winter.
19 [a]"For *in* those days there will be tribulation, such as has
not been since the beginning of the creation which God cre-
ated until this time, nor ever shall be.
20 "And unless the Lord had shortened those days, no flesh
would be saved; but for the elect's sake, whom He chose, He
shortened the days.
21 [a]"Then if anyone says to you, 'Look, here *is* the Christ!' or,
'Look, *He is* there!' do not believe it.
22 "For false christs and false prophets will rise and show
signs and [a]wonders to deceive, if possible, even the elect.
23 "But [a]take heed; see, I have told you all things before-
hand.
24 [a]"But in those days, after that tribulation, the sun will be
darkened, and the moon will not give its light;

13:8[a]Hag. 2:22 [b]Matt. 24:8 [1]NU-Text omits *and troubles.* 13:9[a]Matt. 10:17, 18; 24:9 [1]NU-Text and M-Text read *will stand.* 13:10[a]Matt. 24:14 13:11[a]Luke 12:11; 21:12–17 [b]Acts 2:4; 4:8, 31 [1]NU-Text omits *or premeditate.* 13:12[a]Mic. 7:6 13:13[a]Luke 21:17 [b]Matt. 10:22; 24:13 13:14[a]Matt. 24:15 [b]Dan. 9:27; 11:31; 12:11 [c]Luke 21:21 [1]Daniel 11:31; 12:11 [2]NU-Text omits *spoken of by Daniel the prophet.* 13:17[a]Luke 21:23 13:19[a]Dan. 9:26; 12:1 13:21[a]Luke 17:23; 21:8 13:22[a]Rev. 13:13, 14 13:23[a][2 Pet. 3:17] 13:24[a]Zeph. 1:15

25 "the stars of heaven will fall, and the powers in the heav-
ens will be [a]shaken.
26 [a]"Then they will see the Son of Man coming in the clouds
with great power and glory.
27 "And then He will send His angels, and gather together
His elect from the four winds, from the farthest part of earth
to the farthest part of heaven.
28 [a]"Now learn this parable from the fig tree: When its branch
has already become tender, and puts forth leaves, you know
that summer is near.
29 "So you also, when you see these things happening, know
that it[1] is near—at the doors!
30 "Assuredly, I say to you, this generation will by no means
pass away till all these things take place.
31 "Heaven and earth will pass away, but [a]My words will by
no means pass away.
32 "But of that day and hour [a]no one knows, not even the
angels in heaven, nor the Son, but only the [b]Father.
33 [a]"Take heed, watch and pray; for you do not know when
the time is.
34 [a]"*It is* like a man going to a far country, who left his house
and gave [b]authority to his servants, and to each his work, and
commanded the doorkeeper to watch.
35 [a]"Watch therefore, for you do not know when the master
of the house is coming—in the evening, at midnight, at the
crowing of the rooster, or in the morning—
36 "lest, coming suddenly, he find you sleeping.
37 "And what I say to you, I say to all: Watch!"

13:25[a]Is. 13:10; 34:4 13:26[a][Dan. 7:13, 14] 13:28[a]Luke 21:29 13:29[1]Or *He*
13:31[a]Is. 40:8 13:32[a]Matt. 25:13 [b]Acts 1:7 13:33[a]1 Thess. 5:6 13:34[a]Matt. 24:45;
25:14 [b][Matt. 16:19] 13:35[a]Matt. 24:42, 44

MARK 14

THE BEGINNING OF THE LORD'S SUPPER

They brought in our Lord from the garden bound, but they also kept fast hold upon Him, for we read of "those who had laid hold of Jesus" (Matt. 26:57). They were evidently afraid of their prisoner even when they had Him entirely in their power. He was all gentleness and submission, but conscience made cowards of them all, and they therefore took all a coward's care to hold Him in their grasp.

John 18:19 tells us, "The high priest then asked Jesus about His disciples." I do not know how the crafty Caiaphas put his questions, but the Savior gave no reply to this particular enquiry. What could He have said if He had attempted to answer? What good could He have said of His disciples? He might have said, *Concerning My disciples, one of them has betrayed Me; he has still the blood money in his hand that you gave him as My price. Another of them, down in the hall there, before the cock crows will deny that he ever knew Me and add oaths and cursing to his denial. And as for the rest, they have all forsaken Me and fled.* Therefore our Lord said nothing concerning His disciples, for He will not turn the accuser of His own whom He came not to condemn but to justify.

---

1 After [a]two days it was the Passover and [b]*the Feast* of Un-
leavened Bread. And the chief priests and the scribes sought
how they might take Him by trickery and put *Him* to death.
2 But they said, "Not during the feast, lest there be an uproar
of the people."
3 [a]And being in Bethany at the house of Simon the leper, as
He sat at the table, a woman came having an alabaster flask
of very costly oil of spikenard. Then she broke the flask and
poured *it* on His head.
4 But there were some who were indignant among them-
selves, and said, "Why was this fragrant oil wasted?
5 "For it might have been sold for more than three hundred
[a]denarii and given to the poor." And they [b]criticized her sharp-
ly.
6 But Jesus said, "Let her alone. Why do you trouble her?
She has done a good work for Me.
7 [a]"For you have the poor with you always, and whenever
you wish you may do them good; [b]but Me you do not have
always.
8 "She has done what she could. She has come beforehand
to anoint My body for burial.

14:1 [a]Luke 22:1, 2 [b]Ex. 12:1–27 14:3 [a]Luke 7:37 14:5 [a]Matt. 18:28 [b]John 6:61
14:7 [a]Deut. 15:11 [b][John 7:33; 8:21; 14:2, 12; 16:10, 17, 28]

9 "Assuredly, I say to you, wherever this gospel is [a]preached
in the whole world, what this woman has done will also be
told as a memorial to her."
10 [a]Then Judas Iscariot, one of the twelve, went to the chief
priests to betray Him to them.
11 And when they heard *it,* they were glad, and promised to
give him money. So he sought how he might conveniently
betray Him.
12 [a]Now on the first day of Unleavened Bread, when they killed
the Passover *lamb,* His disciples said to Him, "Where do You
want us to go and prepare, that You may eat the Passover?"
13 And He sent out two of His disciples and said to them,
"Go into the city, and a man will meet you carrying a pitcher
of water; follow him.
14 "Wherever he goes in, say to the master of the house, 'The
Teacher says, "Where is the guest room in which I may eat
the Passover with My disciples?"'
15 "Then he will show you a large upper room, furnished *and*
prepared; there make ready for us."
16 So His disciples went out, and came into the city, and
found it just as He had said to them; and they prepared the
Passover.
17 [a]In the evening He came with the twelve.
18 Now as they sat and ate, Jesus said, "Assuredly, I say to
you, [a]one of you who eats with Me will betray Me."
19 And they began to be sorrowful, and to say to Him one by
one, "*Is* it I?" And another *said,* "*Is* it I?"[1]
20 He answered and said to them, "*It is* one of the twelve,
who dips with Me in the dish.
21 [a]"The Son of Man indeed goes just as it is written of Him,
but woe to that man by whom the Son of Man is betrayed!
It would have been good for that man if he had never been
born."
22 [a]And as they were eating, Jesus took bread, blessed and
broke *it,* and gave *it* to them and said, "Take, eat;[1] this is My
[b]body."
23 Then He took the cup, and when He had given thanks He
gave *it* to them, and they all drank from it.
24 And He said to them, "This is My blood of the new[1] cov-
enant, which is shed for many.
25 "Assuredly, I say to you, I will no longer drink of the fruit
of the vine until that day when I drink it new in the kingdom
of God."
26 [a]And when they had sung a hymn, they went out to the
Mount of Olives.

14:9[a]Luke 24:47 14:10[a]Matt. 10:2–4 14:12[a]Matt. 26:17–19 14:17[a]Matt. 26:20–24 14:18[a]John 6:70, 71; 13:18 14:19[1]NU-Text omits this sentence. 14:21[a]Luke 22:22 14:22[a]1 Cor. 11:23–25 [b][1 Pet. 2:24] [1]NU-Text omits *eat.* 14:24[1]NU-Text omits *new.* 14:26[a]Matt. 26:30

27 [a]Then Jesus said to them, "All of you will be made to stum-
ble because of Me this night,[1] for it is written:

> [b]'I will strike the Shepherd,
> And the sheep will be scattered.'[2]

28 "But [a]after I have been raised, I will go before you to Gal-
ilee."
29 [a]Peter said to Him, "Even if all are made to stumble, yet
I *will* not *be*."
30 Jesus said to him, "Assuredly, I say to you that today, *even*
this night, before the rooster crows twice, you will deny Me
three times."
31 But he spoke more vehemently, "If I have to die with You,
I will not deny You!" And they all said likewise.
32 [a]Then they came to a place which was named Gethsem-
ane; and He said to His disciples, "Sit here while I pray."
33 And He [a]took Peter, James, and John with Him, and He
began to be troubled and deeply distressed.
34 Then He said to them, [a]"My soul is exceedingly sorrow-
ful, *even* to death. Stay here and watch."
35 He went a little farther, and fell on the ground, and prayed
that if it were possible, the hour might pass from Him.
36 And He said, [a]"Abba, Father, [b]all things *are* possible for
You. Take this cup away from Me; [c]nevertheless, not what I
will, but what You *will*."
37 Then He came and found them sleeping, and said to Peter,
"Simon, are you sleeping? Could you not watch one hour?
38 [a]"Watch and pray, lest you enter into temptation. [b]The
spirit indeed *is* willing, but the flesh *is* weak."
39 Again He went away and prayed, and spoke the same
words.
40 And when He returned, He found them asleep again, for
their eyes were heavy; and they did not know what to an-
swer Him.
41 Then He came the third time and said to them, "Are you
still sleeping and resting? It is enough! [a]The hour has come;
behold, the Son of Man is being betrayed into the hands of
sinners.
42 [a]"Rise, let us be going. See, My betrayer is at hand."
43 [a]And immediately, while He was still speaking, Judas, one
of the twelve, with a great multitude with swords and clubs,
came from the chief priests and the scribes and the elders.
44 Now His betrayer had given them a signal, saying,

14:27 [a]Matt. 26:31–35 [b]Zech. 13:7 [1]NU-Text omits *because of Me this night.* [2]Zechariah 13:7 14:28 [a]Mark 16:7 14:29 [a]John 13:37, 38 14:32 [a]Luke 22:40–46 14:33 [a]Mark 5:37; 9:2; 13:3 14:34 [a]John 12:27 14:36 [a]Gal. 4:6 [b][Heb. 5:7] [c]John 5:30; 6:38 14:38 [a]Luke 21:36 [b][Rom. 7:18, 21–24] 14:41 [a]John 13:1; 17:1 14:42 [a]John 13:21; 18:1, 2 14:43 [a]Luke 22:47–53

"Whomever I [a]kiss, He is the One; seize Him and lead *Him* away safely."

45 As soon as he had come, immediately he went up to Him and said to Him, "Rabbi, Rabbi!" and kissed Him.

46 Then they laid their hands on Him and took Him.

47 And one of those who stood by drew his sword and struck the servant of the high priest, and cut off his ear.

48 [a]Then Jesus answered and said to them, "Have you come out, as against a robber, with swords and clubs to take Me?

49 "I was daily with you in the temple [a]teaching, and you did not seize Me. But [b]the Scriptures must be fulfilled."

50 [a]Then they all forsook Him and fled.

51 Now a certain young man followed Him, having a linen cloth thrown around *his* naked *body*. And the young men laid hold of him,

52 and he left the linen cloth and fled from them naked.

53 [a]And they led Jesus away to the high priest; and with him were [b]assembled all the [c]chief priests, the elders, and the scribes.

54 But [a]Peter followed Him at a distance, right into the courtyard of the high priest. And he sat with the servants and warmed himself at the fire.

55 [a]Now the chief priests and all the council sought testimony against Jesus to put Him to death, but found none.

56 For many bore [a]false witness against Him, but their testimonies did not agree.

57 Then some rose up and bore false witness against Him, saying,

58 "We heard Him say, [a]'I will destroy this temple made with hands, and within three days I will build another made without hands.'"

59 But not even then did their testimony agree.

60 [a]And the high priest stood up in the midst and asked Jesus, saying, "Do You answer nothing? What *is it* these men testify against You?"

61 But [a]He kept silent and answered nothing. [b]Again the high priest asked Him, saying to Him, "Are You the Christ, the Son of the Blessed?"

62 Jesus said, "I am. [a]And you will see the Son of Man sitting at the right hand of the Power, and coming with the clouds of heaven."

63 Then the high priest tore his clothes and said, "What further need do we have of witnesses?

64 "You have heard the [a]blasphemy! What do you think?" And they all condemned Him to be deserving of [b]death.

14:44[a][Prov. 27:6] 14:48[a]Matt. 26:55 14:49[a]Matt. 21:23 [b]Is. 53:7 14:50[a]Ps. 88:8 14:53[a]Matt. 26:57–68 [b]Mark 15:1 [c]John 7:32; 18:3; 19:6 14:54[a]John 18:15 14:55[a]Matt. 26:59 14:56[a]Ex. 20:16 14:58[a]John 2:19 14:60[a]Matt. 26:62 14:61[a]Is. 53:7 [b]Luke 22:67–71 14:62[a]Luke 22:69 14:64[a]John 10:33, 36 [b]John 19:7

65 Then some began to [a]spit on Him, and to blindfold Him,
and to beat Him, and to say to Him, "Prophesy!" And the of-
ficers struck Him with the palms of their hands.[1]
66 [a]Now as Peter was below in the courtyard, one of the ser-
vant girls of the high priest came.
67 And when she saw Peter warming himself, she looked at
him and said, "You also were with [a]Jesus of Nazareth."
68 But he denied it, saying, "I neither know nor understand
what you are saying." And he went out on the porch, and a
rooster crowed.
69 [a]And the servant girl saw him again, and began to say to
those who stood by, "This is *one* of them."
70 But he denied it again. [a]And a little later those who stood
by said to Peter again, "Surely you are *one* of them; [b]for you
are a Galilean, and your speech shows *it*."[1]
71 Then he began to curse and swear, "I do not know this
Man of whom you speak!"
72 [a]A second time *the* rooster crowed. Then Peter called to
mind the word that Jesus had said to him, "Before the roost-
er crows twice, you will deny Me three times." And when he
thought about it, he wept.

14:65 [a]Is. 50:6; 52:14 [1]NU-Text reads *received Him with slaps.* 14:66 [a]John 18:16–18, 25–27 14:67 [a]John 1:45 14:69 [a]Matt. 26:71 14:70 [a]Luke 22:59 [b]Acts 2:7 [1]NU-Text omits *and your speech shows it.* 14:72 [a]Matt. 26:75

MARK 15

JESUS IS TRIED AND CRUCIFIED

Consider the abuse. Let me read the words: "Then they spat in His face" (Matt. 26:67) Be astonished, O heavens, and be horribly afraid. His face is the light of the universe, His Person is the glory of heaven, and "they spat in His face." Alas, my God, that man should be so base! Some went further, and they "blindfolded Him" (Luke 22:64). How could they thus put out the sun and shut up bliss? Then when all was dark to Him we read that they began to say, "Prophesy! Who is the one who struck You?" (Luke 22:64). Then another did the like, and many were the cruel cuffs they laid about His blessed face. The medieval writers delighted to talk about the teeth that were broken, the bruises on the checks, the blood that flowed, the flesh that was bruised and blackened—but we dare not thus imagine. Scripture has cast a veil, and there let it abide. Yet it must have been an awful sight to see the Lord of glory with His face stained by their accursed phlegm and bruised by their cruel fists.

Here insult and cruelty were combined: ridicule of His prophetic claims and dishonor to His divine Person. They invented all they could of shame and scorn, and He stood patient there though a single flash of His eye would have consumed them in a moment.

Brothers, sisters, this is what our sin deserved.

---

1 Immediately, [a]in the morning, the chief priests held a consultation with the elders and scribes and the whole council; and they bound Jesus, led *Him* away, and [b]delivered *Him* to Pilate.
2 [a]Then Pilate asked Him, "Are You the King of the Jews?" He answered and said to him, "*It is as* you say."
3 And the chief priests accused Him of many things, but He [a]answered nothing.
4 [a]Then Pilate asked Him again, saying, "Do You answer nothing? See how many things they testify against You!"[1]
5 [a]But Jesus still answered nothing, so that Pilate marveled.
6 Now [a]at the feast he was accustomed to releasing one prisoner to them, whomever they requested.
7 And there was one named Barabbas, *who was* chained with his fellow rebels; they had committed murder in the rebellion.

15:1[a]Ps. 2:2 [b]Acts 3:13 15:2[a]Matt. 27:11–14 15:3[a]John 19:9 15:4[a]Matt. 27:13
[1]NU-Text reads *of which they accuse You.* 15:5[a]Is. 53:7 15:6[a]Matt. 27:15–26

8 Then the multitude, crying aloud,[1] began to ask *him to do*
just as he had always done for them.
9 But Pilate answered them, saying, "Do you want me to re-
lease to you the King of the Jews?"
10 For he knew that the chief priests had handed Him over
because of envy.
11 But [a]the chief priests stirred up the crowd, so that he
should rather release Barabbas to them.
12 Pilate answered and said to them again, "What then do
you want me to do *with Him* whom you call the [a]King of the
Jews?"
13 So they cried out again, "Crucify Him!"
14 Then Pilate said to them, "Why, [a]what evil has He done?"
But they cried out all the more, "Crucify Him!"
15 [a]So Pilate, wanting to gratify the crowd, released Barab-
bas to them; and he delivered Jesus, after he had scourged
Him, to be [b]crucified.
16 [a]Then the soldiers led Him away into the hall called Prae-
torium, and they called together the whole garrison.
17 And they clothed Him with purple; and they twisted a
crown of thorns, put it on His *head,*
18 and began to salute Him, "Hail, King of the Jews!"
19 Then they [a]struck Him on the head with a reed and spat
on Him; and bowing the knee, they worshiped Him.
20 And when they had [a]mocked Him, they took the purple
off Him, put His own clothes on Him, and led Him out to
crucify Him.
21 [a]Then they compelled a certain man, Simon a Cyrenian,
the father of Alexander and Rufus, as he was coming out of
the country and passing by, to bear His cross.
22 [a]And they brought Him to the place Golgotha, which is
translated, Place of a Skull.
23 [a]Then they gave Him wine mingled with myrrh to drink,
but He did not take *it.*
24 And when they crucified Him, [a]they divided His gar-
ments, casting lots for them *to determine* what every man
should take.
25 Now [a]it was the third hour, and they crucified Him.
26 And [a]the inscription of His accusation was written above:

THE KING OF THE JEWS.

27 [a]With Him they also crucified two robbers, one on His
right and the other on His left.

15:8[1] NU-Text reads *going up.* 15:11[a] Acts 3:14 15:12[a] Mic. 5:2 15:14[a] 1 Pet. 2:21–23 15:15[a] Matt. 27:26 [b] [Is. 53:8] 15:16[a] Matt. 27:27–31 15:19[a] [Is. 50:6; 52:14; 53:5] 15:20[a] Luke 22:63; 23:11 15:21[a] Matt. 27:32 15:22[a] John 19:17–24 15:23[a] Matt. 27:34 15:24[a] Ps. 22:18 15:25[a] John 19:14 15:26[a] Matt. 27:37 15:27[a] Luke 22:37

28 So the Scripture was fulfilled[1] which says, [a]"And He was
numbered with the transgressors."[2]
29 And [a]those who passed by blasphemed Him, [b]wagging
their heads and saying, "Aha! [c]*You* who destroy the temple
and build *it* in three days,
30 "save Yourself, and come down from the cross!"
31 Likewise the chief priests also, [a]mocking among them-
selves with the scribes, said, "He saved [b]others; Himself He
cannot save.
32 "Let the Christ, the King of Israel, descend now from the
cross, that we may see and believe."[1] Even [a]those who were
crucified with Him reviled Him.
33 Now [a]when the sixth hour had come, there was darkness
over the whole land until the ninth hour.
34 And at the ninth hour Jesus cried out with a loud voice,
saying, "Eloi, Eloi, lama sabachthani?" which is translated,
[a]"My God, My God, why have You forsaken Me?"[1]
35 Some of those who stood by, when they heard *that,* said,
"Look, He is calling for Elijah!"
36 Then [a]someone ran and filled a sponge full of sour wine,
put *it* on a reed, and [b]offered *it* to Him to drink, saying, "Let
Him alone; let us see if Elijah will come to take Him down."
37 [a]And Jesus cried out with a loud voice, and breathed His
last.
38 Then [a]the veil of the temple was torn in two from top to
bottom.
39 So [a]when the centurion, who stood opposite Him, saw
that He cried out like this and breathed His last,[1] he said,
"Truly this Man was the Son of God!"
40 [a]There were also women looking on [b]from afar, among
whom were Mary Magdalene, Mary the mother of James the
Less and of Joses, and Salome,
41 who also [a]followed Him and ministered to Him when He
was in Galilee, and many other women who came up with
Him to Jerusalem.
42 [a]Now when evening had come, because it was the Prepa-
ration Day, that is, the day before the Sabbath,
43 Joseph of Arimathea, a prominent council member, who
[a]was himself waiting for the kingdom of God, coming and
taking courage, went in to Pilate and asked for the body of
Jesus.
44 Pilate marveled that He was already dead; and summon-
ing the centurion, he asked him if He had been dead for some
time.

15:28[a]Is. 53:12 [1]Isaiah 53:12 [2]NU-Text omits this verse. 15:29[a]Ps. 22:6, 7; 69:7 [b]Ps. 109:25 [c]John 2:19–21 15:31[a]Luke 18:32 [b]John 11:43, 44 15:32[a]Matt. 27:44 [1]M-Text reads *believe Him.* 15:33[a]Luke 23:44–49 15:34[a]Ps. 22:1 [1]Psalm 22:1 15:36[a]John 19:29 [b]Ps. 69:21 15:37[a]Matt. 27:50 15:38[a]Ex. 26:31–33 15:39[a]Luke 23:47 [1]NU-Text reads *that He thus breathed His last.* 15:40[a]Matt. 27:55 [b]Ps. 38:11 15:41[a]Luke 8:2, 3 15:42[a]John 19:38–42 15:43[a]Luke 2:25, 38; 23:51

45 So when he found out from the centurion, he granted the
body to Joseph.
46 [a]Then he bought fine linen, took Him down, and wrapped
Him in the linen. And he laid Him in a tomb which had been
hewn out of the rock, and rolled a stone against the door of
the tomb.
47 And Mary Magdalene and Mary *the mother* of Joses ob-
served where He was laid.

15:46[a] Matt. 27:59, 60

MARK 16

THE RISEN AND ASCENDED CHRIST

Our Lord always told His disciples that He would rise. They were astonished to hear that He would die at all: they could not think it possible that He could die the terrible death He often hinted at. It ran so contrary to all their ideas of a kingdom for a Messiah that they could not somehow grasp it as a reality.

The great cure that our Lord prescribed for the matter of unbelief lies in the fact that He is risen. He is risen from the dead. You will observe everywhere here, where we meet with the unbelief of man, we meet with the fact of the resurrection of Christ brought in like light to subdue the darkness. Here are the women in difficulties: it is the resurrection of Christ that removes the difficulty. "Who will roll away the stone from the door of the tomb for us?" (Mark 16:3). The stone is rolled away because Christ is risen.

Now here the Lord seems to tell us that the best and grandest cure of all our fear about difficulty lies in this: "He is risen!" You serve a living Savior. What is the difficulty? Is it a providential one? He is the Master of providence. That difficulty, then, which would obstruct you in yon pathway to heaven, if you trust in Him, must vanish because Jesus lives.

---

1 Now [a]when the Sabbath was past, Mary Magdalene, Mary
the mother of James, and Salome [b]bought spices, that they
might come and anoint Him.
2 [a]Very early in the morning, on the first *day* of the week,
they came to the tomb when the sun had risen.
3 And they said among themselves, "Who will roll away the
stone from the door of the tomb for us?"
4 But when they looked up, they saw that the stone had been
rolled away—for it was very large.
5 [a]And entering the tomb, they saw a young man clothed
in a long white robe sitting on the right side; and they were
alarmed.
6 [a]But he said to them, "Do not be alarmed. You seek Jesus
of Nazareth, who was crucified. He is risen! He is not here.
See the place where they laid Him.
7 "But go, tell His disciples—and Peter—that He is going
before you into Galilee; there you will see Him, [a]as He said
to you."
8 So they went out quickly[1] and fled from the tomb, for they
trembled and were amazed. [a]And they said nothing to anyone, for they were afraid.

16:1[a]John 20:1–8 [b]Luke 23:56 16:2[a]Luke 24:1 16:5[a]John 20:11, 12 16:6[a]Matt. 28:6 16:7[a]Matt. 26:32; 28:16, 17 16:8[a]Matt. 28:8 [1]NU-Text and M-Text omit *quickly*.

9 Now when *He* rose early on the first *day* of the week, He
appeared first to Mary Magdalene, [a]out of whom He had cast
seven demons.
10 [a]She went and told those who had been with Him, as they
mourned and wept.
11 [a]And when they heard that He was alive and had been
seen by her, they did not believe.
12 After that, He appeared in another form [a]to two of them
as they walked and went into the country.
13 And they went and told *it* to the rest, *but* they did not be-
lieve them either.
14 [a]Later He appeared to the eleven as they sat at the table;
and He rebuked their unbelief and hardness of heart, be-
cause they did not believe those who had seen Him after He
had risen.
15 [a]And He said to them, "Go into all the world [b]and preach
the gospel to every creature.
16 [a]"He who believes and is baptized will be saved; [b]but he
who does not believe will be condemned.
17 "And these [a]signs will follow those who believe: [b]In My
name they will cast out demons; [c]they will speak with new
tongues;
18 [a]"they[1] will take up serpents; and if they drink anything
deadly, it will by no means hurt them; [b]they will lay hands
on the sick, and they will recover."
19 So then, [a]after the Lord had spoken to them, He was [b]re-
ceived up into heaven, and [c]sat down at the right hand of God.
20 And they went out and preached everywhere, the Lord
working with *them* [a]and confirming the word through the
accompanying signs. Amen.[1]

16:9 [a]Luke 8:2 16:10 [a]Luke 24:10 16:11 [a]Luke 24:11, 41 16:12 [a]Luke 24:13–35 16:14 [a]1 Cor. 15:5 16:15 [a]Matt. 28:19 [b][Col. 1:23] 16:16 [a][John 3:18, 36] [b][John 12:48] 16:17 [a]Acts 5:12 [b]Luke 10:17 [c][Acts 2:4] 16:18 [a]Acts 28:3–6 [b]James 5:14 [1]NU-Text reads *and in their hands they will.* 16:19 [a]Acts 1:2, 3 [b]Luke 9:51; 24:51 [c][Ps. 110:1] 16:20 [a][Heb. 2:4] [1]Verses 9–20 are bracketed in NU-Text as not original. They are lacking in Codex Sinaiticus and Codex Vaticanus, although nearly all other manuscripts of Mark contain them.

LUKE

LUKE 1

JOHN THE BAPTIST IS BORN

Mary's Magnificat was a song of faith. You have thought, perhaps, that you could easily have sung this song if you had been as highly favored as she was—but are you sure you could have done so? Have you ever realized the difficulties under which this hymn was composed and sung? The visitation of the angel and all its consequences would seem to be ridiculous and even impossible to many to whom she might venture to mention the circumstances; nay, more than that, telling of this experience would subject her to many cruel insinuations that would scandalize her character! That which conferred upon her the highest honor that ever fell to woman would, in the judgment of many, bring upon her the greatest possible dishonor. Mary must have been sorely troubled if she had been influenced by her natural feelings and swayed by external circumstances.

It was only her wondrous faith that she should be the mother of the holy Child Jesus that sustained her. Truly blessed was she in believing that, and blessed indeed was she in that even before there was an accomplishment of the things that were told her by the angel. So she could sing, "My soul magnifies the Lord, and my spirit has rejoiced in God my Savior." Unbelief would have said, *Wait*. Fear would have said, *Be silent*. But faith could not wait and could not be silent: she must sing, and sing she did most sweetly.

---

1 Inasmuch as many have taken in hand to set in order a nar-
rative of those [a]things which have been fulfilled[1] among us,
2 just as those who [a]from the beginning were [b]eyewitness-
es and ministers of the word [c]delivered them to us,
3 it seemed good to me also, having had perfect understand-
ing of all things from the very first, to write to you an orderly
account, [a]most excellent Theophilus,
4 [a]that you may know the certainty of those things in which
you were instructed.
5 There was [a]in the days of Herod, the king of Judea, a cer-
tain priest named Zacharias, [b]of the division of [c]Abijah. His
[d]wife *was* of the daughters of Aaron, and her name *was* Eliz-
abeth.
6 And they were both righteous before God, walking in all
the commandments and ordinances of the Lord blameless.
7 But they had no child, because Elizabeth was barren, and
they were both well advanced in years.

1:1[a]John 20:31 [1]Or *are most surely believed* 1:2[a]Acts 1:21, 22 [b]Acts 1:2 [c]Heb. 2:3 1:3[a]Acts 1:1 1:4[a][John 20:31] 1:5[a]Matt. 2:1 [b]1 Chr. 24:1, 10 [c]Neh. 12:4 [d]Lev. 21:13, 14

8 So it was, that while he was serving as priest before God in
the order of his division,
9 according to the custom of the priesthood, his lot fell [a]to
burn incense when he went into the temple of the Lord.
10 [a]And the whole multitude of the people was praying out-
side at the hour of incense.
11 Then an angel of the Lord appeared to him, standing on
the right side of [a]the altar of incense.
12 And when Zacharias saw *him,* [a]he was troubled, and fear
fell upon him.
13 But the angel said to him, "Do not be afraid, Zacharias, for
your prayer is heard; and your wife Elizabeth will bear you a
son, and [a]you shall call his name John.
14 "And you will have joy and gladness, and [a]many will re-
joice at his birth.
15 "For he will be [a]great in the sight of the Lord, and [b]shall
drink neither wine nor strong drink. He will also be filled
with the Holy Spirit, [c]even from his mother's womb.
16 "And he will turn many of the children of Israel to the
Lord their God.
17 [a]"He will also go before Him in the spirit and power of
Elijah, 'to turn the hearts of the fathers to the children,'[1] and
the disobedient to the wisdom of the just, to make ready a
people prepared for the Lord."
18 And Zacharias said to the angel, [a]"How shall I know this?
For I am an old man, and my wife is well advanced in years."
19 And the angel answered and said to him, "I am [a]Gabriel,
who stands in the presence of God, and was sent to speak to
you and bring you these glad [b]tidings.
20 "But behold, [a]you will be mute and not able to speak until
the day these things take place, because you did not believe
my words which will be fulfilled in their own time."
21 And the people waited for Zacharias, and marveled that
he lingered so long in the temple.
22 But when he came out, he could not speak to them; and
they perceived that he had seen a vision in the temple, for
he beckoned to them and remained speechless.
23 So it was, as soon as [a]the days of his service were com-
pleted, that he departed to his own house.
24 Now after those days his wife Elizabeth conceived; and
she hid herself five months, saying,
25 "Thus the Lord has dealt with me, in the days when He
looked on *me,* to [a]take away my reproach among people."
26 Now in the sixth month the angel Gabriel was sent by God
to a city of Galilee named Nazareth,

1:9 [a]Ex. 30:7, 8 1:10 [a]Lev. 16:17 1:11 [a]Ex. 30:1 1:12 [a]Luke 2:9 1:13 [a]Luke 1:57, 60, 63 1:14 [a]Luke 1:58 1:15 [a][Luke 7:24–28] [b]Num. 6:3 [c]Jer. 1:5 1:17 [a]Mal. 4:5, 6; Matt. 3:2; 11:14 [1]Malachi 4:5, 6 1:18 [a]Gen. 17:17 1:19 [a]Dan. 8:16 [b]Luke 2:10 1:20 [a]Ezek. 3:26; 24:27 1:23 [a]2 Kin. 11:5 1:25 [a]Gen. 30:23

27 to a virgin [a]betrothed to a man whose name was Joseph,
of the house of David. The virgin's name *was* Mary.
28 And having come in, the angel said to her, [a]"Rejoice, high-
ly favored *one,* [b]the Lord *is* with you; blessed *are* you among
women!"[1]
29 But when she saw *him,*[1] [a]she was troubled at his saying,
and considered what manner of greeting this was.
30 Then the angel said to her, "Do not be afraid, Mary, for
you have found [a]favor with God.
31 [a]"And behold, you will conceive in your womb and bring
forth a Son, and [b]shall call His name JESUS.
32 "He will be great, [a]and will be called the Son of the High-
est; and [b]the Lord God will give Him the [c]throne of His [d]fa-
ther David.
33 [a]"And He will reign over the house of Jacob forever, and
of His kingdom there will be no end."
34 Then Mary said to the angel, "How can this be, since I do
not know a man?"
35 And the angel answered and said to her, [a]"*The* Holy Spirit
will come upon you, and the power of the Highest will over-
shadow you; therefore, also, that Holy One who is to be born
will be called [b]the Son of God.
36 "Now indeed, Elizabeth your relative has also conceived
a son in her old age; and this is now the sixth month for her
who was called barren.
37 "For [a]with God nothing will be impossible."
38 Then Mary said, "Behold the maidservant of the Lord! Let
it be to me according to your word." And the angel departed
from her.
39 Now Mary arose in those days and went into the hill coun-
try with haste, [a]to a city of Judah,
40 and entered the house of Zacharias and greeted Eliza-
beth.
41 And it happened, when Elizabeth heard the greeting of
Mary, that the babe leaped in her womb; and Elizabeth was
[a]filled with the Holy Spirit.
42 Then she spoke out with a loud voice and said, [a]"Blessed
are you among women, and blessed *is* the fruit of your womb!
43 "But why *is* this *granted* to me, that the mother of my Lord
should come to me?
44 "For indeed, as soon as the voice of your greeting sound-
ed in my ears, the babe leaped in my womb for joy.
45 [a]"Blessed *is* she who believed, for there will be a fulfill-
ment of those things which were told her from the Lord."

1:27[a]Matt. 1:18 1:28[a]Dan. 9:23 [b]Judg. 6:12 [1]NU-Text omits *blessed are you among women.* 1:29[a]Luke 1:12 [1]NU-Text omits *when she saw him.* 1:30[a]Luke 2:52
1:31[a]Is. 7:14 [b]Luke 2:21 1:32[a]Mark 5:7 [b]2 Sam. 7:12, 13, 16 [c]2 Sam. 7:14–17 [d]Matt. 1:1
1:33[a][Dan. 2:44] 1:35[a]Matt. 1:20 [b][Heb. 1:2, 8] 1:37[a]Jer. 32:17 1:39[a]Josh. 21:9
1:41[a]Acts 6:3 1:42[a]Judg. 5:24 1:45[a]John 20:29

46 And Mary said:

[a]"My soul magnifies the Lord,
47 And my spirit has [a]rejoiced in [b]God my Savior.
48 For [a]He has regarded the lowly
state of His maidservant;
For behold, henceforth [b]all generations
will call me blessed.
49 For He who is mighty [a]has done
great things for me,
And [b]holy *is* His name.
50 And [a]His mercy *is* on those who fear Him
From generation to generation.
51 [a]He has shown strength with His arm;
[b]He has scattered *the* proud in the
imagination of their hearts.
52 [a]He has put down the mighty from *their* thrones,
And exalted *the* lowly.
53 He has [a]filled *the* hungry with good things,
And *the* rich He has sent away empty.
54 He has helped His [a]servant Israel,
[b]In remembrance of *His* mercy,
55 [a]As He spoke to our [b]fathers,
To Abraham and to his [c]seed forever."

56 And Mary remained with her about three months, and
returned to her house.
57 Now Elizabeth's full time came for her to be delivered,
and she brought forth a son.
58 When her neighbors and relatives heard how the Lord
had shown great mercy to her, they [a]rejoiced with her.
59 So it was, [a]on the eighth day, that they came to circum-
cise the child; and they would have called him by the name
of his father, Zacharias.
60 His mother answered and said, [a]"No; he shall be called
John."
61 But they said to her, "There is no one among your rela-
tives who is called by this name."
62 So they made signs to his father—what he would have
him called.
63 And he asked for a writing tablet, and wrote, saying, "His
name is John." So they all marveled.
64 Immediately his mouth was opened and his tongue *loosed,*
and he spoke, praising God.
65 Then fear came on all who dwelt around them; and all

1:46[a]1 Sam. 2:1–10 1:47[a]Hab. 3:18 [b]1 Tim. 1:1; 2:3 1:48[a]Ps. 138:6 [b]Luke 11:27 1:49[a]Ps. 71:19; 126:2, 3 [b]Ps. 111:9 1:50[a]Ps. 103:17 1:51[a]Ps. 98:1; 118:15 [b][1 Pet. 5:5] 1:52[a]1 Sam. 2:7, 8 1:53[a][Matt. 5:6] 1:54[a]Is. 41:8 [b][Jer. 31:3] 1:55[a]Gen. 17:19 [b][Rom. 11:28] [c]Gen. 17:7 1:58[a][Rom. 12:15] 1:59[a]Gen. 17:12 1:60[a]Luke 1:13, 63

these sayings were discussed throughout all the hill country
of Judea.
66 And all those who heard *them* [a]kept *them* in their hearts,
saying, "What kind of child will this be?" And [b]the hand of
the Lord was with him.
67 Now his father Zacharias [a]was filled with the Holy Spirit,
and prophesied, saying:

68 "Blessed[a] *is* the Lord God of Israel,
For [b]He has visited and redeemed His people,
69 [a]And has raised up a horn of salvation for us
In the house of His servant David,
70 [a]As He spoke by the mouth of His holy prophets,
Who *have been* [b]since the world began,
71 That we should be saved from our enemies
And from the hand of all who hate us,
72 [a]To perform the mercy *promised* to our fathers
And to remember His holy covenant,
73 [a]The oath which He swore to
our father Abraham:
74 To grant us that we,
Being delivered from the hand of our enemies,
Might [a]serve Him without fear,
75 [a]In holiness and righteousness before
Him all the days of our life.

76 "And you, child, will be called the
[a]prophet of the Highest;
For [b]you will go before the face of the
Lord to prepare His ways,
77 To give [a]knowledge of salvation to His people
By the remission of their sins,
78 Through the tender mercy of our God,
With which the Dayspring from
on high has visited[1] us;
79 [a]To give light to those who sit in
darkness and the shadow of death,
To [b]guide our feet into the way of peace."

80 So [a]the child grew and became strong in spirit, and [b]was
in the deserts till the day of his manifestation to Israel.

1:66 [a]Luke 2:19 [b]Acts 11:21 1:67 [a]Joel 2:28 1:68 [a]1 Kin. 1:48 [b]Ex. 3:16 1:69 [a]Ps. 132:17 1:70 [a]Rom. 1:2 [b]Acts 3:21 1:72 [a]Lev. 26:42 1:73 [a]Gen. 12:3; 22:16–18 1:74 [a][Heb. 9:14] 1:75 [a][Eph. 4:24] 1:76 [a]Matt. 3:3; 11:9 [b]Is. 40:3 1:77 [a][Mark 1:4] 1:78 [1]NU-Text reads *shall visit.* 1:79 [a]Is. 9:2 [b][John 10:4; 14:27; 16:33] 1:80 [a]Luke 2:40 [b]Matt. 3:1

LUKE 2

THE BIRTH AND CHILDHOOD OF JESUS

Observe that Simeon found Christ in the temple after being conducted thither by the Holy Ghost. There was an ancient promise, "The Lord, whom you seek, will suddenly come to His temple" (Mal. 3:1), and this probably drew the holy man to the courts of the Lord. Being led by the Spirit, he came to the appointed spot at the very time when the mother of Christ was bringing the Babe in her arms to do for Him according to the law.

In this Simeon is an instance of the truth that they find Christ who are led by the Spirit. No man ever comes to Christ by his own wit and wisdom or by his own unprompted will: he alone who is drawn of the Spirit comes to Christ. We must submit ourselves to divine teaching and divine drawing or else Christ may come in His temple, but we shall not perceive Him. I therefore would earnestly remark how needful it is that we should submit ourselves to the movements of the Holy Spirit upon our souls; let me rather say what a privilege it is to be moved by the Spirit and how gladly we should welcome His divine influences.

---

1 And it came to pass in those days *that* a decree went out
from Caesar Augustus that all the world should be registered.
2 [a]This census first took place while Quirinius was govern-
ing Syria.
3 So all went to be registered, everyone to his own city.
4 Joseph also went up from Galilee, out of the city of Naza-
reth, into Judea, to [a]the city of David, which is called Beth-
lehem, [b]because he was of the house and lineage of David,
5 to be registered with Mary, [a]his betrothed wife,[1] who was
with child.
6 So it was, that while they were there, the days were com-
pleted for her to be delivered.
7 And [a]she brought forth her firstborn Son, and wrapped
Him in swaddling cloths, and laid Him in a manger, because
there was no room for them in the inn.
8 Now there were in the same country shepherds living out
in the fields, keeping watch over their flock by night.
9 And behold,[1] an angel of the Lord stood before them, and
the glory of the Lord shone around them, [a]and they were
greatly afraid.
10 Then the angel said to them, [a]"Do not be afraid, for be-
hold, I bring you good tidings of great joy [b]which will be to
all people.

2:2 [a]Acts 5:37 2:4 [a]1 Sam. 16:1 [b]Matt. 1:16 2:5 [a][Matt. 1:18] [1]NU-Text omits *wife.*
2:7 [a]Matt. 1:25 2:9 [a]Luke 1:12 [1]NU-Text omits *behold.* 2:10 [a]Luke 1:13, 30 [b]Gen. 12:3

11 [a]"For there is born to you this day in the city of David [b]a
Savior, [c]who is Christ the Lord.
12 "And this *will be* the sign to you: You will find a Babe
wrapped in swaddling cloths, lying in a manger."
13 [a]And suddenly there was with the angel a multitude of
the heavenly host praising God and saying:

> 14 "Glory[a] to God in the highest,
> And on earth [b]peace, [c]goodwill toward men!"[1]

15 So it was, when the angels had gone away from them into
heaven, that the shepherds said to one another, "Let us now
go to Bethlehem and see this thing that has come to pass,
which the Lord has made known to us."
16 And they came with haste and found Mary and Joseph,
and the Babe lying in a manger.
17 Now when they had seen *Him,* they made widely[1] known
the saying which was told them concerning this Child.
18 And all those who heard *it* marveled at those things which
were told them by the shepherds.
19 [a]But Mary kept all these things and pondered *them* in her
heart.
20 Then the shepherds returned, glorifying and [a]praising
God for all the things that they had heard and seen, as it was
told them.
21 [a]And when eight days were completed for the circum-
cision of the Child,[1] His name was called [b]JESUS, the name
given by the angel [c]before He was conceived in the womb.
22 Now when [a]the days of her purification according to the
law of Moses were completed, they brought Him to Jerusa-
lem to present *Him* to the Lord
23 [a](as it is written in the law of the Lord, [b]"Every male who
opens the womb shall be called holy to the LORD"),[1]
24 and to offer a sacrifice according to what is said in the law
of the Lord, [a]"A pair of turtledoves or two young pigeons."[1]
25 And behold, there was a man in Jerusalem whose name
was Simeon, and this man was just and devout, [a]waiting for
the Consolation of Israel, and the Holy Spirit was upon him.
26 And it had been revealed to him by the Holy Spirit that
he would not [a]see death before he had seen the Lord's Christ.
27 So he came [a]by the Spirit into the temple. And when the
parents brought in the Child Jesus, to do for Him according
to the custom of the law,

2:11 [a]Is. 9:6 [b]Matt. 1:21 [c]Acts 2:36 2:13 [a]Dan. 7:10 2:14 [a]Luke 19:38 [b]Is. 57:19 [c][Eph. 2:4, 7] [1]NU-Text reads *toward men of goodwill.* 2:17 [1]NU-Text omits *widely.* 2:19 [a]Gen. 37:11 2:20 [a]Luke 19:37 2:21 [a]Lev. 12:3 [b][Matt. 1:21] [c]Luke 1:31 [1]NU-Text reads *for His circumcision.* 2:22 [a]Lev. 12:2–8 2:23 [a]Deut. 18:4 [b]Ex. 13:2, 12, 15 [1]Exodus 13:2, 12, 15 2:24 [a]Lev. 12:2, 8 [1]Leviticus 12:8 2:25 [a]Mark 15:43 2:26 [a][Heb. 11:5] 2:27 [a]Matt. 4:1

28 he took Him up in his arms and blessed God and said:

29 "Lord, [a]now You are letting Your
servant depart in peace,
According to Your word;
30 For my eyes [a]have seen Your salvation
31 Which You have prepared before
the face of all peoples,
32 [a]A light to *bring* revelation to the Gentiles,
And the glory of Your people Israel."

33 And Joseph and His mother[1] marveled at those things
which were spoken of Him.
34 Then Simeon blessed them, and said to Mary His mother,
"Behold, this *Child* is destined for the [a]fall and rising of many
in Israel, and for [b]a sign which will be spoken against
35 "(yes, [a]a sword will pierce through your own soul also),
that the thoughts of many hearts may be revealed."
36 Now there was one, Anna, a prophetess, the daughter of
Phanuel, of the tribe of [a]Asher. She was of a great age, and
had lived with a husband seven years from her virginity;
37 and this woman *was* a widow of about eighty-four years,[1]
who did not depart from the temple, but served *God* with
fastings and prayers [a]night and day.
38 And coming in that instant she gave thanks to the Lord,[1]
and spoke of Him to all those who [a]looked for redemption
in Jerusalem.
39 So when they had performed all things according to the
law of the Lord, they returned to Galilee, to their *own* city,
Nazareth.
40 [a]And the Child grew and became strong in spirit,[1] filled
with wisdom; and the grace of God was upon Him.
41 His parents went to [a]Jerusalem [b]every year at the Feast
of the Passover.
42 And when He was twelve years old, they went up to Jeru-
salem according to the [a]custom of the feast.
43 When they had finished the [a]days, as they returned, the
Boy Jesus lingered behind in Jerusalem. And Joseph and His
mother[1] did not know *it;*
44 but supposing Him to have been in the company, they
went a day's journey, and sought Him among *their* relatives
and acquaintances.
45 So when they did not find Him, they returned to Jerusa-
lem, seeking Him.

2:29 [a]Gen. 46:30 2:30 [a][Is. 52:10] 2:32 [a]Acts 10:45; 13:47; 28:28 2:33 [1]NU-Text reads *And His father and mother.* 2:34 [a][1 Pet. 2:7, 8] [b]Acts 4:2; 17:32; 28:22 2:35 [a]Ps. 42:10 2:36 [a]Josh. 19:24 2:37 [a]1 Tim. 5:5 [1]NU-Text reads *a widow until she was eighty-four.* 2:38 [a]Mark 15:43 [1]NU-Text reads *to God.* 2:40 [a]Luke 1:80; 2:52 [1]NU-Text omits *in spirit.* 2:41 [a]John 4:20 [b]Deut. 16:1, 16 2:42 [a]Ex. 23:14, 15 2:43 [a]Ex. 12:15 [1]NU-Text reads *And His parents.*

46 Now so it was *that* after three days they found Him in the
temple, sitting in the midst of the teachers, both listening to
them and asking them questions.
47 And [a]all who heard Him were astonished at His under-
standing and answers.
48 So when they saw Him, they were amazed; and His mother
said to Him, "Son, why have You done this to us? Look, Your
father and I have sought You anxiously."
49 And He said to them, "Why did you seek Me? Did you not
know that I must be [a]about [b]My Father's business?"
50 But [a]they did not understand the statement which He
spoke to them.
51 Then He went down with them and came to Nazareth, and
was subject to them, but His mother [a]kept all these things in
her heart.
52 And Jesus [a]increased in wisdom and stature, [b]and in fa-
vor with God and men.

2:47[a]Matt. 7:28; 13:54; 22:33 2:49[a]John 9:4 [b][Luke 4:22, 32] 2:50[a]John 7:15, 46 2:51[a]Dan. 7:28 2:52[a][Col. 2:2, 3] [b]1 Sam. 2:26

LUKE 3

JOHN THE BAPTIST PREPARES THE WAY

Prayer seems to be like a silver thread running through the whole of our Savior's life, yet we have the record of His prayers on many special occasions. So we find that it was while Christ was praying at His baptism that the Holy Ghost came upon Him "in bodily form like a dove" to qualify Him for His public service; and it is through prayer that we also receive the spiritual enrichment that equips us as coworkers together with God.

Without prayer, you will remain in a region that is desolate as a desert, but bend your knees in supplication to the Most High and you have reached the Land of Promise, the country of benediction. More prayer, more power: the more pleading with God there is, the more power will there be in pleading with men, for the Holy Ghost will come upon us while we are pleading, and so we shall be fitted and qualified to do the work to which we are called of God.

Let us learn, then, from this first instance of our Savior's preparatory prayer at His baptism the necessity of special supplication on our part in similar circumstances. If we are in any way coming out more distinctly before the world as the servants of Christ, let us set apart special seasons for prayer.

---

1 Now in the fifteenth year of the reign of Tiberius Caesar, [a]Pontius Pilate being governor of Judea, Herod being tetrarch of Galilee, his brother Philip tetrarch of Iturea and the region of Trachonitis, and Lysanias tetrarch of Abilene,
2 while [a]Annas and Caiaphas were high priests,[1] the word of God came to [b]John the son of Zacharias in the wilderness.
3 [a]And he went into all the region around the Jordan, preaching a baptism of repentance [b]for the remission of sins,
4 as it is written in the book of the words of Isaiah the prophet, saying:

> [a]"The voice of one crying in the wilderness:
> 'Prepare the way of the LORD;
> Make His paths straight.
> 5 Every valley shall be filled
> And every mountain and hill brought low;
> The crooked places shall be made straight
> And the rough ways smooth;
> 6 And [a]all flesh shall see the salvation of God.'"[1]

3:1[a]Matt. 27:2 3:2[a]Acts 4:6 [b]Luke 1:13 [1]NU-Text and M-Text read *in the high priesthood of Annas and Caiaphas.* 3:3[a]Mark 1:4 [b]Luke 1:77 3:4[a]Is. 40:3–5 3:6[a]Is. 52:10 [1]Isaiah 40:3–5

7 Then he said to the multitudes that came out to be bap-
tized by him, [a]"Brood of vipers! Who warned you to flee from
the wrath to come?
8 "Therefore bear fruits [a]worthy of repentance, and do not
begin to say to yourselves, 'We have Abraham as *our* father.'
For I say to you that God is able to raise up children to Abra-
ham from these stones.
9 "And even now the ax is laid to the root of the trees. There-
fore [a]every tree which does not bear good fruit is cut down
and thrown into the fire."
10 So the people asked him, saying, [a]"What shall we do
then?"
11 He answered and said to them, [a]"He who has two tunics,
let him give to him who has none; and he who has food, [b]let
him do likewise."
12 Then [a]tax collectors also came to be baptized, and said to
him, "Teacher, what shall we do?"
13 And he said to them, [a]"Collect no more than what is ap-
pointed for you."
14 Likewise the soldiers asked him, saying, "And what shall
we do?" So he said to them, "Do not intimidate anyone [a]or
accuse falsely, and be content with your wages."
15 Now as the people were in expectation, and all reasoned
in their hearts about John, whether he was the Christ *or* not,
16 John answered, saying to all, [a]"I indeed baptize you with
water; but One mightier than I is coming, whose sandal strap
I am not worthy to loose. He will [b]baptize you with the Holy
Spirit and fire.
17 "His winnowing fan *is* in His hand, and He will thoroughly
clean out His threshing floor, and [a]gather the wheat into His
barn; but the chaff He will burn with unquenchable fire."
18 And with many other exhortations he preached to the
people.
19 [a]But Herod the tetrarch, being rebuked by him concern-
ing Herodias, his brother Philip's wife,[1] and for all the evils
which Herod had done,
20 also added this, above all, that he shut John up in prison.
21 When all the people were baptized, [a]it came to pass that
Jesus also was baptized; and while He prayed, the heaven
was opened.
22 And the Holy Spirit descended in bodily form like a dove
upon Him, and a voice came from heaven which said, "You
are My beloved Son; in You I am [a]well pleased."
23 Now Jesus Himself began *His ministry at* [a]about thirty

3:7[a]Matt. 3:7; 12:34; 23:33 3:8[a][2 Cor. 7:9–11] 3:9[a]Matt. 7:19 3:10[a][Acts 2:37, 38; 16:30, 31] 3:11[a]2 Cor. 8:14 [b]Is. 58:7 3:12[a]Luke 7:29 3:13[a]Luke 19:8 3:14[a]Ex. 20:16; 23:1 3:16[a]Matt. 3:11, 12 [b]John 7:39; 20:22 3:17[a]Matt. 13:24–30 3:19[a]Mark 6:17 [1]NU-Text reads *his brother's wife.* 3:21[a]Matt. 3:13–17 3:22[a]2 Pet. 1:17 3:23[a][Num. 4:3, 35, 39, 43, 47]

years of age, being (as was supposed) [b]*the* son of Joseph, *the*
son of Heli,
24 *the son* of Matthat,[1] *the son* of Levi, *the son* of Melchi, *the*
son of Janna, *the son* of Joseph,
25 *the son* of Mattathiah, *the son* of Amos, *the son* of Nahum,
the son of Esli, *the son* of Naggai,
26 *the son* of Maath, *the son* of Mattathiah, *the son* of Semei,
the son of Joseph, *the son* of Judah,
27 *the son* of Joannas, *the son* of Rhesa, *the son* of [a]Zerubba-
bel, *the son* of Shealtiel, *the son* of Neri,
28 *the son* of Melchi, *the son* of Addi, *the son* of Cosam, *the*
son of Elmodam, *the son* of Er,
29 *the son* of Jose, *the son* of Eliezer, *the son* of Jorim, *the son*
of Matthat, *the son* of Levi,
30 *the son* of Simeon, *the son* of Judah, *the son* of Joseph, *the*
son of Jonan, *the son* of Eliakim,
31 *the son* of Melea, *the son* of Menan, *the son* of Mattathah,
the son of [a]Nathan, [b]*the son* of David,
32 [a]*the son* of Jesse, *the son* of Obed, *the son* of Boaz, *the son*
of Salmon, *the son* of Nahshon,
33 *the son* of Amminadab, *the son* of Ram, *the son* of Hezron,
the son of Perez, *the son* of Judah,
34 *the son* of Jacob, *the son* of Isaac, *the son* of Abraham, [a]*the*
son of Terah, *the son* of Nahor,
35 *the son* of Serug, *the son* of Reu, *the son* of Peleg, *the son*
of Eber, *the son* of Shelah,
36 [a]*the son* of Cainan, *the son* of [b]Arphaxad, [c]*the son* of Shem,
the son of Noah, *the son* of Lamech,
37 *the son* of Methuselah, *the son* of Enoch, *the son* of Jared,
the son of Mahalalel, *the son* of Cainan,
38 *the son* of Enosh, *the son* of Seth, *the son* of Adam, [a]*the son*
of God.

3:23 [b]John 6:42 3:24 [1]This and several other names in the genealogy are spelled somewhat differently in the NU-Text. Since the New King James Version uses the Old Testament spelling for persons mentioned in the New Testament, these variations, which come from the Greek, have not been footnoted. 3:27 [a]Ezra 2:2; 3:8 3:31 [a]Zech. 12:12 [b]2 Sam. 5:14; 7:12 3:32 [a]Ruth 4:18–22 3:34 [a]Gen. 11:24, 26–30; 12:3 3:36 [a]Gen. 11:12 [b]Gen. 10:22, 24; 11:10–13 [c]Gen. 5:6–32; 9:27; 11:10 3:38 [a]Gen. 5:1, 2

LUKE 4

THE TEMPTATION OF JESUS

Who were these rejecters of Christ? These people of Nazareth were those who knew most about Christ. They were well acquainted with His mother, His pedigree, His history. The whole story of the wondrous Child was known to them. Now, surely these people, not needing to be taught the rudiments, not requiring to be instructed in the very elements of the faith, must have been a very hopeful people for Jesus to preach to. But alas! They did not prove to be so.

There are many who are wonderfully like them. You know the whole story of the Savior and have known it ever since your childhood. More than that, you well understand the doctrines of the gospel. You can discuss gospel truths, and you delight to do so, for you take a deep interest in them. When you read the Scripture, it is not to you a dark, mysterious volume that you cannot at all comprehend; you are able to teach others what are the first principles of the truth.

And yet, for all that, how strangely sad it is that knowing so much, you should practice so little. I am afraid that some of you know the gospel so well that for this very reason it has lost much of its power with you, for it is as well known as a thrice-told tale. It is sad indeed that men so nearly related to Christianity, who know so much about Christ, should yet reject the Redeemer.

1 Then [a]Jesus, being filled with the Holy Spirit, returned
from the Jordan and [b]was led by the Spirit into[1] the wilder-
ness,
2 being tempted for forty days by the devil. And [a]in those
days He ate nothing, and afterward, when they had ended,
He was hungry.
3 And the devil said to Him, "If You are [a]the Son of God,
command this stone to become bread."
4 But Jesus answered him, saying,[1] "It is written, [a]'Man shall
not live by bread alone, but by every word of God.'"[2]
5 Then the devil, taking Him up on a high mountain, showed
Him[1] all the kingdoms of the world in a moment of time.
6 And the devil said to Him, "All this authority I will give
You, and their glory; for [a]*this* has been delivered to me, and
I give it to whomever I wish.
7 "Therefore, if You will worship before me, all will be Yours."
8 And Jesus answered and said to him, "Get behind Me,

4:1[a]Matt. 4:1–11 [b]Luke 2:27 [1]NU-Text reads *in.* 4:2[a]Ex. 34:28 4:3[a]John 20:31
4:4[a]Deut. 8:3 [1]Deuteronomy 8:3 [2]NU-Text omits *but by every word of God.*
4:5[1]NU-Text reads *And taking Him up, he showed Him.* 4:6[a][Rev. 13:2, 7]

Satan![1] For[2] it is written, [a]'You shall worship the LORD your
God, and Him only you shall serve.'"[3]
9 [a]Then he brought Him to Jerusalem, set Him on the pin-
nacle of the temple, and said to Him, "If You are the Son of
God, throw Yourself down from here.
10 "For it is written:

> [a]'He shall give His angels charge over you,
> To keep you,'

11 "and,

> [a]'In *their* hands they shall bear you up,
> Lest you dash your foot against a stone.'"[1]

12 And Jesus answered and said to him, "It has been said,
[a]'You shall not tempt the LORD your God.'"[1]
13 Now when the devil had ended every temptation, he de-
parted from Him [a]until an opportune time.
14 [a]Then Jesus returned [b]in the power of the Spirit to [c]Gali-
lee, and [d]news of Him went out through all the surrounding
region.
15 And He [a]taught in their synagogues, [b]being glorified by all.
16 So He came to [a]Nazareth, where He had been brought up.
And as His custom was, [b]He went into the synagogue on the
Sabbath day, and stood up to read.
17 And He was handed the book of the prophet Isaiah. And
when He had opened the book, He found the place where it
was written:

> 18 "The[a] Spirit of the LORD *is* upon Me,
> Because He has anointed Me
> To preach the gospel to *the* poor;
> He has sent Me to heal the brokenhearted,[1]
> To proclaim liberty to *the* captives
> And recovery of sight to *the* blind,
> *To* [b]set at liberty those who are oppressed;
> 19 To proclaim the acceptable year of the LORD."[1]

20 Then He closed the book, and gave *it* back to the atten-
dant and sat down. And the eyes of all who were in the syn-
agogue were fixed on Him.
21 And He began to say to them, "Today this Scripture is
[a]fulfilled in your hearing."

4:8[a]Deut. 6:13; 10:20 [1]NU-Text omits *Get behind Me, Satan.* [2]NU-Text and M-Text omit *For.* [3]Deuteronomy 6:13 4:9[a]Matt. 4:5–7 4:10[a]Ps. 91:11 4:11[a]Ps. 91:12 [1]Psalm 91:11, 12 4:12[a]Deut. 6:16 [1]Deuteronomy 6:16 4:13[a][Heb. 4:15] 4:14[a]Matt. 4:12 [b]John 4:43 [c]Acts 10:37 [d]Matt. 4:24 4:15[a]Matt. 4:23 [b]Is. 52:13 4:16[a]Mark 6:1 [b]Acts 13:14–16; 17:2 4:18[a]Is. 49:8, 9; 61:1, 2 [b][Dan. 9:24] [1]NU-Text omits *to heal the brokenhearted.* 4:19[1]Isaiah 61:1, 2 4:21[a]Acts 13:29

22 So all bore witness to Him, and [a]marveled at the gracious
words which proceeded out of His mouth. And they said, [b]"Is
this not Joseph's son?"
23 He said to them, "You will surely say this proverb to Me,
'Physician, heal yourself! Whatever we have heard done in
[a]Capernaum,[1] do also here in [b]Your country.'"
24 Then He said, "Assuredly, I say to you, no [a]prophet is ac-
cepted in his own country.
25 "But I tell you truly, [a]many widows were in Israel in the
days of Elijah, when the heaven was shut up three years and
six months, and there was a great famine throughout all the
land;
26 "but to none of them was Elijah sent except to Zarephath,[1]
in the region of Sidon, to a woman *who was* a widow.
27 [a]"And many lepers were in Israel in the time of Elisha the
prophet, and none of them was cleansed except Naaman the
Syrian."
28 So all those in the synagogue, when they heard these
things, were [a]filled with wrath,
29 [a]and rose up and thrust Him out of the city; and they led
Him to the brow of the hill on which their city was built, that
they might throw Him down over the cliff.
30 Then [a]passing through the midst of them, He went
His way.
31 Then [a]He went down to Capernaum, a city of Galilee, and
was teaching them on the Sabbaths.
32 And they were [a]astonished at His teaching, [b]for His word
was with authority.
33 [a]Now in the synagogue there was a man who had a spirit
of an unclean demon. And he cried out with a loud voice,
34 saying, "Let *us* alone! What have we to do with You, Jesus
of Nazareth? Did You come to destroy us? [a]I know who You
are—[b]the Holy One of God!"
35 But Jesus rebuked him, saying, "Be quiet, and come out
of him!" And when the demon had thrown him in *their* midst,
it came out of him and did not hurt him.
36 Then they were all amazed and spoke among themselves,
saying, "What a word this *is!* For with authority and power
He commands the unclean spirits, and they come out."
37 And the report about Him went out into every place in
the surrounding region.
38 [a]Now He arose from the synagogue and entered Simon's
house. But Simon's wife's mother was sick with a high fever,
and they [b]made request of Him concerning her.

4:22[a][Ps. 45:2] [b]John 6:42 4:23[a]Matt. 4:13; 11:23 [b]Matt. 13:54 [1]Here and elsewhere the NU-Text spelling is *Capharnaum.* 4:24[a]John 4:44 4:25[a]1 Kin. 17:9 4:26[1]Greek *Sarepta* 4:27[a]2 Kin. 5:1–14 4:28[a]Luke 6:11 4:29[a]John 8:37; 10:31 4:30[a]John 8:59; 10:39 4:31[a]Matt. 4:13 4:32[a]Matt. 7:28, 29 [b][John 6:63; 7:46; 8:26, 28, 38, 47; 12:49, 50] 4:33[a]Mark 1:23 4:34[a]Luke 4:41 [b]Ps. 16:10 4:38[a]Mark 1:29–31 [b]Mark 5:23

39 So He stood over her and [a]rebuked the fever, and it left
her. And immediately she arose and served them.
40 [a]When the sun was setting, all those who had any that
were sick with various diseases brought them to Him; and
He laid His hands on every one of them and healed them.
41 [a]And demons also came out of many, crying out and say-
ing, [b]"You are the Christ,[1] the Son of God!" And He, [c]rebuking
them, did not allow them to speak, for they knew that He was
the Christ.
42 [a]Now when it was day, He departed and went into a de-
serted place. And the crowd sought Him and came to Him,
and tried to keep Him from leaving them;
43 but He said to them, "I must [a]preach the kingdom of God
to the other cities also, because for this purpose I have been
sent."
44 [a]And He was preaching in the synagogues of Galilee.[1]

4:39[a]Luke 8:24 4:40[a]Matt. 8:16, 17 4:41[a]Mark 1:34; 3:11 [b]Mark 8:29 [c]Mark 1:25, 34; 3:11 [1]NU-Text omits *the Christ.* 4:42[a]Mark 1:35–38 4:43[a][John 9:4] 4:44[a]Matt. 4:23; 9:35 [1]NU-Text reads *Judea.*

LUKE 5

DISCIPLESHIP, HEALING, AND FORGIVENESS

This man was paralyzed in body, but he was very far from being paralyzed in mind. He would appear to have been earnest, resolute, energetic, and persevering. You very seldom find persons attempting more for you than you yourself desire, and if the four men who carried this paralytic person were so zealous in getting him under the Lord's notice, we may be morally certain that he himself was even more set upon it.

Suppose it to be your own case, my dear hearer. Are you not persuaded that if, broken in spirit, you were to say to your friends, "Let me alone—my case is hopeless," few would dream of exciting themselves to desperate efforts on your behalf? It is a rule that you must yourself be energetic if you are to make other people energetic on your behalf.

Therefore, it seems to me that this man had a resolute and intense spirit and had such influence over his friends that he inspired them by his eagerness, having first won them by his importunity. He besought them to aid him in what had become a necessity of life—he must see Jesus. He must be brought before the great Healing One somehow or other, and because of his personal enthusiasm, his friends made up their minds to help him.

---

1 So [a]it was, as the multitude pressed about Him to [b]hear
the word of God, that He stood by the Lake of Gennesaret,
2 and saw two boats standing by the lake; but the fishermen
had gone from them and were washing *their* nets.
3 Then He got into one of the boats, which was Simon's, and
asked him to put out a little from the land. And He [a]sat down
and taught the multitudes from the boat.
4 When He had stopped speaking, He said to Simon, [a]"Launch
out into the deep and let down your nets for a catch."
5 But Simon answered and said to Him, "Master, we have
toiled all night and caught [a]nothing; nevertheless [b]at Your
word I will let down the net."
6 And when they had done this, they caught a great number
of fish, and their net was breaking.
7 So they signaled to *their* partners in the other boat to come
and help them. And they came and filled both the boats, so
that they began to sink.
8 When Simon Peter saw *it,* he fell down at Jesus' knees, say-
ing, [a]"Depart from me, for I am a sinful man, O Lord!"

5:1 [a]Mark 1:16–20 [b]Acts 13:44 5:3 [a]John 8:2 5:4 [a]John 21:6 5:5 [a]John 21:3 [b]Ps. 33:9 5:8 [a]1 Kin. 17:18

9 For he and all who were with him were [a]astonished at the
catch of fish which they had taken;
10 and so also *were* James and John, the sons of Zebedee,
who were partners with Simon. And Jesus said to Simon, "Do
not be afraid. [a]From now on you will catch men."
11 So when they had brought their boats to land, [a]they for-
sook all and followed Him.
12 [a]And it happened when He was in a certain city, that be-
hold, a man who was full of [b]leprosy saw Jesus; and he fell on
his face and implored Him, saying, "Lord, if You are willing,
You can make me clean."
13 Then He put out *His* hand and touched him, saying, "I am
willing; be cleansed." [a]Immediately the leprosy left him.
14 [a]And He charged him to tell no one, "But go and show
yourself to the priest, and make an offering for your cleans-
ing, as a testimony to them, [b]just as Moses commanded."
15 However, [a]the report went around concerning Him all
the more; and [b]great multitudes came together to hear, and
to be healed by Him of their infirmities.
16 [a]So He Himself *often* withdrew into the wilderness and
[b]prayed.
17 Now it happened on a certain day, as He was teaching,
that there were Pharisees and teachers of the law sitting
by, who had come out of every town of Galilee, Judea, and
Jerusalem. And the power of the Lord was *present* to heal
them.[1]
18 [a]Then behold, men brought on a bed a man who was par-
alyzed, whom they sought to bring in and lay before Him.
19 And when they could not find how they might bring him
in, because of the crowd, they went up on the housetop and
let him down with *his* bed through the tiling into the midst
[a]before Jesus.
20 When He saw their faith, He said to him, "Man, your sins
are forgiven you."
21 [a]And the scribes and the Pharisees began to reason, say-
ing, "Who is this who speaks blasphemies? [b]Who can forgive
sins but God alone?"
22 But when Jesus [a]perceived their thoughts, He answered
and said to them, "Why are you reasoning in your hearts?
23 "Which is easier, to say, 'Your sins are forgiven you,' or to
say, 'Rise up and walk'?
24 "But that you may know that the Son of Man has power
on earth to forgive sins"—He said to the man who was par-
alyzed, [a]"I say to you, arise, take up your bed, and go to your
house."

5:9[a]Mark 5:42; 10:24, 26 5:10[a]Matt. 4:19 5:11[a]Matt. 4:20; 19:27 5:12[a]Mark 1:40–44 [b]Lev. 13:14 5:13[a]John 5:9 5:14[a]Matt. 8:4 [b]Lev. 13:1–3; 14:2–32 5:15[a]Mark 1:45 [b]John 6:2 5:16[a]Luke 9:10 [b]Matt. 14:23 5:17[1]NU-Text reads *present with Him to heal.* 5:18[a]Mark 2:3–12 5:19[a]Matt. 15:30 5:21[a]Mark 2:6, 7 [b]Is. 43:25 5:22[a]John 2:25 5:24[a]Luke 7:14

25 Immediately he rose up before them, took up what he
had been lying on, and departed to his own house, [a]glorify-
ing God.
26 And they were all amazed, and they [a]glorified God and
were filled with fear, saying, "We have seen strange things
today!"
27 [a]After these things He went out and saw a tax collector
named Levi, sitting at the tax office. And He said to him,
[b]"Follow Me."
28 So he left all, rose up, and [a]followed Him.
29 [a]Then Levi gave Him a great feast in his own house. And
[b]there were a great number of tax collectors and others who
sat down with them.
30 And their scribes and the Pharisees[1] complained against
His disciples, saying, [a]"Why do You eat and drink with tax
collectors and sinners?"
31 Jesus answered and said to them, "Those who are well
have no need of a physician, but those who are sick.
32 [a]"I have not come to call *the* righteous, but sinners, to
repentance."
33 Then they said to Him, [a]"Why do[1] the disciples of John
fast often and make prayers, and likewise those of the Phar-
isees, but Yours eat and drink?"
34 And He said to them, "Can you make the friends of the
bridegroom fast while the [a]bridegroom is with them?
35 "But the days will come when the bridegroom will be
taken away from them; then they will fast in those days."
36 [a]Then He spoke a parable to them: "No one puts a piece
from a new garment on an old one;[1] otherwise the new makes
a tear, and also the piece that was *taken* out of the new does
not match the old.
37 "And no one puts new wine into old wineskins; or else
the new wine will burst the wineskins and be spilled, and the
wineskins will be ruined.
38 "But new wine must be put into new wineskins, and both
are preserved.[1]
39 "And no one, having drunk old *wine,* immediately[1] de-
sires new; for he says, 'The old is better.' "[2]

5:25[a]Acts 3:8 5:26[a]Luke 1:65; 7:16 5:27[a]Matt. 9:9–17 [b]John 12:26; 21:19, 22 5:28[a]Mark 10:28 5:29[a]Matt. 9:9, 10 [b]Luke 15:1 5:30[a]Luke 15:2 [1]NU-Text reads *But the Pharisees and their scribes.* 5:32[a]1 Tim. 1:15 5:33[a]Matt. 9:14 [1]NU-Text omits *Why do,* making the verse a statement. 5:34[a]John 3:29 5:36[a]Mark 2:21, 22 [1]NU-Text reads *No one tears a piece from a new garment and puts it on an old one.* 5:38[1]NU-Text omits *and both are preserved.* 5:39[1]NU-Text omits *immediately.* [2]NU-Text reads *good.*

LUKE 6

JESUS CHOOSES TWELVE DISCIPLES

All hearers are builders of houses for their souls; they are each one doing something to set up a spiritual habitation. Some are mistaken builders who fail in the foundation and make nothing sure except that their house will come down about their ears. Others there are who are building rightly, building for eternity: constructing a dwelling place with a basis of rock and walls of well-built stone of which the Lord Christ is both Foundation and Cornerstone.

Dig deep if you do dig a foundation. If it be repentance, let it be an intensely earnest repentance including a vehement hatred of every form of sin. If you make confession before God, confess with your very soul. If it be faith that you talk of, believe right up to the hilt. In the purging of the soul, there is nothing like sweeping out every particle of the old leaven of falsehood and bringing in everything that Christ prescribes, that of His fullness we may receive grace upon grace, all the grace that is needed. The wise builder dug through the earth and continued his digging till he reached the rock. And then he dug into the rock and struck out a trench wherein he might lay his foundation, for he could not be content unless he made sure and thorough work of it.

1 Now [a]it happened on the second Sabbath after the first[1] that
He went through the grainfields. And His disciples plucked
the heads of grain and ate *them,* rubbing *them* in *their* hands.
2 And some of the Pharisees said to them, "Why are you do-
ing [a]what is not lawful to do on the Sabbath?"
3 But Jesus answering them said, "Have you not even read
this, [a]what David did when he was hungry, he and those who
were with him:
4 "how he went into the house of God, took and ate the show-
bread, and also gave some to those with him, [a]which is not
lawful for any but the priests to eat?"
5 And He said to them, "The Son of Man is also Lord of the
Sabbath."
6 [a]Now it happened on another Sabbath, also, that He en-
tered the synagogue and taught. And a man was there whose
right hand was withered.
7 So the scribes and Pharisees watched Him closely, wheth-
er He would [a]heal on the Sabbath, that they might find an
[b]accusation against Him.

6:1 [a]Matt. 12:1–8 [1]NU-Text reads *on a Sabbath.* 6:2 [a]Ex. 20:10 6:3 [a]1 Sam. 21:6 6:4 [a]Lev. 24:9 6:6 [a]Mark 3:1–6 6:7 [a]Luke 13:14; 14:1–6 [b]Luke 20:20

8 But He [a]knew their thoughts, and said to the man who had
the withered hand, "Arise and stand here." And he arose and
stood.
9 Then Jesus said to them, "I will ask you one thing: [a]Is it
lawful on the Sabbath to do good or to do evil, to save life or
to destroy?"[1]
10 And when He had looked around at them all, He said to
the man,[1] "Stretch out your hand." And he did so, and his
hand was restored as whole as the other.[2]
11 But they were filled with rage, and discussed with one an-
other what they might do to Jesus.
12 Now it came to pass in those days that He went out to the
mountain to pray, and continued all night in [a]prayer to God.
13 And when it was day, He called His disciples to *Himself;*
[a]and from them He chose [b]twelve whom He also named
apostles:
14 Simon, [a]whom He also named Peter, and Andrew his
brother; James and John; Philip and Bartholomew;
15 Matthew and Thomas; James the *son* of Alphaeus, and
Simon called the Zealot;
16 Judas [a]*the son* of James, and [b]Judas Iscariot who also be-
came a traitor.
17 And He came down with them and stood on a level place
with a crowd of His disciples [a]and a great multitude of peo-
ple from all Judea and Jerusalem, and from the seacoast of
Tyre and Sidon, who came to hear Him and be healed of their
diseases,
18 as well as those who were tormented with unclean spirits.
And they were healed.
19 And the whole multitude [a]sought to [b]touch Him, for [c]power
went out from Him and healed *them* all.
20 Then He lifted up His eyes toward His disciples, and said:

> [a]"Blessed *are you* poor,
> For yours is the kingdom of God.
> 21 [a]Blessed *are you* who hunger now,
> For you shall be [b]filled.
> [c]Blessed *are you* who weep now,
> For you shall [d]laugh.
> 22 [a]Blessed are you when men hate you,
> And when they [b]exclude you,
> And revile *you,* and cast out your
> name as evil,
> For the Son of Man's sake.

6:8 [a]Matt. 9:4 6:9 [a]John 7:23 [1]M-Text reads *to kill.* 6:10 [1]NU-Text and M-Text read *to him.* [2]NU-Text omits *as whole as the other.* 6:12 [a]Mark 1:35 6:13 [a]John 6:70 [b]Matt. 10:1 6:14 [a]John 1:42 6:16 [a]Jude 1 [b]Luke 22:3–6 6:17 [a]Mark 3:7, 8 6:19 [a]Matt. 9:21; 14:36 [b]Mark 5:27, 28 [c]Luke 8:46 6:20 [a]Matt. 5:3–12; [11:5] 6:21 [a]Is. 55:1; 65:13 [b][Rev. 7:16] [c][Is. 61:3] [d]Ps. 126:5 6:22 [a]1 Pet. 2:19; 3:14; 4:14 [b][John 16:2]

23 [a]Rejoice in that day and leap for joy!
For indeed your reward *is* great in heaven,
For [b]in like manner their fathers
did to the prophets.

24 "But[a] woe to you [b]who are rich,
For [c]you have received your consolation.
25 [a]Woe to you who are full,
For you shall hunger.
[b]Woe to you who laugh now,
For you shall mourn and [c]weep.
26 [a]Woe to you[1] when all[2] men speak well of you,
For so did their fathers to the false prophets.

27 [a]"But I say to you who hear: Love your enemies, do good
to those who hate you,
28 [a]"bless those who curse you, and [b]pray for those who
spitefully use you.
29 [a]"To him who strikes you on the *one* cheek, offer the other
also. [b]And from him who takes away your cloak, do not with-
hold *your* tunic either.
30 [a]"Give to everyone who asks of you. And from him who
takes away your goods do not ask *them* back.
31 [a]"And just as you want men to do to you, you also do to
them likewise.
32 [a]"But if you love those who love you, what credit is that
to you? For even sinners love those who love them.
33 "And if you do good to those who do good to you, what
credit is that to you? For even sinners do the same.
34 [a]"And if you lend *to those* from whom you hope to receive
back, what credit is that to you? For even sinners lend to sin-
ners to receive as much back.
35 "But [a]love your enemies, [b]do good, and [c]lend, hoping for
nothing in return; and your reward will be great, and [d]you
will be sons of the Most High. For He is kind to the unthank-
ful and evil.
36 [a]"Therefore be merciful, just as your Father also is mer-
ciful.
37 [a]"Judge not, and you shall not be judged. Condemn not,
and you shall not be condemned. [b]Forgive, and you will be
forgiven.
38 [a]"Give, and it will be given to you: good measure, pressed
down, shaken together, and running over will be put into your

6:23[a]James 1:2 [b]Acts 7:51 6:24[a]James 5:1–6 [b]Luke 12:21 [c]Luke 16:25 6:25[a][Is. 65:13] [b][Prov. 14:13] [c]James 4:9 6:26[a][John 15:19] [1]NU-Text and M-Text omit *to you.* [2]M-Text omits *all.* 6:27[a]Rom. 12:20 6:28[a]Rom. 12:14 [b]Acts 7:60 6:29[a]Matt. 5:39–42 [b][1 Cor. 6:7] 6:30[a]Deut. 15:7, 8 6:31[a]Matt. 7:12 6:32[a]Matt. 5:46 6:34[a]Matt. 5:42 6:35[a][Rom. 13:10] [b]Heb. 13:16 [c]Ps. 37:26 [d]Matt. 5:46 6:36[a]Matt. 5:48 6:37[a]Matt. 7:1–5 [b]Matt. 18:21–35 6:38[a][Prov. 19:17; 28:27]

[b]bosom. For [c]with the same measure that you use, it will be
measured back to you."
39 And He spoke a parable to them: [a]"Can the blind lead the
blind? Will they not both fall into the ditch?
40 [a]"A disciple is not above his teacher, but everyone who is
perfectly trained will be like his teacher.
41 [a]"And why do you look at the speck in your brother's eye,
but do not perceive the plank in your own eye?
42 "Or how can you say to your brother, 'Brother, let me re-
move the speck that *is* in your eye,' when you yourself do not
see the plank that *is* in your own eye? Hypocrite! First remove
the plank from your own eye, and then you will see clearly
to remove the speck that is in your brother's eye.
43 [a]"For a good tree does not bear bad fruit, nor does a bad
tree bear good fruit.
44 "For [a]every tree is known by its own fruit. For *men* do
not gather figs from thorns, nor do they gather grapes from
a bramble bush.
45 [a]"A good man out of the good treasure of his heart brings
forth good; and an evil man out of the evil treasure of his
heart[1] brings forth evil. For out [b]of the abundance of the
heart his mouth speaks.
46 [a]"But why do you call Me 'Lord, Lord,' and not do the
things which I say?
47 [a]"Whoever comes to Me, and hears My sayings and does
them, I will show you whom he is like:
48 "He is like a man building a house, who dug deep and
laid the foundation on the rock. And when the flood arose,
the stream beat vehemently against that house, and could
not shake it, for it was founded on the rock.[1]
49 "But he who heard and did nothing is like a man who built
a house on the earth without a foundation, against which the
stream beat vehemently; and immediately it fell.[1] And the
ruin of that house was great."

6:38 [b]Ps. 79:12 [c]James 2:13 6:39 [a]Matt. 15:14; 23:16 6:40 [a][John 13:16; 15:20] 6:41 [a]Matt. 7:3 6:43 [a]Matt. 7:16–18, 20 6:44 [a]Matt. 12:33 6:45 [a]Matt. 12:35 [b]Matt. 12:34 [1]NU-Text omits *treasure of his heart.* 6:46 [a]Mal. 1:6 6:47 [a]James 1:22–25 6:48 [1]NU-Text reads *for it was well built.* 6:49 [1]NU-Text reads *collapsed.*

LUKE 7

JESUS HEALS AND TEACHES IN GALILEE

We are all indebted to God first in the matter of obedience to Him as His creatures. He is our Creator, our Preserver, our Provider, our Benefactor. "It is He who has made us, and not we ourselves; we are His people and the sheep of His pasture" (Ps. 100:3). We owe to Him our continued existence; every breath of our nostrils is His gift. Therefore, by our very creation, we are bound to serve Him according to the righteous demands of His holy law.

But as we have not rendered to God the obedience that is due to Him, we have become further indebted because of the penalty incurred by us as sinners. All the Ten Commandments stand up in the court as witnesses against us, for we have broken them all. That debt of penalty involves tremendous results to the body and the soul of man.

My dear friends, it gives me great joy to add that if we are pardoned sinners, we owe to God a deep debt of gratitude. If, through the death of Christ, we are delivered from the death penalty of sin—as we certainly are, for Christ has forever cleared all believers by bearing their punishment in His own body on the tree—then are we debtors to the infinite love and boundless compassion of our covenant-keeping God, His well-beloved Son, and the ever-blessed Spirit. In this debt, let us be willing continually to sink deeper and deeper.

---

1 Now when He concluded all His sayings in the hearing of the people, He [a]entered Capernaum.

2 And a certain centurion's servant, who was dear to him, was sick and ready to die.

3 So when he heard about Jesus, he sent elders of the Jews to Him, pleading with Him to come and heal his servant.

4 And when they came to Jesus, they begged Him earnestly, saying that the one for whom He should do this was deserving,

5 "for he loves our nation, and has built us a synagogue."

6 Then Jesus went with them. And when He was already not far from the house, the centurion sent friends to Him, saying to Him, "Lord, do not trouble Yourself, for I am not worthy that You should enter under my roof.

7 "Therefore I did not even think myself worthy to come to You. But [a]say the word, and my servant will be healed.

8 "For I also am a man placed under [a]authority, having soldiers under me. And I say to one, 'Go,' and he goes; and to

7:1[a]Matt. 8:5–13 7:7[a]Ps. 33:9; 107:20 7:8[a][Mark 13:34]

another, 'Come,' and he comes; and to my servant, 'Do this,'
and he does *it*."
9 When Jesus heard these things, He marveled at him, and
turned around and said to the crowd that followed Him, "I
say to you, I have not found such great faith, not even in Is-
rael!"
10 And those who were sent, returning to the house, found
the servant well who had been sick.[1]
11 Now it happened, the day after, *that* He went into a city
called Nain; and many of His disciples went with Him, and
a large crowd.
12 And when He came near the gate of the city, behold, a dead
man was being carried out, the only son of his mother; and
she was a widow. And a large crowd from the city was with her.
13 When the Lord saw her, He had [a]compassion on her and
said to her, [b]"Do not weep."
14 Then He came and touched the open coffin, and those
who carried *him* stood still. And He said, "Young man, I say
to you, [a]arise."
15 So he who was dead [a]sat up and began to speak. And He
[b]presented him to his mother.
16 [a]Then fear came upon all, and they [b]glorified God, saying,
[c]"A great prophet has risen up among us"; and, [d]"God has vis-
ited His people."
17 And this report about Him went throughout all Judea and
all the surrounding region.
18 [a]Then the disciples of John reported to him concerning
all these things.
19 And John, calling two of his disciples to *him,* sent *them* to
Jesus,[1] saying, "Are You [a]the Coming One, or do we look for
another?"
20 When the men had come to Him, they said, "John the
Baptist has sent us to You, saying, 'Are You the Coming One,
or do we look for another?'"
21 And that very hour He cured many of infirmities, afflic-
tions, and evil spirits; and to many blind He gave sight.
22 [a]Jesus answered and said to them, "Go and tell John the
things you have seen and heard: [b]that *the* blind [c]see, *the* lame
[d]walk, *the* lepers are [e]cleansed, *the* deaf [f]hear, *the* dead are
raised, [g]*the* poor have the gospel preached to them.
23 "And blessed is *he* who is not offended because of Me."
24 [a]When the messengers of John had departed, He began
to speak to the multitudes concerning John: "What did you
go out into the wilderness to see? A reed shaken by the wind?
25 "But what did you go out to see? A man clothed in soft

7:10[1] NU-Text omits *who had been sick.* 7:13[a] John 11:35 [b] Luke 8:52 7:14[a] Acts 9:40 7:15[a] John 11:44 [b] 2 Kin. 4:36 7:16[a] Luke 1:65 [b] Luke 5:26 [c] Luke 24:19 [d] Luke 1:68 7:18[a] Matt. 11:2–19 7:19[a] [Zech. 9:9] [1] NU-Text reads *the Lord.* 7:22[a] Matt. 11:4 [b] Is. 35:5 [c] John 9:7 [d] Matt. 15:31 [e] Luke 17:12–14 [f] Mark 7:37 [g] [Is. 61:1–3] 7:24[a] Matt. 11:7

garments? Indeed those who are gorgeously appareled and
live in luxury are in kings' courts.
26 "But what did you go out to see? A prophet? Yes, I say to
you, and more than a prophet.
27 "This is *he* of whom it is written:

> [a]'Behold, I send My messenger before Your face,
> Who will prepare Your way before You.'[1]

28 "For I say to you, among those born of women there is
not a [a]greater prophet than John the Baptist;[1] but he who is
least in the kingdom of God is greater than he."
29 And when all the people heard *Him,* even the tax collectors
justified God, [a]having been baptized with the baptism of John.
30 But the Pharisees and lawyers rejected [a]the will of God
for themselves, not having been baptized by him.
31 And the Lord said,[1] [a]"To what then shall I liken the men
of this generation, and what are they like?
32 "They are like children sitting in the marketplace and
calling to one another, saying:

> 'We played the flute for you,
> And you did not dance;
> We mourned to you,
> And you did not weep.'

33 "For [a]John the Baptist came [b]neither eating bread nor
drinking wine, and you say, 'He has a demon.'
34 "The Son of Man has come [a]eating and drinking, and you
say, 'Look, a glutton and a winebibber, a friend of tax collec-
tors and sinners!'
35 [a]"But wisdom is justified by all her children."
36 [a]Then one of the Pharisees asked Him to eat with him.
And He went to the Pharisee's house, and sat down to eat.
37 And behold, a woman in the city who was a sinner, when
she knew that *Jesus* sat at the table in the Pharisee's house,
brought an alabaster flask of fragrant oil,
38 and stood at His feet behind *Him* weeping; and she be-
gan to wash His feet with her tears, and wiped *them* with the
hair of her head; and she kissed His feet and anointed *them*
with the fragrant oil.
39 Now when the Pharisee who had invited Him saw *this,* he
spoke to himself, saying, [a]"This Man, if He were a prophet,
would know who and what manner of woman *this is* who is
touching Him, for she is a sinner."

7:27[a]Mal. 3:1 [1]Malachi 3:1 7:28[a][Luke 1:15] [1]NU-Text reads *there is none greater than John.* 7:29[a]Luke 3:12 7:30[a]Acts 20:27 7:31[a]Matt. 11:16 [1]NU-Text and M-Text omit *And the Lord said.* 7:33[a]Matt. 3:1 [b]Luke 1:15 7:34[a]Luke 15:2 7:35[a]Matt. 11:19 7:36[a]John 11:2 7:39[a]Luke 15:2

40 And Jesus answered and said to him, "Simon, I have
something to say to you." So he said, "Teacher, say it."
41 "There was a certain creditor who had two debtors. One
owed five hundred [a]denarii, and the other fifty.
42 "And when they had nothing with which to repay, he free-
ly forgave them both. Tell Me, therefore, which of them will
love him more?"
43 Simon answered and said, "I suppose the *one* whom he
forgave more." And He said to him, "You have rightly judged."
44 Then He turned to the woman and said to Simon, "Do
you see this woman? I entered your house; you gave Me no
[a]water for My feet, but she has washed My feet with her tears
and wiped *them* with the hair of her head.
45 "You gave Me no [a]kiss, but this woman has not ceased to
kiss My feet since the time I came in.
46 [a]"You did not anoint My head with oil, but this woman
has anointed My feet with fragrant oil.
47 [a]"Therefore I say to you, her sins, *which are* many, are
forgiven, for she loved much. But to whom little is forgiven,
the same loves little."
48 Then He said to her, [a]"Your sins are forgiven."
49 And those who sat at the table with Him began to say to
themselves, [a]"Who is this who even forgives sins?"
50 Then He said to the woman, [a]"Your faith has saved you.
Go in peace."

7:41[a]Matt. 18:28 7:44[a]Gen. 18:4; 19:2; 43:24 7:45[a]Rom. 16:16 7:46[a]Ps. 23:5 7:47[a][1 Tim. 1:14] 7:48[a]Matt. 9:2 7:49[a]Luke 5:21 7:50[a]Matt. 9:22

LUKE 8

PARABLES AND THEIR MEANING

The words of good cheer that our Savior spoke to this woman were not given to her while she was coming to Him, for that would have been premature. She had not avowed her desire to be healed; she had uttered no prayer; she had actually as yet sought nothing at the Savior's hands. The Savior was in the press, she joined the throng, and with a holy boldness mixed with a sacred modesty she came behind Him, wishing only to touch His garment or even the fringe of it; she felt persuaded that if she did but come into contact with the Lord, no matter how, she would be healed. According to her faith so was it done to her, and it was after she had been healed that our Lord spoke comfortingly to her.

It is one of the unwisest things under heaven to comfort people who do not require it. When we are dealing with enquirers, our love may bring them loss if we offer words of cheer when they need admonition or rebuke. Any comfort that keeps a soul short of Christ is dangerous. A sinner's main business is to get to Jesus Himself, to exercise personal faith in the personal Savior, and we have no right to a gleam of comfort until we have heartily and honestly trusted in Christ. If encouragements to believe are used as a sort of halfway house to rest in before actually believing, they are mischievously used and may ruin our souls.

---

1 Now it came to pass, afterward, that He went through ev-
ery city and village, preaching and bringing the glad tidings
of the kingdom of God. And the twelve *were* with Him,
2 and [a]certain women who had been healed of evil spirits
and infirmities—Mary called Magdalene, [b]out of whom had
come seven demons,
3 and Joanna the wife of Chuza, Herod's steward, and Su-
sanna, and many others who provided for Him[1] from their
substance.
4 [a]And when a great multitude had gathered, and they had
come to Him from every city, He spoke by a parable:
5 "A sower went out to sow his seed. And as he sowed, some
fell by the wayside; and it was trampled down, and the birds
of the air devoured it.
6 "Some fell on rock; and as soon as it sprang up, it withered
away because it lacked moisture.
7 "And some fell among thorns, and the thorns sprang up
with it and choked it.
8 "But others fell on good ground, sprang up, and yielded

8:2[a]Matt. 27:55 [b]Mark 16:9 8:3[1]NU-Text and M-Text read *them*. 8:4[a]Mark 4:1–9

a crop a hundredfold." When He had said these things He
cried, [a]"He who has ears to hear, let him hear!"
9 [a]Then His disciples asked Him, saying, "What does this
parable mean?"
10 And He said, "To you it has been given to know the mys-
teries of the kingdom of God, but to the rest *it is given* in par-
ables, that

> [a]'Seeing they may not see,
> And hearing they may not understand.'[1]

11 [a]"Now the parable is this: The seed is the [b]word of God.
12 "Those by the wayside are the ones who hear; then the
devil comes and takes away the word out of their hearts, lest
they should believe and be saved.
13 "But the ones on the rock *are those* who, when they hear,
receive the word with joy; and these have no root, who be-
lieve for a while and in time of temptation fall away.
14 "Now the ones *that* fell among thorns are those who, when
they have heard, go out and are choked with cares, [a]riches,
and pleasures of life, and bring no fruit to maturity.
15 "But the ones *that* fell on the good ground are those who,
having heard the word with a noble and good heart, keep *it*
and bear fruit with [a]patience.
16 [a]"No one, when he has lit a lamp, covers it with a vessel
or puts *it* under a bed, but sets *it* on a lampstand, that those
who enter may see the [b]light.
17 [a]"For nothing is secret that will not be [b]revealed, nor *any-
thing* hidden that will not be known and come to light.
18 "Therefore take heed how you hear. [a]For whoever has,
to him *more* will be given; and whoever does not have, even
what he seems to [b]have will be taken from him."
19 [a]Then His mother and brothers came to Him, and could
not approach Him because of the crowd.
20 And it was told Him *by some,* who said, "Your mother and
Your brothers are standing outside, desiring to see You."
21 But He answered and said to them, "My mother and My
brothers are these who hear the word of God and do it."
22 [a]Now it happened, on a certain day, that He got into a boat
with His disciples. And He said to them, "Let us cross over to
the other side of the lake." And they launched out.
23 But as they sailed He fell asleep. And a windstorm came
down on the lake, and they were filling *with water,* and were
in jeopardy.
24 And they came to Him and awoke Him, saying, "Master,

8:8[a]Luke 14:35 8:9[a]Matt. 13:10–23 8:10[a]Is. 6:9 [1]Isaiah 6:9 8:11[a][1 Pet. 1:23] [b]Luke 5:1; 11:28 8:14[a]1 Tim. 6:9, 10 8:15[a][Heb. 10:36–39] 8:16[a]Luke 11:33 [b]Matt. 5:14 8:17[a]Luke 12:2 [b][2 Cor. 5:10] 8:18[a]Matt. 25:29 [b]Matt. 13:12 8:19[a]Mark 3:31–35 8:22[a]Matt. 8:23–27

Master, we are perishing!" Then He arose and rebuked the
wind and the raging of the water. And they ceased, and there
was a calm.
25 But He said to them, [a]"Where is your faith?" And they were
afraid, and marveled, saying to one another, [b]"Who can this
be? For He commands even the winds and water, and they
obey Him!"
26 [a]Then they sailed to the country of the Gadarenes,[1] which
is opposite Galilee.
27 And when He stepped out on the land, there met Him a
certain man from the city who had demons for a long time.
And he wore no clothes,[1] nor did he live in a house but in the
tombs.
28 When he saw Jesus, he [a]cried out, fell down before Him,
and with a loud voice said, [b]"What have I to do with [c]You,
Jesus, Son of the Most High God? I beg You, do not tor-
ment me!"
29 For He had commanded the unclean spirit to come out
of the man. For it had often seized him, and he was kept un-
der guard, bound with chains and shackles; and he broke the
bonds and was driven by the demon into the wilderness.
30 Jesus asked him, saying, "What is your name?" And he
said, "Legion," because many demons had entered him.
31 And they begged Him that He would not command them
to go out [a]into the abyss.
32 Now a herd of many [a]swine was feeding there on the
mountain. So they begged Him that He would permit them
to enter them. And He permitted them.
33 Then the demons went out of the man and entered the
swine, and the herd ran violently down the steep place into
the lake and drowned.
34 When those who fed *them* saw what had happened, they
fled and told *it* in the city and in the country.
35 Then they went out to see what had happened, and came
to Jesus, and found the man from whom the demons had de-
parted, [a]sitting at the [b]feet of Jesus, clothed and in his [c]right
mind. And they were afraid.
36 They also who had seen *it* told them by what means he
who had been demon-possessed was healed.
37 [a]Then the whole multitude of the surrounding region of
the Gadarenes[1] [b]asked Him to [c]depart from them, for they
were seized with great [d]fear. And He got into the boat and
returned.
38 Now [a]the man from whom the demons had departed

8:25 [a]Luke 9:41 [b]Luke 4:36; 5:26 8:26 [a]Mark 5:1–17 [1]NU-Text reads *Gerasenes.*
8:27 [1]NU-Text reads *who had demons and for a long time wore no clothes.*
8:28 [a]Mark 1:26; 9:26 [b]Mark 1:23, 24 [c]Luke 4:41 8:31 [a][Rev. 20:1, 3] 8:32 [a]Lev. 11:7
8:35 [a][Matt. 11:28] [b]Luke 10:39; 17:16 [c][2 Tim. 1:7] 8:37 [a]Matt. 8:34 [b]Luke 4:34
[c]Acts 16:39 [d]Luke 5:26 [1]NU-Text reads *Gerasenes.* 8:38 [a]Mark 5:18–20

begged Him that he might be with Him. But Jesus sent him
away, saying,
39 "Return to your own house, and tell what great things
God has done for you." And he went his way and proclaimed
throughout the whole city what great things Jesus had done
for him.
40 So it was, when Jesus returned, that the multitude wel-
comed Him, for they were all waiting for Him.
41 [a]And behold, there came a man named Jairus, and he
was a ruler of the synagogue. And he fell down at Jesus' feet
and begged Him to come to his house,
42 for he had an only daughter about twelve years of age, and
she [a]was dying. But as He went, the multitudes thronged Him.
43 [a]Now a woman, having a [b]flow of blood for twelve years,
who had spent all her livelihood on physicians and could not
be healed by any,
44 came from behind and [a]touched the border of His gar-
ment. And immediately her flow of blood stopped.
45 And Jesus said, "Who touched Me?" When all denied
it, Peter and those with him[1] said, "Master, the multitudes
throng and press You, and You say, 'Who touched Me?' "[2]
46 But Jesus said, "Somebody touched Me, for I perceived
[a]power going out from Me."
47 Now when the woman saw that she was not hidden, she
came trembling; and falling down before Him, she declared
to Him in the presence of all the people the reason she had
touched Him and how she was healed immediately.
48 And He said to her, "Daughter, be of good cheer;[1] [a]your
faith has made you well. [b]Go in peace."
49 [a]While He was still speaking, someone came from the
ruler of the synagogue's *house,* saying to him, "Your daugh-
ter is dead. Do not trouble the Teacher."[1]
50 But when Jesus heard *it,* He answered him, saying, "Do
not be afraid; [a]only believe, and she will be made well."
51 When He came into the house, He permitted no one to
go in[1] except Peter, James, and John,[2] and the father and
mother of the girl.
52 Now all wept and mourned for her; but He said, [a]"Do not
weep; she is not dead, [b]but sleeping."
53 And they ridiculed Him, knowing that she was dead.
54 But He put them all outside,[1] took her by the hand and
called, saying, "Little girl, [a]arise."

8:41 [a]Mark 5:22–43 8:42 [a]Luke 7:2 8:43 [a]Matt. 9:20 [b]Luke 15:19–22 8:44 [a]Mark 6:56 8:45 [1]NU-Text omits *and those with him.* [2]NU-Text omits *and You say, 'Who touched Me?'* 8:46 [a]Mark 5:30 8:48 [a]Luke 7:50 [b]John 8:11 [1]NU-Text omits *be of good cheer.* 8:49 [a]Mark 5:35 [1]NU-Text adds *anymore.* 8:50 [a][Mark 11:22–24] 8:51 [1]NU-Text adds *with Him.* [2]NU-Text and M-Text read *Peter, John, and James.* 8:52 [a]Luke 7:13 [b][John 11:11, 13] 8:54 [a]John 11:43 [1]NU-Text omits *put them all outside.*

55 Then her spirit returned, and she arose immediately. And
He commanded that she be given *something* to eat.
56 And her parents were astonished, but [a]He charged them
to tell no one what had happened.

8:56[a]Matt. 8:4; 9:30

LUKE 9

JESUS FEEDS FIVE THOUSAND

The first man, a scribe, said, "Lord, I will follow You wherever You go." What that might mean, what that might involve he did not ask and therefore did not know. He was sincere as far as he knew, but then he did not know much.

Like our Lord, we meet with many persons who are great at resolving. They are willing to make that declaration as publicly as you like and stand up, fall down, or do anything else to declare that they have resolved. I frequently hear persons exhorted to give their hearts to Christ, which is a very proper exhortation; but that is not the gospel. Salvation comes from something that Christ gives you, not something that you give to Christ. The giving of your heart to Christ follows after the receiving from Christ of eternal life by faith. We cannot come to Christ unless Christ comes to us and gives us a broken heart and a contrite spirit.

If there be no repentance, depend on it that that faith we think we have is not the faith that will save us. Give me faith with tears in the eyes; I know that to be the true child of God. The faith that makes me feel my ruin, confess my sin, and lay hold of eternal life because otherwise my merits will bring me to eternal death—this is the faith that saves. But some people are very great at resolving rather than repenting and believing.

---

1 Then [a]He called His twelve disciples together and [b]gave
them power and authority over all demons, and to cure diseases.
2 [a]He sent them to preach the kingdom of God and to heal
the sick.
3 [a]And He said to them, "Take nothing for the journey, neither staffs nor bag nor bread nor money; and do not have
two tunics apiece.
4 [a]"Whatever house you enter, stay there, and from there
depart.
5 [a]"And whoever will not receive you, when you go out of
that city, [b]shake off the very dust from your feet as a testimony against them."
6 [a]So they departed and went through the towns, preaching
the gospel and healing everywhere.
7 [a]Now Herod the tetrarch heard of all that was done by Him;
and he was perplexed, because it was said by some that John
had risen from the dead,

9:1[a]Matt. 10:1, 2 [b][John 14:12] 9:2[a]Matt. 10:7, 8 9:3[a]Luke 10:4–12; 22:35 9:4[a]Mark 6:10 9:5[a]Matt. 10:14 [b]Acts 13:51 9:6[a]Mark 6:12 9:7[a]Matt. 14:1, 2

8 and by some that Elijah had appeared, and by others that
one of the old prophets had risen again.
9 Herod said, "John I have beheaded, but who is this of whom
I hear such things?" [a]So he sought to see Him.
10 [a]And the apostles, when they had returned, told Him all that
they had done. [b]Then He took them and went aside privately
into a deserted place belonging to the city called Bethsaida.
11 But when the multitudes knew *it,* they followed Him; and
He received them and spoke to them about the kingdom of
God, and healed those who had need of healing.
12 [a]When the day began to wear away, the twelve came and
said to Him, "Send the multitude away, that they may go into
the surrounding towns and country, and lodge and get pro-
visions; for we are in a deserted place here."
13 But He said to them, "You give them something to eat."
And they said, "We have no more than five loaves and two
fish, unless we go and buy food for all these people."
14 For there were about five thousand men. Then He said to
His disciples, "Make them sit down in groups of fifty."
15 And they did so, and made them all sit down.
16 Then He took the five loaves and the two fish, and looking
up to heaven, He [a]blessed and broke them, and gave *them* to
the disciples to set before the multitude.
17 So they all ate and were filled, and twelve baskets of the
leftover fragments were taken up by them.
18 [a]And it happened, as He was alone praying, *that* His dis-
ciples joined Him, and He asked them, saying, "Who do the
crowds say that I am?"
19 So they answered and said, [a]"John the Baptist, but some
say Elijah; and others *say* that one of the old prophets has
risen again."
20 He said to them, "But who do you say that I am?" [a]Peter
answered and said, "The Christ of God."
21 [a]And He strictly warned and commanded them to tell
this to no one,
22 saying, [a]"The Son of Man must suffer many things, and
be rejected by the elders and chief priests and scribes, and
be killed, and be raised the third day."
23 [a]Then He said to *them* all, "If anyone desires to come af-
ter Me, let him deny himself, and take up his cross daily,[1] and
follow Me.
24 [a]"For whoever desires to save his life will lose it, but who-
ever loses his life for My sake will save it.
25 [a]"For what profit is it to a man if he gains the whole world,
and is himself destroyed or lost?

9:9[a]Luke 23:8 9:10[a]Mark 6:30 [b]Matt. 14:13 9:12[a]John 6:1, 5 9:16[a]Luke 22:19; 24:30 9:18[a]Matt. 16:13–16 9:19[a]Matt. 14:2 9:20[a]John 6:68, 69 9:21[a]Matt. 8:4; 16:20 9:22[a]Matt. 16:21; 17:22 9:23[a]Matt. 10:38; 16:24 [1]M-Text omits *daily.* 9:24[a][John 12:25] 9:25[a]Mark 8:36

26 [a]"For whoever is ashamed of Me and My words, of him
the Son of Man will be [b]ashamed when He comes in His *own*
glory, and *in His* Father's, and of the holy angels.
27 [a]"But I tell you truly, there are some standing here who
shall not taste death till they see the kingdom of God."
28 [a]Now it came to pass, about eight days after these say-
ings, that He took Peter, John, and James and went up on the
mountain to pray.
29 As He prayed, the appearance of His face was altered, and
His robe *became* white *and* glistening.
30 And behold, two men talked with Him, who were [a]Moses
and [b]Elijah,
31 who appeared in glory and spoke of His decease which
He was about to accomplish at Jerusalem.
32 But Peter and those with him [a]were heavy with sleep; and
when they were fully awake, they saw His glory and the two
men who stood with Him.
33 Then it happened, as they were parting from Him, *that*
Peter said to Jesus, "Master, it is good for us to be here; and
let us make three tabernacles: one for You, one for Moses,
and one for Elijah"—not knowing what he said.
34 While he was saying this, a cloud came and overshadowed
them; and they were fearful as they entered the [a]cloud.
35 And a voice came out of the cloud, saying, [a]"This is My
beloved Son.[1] [b]Hear Him!"
36 When the voice had ceased, Jesus was found alone. [a]But
they kept quiet, and told no one in those days any of the
things they had seen.
37 [a]Now it happened on the next day, when they had come
down from the mountain, that a great multitude met Him.
38 Suddenly a man from the multitude cried out, saying,
"Teacher, I implore You, look on my son, for he is my only
child.
39 "And behold, a spirit seizes him, and he suddenly cries
out; it convulses him so that he foams *at the mouth;* and it
departs from him with great difficulty, bruising him.
40 "So I implored Your disciples to cast it out, but they
could not."
41 Then Jesus answered and said, "O faithless and perverse
generation, how long shall I be with you and bear with you?
Bring your son here."
42 And as he was still coming, the demon threw him down
and convulsed *him*. Then Jesus rebuked the unclean spirit,
healed the child, and gave him back to his father.
43 And they were all amazed at the majesty of God. But while

9:26 [a][Rom. 1:16] [b]Matt. 10:33 9:27 [a]Matt. 16:28 9:28 [a]Mark 9:2–8 9:30 [a]Heb. 11:23–29 [b]2 Kin. 2:1–11 9:32 [a]Dan. 8:18; 10:9 9:34 [a]Ex. 13:21 9:35 [a][Matt. 3:17; 12:18] [b]Acts 3:22 [1]NU-Text reads *This is My Son, the Chosen One.*
9:36 [a]Matt. 17:9 9:37 [a]Mark 9:14–27

everyone marveled at all the things which Jesus did, He said
to His disciples,
44 [a]"Let these words sink down into your ears, for the Son
of Man is about to be betrayed into the hands of men."
45 [a]But they did not understand this saying, and it was hid-
den from them so that they did not perceive it; and they were
afraid to ask Him about this saying.
46 [a]Then a dispute arose among them as to which of them
would be greatest.
47 And Jesus, [a]perceiving the thought of their heart, took a
[b]little child and set him by Him,
48 and said to them, [a]"Whoever receives this little child in
My name receives Me; and [b]whoever receives Me [c]receives
Him who sent Me. [d]For he who is least among you all will be
great."
49 [a]Now John answered and said, "Master, we saw someone
casting out demons in Your name, and we forbade him be-
cause he does not follow with us."
50 But Jesus said to him, "Do not forbid *him,* for [a]he who is
not against us[1] is on our[2] side."
51 Now it came to pass, when the time had come for [a]Him
to be received up, that He steadfastly set His face to go to Je-
rusalem,
52 and sent messengers before His face. And as they went,
they entered a village of the Samaritans, to prepare for Him.
53 But [a]they did not receive Him, because His face was *set*
for the journey to Jerusalem.
54 And when His disciples [a]James and John saw *this,* they
said, "Lord, do You want us to command fire to come down
from heaven and consume them, just as [b]Elijah did?"[1]
55 But He turned and rebuked them,[1] and said, "You do not
know what manner of [a]spirit you are of.
56 "For [a]the Son of Man did not come to destroy men's lives
but to save *them.*"[1] And they went to another village.
57 [a]Now it happened as they journeyed on the road, *that*
someone said to Him, "Lord, I will follow You wherever
You go."
58 And Jesus said to him, "Foxes have holes and birds of the
air *have* nests, but the Son of Man [a]has nowhere to lay *His*
head."
59 [a]Then He said to another, "Follow Me." But he said, "Lord,
let me first go and bury my father."

9:44 [a]Matt. 17:22 9:45 [a]Mark 9:32 9:46 [a]Matt. 18:1–5 9:47 [a]Matt. 9:4 [b]Luke 18:17 9:48 [a]Matt. 18:5 [b]John 12:44 [c]John 13:20 [d]Eph. 3:8 9:49 [a]Mark 9:38–40 9:50 [a]Luke 11:23 [1]NU-Text reads *you.* [2]NU-Text reads *your.* 9:51 [a]Mark 16:19 9:53 [a]John 4:4, 9 9:54 [a]Mark 3:17 [b]2 Kin. 1:10, 12 [1]NU-Text omits *just as Elijah did.* 9:55 [a][2 Tim. 1:7] [1]NU-Text omits the rest of this verse. 9:56 [a]John 3:17; 12:47 [1]NU-Text omits the first sentence of this verse. 9:57 [a]Matt. 8:19–22 9:58 [a]Luke 2:7; 8:23 9:59 [a]Matt. 8:21, 22

60 Jesus said to him, "Let the dead bury their own dead, but
you go and preach the kingdom of God."
61 And another also said, "Lord, [a]I will follow You, but let
me first go *and* bid them farewell who are at my house."
62 But Jesus said to him, "No one, having put his hand to
the plow, and looking back, is [a]fit for the kingdom of God."

9:61[a]1 Kin. 19:20 9:62[a]2 Tim. 4:10

LUKE 10

SENDING THE SEVENTY; THE GOOD SAMARITAN

Jesus tells us over and over again the manner in which we are to live toward our fellow men, and He lays great stress upon the love that should shine throughout the Christian character. The story of the good Samaritan is a case in point, for our Lord is there explaining a point that arose out of the question "What shall I do to inherit eternal life?" The question is legal, and the answer is to the point. But let it never be forgotten that what the law demands of us the gospel really produces in us. The law tells us what we ought to be, and it is one object of the gospel to raise us to that condition.

Hence our Savior's teaching, though it be eminently practical, is always evangelical: even in expounding the law He has always a gospel design. Two ends are served by His setting up a high standard of duty: on the one He slays the self-righteousness that claims to have kept the law; He makes men feel the impossibility of salvation by their own works. And, on the other hand, He calls believers away from all contentment with the mere decencies of life and the routine of outward religion and stimulates them to seek after the highest degree of holiness—that excellence of character that only His grace can give. I shall hold up the love of our neighbor not as a condition of salvation but as a fruit of it.

---

1 After these things the Lord appointed seventy others also,[1]
and [a]sent them two by two before His face into every city and
place where He Himself was about to go.
2 Then He said to them, [a]"The harvest truly *is* great, but the
laborers *are* few; therefore [b]pray the Lord of the harvest to
send out laborers into His harvest.
3 "Go your way; [a]behold, I send you out as lambs among
wolves.
4 [a]"Carry neither money bag, knapsack, nor sandals; and
[b]greet no one along the road.
5 [a]"But whatever house you enter, first say, 'Peace to this
house.'
6 "And if a son of peace is there, your peace will rest on it; if
not, it will return to you.
7 [a]"And remain in the same house, [b]eating and drinking such
things as they give, for [c]the laborer is worthy of his wages. Do
not go from house to house.

10:1[a]Mark 6:7 [1]NU-Text reads *seventy-two others.* 10:2[a]John 4:35 [b]2 Thess. 3:1
10:3[a]Matt. 10:16 10:4[a]Luke 9:3–5 [b]2 Kin. 4:29 10:5[a]Matt. 10:12
10:7[a]Matt. 10:11 [b]1 Cor. 10:27 [c]1 Tim. 5:18

8 "Whatever city you enter, and they receive you, eat such things as are set before you.

9 [a]"And heal the sick there, and say to them, [b]'The kingdom of God has come near to you.'

10 "But whatever city you enter, and they do not receive you, go out into its streets and say,

11 [a]'The very dust of your city which clings to us[1] we wipe off against you. Nevertheless know this, that the kingdom of God has come near you.'

12 "But[1] I say to you that [a]it will be more tolerable in that Day for Sodom than for that city.

13 [a]"Woe to you, Chorazin! Woe to you, Bethsaida! [b]For if the mighty works which were done in you had been done in Tyre and Sidon, they would have repented long ago, sitting in sackcloth and ashes.

14 "But it will be more tolerable for Tyre and Sidon at the judgment than for you.

15 [a]"And you, Capernaum, who are [b]exalted to heaven, [c]will be brought down to Hades.[1]

16 [a]"He who hears you hears Me, [b]he who rejects you rejects Me, and [c]he who rejects Me rejects Him who sent Me."

17 Then [a]the seventy[1] returned with joy, saying, "Lord, even the demons are subject to us in Your name."

18 And He said to them, [a]"I saw Satan fall like lightning from heaven.

19 "Behold, [a]I give you the authority to trample on serpents and scorpions, and over all the power of the enemy, and nothing shall by any means hurt you.

20 "Nevertheless do not rejoice in this, that the spirits are subject to you, but rather[1] rejoice because [a]your names are written in heaven."

21 [a]In that hour Jesus rejoiced in the Spirit and said, "I thank You, Father, Lord of heaven and earth, that You have hidden these things from *the* wise and prudent and revealed them to babes. Even so, Father, for so it seemed good in Your sight.

22 [a]"All[1] things have been delivered to Me by My Father, and [b]no one knows who the Son is except the Father, and who the Father is except the Son, and *the one* to whom the Son wills to reveal *Him*."

23 Then He turned to *His* disciples and said privately, [a]"Blessed *are* the eyes which see the things you see;

10:9[a]Mark 3:15 [b]Matt. 3:2; 10:7 10:11[a]Acts 13:51 [1]NU-Text reads *our feet.* 10:12[a]Matt. 10:15; 11:24 [1]NU-Text and M-Text omit *But.* 10:13[a]Matt. 11:21–23 [b]Ezek. 3:6 10:15[a]Matt. 11:23 [b]Is. 14:13–15 [c]Ezek. 26:20 [1]NU-Text reads *will you be exalted to heaven? You will be thrust down to Hades!* 10:16[a]John 13:20 [b]1 Thess. 4:8 [c]John 5:23 10:17[a]Luke 10:1 [1]NU-Text reads *seventy-two.* 10:18[a]John 12:31 10:19[a]Mark 16:18 10:20[a]Is. 4:3 [1]NU-Text and M-Text omit *rather.* 10:21[a]Matt. 11:25–27 10:22[a]John 3:35; 5:27; 17:2 [b][John 1:18; 6:44, 46] [1]M-Text reads *And turning to the disciples He said, "All . . . .* 10:23[a]Matt. 13:16, 17

24 "for I tell you [a]that many prophets and kings have de-
sired to see what you see, and have not seen *it,* and to hear
what you hear, and have not heard *it.*"
25 And behold, a certain lawyer stood up and tested Him,
saying, [a]"Teacher, what shall I do to inherit eternal life?"
26 He said to him, "What is written in the law? What is your
reading *of it?*"
27 So he answered and said, [a]" 'You shall love the LORD
your God with all your heart, with all your soul, with all your
strength, and with all your mind,'[1] and [b]'your neighbor as
yourself.' "[2]
28 And He said to him, "You have answered rightly; do this
and [a]you will live."
29 But he, wanting to [a]justify himself, said to Jesus, "And
who is my neighbor?"
30 Then Jesus answered and said: "A certain *man* went down
from Jerusalem to Jericho, and fell among thieves, who
stripped him of his clothing, wounded *him,* and departed,
leaving *him* half dead.
31 "Now by chance a certain priest came down that road.
And when he saw him, [a]he passed by on the other side.
32 "Likewise a Levite, when he arrived at the place, came
and looked, and passed by on the other side.
33 "But a certain [a]Samaritan, as he journeyed, came where
he was. And when he saw him, he had [b]compassion.
34 "So he went to *him* and bandaged his wounds, pouring
on oil and wine; and he set him on his own animal, brought
him to an inn, and took care of him.
35 "On the next day, when he departed,[1] he took out two [a]de-
narii, gave *them* to the innkeeper, and said to him, 'Take care
of him; and whatever more you spend, when I come again,
I will repay you.'
36 "So which of these three do you think was neighbor to
him who fell among the thieves?"
37 And he said, "He who showed mercy on him." Then Jesus
said to him, [a]"Go and do likewise."
38 Now it happened as they went that He entered a certain
village; and a certain woman named [a]Martha welcomed Him
into her house.
39 And she had a sister called Mary, [a]who also [b]sat at Jesus'[1]
feet and heard His word.
40 But Martha was distracted with much serving, and she
approached Him and said, "Lord, do You not care that my sis-
ter has left me to serve alone? Therefore tell her to help me."

10:24 [a]1 Pet. 1:10, 11 10:25 [a]Matt. 19:16–19; 22:35 10:27 [a]Deut. 6:5 [b]Lev. 19:18 [1]Deuteronomy 6:5 [2]Leviticus 19:18 10:28 [a]Ezek. 20:11, 13, 21 10:29 [a]Luke 16:15 10:31 [a]Ps. 38:11 10:33 [a]John 4:9 [b]Luke 15:20 10:35 [a]Matt. 20:2 [1]NU-Text omits *when he departed.* 10:37 [a]Prov. 14:21 10:38 [a]John 11:1; 12:2, 3 10:39 [a][1 Cor. 7:32–40] [b]Acts 22:3 [1]NU-Text reads *the Lord's.*

41 And Jesus[1] answered and said to her, "Martha, Martha,
you are worried and troubled about many things.
42 "But [a]one thing is needed, and Mary has chosen that good
part, which will not be taken away from her."

10:41[1] NU-Text reads *the Lord.* 10:42[a] [Ps. 27:4]

LUKE 11

JESUS TEACHES HOW TO PRAY

We are shown how to pray, but will God really answer us? Does it end with the benefit that it works in us, or does it really affect the heart of God? Do replies actually come from heaven in answer to the entreaties of God's children?

The answer is given by our Lord with great clearness. We have a parable to show that as importunity does evidently affect men, so importunity will also gain an answer from God, that He will be pleased to give us what we need if we do but know how, with incessant earnestness, to come again and again to Him in prayer. We are assured that asking is attended with receiving, seeking is attended with finding, knocking will lead to opening. It is not a vain thing to pray; our prayers are not lost on the wind or expended merely on ourselves, but there is a connection established by divine decree between the prayer that is raised on earth and the mercy that is given forth from heaven.

But since we are such sinful creatures, these verses deal with a grave doubt that may arise in the troubled mind. The truth here taught is not that God will refuse us evil things if in our mistake we ask for them. The one statement of this verse is that prayers for good things will be answered—and they will be answered not with gifts merely appearing to be good but with the actual good things desired.

---

1 Now it came to pass, as He was praying in a certain place,
when He ceased, *that* one of His disciples said to Him, "Lord,
teach us to pray, as John also taught his disciples."
2 So He said to them, "When you pray, say:

[a]Our Father in heaven,[1]
Hallowed be Your name.
Your kingdom come.[2]
Your will be done
On earth as *it is* in heaven.
3 Give us day by day our daily bread.
4 And [a]forgive us our sins,
For we also forgive everyone
who is indebted to us.
And do not lead us into temptation,
But deliver us from the evil one."[1]

11:2[a]Matt. 6:9–13 [1]NU-Text omits *Our* and *in heaven.* [2]NU-Text omits the rest of this verse. 11:4[a][Eph. 4:32] [1]NU-Text omits *But deliver us from the evil one.*

5 And He said to them, "Which of you shall have a friend,
and go to him at midnight and say to him, 'Friend, lend me
three loaves;
6 'for a friend of mine has come to me on his journey, and I
have nothing to set before him';
7 "and he will answer from within and say, 'Do not trouble
me; the door is now shut, and my children are with me in
bed; I cannot rise and give to you'?
8 "I say to you, [a]though he will not rise and give to him be-
cause he is his friend, yet because of his persistence he will
rise and give him as many as he needs.
9 [a]"So I say to you, ask, and it will be given to you; [b]seek, and
you will find; knock, and it will be opened to you.
10 "For everyone who asks receives, and he who seeks finds,
and to him who knocks it will be opened.
11 [a]"If a son asks for bread[1] from any father among you, will
he give him a stone? Or if *he asks* for a fish, will he give him
a serpent instead of a fish?
12 "Or if he asks for an egg, will he offer him a scorpion?
13 "If you then, being evil, know how to give [a]good gifts to
your children, how much more will *your* heavenly Father
give the Holy Spirit to those who ask Him!"
14 [a]And He was casting out a demon, and it was mute. So
it was, when the demon had gone out, that the mute spoke;
and the multitudes marveled.
15 But some of them said, [a]"He casts out demons by Beelze-
bub,[1] the ruler of the demons."
16 Others, testing *Him,* [a]sought from Him a sign from heaven.
17 [a]But [b]He, knowing their thoughts, said to them: "Every
kingdom divided against itself is brought to desolation, and
a house *divided* against a house falls.
18 "If Satan also is divided against himself, how will his king-
dom stand? Because you say I cast out demons by Beelzebub.
19 "And if I cast out demons by Beelzebub, by whom do your
sons cast *them* out? Therefore they will be your judges.
20 "But if I cast out demons [a]with the finger of God, surely
the kingdom of God has come upon you.
21 [a]"When a strong man, fully armed, guards his own pal-
ace, his goods are in peace.
22 "But [a]when a stronger than he comes upon him and
overcomes him, he takes from him all his armor in which
he trusted, and divides his spoils.
23 [a]"He who is not with Me is against Me, and he who does
not gather with Me scatters.

11:8[a][Luke 18:1–5] 11:9[a][John 15:7] [b]Is. 55:6 11:11[a]Matt. 7:9 [1]NU-Text omits the words from *bread* through *for* in the next sentence. 11:13[a]James 1:17 11:14[a]Matt. 9:32–34; 12:22, 24 11:15[a]Matt. 9:34; 12:24 [1]NU-Text and M-Text read *Beelzebul.* 11:16[a]Matt. 12:38; 16:1 11:17[a]Matt. 12:25–29 [b]John 2:25 11:20[a]Ex. 8:19 11:21[a]Mark 3:27 11:22[a][Is. 53:12] 11:23[a]Matt. 12:30

24 [a]"When an unclean spirit goes out of a man, he goes
through dry places, seeking rest; and finding none, he says,
'I will return to my house from which I came.'
25 "And when he comes, he finds *it* swept and put in order.
26 "Then he goes and takes with *him* seven other spirits
more wicked than himself, and they enter and dwell there;
and [a]the last *state* of that man is worse than the first."
27 And it happened, as He spoke these things, that a certain
woman from the crowd raised her voice and said to Him,
[a]"Blessed *is* the womb that bore You, and *the* breasts which
nursed You!"
28 But He said, [a]"More than that, blessed *are* those who hear
the word of God and keep it!"
29 [a]And while the crowds were thickly gathered together,
He began to say, "This is an evil generation. It seeks a [b]sign,
and no sign will be given to it except the sign of Jonah the
prophet.[1]
30 "For as [a]Jonah became a sign to the Ninevites, so also the
Son of Man will be to this generation.
31 [a]"The queen of the South will rise up in the judgment
with the men of this generation and condemn them, for she
came from the ends of the earth to hear the wisdom of Sol-
omon; and indeed a [b]greater than Solomon *is* here.
32 "The men of Nineveh will rise up in the judgment with
this generation and condemn it, for [a]they repented at the
preaching of Jonah; and indeed a greater than Jonah *is*
here.
33 [a]"No one, when he has lit a lamp, puts *it* in a secret place
or under a [b]basket, but on a lampstand, that those who come
in may see the light.
34 [a]"The lamp of the body is the eye. Therefore, when your
eye is good, your whole body also is full of light. But when
your eye is bad, your body also *is* full of darkness.
35 "Therefore take heed that the light which is in you is not
darkness.
36 "If then your whole body *is* full of light, having no part
dark, *the* whole *body* will be full of light, as when the bright
shining of a lamp gives you light."
37 And as He spoke, a certain Pharisee asked Him to dine
with him. So He went in and sat down to eat.
38 [a]When the Pharisee saw *it,* he marveled that He had not
first washed before dinner.
39 [a]Then the Lord said to him, "Now you Pharisees make
the outside of the cup and dish clean, but [b]your inward part
is full of greed and wickedness.

11:24[a]Matt. 12:43–45 11:26[a][2 Pet. 2:20] 11:27[a]Luke 1:28, 48 11:28[a][Luke 8:21] 11:29[a]Matt. 12:38–42 [b]1 Cor. 1:22 [1]NU-Text omits *the prophet.* 11:30[a]Jon. 1:17; 2:10; 3:3–10 11:31[a]1 Kin. 10:1–9 [b][Rom. 9:5] 11:32[a]Jon. 3:5 11:33[a]Mark 4:21 [b]Matt. 5:15 11:34[a]Matt. 6:22, 23 11:38[a]Mark 7:2, 3 11:39[a]Matt. 23:25 [b]Titus 1:15

40 "Foolish ones! Did not [a]He who made the outside make
the inside also?
41 [a]"But rather give alms of such things as you have; then
indeed all things are clean to you.
42 [a]"But woe to you Pharisees! For you tithe mint and rue
and all manner of herbs, and [b]pass by justice and the [c]love
of God. These you ought to have done, without leaving the
others undone.
43 [a]"Woe to you Pharisees! For you love the best seats in the
synagogues and greetings in the marketplaces.
44 [a]"Woe to you, scribes and Pharisees, hypocrites![1] [b]For you
are like graves which are not seen, and the men who walk
over *them* are not aware *of them*."
45 Then one of the lawyers answered and said to Him,
"Teacher, by saying these things You reproach us also."
46 And He said, "Woe to you also, lawyers! [a]For you load men
with burdens hard to bear, and you yourselves do not touch
the burdens with one of your fingers.
47 [a]"Woe to you! For you build the tombs of the prophets,
and your fathers killed them.
48 "In fact, you bear witness that you approve the deeds of
your fathers; for they indeed killed them, and you build their
tombs.
49 "Therefore the wisdom of God also said, [a]'I will send them
prophets and apostles, and *some* of them they will kill and
persecute,'
50 "that the blood of all the prophets which was shed from
the foundation of the world may be required of this genera-
tion,
51 [a]"from the blood of Abel to [b]the blood of Zechariah who
perished between the altar and the temple. Yes, I say to you,
it shall be required of this generation.
52 [a]"Woe to you lawyers! For you have taken away the key of
knowledge. You did not enter in yourselves, and those who
were entering in you hindered."
53 And as He said these things to them,[1] the scribes and
the Pharisees began to assail *Him* vehemently, and to cross-
examine Him about many things,
54 lying in wait for Him, and [a]seeking to catch Him in some-
thing He might say, that they might accuse Him.[1]

11:40 [a]Gen. 1:26, 27 11:41 [a][Luke 12:33; 16:9] 11:42 [a]Matt. 23:23 [b][Mic. 6:7, 8] [c]John 5:42 11:43 [a]Mark 12:38, 39 11:44 [a]Matt. 23:27 [b]Ps. 5:9 [1]NU-Text omits *scribes and Pharisees, hypocrites.* 11:46 [a]Matt. 23:4 11:47 [a]Matt. 23:29 11:49 [a]Matt. 23:34 11:51 [a]Gen. 4:8 [b]2 Chr. 24:20, 21 11:52 [a]Matt. 23:13 11:53 [1]NU-Text reads *And when He left there.* 11:54 [a]Mark 12:13 [1]NU-Text omits *and seeking* and *that they might accuse Him.*

LUKE 12

JESUS PREACHES TO THE MULTITUDE

A Fear-Not is a plant that grows very plentifully in God's garden. If you look through the lily beds of Scripture, you will continually find by the other flowers the sweet Fear-Nots peering out from among doctrines and precepts even as violets look up from green leaves. If you are a meek and quiet spirit and rather apt to tremble exceedingly, may the Lord often give you a blessed Fear-Not to wear on your chest that its fragrance may comfort your heart. Fear-Nots are scattered throughout the Bible as the stars are sprinkled over the whole of the sky.

Here are a few of His antidotes for the fever of fear: "Say to those who are fearful-hearted, 'Be strong, do not fear!'" (Is. 35:4). "Fear not, for I am with you; be not dismayed, for I am your God" (Is. 41:10). "Fear not, I will help you" (Is. 41:13). "Fear not, for I have redeemed you" (Is. 43:1). "Do not fear, for you will not be ashamed; neither be disgraced, for you will not be put to shame" (Is. 54:4)—and so on, "world without end" (Eph. 3:21 KJV). So abundant are these "Do not fears" that they grow like the kingcups, daisies, and other sweet flowers of the meadows where the little children in the springtime delight themselves. As to gathering them all, no one would attempt the task. The bank that is fullest of these beautiful flowers is that which Isaiah has cast up: go there and pluck them for yourselves.

---

1 In [a]the meantime, when an innumerable multitude of
people had gathered together, so that they trampled one an-
other, He began to say to His disciples first *of all*, [b]"Beware of
the leaven of the Pharisees, which is hypocrisy.
2 [a]"For there is nothing covered that will not be revealed,
nor hidden that will not be known.
3 "Therefore whatever you have spoken in the dark will be
heard in the light, and what you have spoken in the ear in
inner rooms will be proclaimed on the housetops.
4 [a]"And I say to you, [b]My friends, do not be afraid of those who
kill the body, and after that have no more that they can do.
5 "But I will show you whom you should fear: Fear Him who,
after He has killed, has power to cast into hell; yes, I say to
you, [a]fear Him!
6 "Are not five sparrows sold for two copper coins?[1] And [a]not
one of them is forgotten before God.

12:1[a]Mark 8:15 [b]Matt. 16:12 12:2[a]Matt. 10:26; [1 Cor. 4:5] 12:4[a]Is. 51:7, 8, 12, 13 [b][John 15:13–15] 12:5[a]Ps. 119:120 12:6[a]Matt. 6:26 [1]Greek *assarion,* a coin of very small value

7 "But the very hairs of your head are all numbered. Do not
fear therefore; you are of more value than many sparrows.
8 [a]"Also I say to you, whoever confesses Me [b]before men, him
the Son of Man also will confess before the angels of God.
9 "But he who [a]denies Me before men will be denied before
the angels of God.
10 "And [a]anyone who speaks a word against the Son of Man,
it will be forgiven him; but to him who blasphemes against
the Holy Spirit, it will not be forgiven.
11 [a]"Now when they bring you to the synagogues and mag-
istrates and authorities, do not worry about how or what you
should answer, or what you should say.
12 "For the Holy Spirit will [a]teach you in that very hour what
you ought to say."
13 Then one from the crowd said to Him, "Teacher, tell my
brother to divide the inheritance with me."
14 But He said to him, [a]"Man, who made Me a judge or an
arbitrator over you?"
15 And He said to them, [a]"Take heed and beware of covet-
ousness,[1] for one's life does not consist in the abundance of
the things he possesses."
16 Then He spoke a parable to them, saying: "The ground of
a certain rich man yielded plentifully.
17 "And he thought within himself, saying, 'What shall I do,
since I have no room to store my crops?'
18 "So he said, 'I will do this: I will pull down my barns and
build greater, and there I will store all my crops and my goods.
19 'And I will say to my soul, [a]"Soul, you have many goods
laid up for many years; take your ease; [b]eat, drink, *and* be
merry."'
20 "But God said to him, 'Fool! This night [a]your soul will be
required of you; [b]then whose will those things be which you
have provided?'
21 "So *is* he who lays up treasure for himself, [a]and is not rich
toward God."
22 Then He said to His disciples, "Therefore I say to you, [a]do
not worry about your life, what you will eat; nor about the
body, what you will put on.
23 "Life is more than food, and the body *is more* than cloth-
ing.
24 "Consider the ravens, for they neither sow nor reap, which
have neither storehouse nor barn; and [a]God feeds them. Of
how much more value are you than the birds?
25 "And which of you by worrying can add one cubit to his
stature?

12:8[a]Matt. 10:32 [b]Ps. 119:46 12:9[a]Matt. 10:33 12:10[a][Matt. 12:31, 32] 12:11[a]Mark 13:11 12:12[a][John 14:26] 12:14[a][John 18:36] 12:15[a][1 Tim. 6:6–10] [1]NU-Text reads *all covetousness.* 12:19[a]Eccl. 11:9 [b][Eccl. 2:24; 3:13; 5:18; 8:15] 12:20[a]Ps. 52:7 [b]Ps. 39:6 12:21[a][James 2:5; 5:1–5] 12:22[a]Matt. 6:25–33 12:24[a]Job 38:41

26 "If you then are not able to do *the* least, why are you anx-
ious for the rest?
27 "Consider the lilies, how they grow: they neither toil nor
spin; and yet I say to you, even [a]Solomon in all his glory was
not arrayed like one of these.
28 "If then God so clothes the grass, which today is in the
field and tomorrow is thrown into the oven, how much more
will He clothe you, O *you* of [a]little faith?
29 "And do not seek what you should eat or what you should
drink, nor have an anxious mind.
30 "For all these things the nations of the world seek after,
and your Father [a]knows that you need these things.
31 [a]"But seek the kingdom of God, and all these things[1] shall
be added to you.
32 "Do not fear, little flock, for [a]it is your Father's good plea-
sure to give you the kingdom.
33 [a]"Sell what you have and give [b]alms; [c]provide yourselves
money bags which do not grow old, a treasure in the heav-
ens that does not fail, where no thief approaches nor moth
destroys.
34 "For where your treasure is, there your heart will be also.
35 [a]"Let your waist be girded and [b]*your* lamps burning;
36 "and you yourselves be like men who wait for their master,
when he will return from the wedding, that when he comes
and knocks they may open to him immediately.
37 [a]"Blessed *are* those servants whom the master, when he
comes, will find watching. Assuredly, I say to you that he will
gird himself and have them sit down *to eat,* and will come
and serve them.
38 "And if he should come in the second watch, or come
in the third watch, and find *them* so, blessed are those ser-
vants.
39 [a]"But know this, that if the master of the house had known
what hour the thief would come, he would have watched and[1]
not allowed his house to be broken into.
40 [a]"Therefore you also be ready, for the Son of Man is com-
ing at an hour you do not expect."
41 Then Peter said to Him, "Lord, do You speak this parable
only to us, or to all *people?*"
42 And the Lord said, [a]"Who then is that faithful and wise
steward, whom *his* master will make ruler over his house-
hold, to give *them their* portion of food in due season?
43 "Blessed *is* that servant whom his master will find so do-
ing when he comes.

12:27[a]1 Kin. 10:4–7 12:28[a]Matt. 6:30; 8:26; 14:31; 16:8 12:30[a]Matt. 6:31, 32
12:31[a]Matt. 6:33 [1]NU-Text reads *His kingdom, and these things.* 12:32[a][Matt. 11:25, 26] 12:33[a]Matt. 19:21 [b]Luke 11:41 [c]Matt. 6:20 12:35[a][1 Pet. 1:13] [b][Matt. 25:1–13]
12:37[a]Matt. 24:46 12:39[a]Rev. 3:3; 16:15 [1]NU-Text reads *he would not have allowed.*
12:40[a]Mark 13:33 12:42[a]Matt. 24:45, 46; 25:21

44 [a]"Truly, I say to you that he will make him ruler over all
that he has.
45 [a]"But if that servant says in his heart, 'My master is de-
laying his coming,' and begins to beat the male and female
servants, and to eat and drink and be drunk,
46 "the master of that servant will come on a [a]day when he
is not looking for *him,* and at an hour when he is not aware,
and will cut him in two and appoint *him* his portion with the
unbelievers.
47 "And [a]that servant who [b]knew his master's will, and did
not prepare *himself* or do according to his will, shall be beat-
en with many *stripes.*
48 [a]"But he who did not know, yet committed things de-
serving of stripes, shall be beaten with few. For everyone to
whom much is given, from him much will be required; and
to whom much has been committed, of him they will ask the
more.
49 [a]"I came to send fire on the earth, and how I wish it were
already kindled!
50 "But [a]I have a baptism to be baptized with, and how dis-
tressed I am till it is [b]accomplished!
51 [a]"Do *you* suppose that I came to give peace on earth? I
tell you, not at all, [b]but rather division.
52 [a]"For from now on five in one house will be divided: three
against two, and two against three.
53 [a]"Father will be divided against son and son against fa-
ther, mother against daughter and daughter against mother,
mother-in-law against her daughter-in-law and daughter-in-
law against her mother-in-law."
54 Then He also said to the multitudes, [a]"Whenever you see
a cloud rising out of the west, immediately you say, 'A shower
is coming'; and so it is.
55 "And when you see the [a]south wind blow, you say, 'There
will be hot weather'; and there is.
56 "Hypocrites! You can discern the face of the sky and of
the earth, but how *is it* you do not discern [a]this time?
57 "Yes, and why, even of yourselves, do you not judge what
is right?
58 [a]"When you go with your adversary to the magistrate,
make every effort [b]along the way to settle with him, lest he
drag you to the judge, the judge deliver you to the officer, and
the officer throw you into prison.
59 "I tell you, you shall not depart from there till you have
paid the very last mite."

12:44[a]Matt. 24:47; 25:21 12:45[a]2 Pet. 3:3, 4 12:46[a]1 Thess. 5:3 12:47[a]Deut. 25:2 [b][James 4:17] 12:48[a][Lev. 5:17] 12:49[a]Luke 12:51 12:50[a]Mark 10:38 [b]John 12:27; 19:30 12:51[a]Matt. 10:34–36 [b]John 7:43; 9:16; 10:19 12:52[a]Mark 13:12 12:53[a]Matt. 10:21, 36 12:54[a]Matt. 16:2, 3 12:55[a]Job 37:17 12:56[a]Luke 19:41–44 12:58[a]Prov. 25:8 [b][Is. 55:6]

LUKE 13

PARABLES OF THE KINGDOM

In this parable, light is thrown upon the work of those who teach the gospel. Notice a very simple work. The work of teaching the gospel is as the casting of a grain of mustard seed into a garden. The teacher should know what he is going to teach, to have that truth distinctly in his mind's eye, as the man had the grain of mustard seed between his fingers. Depend on it: unless a truth is clearly seen and distinctly recognized by the teacher, little will come of it to the taught.

If a man takes it, understands it, grasps it, and loves it, he will do something with it. Beloved, first and foremost let us ourselves take the gospel, let us believe it, let us appreciate it, let us prize it beyond all things, for truth lives as it is loved, and no hand is so fit for its sowing as the hand that grasps it well.

Further, this man had a garden. Some Christian people have no garden—no personal sphere of service. This man simply cast it into his garden. He did not wrap it around with gold leaf or otherwise adorn it, but he put it into the ground. The naked seed came into contact with the naked soil. O teachers, do not try to make the gospel look fine; do not overlay it with your fine words or elaborate explanations. The gospel seed is to be put into the young heart just as it is.

---

1 There were present at that season some who told Him
about the Galileans whose blood Pilate had mingled with
their sacrifices.
2 And Jesus answered and said to them, "Do you suppose
that these Galileans were worse sinners than all *other* Gali-
leans, because they suffered such things?
3 "I tell you, no; but unless you repent you will all likewise
perish.
4 "Or those eighteen on whom the tower in Siloam fell and
killed them, do you think that they were worse sinners than
all *other* men who dwelt in Jerusalem?
5 "I tell you, no; but unless you repent you will all likewise
perish."
6 He also spoke this parable: [a]"A certain *man* had a fig tree
planted in his vineyard, and he came seeking fruit on it and
found none.
7 "Then he said to the keeper of his vineyard, 'Look, for three
years I have come seeking fruit on this fig tree and find none.
Cut it down; why does it use up the ground?'

13:6[a]Matt. 21:19

8 "But he answered and said to him, 'Sir, let it alone this year
also, until I dig around it and fertilize *it*.
9 'And if it bears fruit, *well*. But if not, after that[1] you can [a]cut
it down.'"
10 Now He was teaching in one of the synagogues on the
Sabbath.
11 And behold, there was a woman who had a spirit of infir-
mity eighteen years, and was bent over and could in no way
raise *herself* up.
12 But when Jesus saw her, He called *her* to *Him* and said to
her, "Woman, you are loosed from your [a]infirmity."
13 [a]And He laid *His* hands on her, and immediately she was
made straight, and glorified God.
14 But the ruler of the synagogue answered with indigna-
tion, because Jesus had [a]healed on the Sabbath; and he said
to the crowd, [b]"There are six days on which men ought to
work; therefore come and be healed on them, and [c]not on
the Sabbath day."
15 The Lord then answered him and said, "Hypocrite![1] [a]Does
not each one of you on the Sabbath loose his ox or donkey
from the stall, and lead *it* away to water it?
16 "So ought not this woman, [a]being a daughter of Abraham,
whom Satan has bound—think of it—for eighteen years, be
loosed from this bond on the Sabbath?"
17 And when He said these things, all His adversaries were
put to shame; and all the multitude rejoiced for all the glo-
rious things that were [a]done by Him.
18 [a]Then He said, "What is the kingdom of God like? And to
what shall I compare it?
19 "It is like a mustard seed, which a man took and put in his
garden; and it grew and became a large[1] tree, and the birds
of the air nested in its branches."
20 And again He said, "To what shall I liken the kingdom
of God?
21 "It is like leaven, which a woman took and hid in three
[a]measures[1] of meal till it was all leavened."
22 [a]And He went through the cities and villages, teaching,
and journeying toward Jerusalem.
23 Then one said to Him, "Lord, are there [a]few who are
saved?" And He said to them,
24 [a]"Strive to enter through the narrow gate, for [b]many, I
say to you, will seek to enter and will not be able.
25 [a]"When once the Master of the house has risen up and

13:9[a][John 15:2] [1]NU-Text reads *And if it bears fruit after that, well. But if not, you can cut it down.* 13:12[a]Luke 7:21; 8:2 13:13[a]Acts 9:17 13:14[a][Luke 6:6–11; 14:1–6] [b]Ex. 20:9; 23:12 [c]Mark 3:2 13:15[a]Luke 14:5 [1]NU-Text and M-Text read *Hypocrites.* 13:16[a]Luke 19:9 13:17[a]Mark 5:19, 20 13:18[a]Mark 4:30–32 13:19[1]NU-Text omits *large.* 13:21[a]Matt. 13:33 [1]Greek *sata,* approximately two pecks in all 13:22[a]Mark 6:6 13:23[a][Matt. 7:14; 20:16] 13:24[a][Matt. 7:13] [b][John 7:34; 8:21; 13:33] 13:25[a]Is. 55:6

[b]shut the door, and you begin to stand outside and knock at
the door, saying, [c]'Lord, Lord, open for us,' and He will answer
and say to you, [d]'I do not know you, where you are from,'
26 "then you will begin to say, 'We ate and drank in Your
presence, and You taught in our streets.'
27 [a]"But He will say, 'I tell you I do not know you, where you
are from. [b]Depart from Me, all you workers of iniquity.'
28 [a]"There will be weeping and gnashing of teeth, [b]when
you see Abraham and Isaac and Jacob and all the prophets
in the kingdom of God, and yourselves thrust out.
29 "They will come from the east and the west, from the
north and the south, and sit down in the kingdom of God.
30 [a]"And indeed there are last who will be first, and there
are first who will be last."
31 On that very day[1] some Pharisees came, saying to Him,
"Get out and depart from here, for Herod wants to kill You."
32 And He said to them, "Go, tell that fox, 'Behold, I cast out
demons and perform cures today and tomorrow, and the
third *day* [a]I shall be perfected.'
33 "Nevertheless I must journey today, tomorrow, and the
day following; for it cannot be that a prophet should perish
outside of Jerusalem.
34 [a]"O Jerusalem, Jerusalem, the one who kills the proph-
ets and stones those who are sent to her! How often I wanted
to gather your children together, as a hen *gathers* her brood
under *her* wings, but you were not willing!
35 "See! [a]Your house is left to you desolate; and assuredly,[1] I
say to you, you shall not see Me until *the time* comes when you
say, [b]'Blessed is He who comes in the name of the LORD!'"[2]

13:25[b]Matt. 25:10 [c]Luke 6:46 [d]Matt. 7:23; 25:12 13:27[a][Matt. 7:23; 25:41] [b]Ps. 6:8 13:28[a]Matt. 8:12; 13:42; 24:51 [b]Matt. 8:11 13:30[a][Matt. 19:30; 20:16] 13:31[1]NU-Text reads *In that very hour.* 13:32[a][Heb. 2:10; 5:9; 7:28] 13:34[a]Matt. 23:37–39 13:35[a]Lev. 26:31, 32 [b]Ps. 118:26; Matt. 21:9 [1]NU-Text and M-Text omit *assuredly.* [2]Psalm 118:26

LUKE 14

THE PARABLE OF THE GREAT SUPPER

"Come, for all things are now ready"—not some, but all. There is nothing you can need between here and heaven but what is provided in Jesus Christ, in His Person and in His work. All things are ready—life for your death, forgiveness for your sin, cleansing for your filth, clothing for your nakedness, joy for your sorrow, strength for your weakness—yea, more than all that ever you can want is stored up in the boundless nature and work of Christ.

You must not say, "I cannot come because I have not this or that." Are you to prepare the feast? Are you to provide anything? Are you the purveyor of even so much as the salt or the water? You know not your true condition, or you would not dream of such a thing. The great Householder Himself has provided the whole of the feast; you have nothing to do with the provision but to partake of it. If you lack, come and take what you lack; the greater your need, the greater reason why you should come where all things you need will be at once supplied. If you be so needy that you have nothing good at all about you, all things are ready. What would you provide more when God has provided all things? All that you want, all is provided and prepared in Jesus Christ the Savior.

---

1 Now it happened, as He went into the house of one of the rulers of the Pharisees to eat bread on the Sabbath, that they watched Him closely.
2 And behold, there was a certain man before Him who had dropsy.
3 And Jesus, answering, spoke to the lawyers and Pharisees, saying, [a]"Is it lawful to heal on the Sabbath?"[1]
4 But they kept silent. And He took *him* and healed him, and let him go.
5 Then He answered them, saying, [a]"Which of you, having a donkey[1] or an ox that has fallen into a pit, will not immediately pull him out on the Sabbath day?"
6 And they could not answer Him regarding these things.
7 So He told a parable to those who were invited, when He noted how they chose the best places, saying to them:
8 "When you are invited by anyone to a wedding feast, do not sit down in the best place, lest one more honorable than you be invited by him;
9 "and he who invited you and him come and say to you,

14:3[a]Matt. 12:10 [1]NU-Text adds *or not.* 14:5[a][Ex. 23:5] [1]NU-Text and M-Text read *son.*

'Give place to this man,' and then you begin with shame to
take the lowest place.
10 [a]"But when you are invited, go and sit down in the lowest
place, so that when he who invited you comes he may say to
you, 'Friend, go up higher.' Then you will have glory in the
presence of those who sit at the table with you.
11 [a]"For whoever exalts himself will be humbled, and he who
humbles himself will be exalted."
12 Then He also said to him who invited Him, "When you give
a dinner or a supper, do not ask your friends, your brothers,
your relatives, nor rich neighbors, lest they also invite you
back, and you be repaid.
13 "But when you give a feast, invite [a]*the* poor, *the* maimed,
the lame, *the* blind.
14 "And you will be [a]blessed, because they cannot repay you;
for you shall be repaid at the resurrection of the just."
15 Now when one of those who sat at the table with Him
heard these things, he said to Him, [a]"Blessed *is* he who shall
eat bread[1] in the kingdom of God!"
16 [a]Then He said to him, "A certain man gave a great supper
and invited many,
17 "and [a]sent his servant at supper time to say to those who
were invited, 'Come, for all things are now ready.'
18 "But they all with one *accord* began to make excuses. The
first said to him, 'I have bought a piece of ground, and I must
go and see it. I ask you to have me excused.'
19 "And another said, 'I have bought five yoke of oxen, and
I am going to test them. I ask you to have me excused.'
20 "Still another said, 'I have married a wife, and therefore
I cannot come.'
21 "So that servant came and reported these things to his
master. Then the master of the house, being angry, said to
his servant, 'Go out quickly into the streets and lanes of the
city, and bring in here *the* poor and *the* maimed and *the* lame
and *the* blind.'
22 "And the servant said, 'Master, it is done as you commanded,
and still there is room.'
23 "Then the master said to the servant, 'Go out into the
highways and hedges, and compel *them* to come in, that my
house may be filled.
24 'For I say to you [a]that none of those men who were invited
shall taste my supper.'"
25 Now great multitudes went with Him. And He turned and
said to them,
26 [a]"If anyone comes to Me [b]and does not hate his father

14:10[a]Prov. 25:6, 7 14:11[a]Matt. 23:12 14:13[a]Neh. 8:10, 12 14:14[a][Matt. 25:34–40] 14:15[a]Rev. 19:9 [1]M-Text reads *dinner.* 14:16[a]Matt. 22:2–14 14:17[a]Prov. 9:2, 5 14:24[a][Acts 13:46] 14:26[a]Deut. 13:6; 33:9 [b]Rom. 9:13

and mother, wife and children, brothers and sisters, [c]yes, and
his own life also, he cannot be My disciple.
27 "And [a]whoever does not bear his cross and come after
Me cannot be My disciple.
28 "For [a]which of you, intending to build a tower, does not
sit down first and count the cost, whether he has *enough* to
finish *it*—
29 "lest, after he has laid the foundation, and is not able to
finish, all who see *it* begin to mock him,
30 "saying, 'This man began to build and was not able to fin-
ish.'
31 "Or what king, going to make war against another king,
does not sit down first and consider whether he is able with
ten thousand to meet him who comes against him with twen-
ty thousand?
32 "Or else, while the other is still a great way off, he sends
a delegation and asks conditions of peace.
33 "So likewise, whoever of you [a]does not forsake all that he
has cannot be My disciple.
34 [a]"Salt *is* good; but if the salt has lost its flavor, how shall
it be seasoned?
35 "It is neither fit for the land nor for the dunghill, *but* men
throw it out. He who has ears to hear, let him hear!"

14:26[c] Rev. 12:11 14:27[a] Luke 9:23 14:28[a] Prov. 24:27 14:33[a] Matt. 19:27
14:34[a] [Mark 9:50]

LUKE 15

THE LOST SHEEP, THE LOST COIN, AND THE LOST SON

Before the prodigal son received his father's kisses of love, he "arose and came to his father." The determination to return home is good, but it is when the wandering boy begins the business of really carrying out the good resolve that he draws near the blessing.

Before the kisses of love were given, this young man was on his way to his father, but he would not have reached him unless his father had come the major part of the way. I do not know that the prodigal saw his father, but his father saw him. The eyes of mercy are quicker than the eyes of repentance.

I do not suppose that the prodigal traveled very fast. He was resolved to come, yet he was half afraid. But we read that his father ran. Slow are the steps of repentance, but swift are the feet of forgiveness. God can run where we can scarcely limp, and if we are limping toward Him, He will run toward us.

His father "ran and fell on his neck and kissed him"—kissed him eagerly. He did not delay a moment. Though he was out of breath, he was not out of love. There stood his son ready to confess his sin: therefore did his father kiss him all the more. The more willing you are to own your sin, the more willing is God to forgive you.

---

1 Then [a]all the tax collectors and the sinners drew near to Him to hear Him.
2 And the Pharisees and scribes complained, saying, "This Man receives sinners [a]and eats with them."
3 So He spoke this parable to them, saying:
4 [a]"What man of you, having a hundred sheep, if he loses one of them, does not leave the ninety-nine in the wilderness, and go after the one which is lost until he finds it?
5 "And when he has found *it,* he lays *it* on his shoulders, rejoicing.
6 "And when he comes home, he calls together *his* friends and neighbors, saying to them, [a]'Rejoice with me, for I have found my sheep [b]which was lost!'
7 "I say to you that likewise there will be more joy in heaven over one sinner who repents [a]than over ninety-nine just persons who [b]need no repentance.
8 "Or what woman, having ten silver coins,[1] if she loses one

15:1[a][Matt. 9:10–13] 15:2[a]Gal. 2:12 15:4[a]Matt. 18:12–14 15:6[a][Rom. 12:15] [b][1 Pet. 2:10, 25] 15:7[a][Luke 5:32] [b][Mark 2:17] 15:8[1]Greek *drachma,* a valuable coin often worn in a ten-piece garland by married women

coin, does not light a lamp, sweep the house, and search care-
fully until she finds *it?*
9 "And when she has found *it,* she calls *her* friends and neigh-
bors together, saying, 'Rejoice with me, for I have found the
piece which I lost!'
10 "Likewise, I say to you, there is joy in the presence of the
angels of God over one sinner who repents."
11 Then He said: "A certain man had two sons.
12 "And the younger of them said to *his* father, 'Father, give
me the portion of goods that falls *to me.'* So he divided to
them [a]*his* livelihood.
13 "And not many days after, the younger son gathered all
together, journeyed to a far country, and there wasted his
possessions with prodigal living.
14 "But when he had spent all, there arose a severe famine
in that land, and he began to be in want.
15 "Then he went and joined himself to a citizen of that coun-
try, and he sent him into his fields to feed swine.
16 "And he would gladly have filled his stomach with the
pods that the swine ate, and no one gave him *anything.*
17 "But when he came to himself, he said, 'How many of my
father's hired servants have bread enough and to spare, and
I perish with hunger!
18 'I will arise and go to my father, and will say to him, "Fa-
ther, [a]I have sinned against heaven and before you,
19 "and I am no longer worthy to be called your son. Make
me like one of your hired servants." '
20 "And he arose and came to his father. But [a]when he was
still a great way off, his father saw him and had compassion,
and ran and fell on his neck and kissed him.
21 "And the son said to him, 'Father, I have sinned against
heaven [a]and in your sight, and am no longer worthy to be
called your son.'
22 "But the father said to his servants, 'Bring[1] out the best
robe and put *it* on him, and put a ring on his hand and san-
dals on *his* feet.
23 'And bring the fatted calf here and kill *it,* and let us eat
and be merry;
24 [a]'for this my son was dead and is alive again; he was lost
and is found.' And they began to be merry.
25 "Now his older son was in the field. And as he came and
drew near to the house, he heard music and dancing.
26 "So he called one of the servants and asked what these
things meant.
27 "And he said to him, 'Your brother has come, and because
he has received him safe and sound, your father has killed
the fatted calf.'

15:12[a]Mark 12:44 15:18[a]2 Sam. 12:13; 24:10, 17 15:20[a][Eph. 2:13, 17] 15:21[a]Ps. 51:4
15:22[1]NU-Text reads *Quickly bring.* 15:24[a]Luke 9:60; 15:32

28 “But he was angry and would not go in. Therefore his fa-
ther came out and pleaded with him.
29 “So he answered and said to *his* father, ‘Lo, these many
years I have been serving you; I never transgressed your com-
mandment at any time; and yet you never gave me a young
goat, that I might make merry with my friends.
30 ‘But as soon as this son of yours came, who has devoured
your livelihood with harlots, you killed the fatted calf for him.’
31 “And he said to him, ‘Son, you are always with me, and
all that I have is yours.
32 ‘It was right that we should make merry and be glad, [a]for
your brother was dead and is alive again, and was lost and is
found.’”

15:32[a] Luke 15:24

LUKE 16

THE PARABLE OF THE DISHONEST SERVANT

Beloved, we do solemnly say again that Holy Scripture is so perfect, so complete, that it cannot want the supplement of any declaration concerning a future state. All that you ought to know concerning the future you may know from Holy Scripture. Though "eye has not seen, nor ear heard" (1 Cor. 2:9), the lost yet have Holy Scripture sufficiently told them so that when they meet with death, it shall be no new thing; for they heard of it before, and it was distinctly revealed to them. Nothing more could we know that would be of any use.

Tattlers, idle curiosity people, and such like would be mightily delighted with such a man. Ah! What a precious preacher he would be to them, if they could get him all the way from heaven and get him to tell all its secrets out! Oh! How would they love him—how would they delight in him! "For," say they, "he knows a great many little details, and it is wonderful to hear him explain them!" But there the matter would end. It would be merely the gratification of curiosity; there would be no conferring of blessing.

If to know more of the future state would be a blessing for us, God would not withhold it; there can be no more told us. If what you know would not persuade you, "neither will [you] be persuaded though one rise from the dead."

---

1 He also said to His disciples: "There was a certain rich man who had a steward, and an accusation was brought to him that this man was wasting his goods.
2 "So he called him and said to him, 'What is this I hear about you? Give an [a]account of your stewardship, for you can no longer be steward.'
3 "Then the steward said within himself, 'What shall I do? For my master is taking the stewardship away from me. I cannot dig; I am ashamed to beg.
4 'I have resolved what to do, that when I am put out of the stewardship, they may receive me into their houses.'
5 "So he called every one of his master's debtors to *him,* and said to the first, 'How much do you owe my master?'
6 "And he said, 'A hundred measures[1] of oil.' So he said to him, 'Take your bill, and sit down quickly and write fifty.'
7 "Then he said to another, 'And how much do you owe?' So he said, 'A hundred measures[1] of wheat.' And he said to him, 'Take your bill, and write eighty.'

16:2[a][Rom. 14:12] 16:6[1]Greek *batos,* eight or nine gallons each (Old Testament *bath*) 16:7[1]Greek *koros,* ten or twelve bushels each (Old Testament *kor*)

8 "So the master commended the unjust steward because
he had dealt shrewdly. For the sons of this world are more
shrewd in their generation than [a]the sons of light.
9 "And I say to you, [a]make friends for yourselves by unrigh-
teous mammon, that when you fail,[1] they may receive you
into an everlasting home.
10 [a]"He who *is* faithful in *what is* least is faithful also in much;
and he who is unjust in *what is* least is unjust also in much.
11 "Therefore if you have not been faithful in the unrighteous
mammon, who will commit to your trust the true *riches?*
12 "And if you have not been faithful in what is another man's,
who will give you what is your [a]own?
13 [a]"No servant can serve two masters; for either he will hate
the one and love the other, or else he will be loyal to the one
and despise the other. You cannot serve God and mammon."
14 Now the Pharisees, [a]who were lovers of money, also heard
all these things, and they derided Him.
15 And He said to them, "You are those who [a]justify your-
selves [b]before men, but [c]God knows your hearts. For [d]what is
highly esteemed among men is an abomination in the sight
of God.
16 [a]"The law and the prophets *were* until John. Since that
time the kingdom of God has been preached, and everyone
is pressing into it.
17 [a]"And it is easier for heaven and earth to pass away than
for one tittle of the law to fail.
18 [a]"Whoever divorces his wife and marries another commits
adultery; and whoever marries her who is divorced from *her*
husband commits adultery.
19 "There was a certain rich man who was clothed in purple
and fine linen and fared sumptuously every day.
20 "But there was a certain beggar named Lazarus, full of
sores, who was laid at his gate,
21 "desiring to be fed with the crumbs which fell[1] from the
rich man's table. Moreover the dogs came and licked his sores.
22 "So it was that the beggar died, and was carried by the an-
gels to [a]Abraham's bosom. The rich man also died and was
buried.
23 "And being in torments in Hades, he lifted up his eyes
and saw Abraham afar off, and Lazarus in his bosom.
24 "Then he cried and said, 'Father Abraham, have mercy
on me, and send Lazarus that he may dip the tip of his finger
in water and [a]cool my tongue; for I [b]am tormented in this
flame.'

16:8[a][Eph. 5:8] 16:9[a]Dan. 4:27 [1]NU-Text reads *it fails.* 16:10[a]Matt. 25:21 16:12[a][1 Pet. 1:3, 4] 16:13[a]Matt. 6:24 16:14[a]Matt. 23:14 16:15[a]Luke 10:29 [b][Matt. 6:2, 5, 16] [c]Ps. 7:9 [d]1 Sam. 16:7 16:16[a]Matt. 3:1–12; 4:17; 11:12, 13 16:17[a]Is. 40:8; 51:6 16:18[a]1 Cor. 7:10, 11 16:21[1]NU-Text reads *with what fell.* 16:22[a]Matt. 8:11 16:24[a]Zech. 14:12 [b][Mark 9:42–48]

25 "But Abraham said, 'Son, [a]remember that in your life-
time you received your good things, and likewise Lazarus
evil things; but now he is comforted and you are tormented.
26 'And besides all this, between us and you there is a great
gulf fixed, so that those who want to pass from here to you
cannot, nor can those from there pass to us.'
27 "Then he said, 'I beg you therefore, father, that you would
send him to my father's house,
28 'for I have five brothers, that he may testify to them, lest
they also come to this place of torment.'
29 "Abraham said to him, [a]'They have Moses and the proph-
ets; let them hear them.'
30 "And he said, 'No, father Abraham; but if one goes to them
from the dead, they will repent.'
31 "But he said to him, [a]'If they do not hear Moses and the
prophets, [b]neither will they be persuaded though one rise
from the dead.'"

16:25 [a]Luke 6:24 16:29 [a]Acts 15:21; 17:11 16:31 [a][John 5:46] [b]John 12:10, 11

LUKE 17

THE COMING OF THE KINGDOM

There is a singular variety in Christ's methods of cure. Sometimes it is a touch; another time, clay and spittle; at other times, a word. This time He said to the lepers, "Go, show yourselves to the priests." They were not yet clean, so they might have turned round and said, *What a foolish errand! Why should we go and exhibit our filthiness to priests? Master, if You will cure us, we can then go to the priests. If You will not, it is a vain errand to go to the priests to be again doomed to seclusion.*

They did not ask questions, however; they were too wise for that. They did just as they were told, and the whole ten set off on their pilgrimage to the priests. And, as they went, suddenly the cure was wrought and they were every one of them clean.

Oh, what a beautiful picture is this of the plan of salvation! Jesus Christ says, *Believe on Me and live.* Oh, be not foolish; do not say, "Lord, make me whole, and then I will believe." Do not say, "Lord, give me a tender heart, and then I will come"; "Lord, forgive my sin, and then I will love You." He bids you to trust Him, so do as He bids you; and while you are trusting Him, while you are going to Him with the white leprosy still on your skin, while you are yet upon the way, He will heal you.

---

1 Then He said to the disciples, [a]"It is impossible that no of-
fenses should come, but [b]woe *to him* through whom they do
come!
2 "It would be better for him if a millstone were hung around
his neck, and he were thrown into the sea, than that he should
offend one of these little ones.
3 "Take heed to yourselves. [a]If your brother sins against
you,[1] [b]rebuke him; and if he repents, forgive him.
4 "And if he sins against you seven times in a day, and seven
times in a day returns to you,[1] saying, 'I repent,' you shall for-
give him."
5 And the apostles said to the Lord, "Increase our faith."
6 [a]So the Lord said, "If you have faith as a mustard seed, you
can say to this mulberry tree, 'Be pulled up by the roots and
be planted in the sea,' and it would obey you.
7 "And which of you, having a servant plowing or tending
sheep, will say to him when he has come in from the field,
'Come at once and sit down to eat'?
8 "But will he not rather say to him, 'Prepare something for

17:1 [a][1 Cor. 11:19] [b][2 Thess. 1:6] 17:3 [a][Matt. 18:15, 21] [b][Prov. 17:10] [1]NU-Text omits *against you.* 17:4 [1]M-Text omits *to you.* 17:6 [a][Mark 9:23; 11:23]

my supper, and gird yourself [a]and serve me till I have eaten
and drunk, and afterward you will eat and drink'?
9 "Does he thank that servant because he did the things that
were commanded him? I think not.[1]
10 "So likewise you, when you have done all those things
which you are commanded, say, 'We are [a]unprofitable ser-
vants. We have done what was our duty to do.'"
11 Now it happened [a]as He went to Jerusalem that He passed
through the midst of Samaria and Galilee.
12 Then as He entered a certain village, there met Him ten
men who were lepers, [a]who stood afar off.
13 And they lifted up *their* voices and said, "Jesus, Master,
have mercy on us!"
14 So when He saw *them,* He said to them, [a]"Go, show your-
selves to the priests." And so it was that as they went, they
were cleansed.
15 And one of them, when he saw that he was healed, re-
turned, and with a loud voice [a]glorified God,
16 and fell down on *his* face at His feet, giving Him thanks.
And he was a [a]Samaritan.
17 So Jesus answered and said, "Were there not ten cleansed?
But where *are* the nine?
18 "Were there not any found who returned to give glory to
God except this foreigner?"
19 [a]And He said to him, "Arise, go your way. Your faith has
made you well."
20 Now when He was asked by the Pharisees when the king-
dom of God would come, He answered them and said, "The
kingdom of God does not come with observation;
21 [a]"nor will they say, 'See here!' or 'See there!'[1] For indeed,
[b]the kingdom of God is within you."
22 Then He said to the disciples, [a]"The days will come when
you will desire to see one of the days of the Son of Man, and
you will not see *it.*
23 [a]"And they will say to you, 'Look here!' or 'Look there!'[1]
Do not go after *them* or follow *them.*
24 [a]"For as the lightning that flashes out of one *part* under
heaven shines to the other *part* under heaven, so also the
Son of Man will be in His day.
25 [a]"But first He must suffer many things and be [b]rejected
by this generation.
26 [a]"And as it [b]was in the [c]days of [d]Noah, so it will be also in
the days of the Son of Man:

17:8[a][Luke 12:37] 17:9[1]NU-Text ends verse with *commanded;* M-Text omits *him.* 17:10[a]Rom. 3:12; 11:35 17:11[a]Luke 9:51, 52 17:12[a]Lev. 13:46 17:14[a]Matt. 8:4 17:15[a]Luke 5:25; 18:43 17:16[a]2 Kin. 17:24 17:19[a]Matt. 9:22 17:21[a]Luke 17:23 [b][Rom. 14:17] [1]NU-Text reverses *here* and *there.* 17:22[a]Matt. 9:15 17:23[a]Matt. 24:23 [1]NU-Text reverses *here* and *there.* 17:24[a]Matt. 24:27 17:25[a]Mark 8:31; 9:31; 10:33 [b]Luke 9:22 17:26[a]Matt. 24:37–39 [b][Gen. 6:5–7] [c][Gen. 6:8–13] [d]1 Pet. 3:20

27 "They ate, they drank, they married wives, they were given
in marriage, until the [a]day that Noah entered the ark, and the
flood came and [b]destroyed them all.
28 [a]"Likewise as it was also in the days of Lot: They ate, they
drank, they bought, they sold, they planted, they built;
29 "but on [a]the day that Lot went out of Sodom it rained fire
and brimstone from heaven and destroyed *them* all.
30 "Even so will it be in the day when the Son of Man [a]is re-
vealed.
31 "In that day, he [a]who is on the housetop, and his goods
are in the house, let him not come down to take them away.
And likewise the one who is in the field, let him not turn back.
32 [a]"Remember Lot's wife.
33 [a]"Whoever seeks to save his life will lose it, and whoever
loses his life will preserve it.
34 [a]"I tell you, in that night there will be two *men* in one bed:
the one will be taken and the other will be left.
35 [a]"Two *women* will be grinding together: the one will be
taken and the other left.
36 "Two *men* will be in the field: the one will be taken and
the other left."[1]
37 And they answered and said to Him, [a]"Where, Lord?" So
He said to them, "Wherever the body is, there the eagles will
be gathered together."

17:27[a]Gen. 7:1–16 [b]Gen. 7:19–23 17:28[a]Gen. 19 17:29[a]Gen. 19:16, 24, 29 17:30[a][2 Thess. 1:7] 17:31[a]Mark 13:15 17:32[a]Gen. 19:26 17:33[a]Matt. 10:39; 16:25 17:34[a][1 Thess. 4:17] 17:35[a]Matt. 24:40, 41 17:36[1]NU-Text and M-Text omit verse 36. 17:37[a]Matt. 24:28

LUKE 18

THE PARABLE OF THE PERSISTENT WIDOW

Our Savior bids you not neglect this all-conquering instrument of importunity. God will be more easily moved than this unjust judge—only be you as importunate as this widow was. If you are sure it is a right thing for which you are asking, plead now, plead at noon, plead at night, plead on; with cries and tears spread out your case, order your arguments, back up your pleas with reasons, urge the precious blood of Jesus, set the wounds of Christ before the Father's eyes, bring out the atoning sacrifice, point to Calvary, enlist the crowned Prince, the Priest who stands at the right hand of God. Resolve in your very soul that you will die with the plea upon your lips and with the importunate wish upon your spirit.

If you should die with your prayers unanswered, you need not conclude that God has disappointed you. You cannot tell but what, when you are in glory, you should look down from the windows of heaven and receive a double heaven in beholding your dear loved ones converted by the words you left behind. I do not say this to make you cease pleading for their immediate conversion but to encourage you. Never give up prayer; never be tempted to cease from it. So long as there is breath in your body and breath in their bodies, continue still to pray, for I tell you that He will avenge you speedily though He bear long with you.

---

1 Then He spoke a parable to them, that men [a]always ought
to pray and not lose heart,
2 saying: "There was in a certain city a judge who did not
fear God nor regard man.
3 "Now there was a widow in that city; and she came to him,
saying, 'Get justice for me from my adversary.'
4 "And he would not for a while; but afterward he said with-
in himself, 'Though I do not fear God nor regard man,
5 [a]'yet because this widow troubles me I will avenge her, lest
by her continual coming she weary me.'"
6 Then the Lord said, "Hear what the unjust judge said.
7 "And [a]shall God not avenge His own elect who cry out day
and night to Him, though He bears long with them?
8 "I tell you [a]that He will avenge them speedily. Neverthe-
less, when the Son of Man comes, will He really find faith on
the earth?"
9 Also He spoke this parable to some [a]who trusted in them-
selves that they were righteous, and despised others:

18:1[a]Luke 11:5–10 18:5[a]Luke 11:8 18:7[a]Rev. 6:10 18:8[a]Heb. 10:37
18:9[a]Luke 10:29; 16:15

10 "Two men went up to the temple to pray, one a Pharisee
and the other a tax collector.
11 "The Pharisee [a]stood and prayed thus with himself, [b]'God,
I thank You that I am not like other men—extortioners, un-
just, adulterers, or even as this tax collector.
12 'I fast twice a week; I give tithes of all that I possess.'
13 "And the tax collector, standing afar off, would not so
much as raise *his* eyes to heaven, but beat his breast, saying,
'God, be merciful to me a sinner!'
14 "I tell you, this man went down to his house justified *rath-
er* than the other; [a]for everyone who exalts himself will be
humbled, and he who humbles himself will be exalted."
15 [a]Then they also brought infants to Him that He might
touch them; but when the disciples saw *it,* they rebuked
them.
16 But Jesus called them to *Him* and said, "Let the little chil-
dren come to Me, and do not forbid them; for [a]of such is the
kingdom of God.
17 [a]"Assuredly, I say to you, whoever does not receive the
kingdom of God as a little child will by no means enter it."
18 [a]Now a certain ruler asked Him, saying, "Good Teacher,
what shall I do to inherit eternal life?"
19 So Jesus said to him, "Why do you call Me good? No one
is good but [a]One, *that is,* God.
20 "You know the commandments: [a]'Do not commit adul-
tery,' 'Do not murder,' 'Do not steal,' 'Do not bear false wit-
ness,' [b]'Honor your father and your mother.'"[1]
21 And he said, "All [a]these things I have kept from my youth."
22 So when Jesus heard these things, He said to him, "You
still lack one thing. [a]Sell all that you have and distribute to
the poor, and you will have treasure in heaven; and come,
follow Me."
23 But when he heard this, he became very sorrowful, for
he was very rich.
24 And when Jesus saw that he became very sorrowful, He
said, [a]"How hard it is for those who have riches to enter the
kingdom of God!
25 "For it is easier for a camel to go through the eye of a nee-
dle than for a rich man to enter the kingdom of God."
26 And those who heard it said, "Who then can be saved?"
27 But He said, [a]"The things which are impossible with men
are possible with God."
28 [a]Then Peter said, "See, we have left all[1] and followed You."
29 So He said to them, "Assuredly, I say to you, [a]there is no

18:11[a]Ps. 135:2 [b]Is. 1:15; 58:2 18:14[a]Luke 14:11 18:15[a]Mark 10:13–16 18:16[a]1 Pet. 2:2 18:17[a]Mark 10:15 18:18[a]Matt. 19:16–29 18:19[a]Ps. 86:5; 119:68 18:20[a]Ex. 20:12–16; Deut. 5:16–20 [b]Eph. 6:2; Col. 3:20 [1]Exodus 20:12–16; Deuteronomy 5:16–20 18:21[a]Phil. 3:6 18:22[a]Matt. 6:19, 20; 19:21 18:24[a]Mark 10:23 18:27[a]Jer. 32:17 18:28[a]Matt. 19:27 [1]NU-Text reads *our own.* 18:29[a]Deut. 33:9

one who has left house or parents or brothers or wife or chil-
dren, for the sake of the kingdom of God,
30 [a]"who shall not receive many times more in this present
time, and in the age to come eternal life."
31 [a]Then He took the twelve aside and said to them, "Be-
hold, we are going up to Jerusalem, and all things [b]that are
written by the prophets concerning the Son of Man will be
accomplished.
32 "For [a]He will be delivered to the Gentiles and will be
mocked and insulted and spit upon.
33 "They will scourge *Him* and kill Him. And the third day
He will rise again."
34 [a]But they understood none of these things; this saying
was hidden from them, and they did not know the things
which were spoken.
35 [a]Then it happened, as He was coming near Jericho, that
a certain blind man sat by the road begging.
36 And hearing a multitude passing by, he asked what it
meant.
37 So they told him that Jesus of Nazareth was passing by.
38 And he cried out, saying, "Jesus, [a]Son of David, have mercy
on me!"
39 Then those who went before warned him that he should
be quiet; but he cried out all the more, "Son of David, have
mercy on me!"
40 So Jesus stood still and commanded him to be brought
to Him. And when he had come near, He asked him,
41 saying, "What do you want Me to do for you?" He said,
"Lord, that I may receive my sight."
42 Then Jesus said to him, "Receive your sight; [a]your faith
has made you well."
43 And immediately he received his sight, and followed
Him, [a]glorifying God. And all the people, when they saw *it,*
gave praise to God.

18:30[a]Job 42:10 18:31[a]Matt. 16:21; 17:22; 20:17 [b]Ps. 22 18:32[a]Acts 3:13
18:34[a]Luke 2:50; 9:45 18:35[a]Matt. 20:29–34 18:38[a]Matt. 9:27
18:42[a]Luke 17:19 18:43[a]Luke 5:26

LUKE 19

JESUS RIDES INTO JERUSALEM

Christ's main intent in coming here bore upon the lost. We may well be excused if our preaching seeks the lost, for these are the persons whom our Lord has come to seek and to save. The main stress and intent of the incarnation of God in the Person of Christ lies with the guilty, the fallen, the unworthy, the lost. His errand of mercy has nothing to do with those who are good and righteous in themselves, if such there be; it has to do with sinners, real sinners guilty not of nominal but of actual sins who have gone so far therein as to be lost.

Why should He come to seek and to save that which is not lost? Should the Shepherd seek the sheep that has not gone astray? Wherefore should He come to be the Physician of those who are not lost? Should He light a candle and sweep the house to look for pieces of silver that are not lost but lie bright and untarnished in His hand? To what purpose would this be? Would you have Him paint the lily and gild refined gold? Would you make Him a mere busybody offering superfluous aid?

With those who think themselves pure, what has the cleansing blood of Jesus to do? Is a Savior a needless Person, and was His work a needless business? It must be so if it be intended for those who do not need it.

---

1 Then *Jesus* entered and passed through [a]Jericho.
2 Now behold, *there was* a man named Zacchaeus who was
a chief tax collector, and he was rich.
3 And he sought to [a]see who Jesus was, but could not be-
cause of the crowd, for he was of short stature.
4 So he ran ahead and climbed up into a sycamore tree to
see Him, for He was going to pass that *way*.
5 And when Jesus came to the place, He looked up and saw
him,[1] and said to him, "Zacchaeus, make haste and come
down, for today I must stay at your house."
6 So he made haste and came down, and received Him joy-
fully.
7 But when they saw *it*, they all complained, saying, [a]"He has
gone to be a guest with a man who is a sinner."
8 Then Zacchaeus stood and said to the Lord, "Look, Lord,
I give half of my goods to the [a]poor; and if I have taken any-
thing from anyone by [b]false accusation, [c]I restore fourfold."

19:1[a]Josh. 6:26 19:3[a]John 12:21 19:5[1]NU-Text omits *and saw him.* 19:7[a]Luke 5:30; 15:2 19:8[a][Ps. 41:1] [b]Luke 3:14 [c]Ex. 22:1

9 And Jesus said to him, "Today salvation has come to this
house, because [a]he also is [b]a son of Abraham;
10 [a]"for the Son of Man has come to seek and to save that
which was lost."
11 Now as they heard these things, He spoke another parable,
because He was near Jerusalem and because [a]they thought
the kingdom of God would appear immediately.
12 [a]Therefore He said: "A certain nobleman went into a far
country to receive for himself a kingdom and to return.
13 "So he called ten of his servants, delivered to them ten
minas,[1] and said to them, 'Do business till I come.'
14 [a]"But his citizens hated him, and sent a delegation after
him, saying, 'We will not have this *man* to reign over us.'
15 "And so it was that when he returned, having received the
kingdom, he then commanded these servants, to whom he
had given the money, to be called to him, that he might know
how much every man had gained by trading.
16 "Then came the first, saying, 'Master, your mina has earned
ten minas.'
17 "And he said to him, [a]'Well *done*, good servant; because you
were [b]faithful in a very little, have authority over ten cities.'
18 "And the second came, saying, 'Master, your mina has
earned five minas.'
19 "Likewise he said to him, 'You also be over five cities.'
20 "Then another came, saying, 'Master, here is your mina,
which I have kept put away in a handkerchief.
21 [a]'For I feared you, because you are an austere man. You
collect what you did not deposit, and reap what you did not
sow.'
22 "And he said to him, [a]'Out of your own mouth I will judge
you, *you* wicked servant. [b]You knew that I was an austere
man, collecting what I did not deposit and reaping what I
did not sow.
23 'Why then did you not put my money in the bank, that at
my coming I might have collected it with interest?'
24 "And he said to those who stood by, 'Take the mina from
him, and give *it* to him who has ten minas.'
25 ("But they said to him, 'Master, he has ten minas.')
26 'For I say to you, [a]that to everyone who has will be given;
and from him who does not have, even what he has will be
taken away from him.
27 'But bring here those enemies of mine, who did not want
me to reign over them, and slay *them* before me.'"
28 When He had said this, [a]He went on ahead, going up to
Jerusalem.

19:9 [a][Gal. 3:7] [b][Luke 13:16] 19:10 [a]Matt. 18:11 19:11 [a]Acts 1:6 19:12 [a]Matt. 25:14–30
19:13 [1]The *mina* (Greek *mna,* Hebrew *minah*) was worth about three months' salary.
19:14 [a][John 1:11] 19:17 [a]Matt. 25:21, 23 [b]Luke 16:10 19:21 [a]Matt. 25:24 19:22 [a]Job 15:6 [b]Matt. 25:26 19:26 [a]Luke 8:18 19:28 [a]Mark 10:32

29 [a]And it came to pass, when He drew near to Bethphage[1]
and [b]Bethany, at the mountain called [c]Olivet, *that* He sent
two of His disciples,
30 saying, "Go into the village opposite *you,* where as you
enter you will find a colt tied, on which no one has ever sat.
Loose it and bring *it here.*
31 "And if anyone asks you, 'Why are you loosing *it?*' thus
you shall say to him, 'Because the Lord has need of it.'"
32 So those who were sent went their way and found *it* just
[a]as He had said to them.
33 But as they were loosing the colt, the owners of it said to
them, "Why are you loosing the colt?"
34 And they said, "The Lord has need of him."
35 Then they brought him to Jesus. [a]And they threw their
own clothes on the colt, and they set Jesus on him.
36 And as He went, *many* spread their clothes on the road.
37 Then, as He was now drawing near the descent of the
Mount of Olives, the whole multitude of the disciples began
to [a]rejoice and praise God with a loud voice for all the mighty
works they had seen,
38 saying:

> [a]"'Blessed *is* the King who comes in
> the name of the LORD!'[1]
> [b]Peace in heaven and glory
> in the highest!"

39 And some of the Pharisees called to Him from the crowd,
"Teacher, rebuke Your disciples."
40 But He answered and said to them, "I tell you that if
these should keep silent, [a]the stones would immediately
cry out."
41 Now as He drew near, He saw the city and [a]wept over it,
42 saying, "If you had known, even you, especially in this
[a]your day, the things *that* [b]*make* for your [c]peace! But now
they are hidden from your eyes.
43 "For days will come upon you when your enemies will
[a]build an embankment around you, surround you and close
you in on every side,
44 [a]"and level you, and your children within you, to the
ground; and [b]they will not leave in you one stone upon another, [c]because you did not know the time of your visitation."
45 [a]Then He went into the temple and began to drive out
those who bought and sold in it,[1]

19:29[a]Matt. 21:1 [b]John 12:1 [c]Acts 1:12 [1]M-Text reads *Bethsphage.* 19:32[a]Luke 22:13 19:35[a]2 Kin. 9:13 19:37[a]Luke 13:17; 18:43 19:38[a]Ps. 118:26 [b][Eph. 2:14] [1]Psalm 118:26 19:40[a]Hab. 2:11 19:41[a]John 11:35 19:42[a]Heb. 3:13 [b][Acts 10:36] [c][Rom. 5:1] 19:43[a]Jer. 6:3, 6 19:44[a]1 Kin. 9:7, 8 [b]Matt. 24:2 [c][1 Pet. 2:12] 19:45[a]Mark 11:11, 15–17 [1]NU-Text reads *those who were selling.*

46 saying to them, "It is written, [a]'My house is[1] a house of
prayer,'[2] but you have made it a [b]'den of thieves.'"[3]
47 And He [a]was teaching daily in the temple. But [b]the chief
priests, the scribes, and the leaders of the people sought to
destroy Him,
48 and were unable to do anything; for all the people were
very attentive to [a]hear Him.

19:46 [a]Is. 56:7 [b]Jer. 7:11 [1]NU-Text reads *shall be.* [2]Isaiah 56:7 [3]Jeremiah 7:11
19:47 [a]Luke 21:37; 22:53 [b]John 7:19; 8:37 19:48 [a]Luke 21:38

LUKE 20

DISPUTES IN JERUSALEM

While Moses is in the desert, he is thinking about Israel in Egypt. And so, while Moses in the desert is thinking of his people's plight in Egypt, he sees a bush, and that bush is all ablaze. Yet here was an extraordinary thing—a bush that continued to burn and was not consumed. Here was life in the midst of death, continuance in the midst of destruction. This was an emblem of God's abiding with a people and yet suffering them to live. He who then spoke to Moses was the God of life, the God who could sustain in the midst of destruction, the God who could preserve even a bush from being devoured by the intense fury of flame.

Out of the midst of the bush there came a mysterious and divine voice that said, "I am . . . the God of Abraham, the God of Isaac, and the God of Jacob" (Ex. 3:6). From this voice our divine Lord teaches us that God's people live when they appear to have been long dead—for He who cannot be the God of the dead or nonexistent still avows Himself to be the God of the long-buried patriarchs. Our Lord proved from that utterance at the bush the continued life of the Lord's chosen and also their resurrection.

---

1 Now [a]it happened on one of those days, as He taught the
people in the temple and preached the gospel, *that* the chief
priests and the scribes, together with the elders, confront-
ed *Him*
2 and spoke to Him, saying, "Tell us, [a]by what authority are
You doing these things? Or who is he who gave You this au-
thority?"
3 But He answered and said to them, "I also will ask you one
thing, and answer Me:
4 "The [a]baptism of John—was it from heaven or from men?"
5 And they reasoned among themselves, saying, "If we
say, 'From heaven,' He will say, 'Why then[1] did you not be-
lieve him?'
6 "But if we say, 'From men,' all the people will stone us, [a]for
they are persuaded that John was a prophet."
7 So they answered that they did not know where *it was* from.
8 And Jesus said to them, "Neither will I tell you by what au-
thority I do these things."
9 Then He began to tell the people this parable: [a]"A certain
man planted a vineyard, leased it to vinedressers, and went
into a far country for a long time.

20:1[a]Matt. 21:23–27 20:2[a]Acts 4:7; 7:27 20:4[a]John 1:26, 31 20:5[1]NU-Text and M-Text omit *then.* 20:6[a]Luke 7:24–30 20:9[a]Mark 12:1–12

10 "Now at vintage-time he [a]sent a servant to the vinedressers,
that they might give him some of the fruit of the vineyard.
But the vinedressers beat him and sent *him* away empty-
handed.
11 "Again he sent another servant; and they beat him also,
treated *him* shamefully, and sent *him* away empty-handed.
12 "And again he sent a third; and they wounded him also
and cast *him* out.
13 "Then the owner of the vineyard said, 'What shall I do?
I will send my beloved son. Probably they will respect *him*
when they see him.'
14 "But when the vinedressers saw him, they reasoned among
themselves, saying, 'This is the [a]heir. Come, [b]let us kill him,
that the inheritance may be [c]ours.'
15 "So they cast him out of the vineyard and [a]killed *him*.
Therefore what will the owner of the vineyard do to them?
16 "He will come and destroy those vinedressers and give
the vineyard to [a]others." And when they heard *it* they said,
"Certainly not!"
17 Then He looked at them and said, "What then is this that
is written:

> [a]'The stone which the builders rejected
> Has become the chief cornerstone'?[1]

18 "Whoever falls on that stone will be [a]broken; but [b]on
whomever it falls, it will grind him to powder."
19 And the chief priests and the scribes that very hour sought
to lay hands on Him, but they feared the people[1]—for they
knew He had spoken this parable against them.
20 [a]So they watched *Him*, and sent spies who pretended to
be righteous, that they might seize on His words, in order to
deliver Him to the power and the authority of the governor.
21 Then they asked Him, saying, [a]"Teacher, we know that
You say and teach rightly, and You do not show personal fa-
voritism, but teach the way of God in truth:
22 "Is it lawful for us to pay taxes to Caesar or not?"
23 But He perceived their craftiness, and said to them, "Why
do you test Me?[1]
24 "Show Me a denarius. Whose image and inscription does
it have?" They answered and said, "Caesar's."
25 And He said to them, [a]"Render therefore to Caesar the
things that are Caesar's, and to God the things that are God's."
26 But they could not catch Him in His words in the presence

20:10[a][1 Thess. 2:15] 20:14[a][Heb. 1:1–3] [b]Matt. 27:21–23 [c]John 11:47, 48 20:15[a]Luke 23:33 20:16[a]Rom. 11:1, 11 20:17[a]Ps. 118:22 [1]Psalm 118:22 20:18[a]Is. 8:14, 15 [b][Dan. 2:34, 35, 44, 45] 20:19[1]M-Text reads *but they were afraid*. 20:20[a]Matt. 22:15 20:21[a]Mark 12:14 20:23[1]NU-Text omits *Why do you test Me?* 20:25[a][1 Pet. 2:13–17]

of the people. And they marveled at His answer and kept
silent.
27 [a]Then some of the Sadducees, [b]who deny that there is a
resurrection, came to *Him* and asked Him,
28 saying: "Teacher, Moses wrote to us *that* if a man's
brother dies, having a wife, and he dies without children,
his brother should take his wife and raise up offspring for
his brother.
29 "Now there were seven brothers. And the first took a wife,
and died without children.
30 "And the second[1] took her as wife, and he died childless.
31 "Then the third took her, and in like manner the seven
also; and they left no children,[1] and died.
32 "Last of all the woman died also.
33 "Therefore, in the resurrection, whose wife does she be-
come? For all seven had her as wife."
34 Jesus answered and said to them, "The sons of this age
marry and are given in marriage.
35 "But those who are [a]counted worthy to attain that age,
and the resurrection from the dead, neither marry nor are
given in marriage;
36 "nor can they die anymore, for [a]they are equal to the an-
gels and are sons of God, [b]being sons of the resurrection.
37 "But even Moses showed in the *burning* bush *passage*
that the dead are raised, when he called the Lord [a]'the God
of Abraham, the God of Isaac, and the God of Jacob.'[1]
38 "For He is not the God of the dead but of the living, for
[a]all live to Him."
39 Then some of the scribes answered and said, "Teacher,
You have spoken well."
40 But after that they dared not question Him anymore.
41 And He said to them, [a]"How can they say that the Christ
is the Son of David?
42 "Now David himself said in the Book of Psalms:

> [a]'The LORD said to my Lord,
> "Sit at My right hand,
> 43 Till I make Your enemies Your footstool." '[1]

44 "Therefore David calls Him 'Lord'; [a]how is He then
his Son?"
45 [a]Then, in the hearing of all the people, He said to His dis-
ciples,
46 [a]"Beware of the scribes, who desire to go around in long

20:27 [a]Mark 12:18–27 [b]Acts 23:6, 8 20:30 [1]NU-Text ends verse 30 here. 20:31 [1]NU-Text and M Text read *the seven also left no children.* 20:35 [a]Phil. 3:11 20:36 [a][1 John 3:2] [b]Rom. 8:23 20:37 [a]Ex. 3:1–6, 15 [1]Exodus 3:6, 15 20:38 [a][Rom. 6:10, 11; 14:8, 9] 20:41 [a]Matt. 22:41–46 20:42 [a]Ps. 110:1 20:43 [1]Psalm 110:1 20:44 [a]Rom. 1:3; 9:4, 5 20:45 [a]Matt. 23:1–7 20:46 [a]Matt. 23:5

robes, [b]love greetings in the marketplaces, the best seats in the synagogues, and the best places at feasts,
47 [a]"who devour widows' houses, and for a [b]pretense make long prayers. These will receive greater condemnation."

20:46[b] Luke 11:43; 14:7 20:47[a] Matt. 23:14 [b][Matt. 6:5, 6]

LUKE 21

THE RETURN OF CHRIST IN JUDGMENT

You know that fear is contagious; when one person trembles, many begin to feel the same sort of tremor. And when all the people, wherever we shall go, at home or abroad, shall be in distress—when everywhere the hearts of men shall seem to die within them—if it should ever come to that, then you who have Christ for your Master, God for your Father, eternity for your heritage, and heaven for your home, even then you may "look up and lift up your heads."

You ask, perhaps, "How shall we do that?" You cannot do it without your Lord. In Christ, you can do all things; without Him, you can do nothing. If you live away from your Lord and Master, in those days of terror that are yet to come your heart will quail for fear, and you will be like other men. If you run with them, you shall fear with them. If your strength is where their strength is, you shall be as weak as they; but if you have learned to look up, why, even in those stormy times you shall keep to the habit of looking up. If your portion is in heaven, it shall not be shaken when the earth rocks and reels to its very foundations; if your treasure is in heaven, then your treasure shall not be lost.

---

1 And He looked up [a]and saw the rich putting their gifts into
the treasury,
2 and He saw also a certain [a]poor widow putting in two [b]mites.
3 So He said, "Truly I say to you [a]that this poor widow has
put in more than all;
4 "for all these out of their abundance have put in offerings
for God,[1] but she out of her poverty put in [a]all the livelihood
that she had."
5 [a]Then, as some spoke of the temple, how it was adorned
with beautiful stones and donations, He said,
6 "These things which you see—the days will come in which
[a]not *one* stone shall be left upon another that shall not be
thrown down."
7 So they asked Him, saying, "Teacher, but when will these
things be? And what sign *will there be* when these things are
about to take place?"
8 And He said: [a]"Take heed that you not be deceived. For
many will come in My name, saying, 'I am *He*,' and, 'The time
has drawn near.' Therefore[1] do not go after them.

21:1[a]Mark 12:41–44 21:2[a][2 Cor. 6:10] [b]Mark 12:42 21:3[a][2 Cor. 8:12] 21:4[a][2 Cor. 8:12] [1]NU-Text omits *for God.* 21:5[a]Mark 13:1 21:6[a]Luke 19:41–44 21:8[a]Eph. 5:6 [1]NU-Text omits *Therefore.*

9 "But when you hear of [a]wars and commotions, do not be
terrified; for these things must come to pass first, but the
end *will not come* immediately."
10 [a]Then He said to them, "Nation will rise against nation,
and kingdom against kingdom.
11 "And there will be great [a]earthquakes in various places,
and famines and pestilences; and there will be fearful sights
and great signs from heaven.
12 [a]"But before all these things, they will lay their hands on
you and persecute *you,* delivering *you* up to the synagogues
and [b]prisons. [c]You will be brought before kings and rulers
[d]for My name's sake.
13 "But [a]it will turn out for you as an occasion for testimony.
14 [a]"Therefore settle *it* in your hearts not to meditate before-
hand on what you will answer;
15 "for I will give you a mouth and wisdom [a]which all your
adversaries will not be able to contradict or resist.
16 [a]"You will be betrayed even by parents and brothers, rel-
atives and friends; and they will put [b]*some* of you to death.
17 "And [a]you will be hated by all for My name's sake.
18 [a]"But not a hair of your head shall be lost.
19 "By your patience possess your souls.
20 [a]"But when you see Jerusalem surrounded by armies,
then know that its desolation is near.
21 "Then let those who are in Judea flee to the mountains,
let those who are in the midst of her depart, and let not those
who are in the country enter her.
22 "For these are the days of vengeance, that [a]all things which
are written may be fulfilled.
23 [a]"But woe to those who are pregnant and to those who
are nursing babies in those days! For there will be great dis-
tress in the land and wrath upon this people.
24 "And they will fall by the edge of the sword, and be led
away captive into all nations. And Jerusalem will be tram-
pled by Gentiles [a]until the times of the Gentiles are fulfilled.
25 [a]"And there will be signs in the sun, in the moon, and in
the stars; and on the earth distress of nations, with perplex-
ity, the sea and the waves roaring;
26 "men's hearts failing them from fear and the expectation
of those things which are coming on the earth, [a]for the pow-
ers of the heavens will be shaken.
27 "Then they will see the Son of Man [a]coming in a cloud
with power and great glory.

21:9[a]Rev. 6:4 21:10[a]Matt. 24:7 21:11[a]Rev. 6:12 21:12[a][Rev. 2:10] [b]Acts 4:3; 5:18; 12:4; 16:24 [c]Acts 25:23 [d]1 Pet. 2:13 21:13[a][Phil. 1:12–14, 28] 21:14[a]Luke 12:11 21:15[a]Acts 6:10 21:16[a]Mic. 7:6 [b]Acts 7:59; 12:2 21:17[a]Matt. 10:22 21:18[a]Matt. 10:30 21:20[a]Mark 13:14 21:22[a][Dan. 9:24–27] 21:23[a]Matt. 24:19 21:24[a][Dan. 9:27; 12:7] 21:25[a][2 Pet. 3:10–12] 21:26[a]Matt. 24:29 21:27[a]Rev. 1:7; 14:14

28 "Now when these things begin to happen, look up and
lift up your heads, because [a]your redemption draws near."
29 [a]Then He spoke to them a parable: "Look at the fig tree,
and all the trees.
30 "When they are already budding, you see and know for
yourselves that summer is now near.
31 "So you also, when you see these things happening, know
that the kingdom of God is near.
32 "Assuredly, I say to you, this generation will by no means
pass away till all things take place.
33 [a]"Heaven and earth will pass away, but My [b]words will by
no means pass away.
34 "But [a]take heed to yourselves, lest your hearts be weighed
down with carousing, drunkenness, and [b]cares of this life,
and that Day come on you unexpectedly.
35 "For [a]it will come as a snare on all those who dwell on the
face of the whole earth.
36 [a]"Watch therefore, and [b]pray always that you may be
counted [c]worthy[1] to escape all these things that will come
to pass, and [d]to stand before the Son of Man."
37 [a]And in the daytime He was teaching in the temple, but
[b]at night He went out and stayed on the mountain called
Olivet.
38 Then early in the morning all the people came to Him in
the temple to hear Him.

21:28[a][Rom. 8:19, 23] 21:29[a]Mark 13:28 21:33[a]Matt. 24:35 [b]Is. 40:8
21:34[a]1 Thess. 5:6 [b]Luke 8:14 21:35[a]Rev. 3:3; 16:15 21:36[a]Matt. 24:42; 25:13 [b]Luke 18:1 [c]Luke 20:35 [d][Eph. 6:13] [1]NU-Text reads *may have strength.*
21:37[a]John 8:1, 2 [b]Luke 22:39

LUKE 22

THE BEGINNING OF THE LORD'S SUPPER

Now note that, on the night before His Passion, our Lord led His friends a step beyond ordinary friendship. The servant is seldom entertained at the same table with his lord, but here the Lord Jesus made His chosen ones to be His table companions; He lifted them up to sit with Him at the same table, to eat of the same bread, to drink of the same cup with Himself.

All the Lord's believing people are sitting, by sacred privilege and calling, at the same table with Jesus, for "truly our fellowship is with the Father and with His Son Jesus Christ" (1 John 1:3). He has come into our hearts, and He sups with us, and we with Him; we are His table companions and shall eat bread with Him in the kingdom of God.

Remember that there is, in this solemn eating and drinking together, a pledge of fidelity between the disciples themselves as well as between the disciples and their Lord. You are members one of another, so see that you love each other with a pure heart fervently. Drinking of the same cup and eating of the same bread, you set forth before the world a token that I trust is not meant to be a lie. As it truly shows Christ's faithfulness to you, so let it typify your faithfulness to Christ and to one another.

1 Now [a]the Feast of Unleavened Bread drew near, which is
called Passover.
2 And [a]the chief priests and the scribes sought how they
might kill Him, for they feared the people.
3 [a]Then Satan entered Judas, surnamed Iscariot, who was
numbered among the [b]twelve.
4 So he went his way and conferred with the chief priests
and captains, how he might betray Him to them.
5 And they were glad, and [a]agreed to give him money.
6 So he promised and sought opportunity to [a]betray Him
to them in the absence of the multitude.
7 [a]Then came the Day of Unleavened Bread, when the Pass-
over must be killed.
8 And He sent Peter and John, saying, "Go and prepare the
Passover for us, that we may eat."
9 So they said to Him, "Where do You want us to prepare?"
10 And He said to them, "Behold, when you have entered the
city, a man will meet you carrying a pitcher of water; follow
him into the house which he enters.

22:1[a]Matt. 26:2–5 22:2[a]John 11:47 22:3[a]Mark 14:10, 11 [b]Matt. 10:2–4 22:5[a]Zech. 11:12 22:6[a]Ps. 41:9 22:7[a]Matt. 26:17–19

11 "Then you shall say to the master of the house, 'The Teach-
er says to you, "Where is the guest room where I may eat the
Passover with My disciples?"'
12 "Then he will show you a large, furnished upper room;
there make ready."
13 So they went and [a]found it just as He had said to them,
and they prepared the Passover.
14 [a]When the hour had come, He sat down, and the twelve[1]
apostles with Him.
15 Then He said to them, "With *fervent* desire I have desired
to eat this Passover with you before I suffer;
16 "for I say to you, I will no longer eat of it [a]until it is ful-
filled in the kingdom of God."
17 Then He took the cup, and gave thanks, and said, "Take
this and divide *it* among yourselves;
18 "for [a]I say to you,[1] I will not drink of the fruit of the vine
until the kingdom of God comes."
19 [a]And He took bread, gave thanks and broke *it*, and gave
it to them, saying, "This is My [b]body which is given for you;
[c]do this in remembrance of Me."
20 Likewise He also *took* the cup after supper, saying, [a]"This
cup *is* the new covenant in My blood, which is shed for you.
21 [a]"But behold, the hand of My betrayer *is* with Me on the
table.
22 [a]"And truly the Son of Man goes [b]as it has been deter-
mined, but woe to that man by whom He is betrayed!"
23 [a]Then they began to question among themselves, which
of them it was who would do this thing.
24 [a]Now there was also a dispute among them, as to which
of them should be considered the greatest.
25 [a]And He said to them, "The kings of the Gentiles exercise
lordship over them, and those who exercise authority over
them are called 'benefactors.'
26 [a]"But not so *among* you; on the contrary, [b]he who is great-
est among you, let him be as the younger, and he who gov-
erns as he who serves.
27 [a]"For who *is* greater, he who sits at the table, or he who
serves? *Is* it not he who sits at the table? Yet [b]I am among you
as the One who serves.
28 "But you are those who have continued with Me in [a]My
trials.
29 "And [a]I bestow upon you a kingdom, just as My Father
bestowed *one* upon Me,

22:13[a]Luke 19:32 22:14[a]Mark 14:17 [1]NU-Text omits *twelve.* 22:16[a][Rev. 19:9] 22:18[a]Mark 14:25 [1]NU-Text adds *from now on.* 22:19[a]Matt. 26:26 [b][1 Pet. 2:24] [c]1 Cor. 11:23–26 22:20[a]1 Cor. 10:16 22:21[a]John 13:21, 26, 27 22:22[a]Matt. 26:24 [b]Acts 2:23 22:23[a]John 13:22, 25 22:24[a]Mark 9:34 22:25[a]Mark 10:42–45 22:26[a][1 Pet. 5:3] [b]Luke 9:48 22:27[a][Luke 12:37] [b]Phil. 2:7 22:28[a][Heb. 2:18; 4:15] 22:29[a]Matt. 24:47

30 "that [a]you may eat and drink at My table in My kingdom,
[b]and sit on thrones judging the twelve tribes of Israel."
31 And the Lord said,[1] "Simon, Simon! Indeed, [a]Satan has
asked for you, that he may [b]sift *you* as wheat.
32 "But [a]I have prayed for you, that your faith should not
fail; and when you have returned to *Me,* [b]strengthen your
brethren."
33 But he said to Him, "Lord, I am ready to go with You, both
to prison and to death."
34 [a]Then He said, "I tell you, Peter, the rooster shall not
crow this day before you will deny three times that you
know Me."
35 [a]And He said to them, "When I sent you without money
bag, knapsack, and sandals, did you lack anything?" So they
said, "Nothing."
36 Then He said to them, "But now, he who has a money bag,
let him take *it,* and likewise a knapsack; and he who has no
sword, let him sell his garment and buy one.
37 "For I say to you that this which is written must still be
accomplished in Me: [a]'And He was numbered with the trans-
gressors.'[1] For the things concerning Me have an end."
38 So they said, "Lord, look, here *are* two swords." And He
said to them, "It is enough."
39 [a]Coming out, [b]He went to the Mount of Olives, as He was
accustomed, and His disciples also followed Him.
40 [a]When He came to the place, He said to them, "Pray that
you may not enter into temptation."
41 [a]And He was withdrawn from them about a stone's throw,
and He knelt down and prayed,
42 saying, "Father, if it is Your will, take this cup away from
Me; nevertheless [a]not My will, but Yours, be done."
43 Then [a]an angel appeared to Him from heaven, strength-
ening Him.
44 [a]And being in agony, He prayed more earnestly. Then His
sweat became like great drops of blood falling down to the
ground.[1]
45 When He rose up from prayer, and had come to His dis-
ciples, He found them sleeping from sorrow.
46 Then He said to them, "Why [a]do you sleep? Rise and [b]pray,
lest you enter into temptation."
47 And while He was still speaking, [a]behold, a multitude;
and he who was called [b]Judas, one of the twelve, went before
them and drew near to Jesus to kiss Him.

22:30[a][Matt. 8:11] [b][Rev. 3:21] 22:31[a]1 Pet. 5:8 [b]Amos 9:9 [1]NU-Text omits *And the Lord said.* 22:32[a][John 17:9, 11, 15] [b]John 21:15–17 22:34[a]John 13:37, 38 22:35[a]Matt. 10:9 22:37[a]Is. 53:12 [1]Isaiah 53:12 22:39[a]John 18:1 [b]Luke 21:37 22:40[a]Mark 14:32–42 22:41[a]Matt. 26:39 22:42[a]John 4:34; 5:30; 6:38; 8:29 22:43[a]Matt. 4:11 22:44[a][Heb. 5:7] [1]NU-Text brackets verses 43 and 44 as not in the original text. 22:46[a]Luke 9:32 [b]Luke 22:40 22:47[a]John 18:3–11 [b]Acts 1:16, 17

48 But Jesus said to him, "Judas, are you betraying the Son
of Man with a [a]kiss?"
49 When those around Him saw what was going to happen,
they said to Him, "Lord, shall we strike with the sword?"
50 And [a]one of them struck the servant of the high priest
and cut off his right ear.
51 But Jesus answered and said, "Permit even this." And He
touched his ear and healed him.
52 [a]Then Jesus said to the chief priests, captains of the tem-
ple, and the elders who had come to Him, "Have you come
out, as against a [b]robber, with swords and clubs?
53 "When I was with you daily in the [a]temple, you did not try
to seize Me. But this is your [b]hour, and the power of darkness."
54 [a]Having arrested Him, they led *Him* and brought Him
into the high priest's house. [b]But Peter followed at a distance.
55 [a]Now when they had kindled a fire in the midst of the
courtyard and sat down together, Peter sat among them.
56 And a certain servant girl, seeing him as he sat by the
fire, looked intently at him and said, "This man was also
with Him."
57 But he denied Him,[1] saying, "Woman, I do not know Him."
58 [a]And after a little while another saw him and said, "You
also are of them." But Peter said, "Man, I am not!"
59 [a]Then after about an hour had passed, another confident-
ly affirmed, saying, "Surely this *fellow* also was with Him, for
he is a [b]Galilean."
60 But Peter said, "Man, I do not know what you are saying!"
Immediately, while he was still speaking, the rooster[1] crowed.
61 And the Lord turned and looked at Peter. Then [a]Peter
remembered the word of the Lord, how He had said to him,
[b]"Before the rooster crows,[1] you will deny Me three times."
62 So Peter went out and wept bitterly.
63 [a]Now the men who held Jesus mocked Him and [b]beat Him.
64 And having blindfolded Him, they [a]struck Him on the
face and asked Him,[1] saying, "Prophesy! Who is the one who
struck You?"
65 And many other things they blasphemously spoke
against Him.
66 [a]As soon as it was day, [b]the elders of the people, both
chief priests and scribes, came together and led Him into
their council, saying,
67 [a]"If You are the Christ, tell us." But He said to them, "If I
tell you, you will [b]by no means believe.

22:48 [a][Prov. 27:6] 22:50 [a]Matt. 26:51 22:52 [a]Matt. 26:55 [b]Luke 23:32 22:53 [a]Luke 19:47, 48 [b][John 12:27] 22:54 [a]Matt. 26:57 [b]John 18:15 22:55 [a]Mark 14:66–72 22:57 [1]NU-Text reads *denied it.* 22:58 [a]John 18:25 22:59 [a]Mark 14:70 [b]Acts 1:11; 2:7 22:60 [1]NU-Text and M-Text read *a rooster.* 22:61 [a]Matt. 26:75 [b]John 13:38 [1]NU-Text adds *today.* 22:63 [a]Ps. 69:1, 4, 7–9 [b]Is. 50:6 22:64 [a]Zech. 13:7 [1]NU-Text reads *And having blindfolded Him, they asked Him.* 22:66 [a]Matt. 27:1 [b]Acts 4:26 22:67 [a]Matt. 26:63–66 [b]Luke 20:5–7

68 "And if I also ask *you,* you will by no means answer Me or
let *Me* go.[1]
69 [a]"Hereafter the Son of Man will sit on the right hand of
the power of God."
70 Then they all said, "Are You then the Son of God?" So He
said to them, [a]"You *rightly* say that I am."
71 [a]And they said, "What further testimony do we need? For
we have heard it ourselves from His own mouth."

22:68[1] NU-Text omits *also* and *Me or let Me go.* 22:69[a] Heb. 1:3; 8:1
22:70[a] Matt. 26:64; 27:11 22:71[a] Mark 14:63

LUKE 23

JESUS IS TRIED AND CRUCIFIED

It is Jesus' last hour, but He thinks of them. He is about to die, but the ruling passion is strong in death. He is seeking sinners still, and if He can preach no more yet He can pray, and if He will not speak to them yet He can speak to God for them, and so He continues still to show which way His heart runs by the prayer for those who nailed Him to the wood: "Father, forgive them, for they do not know what they do."

What love is this! One would suppose that the pain He then felt might have distracted His mind from others, and His prayer might have been for Himself, that patience might be given, that strength might be sustained. But no, oblivious of Himself, He reveals His care is still for those He seeks—the sinful sons of men.

Just as an arrow from a bow shot forth with such force that it speeds onward to its target, His whole strength and soul speed onward to the mark of the salvation of the sons of men. One thing, one thing only, does He do—He seeks still their good, and I say again, if not now by active ministering to them yet by ministering for them He prays, "Father, forgive them."

---

1 Then [a]the whole multitude of them arose and led Him to
[b]Pilate.
2 And they began to [a]accuse Him, saying, "We found this
fellow [b]perverting the[1] nation, and [c]forbidding to pay taxes
to Caesar, saying [d]that He Himself is Christ, a King."
3 [a]Then Pilate asked Him, saying, "Are You the King of the
Jews?" He answered him and said, "*It is as* you say."
4 So Pilate said to the chief priests and the crowd, [a]"I find
no fault in this Man."
5 But they were the more fierce, saying, "He stirs up the peo-
ple, teaching throughout all Judea, beginning from [a]Galilee
to this place."
6 When Pilate heard of Galilee,[1] he asked if the Man were a
Galilean.
7 And as soon as he knew that He belonged to [a]Herod's ju-
risdiction, he sent Him to Herod, who was also in Jerusalem
at that time.
8 Now when Herod saw Jesus, [a]he was exceedingly glad; for
he had desired for a long *time* to see Him, because [b]he had
heard many things about Him, and he hoped to see some
miracle done by Him.

23:1[a]John 18:28 [b]Luke 3:1; 13:1 23:2[a]Acts 24:2 [b]Acts 17:7 [c]Matt. 17:27 [d]John 19:12 [1]NU-Text reads *our.* 23:3[a]1 Tim. 6:13 23:4[a][1 Pet. 2:22] 23:5[a]John 7:41 23:6[1]NU-Text omits *of Galilee.* 23:7[a]Luke 3:1; 9:7; 13:31 23:8[a]Luke 9:9 [b]Matt. 14:1

9 Then he questioned Him with many words, but He an-
swered him [a]nothing.
10 And the chief priests and scribes stood and vehemently
accused Him.
11 [a]Then Herod, with his men of war, treated Him with con-
tempt and mocked *Him,* arrayed Him in a gorgeous robe, and
sent Him back to Pilate.
12 That very day [a]Pilate and Herod became friends with each
other, for previously they had been at enmity with each other.
13 [a]Then Pilate, when he had called together the chief priests,
the rulers, and the people,
14 said to them, [a]"You have brought this Man to me, as one
who misleads the people. And indeed, [b]having examined *Him*
in your presence, I have found no fault in this Man concern-
ing those things of which you accuse Him;
15 "no, neither did Herod, for I sent you back to him;[1] and
indeed nothing deserving of death has been done by Him.
16 [a]"I will therefore chastise Him and release *Him*"
17 [a](for it was necessary for him to release one to them at
the feast).[1]
18 And [a]they all cried out at once, saying, "Away with this
Man, and release to us Barabbas"—
19 who had been thrown into prison for a certain rebellion
made in the city, and for murder.
20 Pilate, therefore, wishing to release Jesus, again called
out to them.
21 But they shouted, saying, "Crucify *Him,* crucify Him!"
22 Then he said to them the third time, "Why, what evil has
He done? I have found no reason for death in Him. I will
therefore chastise Him and let *Him* go."
23 But they were insistent, demanding with loud voices that
He be crucified. And the voices of these men and of the chief
priests prevailed.[1]
24 So [a]Pilate gave sentence that it should be as they request-
ed.
25 [a]And he released to them[1] the one they requested, who
for rebellion and murder had been thrown into prison; but
he delivered Jesus to their will.
26 [a]Now as they led Him away, they laid hold of a certain man,
Simon a Cyrenian, who was coming from the country, and
on him they laid the cross that he might bear *it* after Jesus.
27 And a great multitude of the people followed Him, and
women who also mourned and lamented Him.
28 But Jesus, turning to them, said, "Daughters of Jerusalem,

23:9[a]John 19:9 23:11[a]Is. 53:3 23:12[a]Acts 4:26, 27 23:13[a]Mark 15:14 23:14[a]Luke 23:1, 2 [b]Luke 23:4 23:15[1]NU-Text reads *for he sent Him back to us.* 23:16[a]John 19:1 23:17[a]John 18:39 [1]NU-Text omits verse 17. 23:18[a]Acts 3:13–15 23:23[1]NU-Text omits *and of the chief priests.* 23:24[a]Mark 15:15 23:25[a]Is. 53:8 [1]NU-Text and M-Text omit *to them.* 23:26[a]Matt. 27:32

do not weep for Me, but weep for yourselves and for your
children.
29 [a]"For indeed the days are coming in which they will say,
'Blessed *are* the barren, wombs that never bore, and breasts
which never nursed!'
30 "Then they will begin [a]'to say to the mountains, "Fall on
us!" and to the hills, "Cover us!"'[1]
31 [a]"For if they do these things in the green wood, what will
be done in the dry?"
32 [a]There were also two others, criminals, led with Him to
be put to death.
33 And [a]when they had come to the place called Calvary,
there they crucified Him, and the criminals, one on the right
hand and the other on the left.
34 Then Jesus said, "Father, [a]forgive them, for [b]they do not
know what they do."[1] And [c]they divided His garments and
cast lots.
35 And [a]the people stood looking on. But even the [b]rulers
with them sneered, saying, "He saved others; let Him save
Himself if He is the Christ, the chosen of God."
36 The soldiers also mocked Him, coming and offering Him
[a]sour wine,
37 and saying, "If You are the King of the Jews, save Your-
self."
38 [a]And an inscription also was written over Him in letters
of Greek, Latin, and Hebrew:[1]

THIS IS THE KING
OF THE JEWS.

39 [a]Then one of the criminals who were hanged blasphemed
Him, saying, "If You are the Christ,[1] save Yourself and us."
40 But the other, answering, rebuked him, saying, "Do you
not even fear God, seeing you are under the same condem-
nation?
41 "And we indeed justly, for we receive the due reward of
our deeds; but this Man has done [a]nothing wrong."
42 Then he said to Jesus, "Lord,[1] remember me when You
come into Your kingdom."
43 And Jesus said to him, "Assuredly, I say to you, today you
will be with Me in [a]Paradise."
44 [a]Now it was[1] about the sixth hour, and there was darkness
over all the earth until the ninth hour.

23:29 [a]Matt. 24:19 23:30 [a]Hos. 10:8; Rev. 6:16, 17; 9:6 [1]Hosea 10:8 23:31 [a][Jer. 25:29] 23:32 [a]Is. 53:9, 12 23:33 [a]John 19:17–24 23:34 [a]1 Cor. 4:12 [b]Acts 3:17 [c]Matt. 27:35 [1]NU-Text brackets the first sentence as a later addition. 23:35 [a]Ps. 22:17 [b]Matt. 27:39 23:36 [a]Ps. 69:21 23:38 [a]John 19:19 [1]NU-Text omits *written* and *in letters of Greek, Latin, and Hebrew.* 23:39 [a]Mark 15:32 [1]NU-Text reads *Are You not the Christ?* 23:41 [a][Heb. 7:26] 23:42 [1]NU-Text reads *And he said, "Jesus, remember me.* 23:43 [a][Rev. 2:7] 23:44 [a]Matt. 27:45–56 [1]NU-Text adds *already.*

45 Then the sun was darkened,[1] and [a]the veil of the temple
was torn in two.
46 And when Jesus had cried out with a loud voice, He said,
"Father, [a]'into Your hands I commit My spirit.'"[1] [b]Having said
this, He breathed His last.
47 [a]So when the centurion saw what had happened, he glo-
rified God, saying, "Certainly this was a righteous Man!"
48 And the whole crowd who came together to that sight,
seeing what had been done, beat their breasts and returned.
49 [a]But all His acquaintances, and the women who followed
Him from Galilee, stood at a distance, watching these things.
50 [a]Now behold, *there was* a man named Joseph, a council
member, a good and just man.
51 He had not consented to their decision and deed. *He was*
from Arimathea, a city of the Jews, [a]who himself was also
waiting[1] for the kingdom of God.
52 This man went to Pilate and asked for the body of Jesus.
53 [a]Then he took it down, wrapped it in linen, and laid it in
a tomb *that was* hewn out of the rock, where no one had ever
lain before.
54 That day was [a]the Preparation, and the Sabbath drew
near.
55 And the women [a]who had come with Him from Galilee
followed after, and [b]they observed the tomb and how His
body was laid.
56 Then they returned and [a]prepared spices and fragrant
oils. And they rested on the Sabbath [b]according to the com-
mandment.

23:45[a]Matt. 27:51 [1]NU-Text reads *obscured.* 23:46[a]Ps. 31:5 [b]John 19:30 [1]Psalm 31:5 23:47[a]Mark 15:39 23:49[a]Ps. 38:11 23:50[a]Matt. 27:57–61 23:51[a]Luke 2:25, 38 [1]NU-Text reads *who was waiting.* 23:53[a]Mark 15:46 23:54[a]Matt. 27:62 23:55[a]Luke 8:2 [b]Mark 15:47 23:56[a]Mark 16:1 [b]Ex. 20:10

LUKE 24

THE RISEN AND ASCENDED CHRIST

What a blessed walk was that from Jerusalem to Emmaus! Were they not highly favored men to have such a companion as the Lord Jesus, to feel their hearts burning within them with so divine a flame? Brethren, these are not the only men who have walked with the Lord Jesus. We have heard the words of Holy Scripture as though they fell fresh from His lips, and thus they have, by the power of the Holy Spirit, made our hearts to burn like coals of juniper that have a most vehement flame.

Thank God, our divine Master is still the familiar Friend of His disciples. In one sense "He is not here, but is risen"; but in another sense He is more peculiarly here because He has risen. Unrisen He could have been in only one place at a time; now that He is risen He is by His Spirit present with thousands of His people at the same moment, and He walks not only from Jerusalem to Emmaus but to many a village. Jesus delights to manifest Himself unto His people: He is not strange unto His own flesh. We are bound to bear witness to the fact that He is not ashamed to call us brethren and to be found walking with us.

---

1 Now [a]on the first *day* of the week, very early in the morn-
ing, they, and certain *other women* with them,[1] came to the
tomb [b]bringing the spices which they had prepared.
2 [a]But they found the stone rolled away from the tomb.
3 [a]Then they went in and did not find the body of the Lord
Jesus.
4 And it happened, as they were greatly[1] perplexed about this,
that [a]behold, two men stood by them in shining garments.
5 Then, as they were afraid and bowed *their* faces to the earth,
they said to them, "Why do you seek the living among the dead?
6 "He is not here, but is risen! [a]Remember how He spoke to
you when He was still in Galilee,
7 "saying, 'The Son of Man must be [a]delivered into the hands
of sinful men, and be crucified, and the third day rise again.'"
8 And [a]they remembered His words.
9 [a]Then they returned from the tomb and told all these
things to the eleven and to all the rest.
10 It was Mary Magdalene, [a]Joanna, Mary *the mother* of James,
and the other *women* with them, who told these things to the
apostles.

24:1 [a]John 20:1–8 [b]Luke 23:56 [1]NU Text omits *and certain other women with them.* 24:2 [a]Mark 16:4 24:3 [a]Mark 16:5 24:4 [a]John 20:12 [1]NU-Text omits *greatly.* 24:6 [a]Luke 9:22 24:7 [a]Luke 9:44; 11:29, 30; 18:31–33 24:8 [a]John 2:19–22 24:9 [a]Mark 16:10 24:10 [a]Luke 8:3

11 [a]And their words seemed to them like idle tales, and they
did not believe them.
12 [a]But Peter arose and ran to the tomb; and stooping down,
he saw the linen cloths lying[1] by themselves; and he departed,
marveling to himself at what had happened.
13 [a]Now behold, two of them were traveling that same day
to a village called Emmaus, which was seven miles[1] from Je-
rusalem.
14 And they talked together of all these things which had
happened.
15 So it was, while they conversed and reasoned, that [a]Jesus
Himself drew near and went with them.
16 But [a]their eyes were restrained, so that they did not
know Him.
17 And He said to them, "What kind of conversation *is* this
that you have with one another as you walk and are sad?"[1]
18 Then the one [a]whose name was Cleopas answered and said
to Him, "Are You the only stranger in Jerusalem, and have You
not known the things which happened there in these days?"
19 And He said to them, "What things?" So they said to Him,
"The things concerning Jesus of Nazareth, [a]who was a Proph-
et [b]mighty in deed and word before God and all the people,
20 [a]"and how the chief priests and our rulers delivered Him
to be condemned to death, and crucified Him.
21 "But we were hoping [a]that it was He who was going to re-
deem Israel. Indeed, besides all this, today is the third day
since these things happened.
22 "Yes, and [a]certain women of our company, who arrived
at the tomb early, astonished us.
23 "When they did not find His body, they came saying that
they had also seen a vision of angels who said He was alive.
24 "And [a]certain of those *who were* with us went to the tomb
and found *it* just as the women had said; but Him they did
not see."
25 Then He said to them, "O foolish ones, and slow of heart
to believe in all that the prophets have spoken!
26 [a]"Ought not the Christ to have suffered these things and
to enter into His [b]glory?"
27 And beginning at [a]Moses and [b]all the Prophets, He ex-
pounded to them in all the Scriptures the things concerning
Himself.
28 Then they drew near to the village where they were go-
ing, and [a]He indicated that He would have gone farther.

24:11[a]Luke 24:25 24:12[a]John 20:3–6 [1]NU-Text omits *lying.* 24:13[a]Mark 16:12 [1]Literally *sixty stadia* 24:15[a][Matt. 18:20] 24:16[a]John 20:14; 21:4 24:17[1]NU-Text reads *as you walk? And they stood still, looking sad.* 24:18[a]John 19:25 24:19[a]Matt. 21:11 [b]Acts 7:22 24:20[a]Acts 13:27, 28 24:21[a]Luke 1:68; 2:38 24:22[a]Mark 16:10 24:24[a]Luke 24:12 24:26[a]Acts 17:2, 3 [b][1 Pet. 1:10–12] 24:27[a][Deut. 18:15] [b][Is. 7:14; 9:6] 24:28[a]Mark 6:48

29 But [a]they constrained Him, saying, [b]"Abide with us, for
it is toward evening, and the day is far spent." And He went
in to stay with them.
30 Now it came to pass, as [a]He sat at the table with them,
that He took bread, blessed and broke *it,* and gave it to them.
31 Then their eyes were opened and they knew Him; and He
vanished from their sight.
32 And they said to one another, "Did not our heart burn
within us while He talked with us on the road, and while He
opened the Scriptures to us?"
33 So they rose up that very hour and returned to Jerusa-
lem, and found the eleven and those *who were* with them
gathered together,
34 saying, "The Lord is risen indeed, and [a]has appeared to
Simon!"
35 And they told about the things *that had happened* on
the road, and how He was known to them in the breaking of
bread.
36 [a]Now as they said these things, Jesus Himself stood in
the midst of them, and said to them, "Peace to you."
37 But they were terrified and frightened, and supposed
they had seen [a]a spirit.
38 And He said to them, "Why are you troubled? And why
do doubts arise in your hearts?
39 "Behold My hands and My feet, that it is I Myself. [a]Han-
dle Me and see, for a [b]spirit does not have flesh and bones
as you see I have."
40 When He had said this, He showed them His hands and
His feet.[1]
41 But while they still did not believe [a]for joy, and marveled,
He said to them, [b]"Have you any food here?"
42 So they gave Him a piece of a broiled fish and some honey-
comb.[1]
43 [a]And He took *it* and ate in their presence.
44 Then He said to them, [a]"These *are* the words which I
spoke to you while I was still with you, that all things must
be fulfilled which were written in the Law of Moses and *the*
Prophets and *the* Psalms concerning Me."
45 And [a]He opened their understanding, that they might
comprehend the Scriptures.
46 Then He said to them, [a]"Thus it is written, and thus it was
necessary for the Christ to suffer and to rise[1] from the dead
the third day,

24:29 [a]Gen. 19:2, 3 [b][John 14:23] 24:30 [a]Matt. 14:19 24:34 [a]1 Cor. 15:5 24:36 [a]Mark 16:14 24:37 [a]Mark 6:49 24:39 [a]John 20:20, 27 [b][1 Cor. 15:50] 24:40 [1]Some printed New Testaments omit this verse. It is found in nearly all Greek manuscripts. 24:41 [a]Gen. 45:26 [b]John 21:5 24:42 [1]NU-Text omits *and some honeycomb.* 24:43 [a]Acts 10:39–41 24:44 [a]Matt. 16:21; 17:22; 20:18 24:45 [a]Acts 16:14 24:46 [a]Acts 17:3 [1]NU-Text reads *written, that the Christ should suffer and rise.*

47 "and that repentance and [a]remission of sins should be
preached in His name [b]to all nations, beginning at Jerusa-
lem.
48 "And [a]you are witnesses of these things.
49 [a]"Behold, I send the Promise of My Father upon you;
but tarry in the city of Jerusalem[1] until you are endued with
power from on high."
50 And He led them out [a]as far as Bethany, and He lifted up
His hands and blessed them.
51 [a]Now it came to pass, while He blessed them, that He was
parted from them and carried up into heaven.
52 [a]And they worshiped Him, and returned to Jerusalem
with great joy,
53 and were continually [a]in the temple praising and[1] bless-
ing God. Amen.[2]

24:47 [a]Acts 5:31; 10:43; 13:38; 26:18 [b][Jer. 31:34] 24:48 [a][Acts 1:8] 24:49 [a]Joel 2:28 [1]NU-Text omits *of Jerusalem.* 24:50 [a]Acts 1:12 24:51 [a]Mark 16:19 24:52 [a]Matt. 28:9 24:53 [a]Acts 2:46 [1]NU-Text omits *praising and.* [2]NU-Text omits *Amen.*

JOHN

JOHN 1

TESTIMONY OF JOHN THE BAPTIST

The text informs us that there is a fullness in Christ. There is a fullness of essential deity, for "in Him dwells all the fullness of the Godhead" (Col. 2:9). There is a fullness of perfect Manhood, for in Him bodily that Godhead was revealed. In Him there was nothing lacking that was necessary to the perfection of humankind. There is a fullness of atoning efficacy in His blood, for "the blood of Jesus Christ His Son cleanses us from all sin" (1 John 1:7). There is a fullness of justifying righteousness in His life, for "there is therefore now no condemnation to those who are in Christ Jesus" (Rom. 8:1). There is a fullness of divine providence in His plea, for "He is also able to save to the uttermost those who come to God through Him, since He always lives to make intercession for them" (Heb. 7:25). There is a fullness of victory in His death, for He destroyed him who had the power of death. There is a fullness of efficacy in His resurrection from the dead, for by it He "has begotten us again to a living hope" (1 Pet. 1:3). There is a fullness of triumph in His ascension, for "when He ascended on high, He led captivity captive, and gave gifts to men" (Eph. 4:8). There is a fullness of blessings unspeakable, unknown; a fullness of grace to pardon, to regenerate, to sanctify, to preserve, and to perfect. There is a fullness at all times.

---

1 In the beginning [a]was the Word, and the [b]Word was [c]with
God, and the Word was [d]God.
2 [a]He was in the beginning with God.
3 [a]All things were made through Him, and without Him
nothing was made that was made.
4 [a]In Him was life, and [b]the life was the light of men.
5 And [a]the light shines in the darkness, and the darkness
did not comprehend[1] it.
6 There was a [a]man sent from God, whose name *was* John.
7 This man came for a [a]witness, to bear witness of the Light,
that all through him might [b]believe.
8 He was not that Light, but *was sent* to bear witness of that
[a]Light.
9 [a]That was the true Light which gives light to every man
coming into the world.[1]
10 He was in the world, and the world was made through
Him, and [a]the world did not know Him.

1:1[a]1 John 1:1 [b]Rev. 19:13 [c][John 17:5] [d][1 John 5:20] 1:2[a]Gen. 1:1 1:3[a][Col. 1:16, 17] 1:4[a][1 John 5:11] [b]John 8:12; 9:5; 12:46 1:5[a][John 3:19] [1]Or *overcome* 1:6[a]Matt. 3:1–17 1:7[a]John 3:25–36; 5:33–35 [b][John 3:16] 1:8[a]Is. 9:2; 49:6 1:9[a]Is. 49:6 [1]Or *That was the true Light which, coming into the world, gives light to every man.* 1:10[a]Heb. 1:2

11 [a]He came to His own,[1] and His own[2] did not receive Him.
12 But [a]as many as received Him, to them He gave the right
to become children of God, to those who believe in His name:
13 [a]who were born, not of blood, nor of the will of the flesh,
nor of the will of man, but of God.
14 [a]And the Word [b]became [c]flesh and dwelt among us, and
[d]we beheld His glory, the glory as of the only begotten of the
Father, [e]full of grace and truth.
15 [a]John bore witness of Him and cried out, saying, "This
was He of whom I said, [b]'He who comes after me is preferred
before me, [c]for He was before me.'"
16 And[1] of His [a]fullness we have all received, and grace for
grace.
17 For [a]the law was given through Moses, *but* [b]grace and
[c]truth came through Jesus Christ.
18 [a]No one has seen God at any time. [b]The only begotten Son,[1]
who is in the bosom of the Father, He has declared *Him*.
19 Now this is [a]the testimony of John, when the Jews sent
priests and Levites from Jerusalem to ask him, "Who are you?"
20 [a]He confessed, and did not deny, but confessed, "I am
not the Christ."
21 And they asked him, "What then? Are you Elijah?" He said,
"I am not." "Are you [a]the Prophet?" And he answered, "No."
22 Then they said to him, "Who are you, that we may give an
answer to those who sent us? What do you say about your-
self?"
23 He said: [a]"I *am*

> [b]'The voice of one crying in the wilderness:
> "Make straight the way of the LORD,"'[1]

as the prophet Isaiah said."
24 Now those who were sent were from the Pharisees.
25 And they asked him, saying, "Why then do you baptize if
you are not the Christ, nor Elijah, nor the Prophet?"
26 John answered them, saying, [a]"I baptize with water, [b]but
there stands One among you whom you do not know.
27 [a]"It is He who, coming after me, is preferred before me,
whose sandal strap I am not worthy to loose."
28 These things were done [a]in Bethabara[1] beyond the Jor-
dan, where John was baptizing.
29 The next day John saw Jesus coming toward him, and

1:11[a] Is. 53:3; [Luke 19:14] [1]That is, His own things or domain [2]That is, His own people 1:12[a] Gal. 3:26 1:13[a] [1 Pet. 1:23] 1:14[a] Rev. 19:13 [b]Gal. 4:4 [c]Heb. 2:11 [d]Is. 40:5 [e][John 8:32; 14:6; 18:37] 1:15[a] John 3:32 [b][Matt. 3:11] [c][Col. 1:17] 1:16[a] [Col. 1:19; 2:9] [1]NU-Text reads *For.* 1:17[a] [Ex. 20:1] [b][Rom. 5:21; 6:14] [c][John 8:32; 14:6; 18:37] 1:18[a] Ex. 33:20 [b]1 John 4:9 [1]NU-Text reads *only begotten God.* 1:19[a] John 5:33 1:20[a] Luke 3:15 1:21[a] Deut. 18:15, 18 1:23[a] Matt. 3:3 [b]Is. 40:3 [1]Isaiah 40:3 1:26[a] Matt. 3:11 [b]Mal. 3:1 1:27[a] Acts 19:4 1:28[a] Judg. 7:24 [1]NU-Text and M-Text read *Bethany.*

said, "Behold! [a]The Lamb of God [b]who takes away the sin of
the world!
30 "This is He of whom I said, 'After me comes a Man who
is preferred before me, for He was before me.'
31 "I did not know Him; but that He should be revealed to
Israel, [a]therefore I came baptizing with water."
32 [a]And John bore witness, saying, "I saw the Spirit descend-
ing from heaven like a dove, and He remained upon Him.
33 "I did not know Him, but He who sent me to baptize with
water said to me, 'Upon whom you see the Spirit descend-
ing, and remaining on Him, [a]this is He who baptizes with the
Holy Spirit.'
34 "And I have seen and testified that this is the [a]Son of God."
35 Again, the next day, John stood with two of his disciples.
36 And looking at Jesus as He walked, he said, [a]"Behold the
Lamb of God!"
37 The two disciples heard him speak, and they [a]followed
Jesus.
38 Then Jesus turned, and seeing them following, said to
them, "What do you seek?" They said to Him, "Rabbi" (which
is to say, when translated, Teacher), "where are You staying?"
39 He said to them, "Come and see." They came and saw
where He was staying, and remained with Him that day (now
it was about the tenth hour).
40 One of the two who heard John *speak,* and followed Him,
was [a]Andrew, Simon Peter's brother.
41 He first found his own brother Simon, and said to him,
"We have found the Messiah" (which is translated, the Christ).
42 And he brought him to Jesus. Now when Jesus looked at
him, He said, "You are Simon the son of Jonah.[1] [a]You shall
be called Cephas" (which is translated, A Stone).
43 The following day Jesus wanted to go to Galilee, and He
found [a]Philip and said to him, "Follow Me."
44 Now [a]Philip was from Bethsaida, the city of Andrew and
Peter.
45 Philip found [a]Nathanael and said to him, "We have found
Him of whom [b]Moses in the law, and also the [c]prophets,
wrote—Jesus [d]of Nazareth, the [e]son of Joseph."
46 And Nathanael said to him, [a]"Can anything good come
out of Nazareth?" Philip said to him, "Come and see."
47 Jesus saw Nathanael coming toward Him, and said of
him, "Behold, [a]an Israelite indeed, in whom is no deceit!"
48 Nathanael said to Him, "How do You know me?" Jesus
answered and said to him, "Before Philip called you, when
you were under the fig tree, I saw you."

1:29 [a]Rev. 5:6–14 [b][1 Pet. 2:24] 1:31 [a]Matt. 3:6 1:32 [a]Mark 1:10 1:33 [a]Is. 42:1; 61:1; Matt. 3:11 1:34 [a]John 11:27 1:36 [a]John 1:29 1:37 [a]Matt. 4:20, 22 1:40 [a]Matt. 4:18 1:42 [a]Matt. 16:18 [1]NU-Text reads *John.* 1:43 [a]John 6:5; 12:21, 22; 14:8, 9 1:44 [a]John 12:21 1:45 [a]John 21:2 [b]Luke 24:27 [c][Zech. 6:12] [d][Matt. 2:23] [e]Luke 3:23 1:46 [a]John 7:41, 42, 52 1:47 [a]Ps. 32:2; 73:1

49 Nathanael answered and said to Him, "Rabbi, [a]You are
the Son of God! You are [b]the King of Israel!"
50 Jesus answered and said to him, "Because I said to you,
'I saw you under the fig tree,' do you believe? You will see
greater things than these."
51 And He said to him, "Most assuredly, I say to you, [a]here-
after[1] you shall see heaven open, and the angels of God as-
cending and descending upon the Son of Man."

1:49 [a]Matt. 14:33 [b]Matt. 21:5 1:51 [a]Gen. 28:12 [1]NU-Text omits *hereafter.*

JOHN 2

JESUS' FIRST MIRACLE AT CANA

Jesus Christ commenced the gospel dispensation, not with a miracle of vengeance like that of Moses, who turned water into blood, but with a miracle of liberality, turning water into wine. He supplies not only necessaries but luxuries, and this is highly significant of the kingdom of His grace. Here He not only gives sinners enough to save them, but He gives abundantly, grace upon grace. The gifts of the covenant are not stinted or stunted, they are neither small in quantity nor in quality. He gives to men not only the water of life that they may drink and be refreshed but "wines on the lees" (Is. 25:6) that they may rejoice exceedingly. And He gives like a king who gives lavishly without counting the cups and bottles.

As to 120 gallons, how little is that in comparison with the rivers of love and mercy that He is pleased to bestow freely out of His bountiful heart upon the neediest souls? And now let us think about our Lord's mercy: let the wine stand as a type of His grace and the abundance of it as the type of the abundance of His grace that He so liberally bestows. He goes to a simple wedding among poor people, and there in the simplest and most natural way He displays His glory.

1 On the third day there was a [a]wedding in [b]Cana of Galilee,
and the [c]mother of Jesus was there.
2 Now both Jesus and His disciples were invited to the wed-
ding.
3 And when they ran out of wine, the mother of Jesus said
to Him, "They have no wine."
4 Jesus said to her, [a]"Woman, [b]what does your concern have
to do with Me? [c]My hour has not yet come."
5 His mother said to the servants, "Whatever He says to you,
do *it*."
6 Now there were set there six waterpots of stone, [a]according
to the manner of purification of the Jews, containing twenty
or thirty gallons apiece.
7 Jesus said to them, "Fill the waterpots with water." And
they filled them up to the brim.
8 And He said to them, "Draw *some* out now, and take *it* to
the master of the feast." And they took *it*.
9 When the master of the feast had tasted [a]the water that
was made wine, and did not know where it came from (but

2:1[a][Heb. 13:4] [b]John 4:46 [c]John 19:25 2:4[a]John 19:26 [b]2 Sam. 16:10 [c]John 7:6, 8, 30; 8:20 2:6[a][Mark 7:3] 2:9[a]John 4:46

the servants who had drawn the water knew), the master of
the feast called the bridegroom.
10 And he said to him, "Every man at the beginning sets out
the good wine, and when the *guests* have well drunk, then the
inferior. You have kept the good wine until now!"
11 This [a]beginning of signs Jesus did in Cana of Galilee, [b]and
manifested His glory; and His disciples believed in Him.
12 After this He went down to [a]Capernaum, He, His mother,
[b]His brothers, and His disciples; and they did not stay there
many days.
13 [a]Now the Passover of the Jews was at hand, and Jesus went
up to Jerusalem.
14 [a]And He found in the temple those who sold oxen and
sheep and doves, and the money changers doing business.
15 When He had made a whip of cords, He drove them all
out of the temple, with the sheep and the oxen, and poured
out the changers' money and overturned the tables.
16 And He said to those who sold doves, "Take these things
away! Do not make [a]My Father's house a house of merchan-
dise!"
17 Then His disciples remembered that it was written, [a]"Zeal
for Your house has eaten[1] Me up."[2]
18 So the Jews answered and said to Him, [a]"What sign do
You show to us, since You do these things?"
19 Jesus answered and said to them, [a]"Destroy this temple,
and in three days I will raise it up."
20 Then the Jews said, "It has taken forty-six years to build
this temple, and will You raise it up in three days?"
21 But He was speaking [a]of the temple of His body.
22 Therefore, when He had risen from the dead, [a]His dis-
ciples remembered that He had said this to them;[1] and they
believed the Scripture and the word which Jesus had said.
23 Now when He was in Jerusalem at the Passover, during the
feast, many believed in His name when they saw the [a]signs
which He did.
24 But Jesus did not commit Himself to them, because He
[a]knew all *men,*
25 and had no need that anyone should testify of man, for
[a]He knew what was in man.

2:11[a]John 4:54 [b][John 1:14] 2:12[a]Matt. 4:13 [b]Matt. 12:46; 13:55 2:13[a]Deut. 16:1–6 2:14[a]Mark 11:15, 17 2:16[a]Luke 2:49 2:17[a]Ps. 69:9 [1]NU-Text and M-Text read *will eat.* [2]Psalm 69:9 2:18[a]Matt. 12:38 2:19[a]Matt. 26:61; 27:40 2:21[a][1 Cor. 3:16; 6:19] 2:22[a]Luke 24:8 [1]NU-Text and M-Text omit *to them.* 2:23[a][Acts 2:22] 2:24[a]Rev. 2:23 2:25[a]Matt. 9:4

JOHN 3

YOU MUST BE BORN AGAIN

Men who love much will give much, and you may usually measure the truth of love by its self-denials and sacrifices. The love that spares nothing but spends itself to help and bless its object is love indeed and not the mere name of it. Little love forgets to bring water for the feet, but great love breaks its box of alabaster and lavishes its precious ointment.

Consider what this gift was that God gave. I should have to labor for expression if I were to attempt to set forth to the full this priceless boon, and I will not court a failure by attempting the impossible. I will only invite you to think of the sacred Person whom the Great Father gave in order that He might prove His love to men. It was His only begotten Son—His beloved Son in whom He was well pleased. None of us had ever such a son to give. Ours are the sons of men; His was the Son of God. The Father gave His other self, one with Himself. When the great God gave His Son He gave God Himself, for Jesus is not in His eternal nature less than God. What more could He give? Who can measure this love?

---

1 There was a man of the Pharisees named Nicodemus, a
ruler of the Jews.
2 [a]This man came to Jesus by night and said to Him, "Rabbi,
we know that You are a teacher come from God; for [b]no one
can do these signs that You do unless [c]God is with him."
3 Jesus answered and said to him, "Most assuredly, I say to
you, [a]unless one is born again, he cannot see the kingdom
of God."
4 Nicodemus said to Him, "How can a man be born when he
is old? Can he enter a second time into his mother's womb
and be born?"
5 Jesus answered, "Most assuredly, I say to you, [a]unless one
is born of water and the Spirit, he cannot enter the kingdom
of God.
6 "That which is born of the flesh is [a]flesh, and that which is
born of the Spirit is spirit.
7 "Do not marvel that I said to you, 'You must be born again.'
8 [a]"The wind blows where it wishes, and you hear the sound
of it, but cannot tell where it comes from and where it goes.
So is everyone who is born of the Spirit."
9 Nicodemus answered and said to Him, [a]"How can these
things be?"

3:2[a]John 7:50; 19:39 [b]John 9:16, 33 [c][Acts 10:38] 3:3[a][1 Pet. 1:23] 3:5[a][Acts 2:38] 3:6[a]1 Cor. 15:50 3:8[a]Eccl. 11:5 3:9[a]John 6:52, 60

10 Jesus answered and said to him, "Are you the teacher of
Israel, and do not know these things?
11 [a]"Most assuredly, I say to you, We speak what We know
and testify what We have seen, and [b]you do not receive Our
witness.
12 "If I have told you earthly things and you do not believe,
how will you believe if I tell you heavenly things?
13 [a]"No one has ascended to heaven but He who came down
from heaven, *that is,* the Son of Man who is in heaven.[1]
14 [a]"And as Moses lifted up the serpent in the wilderness,
even so [b]must the Son of Man be lifted up,
15 "that whoever [a]believes in Him should not perish but[1]
[b]have eternal life.
16 [a]"For God so loved the world that He gave His only begot-
ten [b]Son, that whoever believes in Him should not perish but
have everlasting life.
17 [a]"For God did not send His Son into the world to condemn
the world, but that the world through Him might be saved.
18 [a]"He who believes in Him is not condemned; but he who
does not believe is condemned already, because he has not
believed in the name of the only begotten Son of God.
19 "And this is the condemnation, [a]that the light has come
into the world, and men loved darkness rather than light,
because their deeds were evil.
20 "For [a]everyone practicing evil hates the light and does
not come to the light, lest his deeds should be exposed.
21 "But he who does the truth comes to the light, that his
deeds may be clearly seen, that they have been [a]done in God."
22 After these things Jesus and His disciples came into the
land of Judea, and there He remained with them [a]and bap-
tized.
23 Now John also was baptizing in Aenon near [a]Salim, be-
cause there was much water there. [b]And they came and were
baptized.
24 For [a]John had not yet been thrown into prison.
25 Then there arose a dispute between *some* of John's dis-
ciples and the Jews about purification.
26 And they came to John and said to him, "Rabbi, He
who was with you beyond the Jordan, [a]to whom you have
testified—behold, He is baptizing, and all [b]are coming
to Him!"
27 John answered and said, [a]"A man can receive nothing
unless it has been given to him from heaven.

3:11 [a][Matt. 11:27] [b]John 3:32; 8:14 3:13 [a]Eph. 4:9 [1]NU-Text omits *who is in heaven.* 3:14 [a]Num. 21:9 [b]John 8:28; 12:34; 19:18 3:15 [a]John 6:47 [b]John 3:36 [1]NU-Text omits *not perish but.* 3:16 [a]Rom. 5:8 [b][Is. 9:6] 3:17 [a]Luke 9:56 3:18 [a]John 5:24; 6:40, 47; 20:31 3:19 [a][John 1:4, 9–11] 3:20 [a]Eph. 5:11, 13 3:21 [a]1 Cor. 15:10 3:22 [a]John 4:1, 2 3:23 [a]1 Sam. 9:4 [b]Matt. 3:5, 6 3:24 [a]Matt. 4:12; 14:3 3:26 [a]John 1:7, 15, 27, 34 [b]Mark 2:2; 3:10; 5:24 3:27 [a]1 Cor. 3:5, 6; 4:7

28 "You yourselves bear me witness, that I said, [a]'I am not
the Christ,' but, [b]'I have been sent before Him.'
29 [a]"He who has the bride is the bridegroom; but [b]the friend
of the bridegroom, who stands and hears him, rejoices great-
ly because of the bridegroom's voice. Therefore this joy of
mine is fulfilled.
30 [a]"He must increase, but I *must* decrease.
31 [a]"He who comes from above [b]is above all; [c]he who is of
the earth is earthly and speaks of the earth. [d]He who comes
from heaven is above all.
32 "And [a]what He has seen and heard, that He testifies; and
no one receives His testimony.
33 "He who has received His testimony [a]has certified that
God is true.
34 [a]"For He whom God has sent speaks the words of God,
for God does not give the Spirit [b]by measure.
35 [a]"The Father loves the Son, and has given all things into
His hand.
36 [a]"He who believes in the Son has everlasting life; and he
who does not believe the Son shall not see life, but the [b]wrath
of God abides on him."

3:28 [a]John 1:19–27 [b]Mal. 3:1 3:29 [a][2 Cor. 11:2] [b]Song 5:1 3:30 [a][Is. 9:7] 3:31 [a]John 3:13; 8:23 [b]Matt. 28:18 [c]1 Cor. 15:47 [d]John 6:33 3:32 [a]John 3:11; 15:15 3:33 [a]1 John 5:10 3:34 [a]Deut. 18:18; John 7:16 [b]John 1:16 3:35 [a][Heb. 2:8] 3:36 [a]John 3:16, 17; 6:47 [b]Rom. 1:18

JOHN 4

JESUS IN SAMARIA AND GALILEE

The woman said to the men, "Come, see a Man who told me all things that I ever did. Could this be the Christ?" Observe first, when she went to the men she had but one aim, and that was to bring them to Jesus. She cries, "Come, see." She did not tell them anything about their sin at the time or try to reform their habits; she called them to Him who could set them right. She knew that if she could bring them to Christ, all things would come right inevitably.

It is good for you to shoot at only one target. Choose your design and aim at it. Drive away at the souls of men in the name of God to get them to Christ and nothing short of Him. Labor for this; He was willing to live for this and to die for this that men may be saved by Immanuel's love, and blood, and Spirit. This Samaritan woman aimed at this object and tried to gain it by an exceedingly earnest address.

I warrant you she said it very prettily, perhaps with all her charms. If you go upon the Lord's errands take your heart with you; speak every single syllable earnestly; and if you are thoroughly alive you will not need to be taught the way of doing it. The way comes naturally to those whose hearts are set upon the end.

---

1 Therefore, when the Lord knew that the Pharisees had
heard that Jesus made and [a]baptized more disciples than
John
2 (though Jesus Himself did not baptize, but His disciples),
3 He left Judea and departed again to Galilee.
4 But He needed to go through Samaria.
5 So He came to a city of Samaria which is called Sychar,
near the plot of ground that [a]Jacob [b]gave to his son Joseph.
6 Now Jacob's well was there. Jesus therefore, being wearied
from *His* journey, sat thus by the well. It was about the sixth
hour.
7 A woman of Samaria came to draw water. Jesus said to her,
"Give Me a drink."
8 For His disciples had gone away into the city to buy food.
9 Then the woman of Samaria said to Him, "How is it that
You, being a Jew, ask a drink from me, a Samaritan woman?"
For [a]Jews have no dealings with [b]Samaritans.
10 Jesus answered and said to her, "If you knew the [a]gift of
God, and who it is who says to you, 'Give Me a drink,' you would
have asked Him, and He would have given you [b]living water."

4:1[a]John 3:22, 26 4:5[a]Gen. 33:19 [b]Gen. 48:22 4:9[a]Acts 10:28 [b]2 Kin. 17:24
4:10[a][Rom. 5:15] [b]Is. 12:3; 44:3

11 The woman said to Him, "Sir, You have nothing to draw
with, and the well is deep. Where then do You get that living
water?
12 "Are You greater than our father Jacob, who gave us the
well, and drank from it himself, as well as his sons and his
livestock?"
13 Jesus answered and said to her, "Whoever drinks of this
water will thirst again,
14 "but [a]whoever drinks of the water that I shall give him will
never thirst. But the water that I shall give him [b]will become
in him a fountain of water springing up into everlasting life."
15 [a]The woman said to Him, "Sir, give me this water, that I
may not thirst, nor come here to draw."
16 Jesus said to her, "Go, call your husband, and come here."
17 The woman answered and said, "I have no husband." Jesus
said to her, "You have well said, 'I have no husband,'
18 "for you have had five husbands, and the one whom you
now have is not your husband; in that you spoke truly."
19 The woman said to Him, "Sir, [a]I perceive that You are a
prophet.
20 "Our fathers worshiped on [a]this mountain, and you *Jews*
say that in [b]Jerusalem is the place where one ought to wor-
ship."
21 Jesus said to her, "Woman, believe Me, the hour is com-
ing [a]when you will neither on this mountain, nor in Jerusa-
lem, worship the Father.
22 "You worship [a]what you do not know; we know what we
worship, for [b]salvation is of the Jews.
23 "But the hour is coming, and now is, when the true wor-
shipers will [a]worship the Father in [b]spirit [c]and truth; for the
Father is seeking such to worship Him.
24 [a]"God *is* Spirit, and those who worship Him must worship
in spirit and truth."
25 The woman said to Him, "I know that Messiah [a]is com-
ing" (who is called Christ). "When He comes, [b]He will tell us
all things."
26 Jesus said to her, [a]"I who speak to you am *He*."
27 And at this *point* His disciples came, and they marveled
that He talked with a woman; yet no one said, "What do You
seek?" or, "Why are You talking with her?"
28 The woman then left her waterpot, went her way into the
city, and said to the men,
29 "Come, see a Man [a]who told me all things that I ever did.
Could this be the Christ?"
30 Then they went out of the city and came to Him.

4:14[a][John 6:35, 58] [b]John 7:37, 38 4:15[a]John 6:34, 35; 17:2, 3 4:19[a]Luke 7:16, 39; 24:19 4:20[a]Judg. 9:7 [b]Deut. 12:5, 11 4:21[a]1 Tim. 2:8 4:22[a][2 Kin. 17:28–41] [b][Rom. 3:1; 9:4, 5] 4:23[a][Heb. 13:10–14] [b]Phil. 3:3 [c][John 1:17] 4:24[a]2 Cor. 3:17 4:25[a]Deut. 18:15 [b]John 4:29, 39 4:26[a]Matt. 26:63, 64 4:29[a]John 4:25

31 In the meantime His disciples urged Him, saying,
"Rabbi, eat."
32 But He said to them, "I have food to eat of which you do
not know."
33 Therefore the disciples said to one another, "Has anyone
brought Him *anything* to eat?"
34 Jesus said to them, [a]"My food is to do the will of Him who
sent Me, and to [b]finish His work.
35 "Do you not say, 'There are still four months and *then*
comes [a]the harvest'? Behold, I say to you, lift up your eyes
and look at the fields, [b]for they are already white for harvest!
36 [a]"And he who reaps receives wages, and gathers fruit for
eternal life, that [b]both he who sows and he who reaps may
rejoice together.
37 "For in this the saying is true: [a]'One sows and another
reaps.'
38 "I sent you to reap that for which you have not labored;
[a]others have labored, and you have entered into their labors."
39 And many of the Samaritans of that city believed in Him
[a]because of the word of the woman who testified, "He told
me all that I *ever* did."
40 So when the Samaritans had come to Him, they urged
Him to stay with them; and He stayed there two days.
41 And many more believed because of His own [a]word.
42 Then they said to the woman, "Now we believe, not be-
cause of what you said, for [a]we ourselves have heard *Him*
and we know that this is indeed the Christ,[1] the Savior of the
world."
43 Now after the two days He departed from there and went
to Galilee.
44 For [a]Jesus Himself testified that a prophet has no honor
in his own country.
45 So when He came to Galilee, the Galileans received Him,
[a]having seen all the things He did in Jerusalem at the feast;
[b]for they also had gone to the feast.
46 So Jesus came again to Cana of Galilee [a]where He had
made the water wine. And there was a certain nobleman
whose son was sick at Capernaum.
47 When he heard that Jesus had come out of Judea into
Galilee, he went to Him and implored Him to come down
and heal his son, for he was at the point of death.
48 Then Jesus said to him, [a]"Unless you *people* see signs and
wonders, you will by no means believe."
49 The nobleman said to Him, "Sir, come down before my
child dies!"

4:34 [a]Ps. 40:7, 8 [b][John 6:38; 17:4; 19:30] 4:35 [a]Gen. 8:22 [b]Matt. 9:37 4:36 [a]Dan. 12:3 [b]1 Thess. 2:19 4:37 [a]1 Cor. 3:5–9 4:38 [a][1 Pet. 1:12] 4:39 [a]John 4:29 4:41 [a]Luke 4:32 4:42 [a]1 John 4:14 [1]NU-Text omits *the Christ*. 4:44 [a]Matt. 13:57 4:45 [a]John 2:13, 23; 3:2 [b]Deut. 16:16 4:46 [a]John 2:1, 11 4:48 [a]1 Cor. 1:22

50 Jesus said to him, "Go your way; your son lives." So the
man believed the word that Jesus spoke to him, and he went
his way.
51 And as he was now going down, his servants met him and
told *him,* saying, "Your son lives!"
52 Then he inquired of them the hour when he got better.
And they said to him, "Yesterday at the seventh hour the fe-
ver left him."
53 So the father knew that *it was* at the same hour in which
Jesus said to him, "Your son lives." And he himself believed,
and his whole household.
54 This again *is* the second sign Jesus did when He had come
out of Judea into Galilee.

JOHN 5

HEALING AT THE BETHESDA POOL

The doctrine of the resurrection of the dead is a peculiarly Christian belief. With natural reason assisted by some little light lingering in tradition or borrowed, a few philosophers spelled out the immortality of the soul; but that the body should rise again, that there should be another life for this corporeal frame, was a hope brought to light by the revelation of Christ Jesus. Men could not have imagined so great a wonder, and they prove their powerlessness to have invented it by the fact that still, as at Athens, when they heard of it for the first time, "some mocked" (Acts 17:32). "Can these bones live?" (Ezek. 37:3) is still the unbeliever's sneer.

The doctrine of the resurrection is a lamp kindled by the hand that once was pierced. It is indeed in some respects the keystone of the Christian arch. It is linked in our holy faith with the Person of Jesus Christ and is one of the brightest gems in His crown. The doctrine of the resurrection ought to be preached much more commonly than it is as vital to the gospel.

The doctrine of the resurrection in the early church was the main battle-ax and weapon of war of the preacher. Wherever the first missionaries went they made this prominent—that according to their gospel there would be a judgment, and the dead should rise again to be judged by the Man Christ Jesus. If we would honor Christ Jesus the Risen One, we must give prominence to this truth.

---

1 After [a]this there was a feast of the Jews, and Jesus [b]went
up to Jerusalem.
2 Now there is in Jerusalem [a]by the Sheep *Gate* a pool, which
is called in Hebrew, Bethesda,[1] having five porches.
3 In these lay a great multitude of sick people, blind, lame,
paralyzed, waiting for the moving of the water.
4 For an angel went down at a certain time into the pool and
stirred up the water; then whoever stepped in first, after the
stirring of the water, was made well of whatever disease he
had.[1]
5 Now a certain man was there who had an infirmity thirty-
eight years.
6 When Jesus saw him lying there, and knew that he already
had been *in that condition* a long time, He said to him, "Do
you want to be made well?"
7 The sick man answered Him, "Sir, I have no man to put

5:1[a]Deut. 16:16 [b]John 2:13 5:2[a]Neh. 3:1, 32; 12:39 [1]NU-Text reads *Bethzatha*.
5:4[1]NU-Text omits *waiting for the moving of the water* at the end of verse 3, and all of verse 4.

me into the pool when the water is stirred up; but while I am
coming, another steps down before me."
8 Jesus said to him, [a]"Rise, take up your bed and walk."
9 And immediately the man was made well, took up his bed,
and walked. And [a]that day was the Sabbath.
10 The Jews therefore said to him who was cured, "It is the
Sabbath; [a]it is not lawful for you to carry your bed."
11 He answered them, "He who made me well said to me,
'Take up your bed and walk.'"
12 Then they asked him, "Who is the Man who said to you,
'Take up your bed and walk'?"
13 But the one who was [a]healed did not know who it was, for
Jesus had withdrawn, a multitude being in *that* place.
14 Afterward Jesus found him in the temple, and said to him,
"See, you have been made well. [a]Sin no more, lest a worse
thing come upon you."
15 The man departed and told the Jews that it was Jesus who
had made him well.
16 For this reason the Jews [a]persecuted Jesus, and sought to
kill Him,[1] because He had done these things on the Sabbath.
17 But Jesus answered them, [a]"My Father has been working
until now, and I have been working."
18 Therefore the Jews [a]sought all the more to kill Him, be-
cause He not only broke the Sabbath, but also said that God
was His Father, [b]making Himself equal with God.
19 Then Jesus answered and said to them, "Most assuredly, I
say to you, [a]the Son can do nothing of Himself, but what He
sees the Father do; for whatever He does, the Son also does
in like manner.
20 "For [a]the Father loves the Son, and [b]shows Him all things
that He Himself does; and He will show Him greater works
than these, that you may marvel.
21 "For as the Father raises the dead and gives life to *them,*
[a]even so the Son gives life to whom He will.
22 "For the Father judges no one, but [a]has committed all
judgment to the Son,
23 "that all should honor the Son just as they honor the Fa-
ther. [a]He who does not honor the Son does not honor the
Father who sent Him.
24 "Most assuredly, I say to you, [a]he who hears My word and
believes in Him who sent Me has everlasting life, and shall
not come into judgment, [b]but has passed from death into
life.
25 "Most assuredly, I say to you, the hour is coming, and now

5:8[a]Luke 5:24 5:9[a]John 9:14 5:10[a]Jer. 17:21, 22 5:13[a]Luke 13:14; 22:51 5:14[a]John 8:11 5:16[a]John 8:37; 10:39 [1]NU-Text omits *and sought to kill Him.* 5:17[a][John 9:4; 17:4] 5:18[a]John 7:1, 19 [b]John 10:30 5:19[a]John 5:30; 6:38; 8:28; 12:49; 14:10 5:20[a]Matt. 3:17 [b][Matt. 11:27] 5:21[a][John 11:25] 5:22[a][Acts 17:31] 5:23[a]1 John 2:23 5:24[a]John 3:16, 18; 6:47 [b][1 John 3:14]

is, when [a]the dead will hear the voice of the Son of God; and
those who hear will live.
26 "For [a]as the Father has life in Himself, so He has granted
the Son to have [b]life in Himself,
27 "and [a]has given Him authority to execute judgment also,
[b]because He is the Son of Man.
28 "Do not marvel at this; for the hour is coming in which
all who are in the graves will [a]hear His voice
29 [a]"and come forth—[b]those who have done good, to the
resurrection of life, and those who have done evil, to the res-
urrection of condemnation.
30 [a]"I can of Myself do nothing. As I hear, I judge; and My
judgment is righteous, because [b]I do not seek My own will
but the will of the Father who sent Me.
31 [a]"If I bear witness of Myself, My witness is not true.
32 [a]"There is another who bears witness of Me, and I know
that the witness which He witnesses of Me is true.
33 "You have sent to John, [a]and he has borne witness to the
truth.
34 "Yet I do not receive testimony from man, but I say these
things that you may be saved.
35 "He was the burning and [a]shining lamp, and [b]you were
willing for a time to rejoice in his light.
36 "But [a]I have a greater witness than John's; for [b]the works
which the Father has given Me to finish—the very [c]works that
I do—bear witness of Me, that the Father has sent Me.
37 "And the Father Himself, who sent Me, [a]has testified of
Me. You have neither heard His voice at any time, [b]nor seen
His form.
38 "But you do not have His word abiding in you, because
whom He sent, Him you do not believe.
39 [a]"You search the Scriptures, for in them you think you
have eternal life; and [b]these are they which testify of Me.
40 [a]"But you are not willing to come to Me that you may have
life.
41 [a]"I do not receive honor from men.
42 "But I know you, that you do not have the love of God
in you.
43 "I have come in My Father's name, and you do not re-
ceive Me; if another comes in his own name, him you will
receive.
44 [a]"How can you believe, who receive honor from one anoth-
er, and do not seek [b]the honor that *comes* from the only God?

5:25[a][Col. 2:13] 5:26[a]Ps. 36:9 [b]1 Cor. 15:45 5:27[a][Acts 10:42; 17:31] [b]Dan. 7:13
5:28[a][1 Thess. 4:15–17] 5:29[a]Is. 26:19 [b]Dan. 12:2 5:30[a]John 5:19 [b]Matt. 26:39
5:31[a]John 8:14 5:32[a][Matt. 3:17] 5:33[a][John 1:15, 19, 27, 32] 5:35[a]2 Pet. 1:19
[b]Mark 6:20 5:36[a]1 John 5:9 [b]John 3:2; 10:25; 17:4 [c]John 9:16; 10:38 5:37[a]Matt.
3:17 [b]1 John 4:12 5:39[a]Is. 8:20; 34:16 [b]Luke 24:27 5:40[a][John 1:11; 3:19]
5:41[a]1 Thess. 2:6 5:44[a]John 12:43 [b][Rom. 2:29]

45 "Do not think that I shall accuse you to the Father; [a]there
is *one* who accuses you—Moses, in whom you trust.
46 "For if you believed Moses, you would believe Me; [a]for he
wrote about Me.
47 "But if you [a]do not believe his writings, how will you be-
lieve My words?"

5:45[a] Rom. 2:12 5:46[a] Deut. 18:15, 18 5:47[a] Luke 16:29, 31

JOHN 6

JESUS FEEDS FIVE THOUSAND

Let it be evermore remembered that the words of Jesus Christ are full of truth and grace and that in each of the two sentences in John 6:37 there is the surest truth and the freest grace. There will be some who from the peculiarity of their minds will prize most the first sentence. They will say, as they read these words, "All that the Father gives Me will come to Me," "Why! Here is high doctrine; here is the security of the covenant, the purpose of God effectually carried out. Herein is the truth that we love and the grace in which we glory."

Other brethren, overlooking the first sentence, will rather grasp at the second sentence, "The one who comes to Me I will by no means cast out." "Why!" say they, "here is universality of description; here is a freeness of invitation; here is a gracious overflow of liberality. This is good free gospel indeed," and they will therefore fall to proclaiming the second sentence to the neglect of the first.

But brethren, let us not sin by setting one Scripture over against another or attempting to divide the living child of revelation. You who love to hear the gospel preached to sinners, do not be afraid of the doctrines of sovereign grace. And you who love sovereign grace, do not be afraid of the free invitations of the gospel and the wide door that Jesus opens for needy sinners in many passages of Scripture.

---

1 After [a]these things Jesus went over the Sea of Galilee, which is *the Sea* of [b]Tiberias.
2 Then a great multitude followed Him, because they saw His signs which He performed on those who were [a]diseased.
3 And Jesus went up on the mountain, and there He sat with His disciples.
4 [a]Now the Passover, a feast of the Jews, was near.
5 [a]Then Jesus lifted up *His* eyes, and seeing a great multitude coming toward Him, He said to [b]Philip, "Where shall we buy bread, that these may eat?"
6 But this He said to test him, for He Himself knew what He would do.
7 Philip answered Him, [a]"Two hundred denarii worth of bread is not sufficient for them, that every one of them may have a little."
8 One of His disciples, [a]Andrew, Simon Peter's brother, said to Him,

6:1[a]Mark 6:32 [b]John 6:23; 21:1 6:2[a]Matt. 4:23; 8:16; 9:35; 14:36; 15:30; 19:2 6:4[a]Deut. 16:1 6:5[a]Matt. 14:14 [b]John 1:43 6:7[a]Num. 11:21, 22 6:8[a]John 1:40

9 "There is a lad here who has five barley loaves and two
small fish, [a]but what are they among so many?"
10 Then Jesus said, "Make the people sit down." Now there
was much grass in the place. So the men sat down, in num-
ber about five thousand.
11 And Jesus took the loaves, and when He had given thanks
He distributed *them* to the disciples, and the disciples[1] to
those sitting down; and likewise of the fish, as much as they
wanted.
12 So when they were filled, He said to His disciples, "Gather
up the fragments that remain, so that nothing is lost."
13 Therefore they gathered *them* up, and filled twelve bas-
kets with the fragments of the five barley loaves which were
left over by those who had eaten.
14 Then those men, when they had seen the sign that Jesus
did, said, "This is truly [a]the Prophet who is to come into the
world."
15 Therefore when Jesus perceived that they were about to
come and take Him by force to make Him [a]king, He departed
again to the mountain by Himself alone.
16 [a]Now when evening came, His disciples went down to
the sea,
17 got into the boat, and went over the sea toward Caper-
naum. And it was already dark, and Jesus had not come to
them.
18 Then the sea arose because a great wind was blowing.
19 So when they had rowed about three or four miles,[1] they
saw Jesus walking on the sea and drawing near the boat; and
they were [a]afraid.
20 But He said to them, [a]"It is I; do not be afraid."
21 Then they willingly received Him into the boat, and im-
mediately the boat was at the land where they were going.
22 On the following day, when the people who were stand-
ing on the other side of the sea saw that there was no other
boat there, except that one which His disciples had entered,[1]
and that Jesus had not entered the boat with His disciples,
but His disciples had gone away alone—
23 however, other boats came from Tiberias, near the place
where they ate bread after the Lord had given thanks—
24 when the people therefore saw that Jesus was not there,
nor His disciples, they also got into boats and came to Ca-
pernaum, [a]seeking Jesus.
25 And when they found Him on the other side of the sea,
they said to Him, "Rabbi, when did You come here?"
26 Jesus answered them and said, "Most assuredly, I say to

6:9 [a]2 Kin. 4:43 6:11 [1]NU-Text omits *to the disciples, and the disciples.* 6:14 [a]Gen. 49:10 6:15 [a][John 18:36] 6:16 [a]Matt. 14:23 6:19 [a]Matt. 17:6 [1]Literally *twenty-five or thirty stadia* 6:20 [a]Is. 43:1, 2 6:22 [1]NU-Text omits *that and which His disciples had entered.* 6:24 [a]Luke 4:42

you, you seek Me, not because you saw the signs, but because
you ate of the loaves and were filled.
27 [a]"Do not labor for the food which perishes, but [b]for the
food which endures to everlasting life, which the Son of
Man will give you, [c]because God the Father has set His seal
on Him."
28 Then they said to Him, "What shall we do, that we may
work the works of God?"
29 Jesus answered and said to them, [a]"This is the work of
God, that you believe in Him whom He sent."
30 Therefore they said to Him, [a]"What sign will You per-
form then, that we may see it and believe You? What work
will You do?
31 [a]"Our fathers ate the manna in the desert; as it is written,
[b]'He gave them bread from heaven to eat.'"[1]
32 Then Jesus said to them, "Most assuredly, I say to you,
Moses did not give you the bread from heaven, but [a]My Fa-
ther gives you the true bread from heaven.
33 "For the bread of God is He who comes down from heav-
en and gives life to the world."
34 [a]Then they said to Him, "Lord, give us this bread always."
35 And Jesus said to them, [a]"I am the bread of life. [b]He who
comes to Me shall never hunger, and he who believes in Me
shall never [c]thirst.
36 [a]"But I said to you that you have seen Me and yet [b]do not
believe.
37 [a]"All that the Father gives Me will come to Me, and [b]the
one who comes to Me I will by no means cast out.
38 "For I have come down from heaven, [a]not to do My own
will, [b]but the will of Him who sent Me.
39 "This is the will of the Father who sent Me, [a]that of all He
has given Me I should lose nothing, but should raise it up at
the last day.
40 "And this is the will of Him who sent Me, [a]that everyone
who sees the Son and believes in Him may have everlasting
life; and I will raise him up at the last day."
41 The Jews then complained about Him, because He said,
"I am the bread which came down from heaven."
42 And they said, [a]"Is not this Jesus, the son of Joseph, whose
father and mother we know? How is it then that He says, 'I
have come down from heaven'?"
43 Jesus therefore answered and said to them, "Do not mur-
mur among yourselves.

6:27[a]Matt. 6:19 [b]John 4:14 [c]Acts 2:22 6:29[a][1 John 3:23] 6:30[a]Matt. 12:38; 16:1 6:31[a]Ex. 16:15 [b]Ex. 16:4, 15; Neh. 9:15; Ps. 78:24 [1]Exodus 16:4; Nehemiah 9:15; Psalm 78:24 6:32[a]John 3:13, 16 6:34[a]John 4:15 6:35[a]John 6:48, 58 [b]John 4:14; 7:37 [c]Is. 55:1, 2 6:36[a]John 6:26, 64; 15:24 [b]John 10:26 6:37[a]John 6:45 [b]2 Tim. 2:19 6:38[a]Matt. 26:39 [b]John 4:34 6:39[a]John 10:28; 17:12; 18:9 6:40[a]John 3:15, 16; 4:14; 6:27, 47, 54 6:42[a]Matt. 13:55

44 [a]"No one can come to Me unless the Father who sent Me
[b]draws him; and I will raise him up at the last day.
45 "It is written in the prophets, [a]'And they shall all be taught
by God.'[1] [b]Therefore everyone who has heard and learned[2]
from the Father comes to Me.
46 [a]"Not that anyone has seen the Father, [b]except He who is
from God; He has seen the Father.
47 "Most assuredly, I say to you, [a]he who believes in Me[1] has
everlasting life.
48 [a]"I am the bread of life.
49 [a]"Your fathers ate the manna in the wilderness, and are
dead.
50 [a]"This is the bread which comes down from heaven, that
one may eat of it and not die.
51 "I am the living bread [a]which came down from heaven. If
anyone eats of this bread, he will live forever; and [b]the bread
that I shall give is My flesh, which I shall give for the life of
the world."
52 The Jews therefore [a]quarreled among themselves, say-
ing, "How can this Man give us *His* flesh to eat?"
53 Then Jesus said to them, "Most assuredly, I say to you,
unless [a]you eat the flesh of the Son of Man and drink His
blood, you have no life in you.
54 [a]"Whoever eats My flesh and drinks My blood has eternal
life, and I will raise him up at the last day.
55 "For My flesh is food indeed,[1] and My blood is drink in-
deed.
56 "He who eats My flesh and drinks My blood [a]abides in
Me, and I in him.
57 "As the living Father sent Me, and I live because of the
Father, so he who feeds on Me will live because of Me.
58 [a]"This is the bread which came down from heaven—not
[b]as your fathers ate the manna, and are dead. He who eats
this bread will live forever."
59 These things He said in the synagogue as He taught in
Capernaum.
60 [a]Therefore many of His disciples, when they heard *this,*
said, "This is a hard saying; who can understand it?"
61 When Jesus knew in Himself that His disciples com-
plained about this, He said to them, "Does this offend you?
62 [a]"*What* then if you should see the Son of Man ascend
where He was before?

6:44[a]Song 1:4 [b][Phil. 1:29; 2:12, 13] 6:45[a]Is. 54:13 [b]John 6:37 [1]Isaiah 54:13 [2]M-Text reads *hears and has learned.* 6:46[a]John 1:18 [b]Matt. 11:27 6:47[a][John 3:16, 18] [1]NU-Text omits *in Me.* 6:48[a]John 6:33, 35 6:49[a]John 6:31, 58 6:50[a]John 6:51, 58 6:51[a]John 3:13 [b]Heb. 10:5 6:52[a]John 7:43; 9:16; 10:19 6:53[a]Matt. 26:26 6:54[a]John 4:14; 6:27, 40 6:55[1]NU-Text reads *true food* and *true drink.* 6:56[a][1 John 3:24; 4:15, 16] 6:58[a]John 6:49–51 [b]Ex. 16:14–35 6:60[a]John 6:66 6:62[a]Acts 1:9; 2:32, 33

63 [a]"It is the Spirit who gives life; the [b]flesh profits nothing.
The [c]words that I speak to you are spirit, and *they* are life.
64 "But [a]there are some of you who do not believe." For
[b]Jesus knew from the beginning who they were who did not
believe, and who would betray Him.
65 And He said, "Therefore [a]I have said to you that no one
can come to Me unless it has been granted to him by My Fa-
ther."
66 [a]From that *time* many of His disciples went back and
walked with Him no more.
67 Then Jesus said to the twelve, "Do you also want to go
away?"
68 But Simon Peter answered Him, "Lord, to whom shall we
go? You have [a]the words of eternal life.
69 [a]"Also we have come to believe and know that You are
the Christ, the Son of the living God."[1]
70 Jesus answered them, [a]"Did I not choose you, the twelve,
[b]and one of you is a devil?"
71 He spoke of [a]Judas Iscariot, *the son* of Simon, for it was
he who would [b]betray Him, being one of the twelve.

6:63 [a]2 Cor. 3:6 [b]John 3:6 [c][John 6:68; 14:24] 6:64 [a]John 6:36 [b]John 2:24, 25; 13:11 6:65 [a]John 6:37, 44, 45 6:66 [a]Luke 9:62 6:68 [a]Acts 5:20 6:69 [a]Luke 9:20 [1]NU-Text reads *You are the Holy One of God.* 6:70 [a]Luke 6:13 [b][John 13:27] 6:71 [a]John 12:4; 13:2, 26 [b]Matt. 26:14–16

JOHN 7

JESUS TEACHES IN THE TEMPLE

The true God has manifested Himself to us in the Trinity of His sacred Persons. If then I worship the Father and the Son but forget or neglect to adore the Holy Spirit, I worship less than God.

What a grievous thing it will be if we do not pay that loving homage and reverence to the Holy Spirit that is so justly His due. May it not be the fact that we enjoy less of His power and see less of His working in the world because the church of God has not been sufficiently mindful of Him. It is a blessed thing to preach the work of Jesus Christ, but it is an evil thing to omit the work of the Holy Ghost, for the work of the Lord Jesus itself is no blessing to that man who does not know the work of the Holy Spirit. There is the ransom price, but it is only through the Spirit that we know the redemption; there is the precious blood, but it is as though the fountain had never been filled unless the Spirit of God lead us with repenting faith to wash therein. The bandage is soft and the ointment is effectual, but the wound will never be healed till the Holy Spirit shall apply that which the great Physician has provided.

Let us not therefore be found neglectful of the work of the divine Spirit lest we incur guilt and inflict upon ourselves serious damage.

---

1 After these things Jesus walked in Galilee; for He did not
want to walk in Judea, [a]because the Jews[1] sought to kill Him.
2 [a]Now the Jews' Feast of Tabernacles was at hand.
3 [a]His brothers therefore said to Him, "Depart from here
and go into Judea, that Your disciples also may see the works
that You are doing.
4 "For no one does anything in secret while he himself seeks
to be known openly. If You do these things, show Yourself to
the world."
5 For [a]even His [b]brothers did not believe in Him.
6 Then Jesus said to them, [a]"My time has not yet come, but
your time is always ready.
7 [a]"The world cannot hate you, but it hates Me [b]because I
testify of it that its works are evil.
8 "You go up to this feast. I am not yet[1] going up to this feast,
[a]for My time has not yet fully come."
9 When He had said these things to them, He remained in
Galilee.

7:1[a]John 5:18; 7:19, 25; 8:37, 40 [1]That is, the ruling authorities 7:2[a]Lev. 23:34 7:3[a]Matt. 12:46 7:5[a]Ps. 69:8; Mic. 7:6 [b]Mark 3:21 7:6[a]John 2:4; 8:20 7:7[a][John 15:19] [b]John 3:19 7:8[a]John 8:20 [1]NU-Text omits *yet.*

10 But when His brothers had gone up, then He also went
up to the feast, not openly, but as it were in secret.
11 Then [a]the Jews sought Him at the feast, and said, "Where
is He?"
12 And [a]there was much complaining among the people
concerning Him. [b]Some said, "He is good"; others said, "No,
on the contrary, He deceives the people."
13 However, no one spoke openly of Him [a]for fear of the
Jews.
14 Now about the middle of the feast Jesus went up into the
temple and [a]taught.
15 [a]And the Jews marveled, saying, "How does this Man
know letters, having never studied?"
16 Jesus[1] answered them and said, [a]"My doctrine is not Mine,
but His who sent Me.
17 [a]"If anyone wills to do His will, he shall know concerning
the doctrine, whether it is from God or *whether* I speak on
My own *authority*.
18 [a]"He who speaks from himself seeks his own glory; but
He who [b]seeks the glory of the One who sent Him is true, and
[c]no unrighteousness is in Him.
19 [a]"Did not Moses give you the law, yet none of you keeps
the law? [b]Why do you seek to kill Me?"
20 The people answered and said, [a]"You have a demon. Who
is seeking to kill You?"
21 Jesus answered and said to them, "I did one work, and
you all marvel.
22 [a]"Moses therefore gave you circumcision (not that it is
from Moses, [b]but from the fathers), and you circumcise a
man on the Sabbath.
23 "If a man receives circumcision on the Sabbath, so that
the law of Moses should not be broken, are you angry with
Me because [a]I made a man completely well on the Sabbath?
24 [a]"Do not judge according to appearance, but judge with
righteous judgment."
25 Now some of them from Jerusalem said, "Is this not He
whom they seek to [a]kill?
26 "But look! He speaks boldly, and they say nothing to Him.
[a]Do the rulers know indeed that this is truly[1] the Christ?
27 [a]"However, we know where this Man is from; but when
the Christ comes, no one knows where He is from."
28 Then Jesus cried out, as He taught in the temple, saying,
[a]"You both know Me, and you know where I am from; and [b]I

7:11[a]John 11:56 7:12[a]John 9:16; 10:19 [b]Luke 7:16 7:13[a][John 9:22; 12:42; 19:38] 7:14[a]Ps. 22:22; Mark 6:34 7:15[a]Matt. 13:54 7:16[a]John 3:11 [1]NU-Text and M-Text read *So Jesus*. 7:17[a]John 3:21; 8:43 7:18[a]John 5:41 [b]John 8:50 [c][2 Cor. 5:21] 7:19[a]Deut. 33:4 [b]Matt. 12:14 7:20[a]John 8:48, 52 7:22[a]Lev. 12:3 [b]Gen. 17:9–14 7:23[a]John 5:8, 9, 16 7:24[a]Prov. 24:23 7:25[a]Matt. 21:38; 26:4 7:26[a]John 7:48 [1]NU-Text omits *truly*. 7:27[a]Luke 4:22 7:28[a]John 8:14 [b]John 5:43

have not come of Myself, but He who sent Me [c]is true, [d]whom
you do not know.
29 "But[1] [a]I know Him, for I am from Him, and He sent Me."
30 Therefore [a]they sought to take Him; but [b]no one laid a
hand on Him, because His hour had not yet come.
31 And [a]many of the people believed in Him, and said, "When
the Christ comes, will He do more signs than these which this
Man has done?"
32 The Pharisees heard the crowd murmuring these things
concerning Him, and the Pharisees and the chief priests sent
officers to take Him.
33 Then Jesus said to them,[1] [a]"I shall be with you a little while
longer, and *then* I [b]go to Him who sent Me.
34 "You [a]will seek Me and not find *Me,* and where I am you
[b]cannot come."
35 Then the Jews said among themselves, "Where does He
intend to go that we shall not find Him? Does He intend to go
to [a]the Dispersion among the Greeks and teach the Greeks?
36 "What is this thing that He said, 'You will seek Me and not
find Me, and where I am you cannot come'?"
37 [a]On the last day, that great *day* of the feast, Jesus stood
and cried out, saying, [b]"If anyone thirsts, let him come to Me
and drink.
38 [a]"He who believes in Me, as the Scripture has said, [b]out
of his heart will flow rivers of living water."
39 [a]But this He spoke concerning the Spirit, whom those
believing[1] in Him would receive; for the Holy[2] Spirit was not
yet *given,* because Jesus was not yet [b]glorified.
40 Therefore many[1] from the crowd, when they heard this
saying, said, "Truly this is [a]the Prophet."
41 Others said, "This is [a]the Christ." But some said, "Will the
Christ come out of Galilee?
42 [a]"Has not the Scripture said that the Christ comes from
the seed of David and from the town of Bethlehem, [b]where
David was?"
43 So [a]there was a division among the people because of Him.
44 Now [a]some of them wanted to take Him, but no one laid
hands on Him.
45 Then the officers came to the chief priests and Pharisees,
who said to them, "Why have you not brought Him?"
46 The officers answered, [a]"No man ever spoke like this Man!"
47 Then the Pharisees answered them, "Are you also de-
ceived?

7:28 [c]Rom. 3:4 [d]John 1:18; 8:55 7:29 [a]Matt. 11:27 [1]NU-Text and M-Text omit *But.* 7:30 [a]Mark 11:18 [b]John 7:32, 44; 8:20; 10:39 7:31 [a]Matt. 12:23 7:33 [a]John 13:33 [b][1 Pet. 3:22] [1]NU-Text and M-Text omit *to them.* 7:34 [a]Hos. 5:6 [b][Matt. 5:20] 7:35 [a]James 1:1 7:37 [a]Lev. 23:36 [b][Is. 55:1] 7:38 [a]Deut. 18:15 [b]Is. 12:3; 43:20; 44:3; 55:1 7:39 [a]Is. 44:3 [b]John 12:16; 13:31; 17:5 [1]NU-Text reads *who believed.* [2]NU-Text omits *Holy.* 7:40 [a]Deut. 18:15, 18 [1]NU-Text reads *some.* 7:41 [a]John 4:42; 6:69 7:42 [a]Mic. 5:2 [b]1 Sam. 16:1, 4 7:43 [a]John 7:12 7:44 [a]John 7:30 7:46 [a]Luke 4:22

48 “Have any of the rulers or the Pharisees believed in Him?
49 “But this crowd that does not know the law is accursed.”
50 Nicodemus [a](he who came to Jesus by night,[1] being one
of them) said to them,
51 [a]“Does our law judge a man before it hears him and knows
what he is doing?”
52 They answered and said to him, “Are you also from Gali-
lee? Search and look, for [a]no prophet has arisen[1] out of Gal-
ilee.”
53 And everyone went to his *own* house.[1]

7:50[a]John 3:1, 2; 19:39 [1]NU-Text reads *before.* 7:51[a]Deut. 1:16, 17; 19:15 7:52[a][Is. 9:1, 2] [1]NU-Text reads *is to rise.* 7:53[1]The words *And everyone* through *sin no more* (8:11) are bracketed by NU-Text as not original. They are present in over 900 manuscripts.

JOHN 8

JESUS THE LIGHT OF THE WORLD

Jesus Christ was the true Light in opposition to the smoking flax of tradition. Some philosophers think themselves the light of the world, but they are meteors that dissolve into mist. Their sophism is an endless strife of words; their research is not worth your study; their knowledge is not worth the knowing. They discuss their paradoxes till they become addle-headed. They refine their subtleties till doctrine dwindles down into doubt; simple truth is degraded into silly twaddle; their translations of Scripture are a travesty and their commentaries an outrage upon commonsense. They make void the Word of God through their traditions or their conjectures. Flee away from the nebulous forms and noxious fumes of their old traditions and new discoveries. Believe what Jesus said and His apostles taught and what you have had revealed to you in His own pure Word: Christ is the true Light. He extinguishes all your earthly luminaries.

Thus, then, is He a Light who is to be followed. To follow Him means to commit yourselves to Him, to believe Him, and to yield yourselves up, obediently doing what He bids and implicitly accepting what He says. You must have no other Master. Jesus Christ only must be your Light. His Word, by the testimony of his Spirit, must be your sole authority.

---

1 But Jesus went to the Mount of Olives.
2 Now early[1] in the morning He came again into the temple, and all the people came to Him; and He sat down and
[a]taught them.
3 Then the scribes and Pharisees brought to Him a woman caught in adultery. And when they had set her in the midst,
4 they said to Him, "Teacher, this woman was caught[1] in
[a]adultery, in the very act.
5 [a]"Now Moses, in the law, commanded[1] us that such should be stoned.[2] But what do You say?"[3]
6 This they said, testing Him, that they [a]might have *something* of which to accuse Him. But Jesus stooped down and wrote on the ground with *His* finger, as though He did not hear.[1]
7 So when they continued asking Him, He raised Himself up[1] and said to them, [a]"He who is without sin among you, let him throw a stone at her first."

8:2 [a]John 8:20; 18:20 [1]M-Text reads *very early.* 8:4 [a]Ex. 20:14 [1]M-Text reads *we found this woman.* 8:5 [a]Lev. 20:10 [1]M-Text reads *in our law Moses commanded.* [2]NU-Text and M-Text read *to stone such.* [3]M-Text adds *about her.* 8:6 [a]Matt. 22:15 [1]NU-Text and M-Text omit *as though He did not hear.* 8:7 [a]Deut. 17:7 [1]M-Text reads *He looked up.*

8 And again He stooped down and wrote on the ground.
9 Then those who heard *it,* [a]being convicted by *their* con-
science,[1] went out one by one, beginning with the oldest *even*
to the last. And Jesus was left alone, and the woman standing
in the midst.
10 When Jesus had raised Himself up and saw no one but the
woman, He said to her,[1] "Woman, where are those accusers
of yours?[2] Has no one condemned you?"
11 She said, "No one, Lord." And Jesus said to her, [a]"Neither
do I condemn you; go and[1] [b]sin no more."
12 Then Jesus spoke to them again, saying, [a]"I am the light
of the world. He who [b]follows Me shall not walk in darkness,
but have the light of life."
13 The Pharisees therefore said to Him, [a]"You bear witness
of Yourself; Your witness is not true."
14 Jesus answered and said to them, "Even if I bear witness
of Myself, My witness is true, for I know where I came from
and where I am going; but [a]you do not know where I come
from and where I am going.
15 [a]"You judge according to the flesh; [b]I judge no one.
16 "And yet if I do judge, My judgment is true; for [a]I am not
alone, but I *am* with the Father who sent Me.
17 [a]"It is also written in your law that the testimony of two
men is true.
18 "I am One who bears witness of Myself, and [a]the Father
who sent Me bears witness of Me."
19 Then they said to Him, "Where is Your Father?" Jesus an-
swered, [a]"You know neither Me nor My Father. [b]If you had
known Me, you would have known My Father also."
20 These words Jesus spoke in [a]the treasury, as He taught
in the temple; and [b]no one laid hands on Him, for [c]His hour
had not yet come.
21 Then Jesus said to them again, "I am going away, and
[a]you will seek Me, and [b]will die in your sin. Where I go you
cannot come."
22 So the Jews said, "Will He kill Himself, because He says,
'Where I go you cannot come'?"
23 And He said to them, [a]"You are from beneath; I am from
above. [b]You are of this world; I am not of this world.
24 [a]"Therefore I said to you that you will die in your sins; [b]for
if you do not believe that I am *He,* you will die in your sins."
25 Then they said to Him, "Who are You?" And Jesus said to

8:9 [a]Rom. 2:22 [1]NU-Text and M-Text omit *being convicted by their conscience.* 8:10 [1]NU-Text omits *and saw no one but the woman;* M-Text reads *He saw her and said.* [2]NU-Text and M-Text omit *of yours.* 8:11 [a][John 3:17] [b][John 5:14] [1]NU-Text and M-Text add *from now on.* 8:12 [a]John 1:4; 9:5; 12:35 [b]1 Thess. 5:5 8:13 [a]John 5:31 8:14 [a]John 7:28; 9:29 8:15 [a]John 7:24 [b][John 3:17; 12:47; 18:36] 8:16 [a]John 16:32 8:17 [a]Deut. 17:6; 19:15 8:18 [a]John 5:37 8:19 [a]John 16:3 [b]John 14:7 8:20 [a]Mark 12:41, 43 [b]John 2:4; 7:30 [c]John 7:8 8:21 [a]John 7:34; 13:33 [b]John 8:24 8:23 [a]John 3:31 [b]1 John 4:5 8:24 [a]John 8:21 [b][Mark 16:16]

them, "Just what I [a]have been saying to you from the begin-
ning.
26 "I have many things to say and to judge concerning you,
but [a]He who sent Me is true; and [b]I speak to the world those
things which I heard from Him."
27 They did not understand that He spoke to them of the
Father.
28 Then Jesus said to them, "When you [a]lift up the Son of
Man, [b]then you will know that I am *He,* and [c]*that* I do noth-
ing of Myself; but [d]as My Father taught Me, I speak these
things.
29 "And [a]He who sent Me is with Me. [b]The Father has not left
Me alone, [c]for I always do those things that please Him."
30 As He spoke these words, [a]many believed in Him.
31 Then Jesus said to those Jews who believed Him, "If you
[a]abide in My word, you are My disciples indeed.
32 "And you shall know the [a]truth, and [b]the truth shall make
you free."
33 They answered Him, [a]"We are Abraham's descendants,
and have never been in bondage to anyone. How *can* You say,
'You will be made free'?"
34 Jesus answered them, "Most assuredly, I say to you, [a]who-
ever commits sin is a slave of sin.
35 "And [a]a slave does not abide in the house forever, *but* a
son abides forever.
36 [a]"Therefore if the Son makes you free, you shall be free
indeed.
37 "I know that you are Abraham's descendants, but [a]you
seek to kill Me, because My word has no place in you.
38 [a]"I speak what I have seen with My Father, and you do
what you have seen with[1] your father."
39 They answered and said to Him, [a]"Abraham is our fa-
ther." Jesus said to them, [b]"If you were Abraham's children,
you would do the works of Abraham.
40 [a]"But now you seek to kill Me, a Man who has told you the
truth [b]which I heard from God. Abraham did not do this.
41 "You do the deeds of your father." Then they said to Him,
"We were not born of fornication; [a]we have one Father—God."
42 Jesus said to them, [a]"If God were your Father, you would
love Me, for [b]I proceeded forth and came from God; [c]nor have
I come of Myself, but He sent Me.
43 [a]"Why do you not understand My speech? Because you
are not able to listen to My word.

8:25[a] John 4:26 8:26[a] John 7:28 [b] John 3:32; 15:15 8:28[a] John 3:14; 12:32; 19:18 [b] [Rom. 1:4] [c] John 5:19, 30 [d] John 3:11 8:29[a] John 14:10 [b] John 8:16; 16:32 [c] John 4:34; 5:30; 6:38 8:30[a] John 7:31; 10:42; 11:45 8:31[a] [John 14:15, 23] 8:32[a] [John 1:14, 17; 14:6] [b] [Rom. 6:14, 18, 22] 8:33[a] [Matt. 3:9] 8:34[a] 2 Pet. 2:19 8:35[a] Gal. 4:30 8:36[a] Gal. 5:1 8:37[a] John 7:19 8:38[a] [John 3:32; 5:19, 30; 14:10, 24] [1] NU-Text reads *heard from.* 8:39[a] Matt. 3:9 [b] [Rom. 2:28] 8:40[a] John 8:37 [b] John 8:26 8:41[a] Is. 63:16 8:42[a] 1 John 5:1 [b] John 16:27; 17:8, 25 [c] Gal. 4:4 8:43[a] [John 7:17]

44 [a]"You are of *your* father the devil, and the [b]desires of your
father you want to [c]do. He was a murderer from the begin-
ning, and [d]does not stand in the truth, because there is no
truth in him. When he speaks a lie, he speaks from his own
resources, for he is a liar and the father of it.
45 "But because I tell the truth, you do not believe Me.
46 "Which of you convicts Me of sin? And if I tell the truth,
why do you not believe Me?
47 [a]"He who is of God hears God's words; therefore you do
not hear, because you are not of God."
48 Then the Jews answered and said to Him, "Do we not say
rightly that You are a Samaritan and [a]have a demon?"
49 Jesus answered, "I do not have a demon; but I honor My
Father, and [a]you dishonor Me.
50 "And [a]I do not seek My *own* glory; there is One who seeks
and judges.
51 "Most assuredly, I say to you, [a]if anyone keeps My word
he shall never see death."
52 Then the Jews said to Him, "Now we know that You [a]have
a demon! [b]Abraham is dead, and the prophets; and You say,
'If anyone keeps My word he shall never taste death.'
53 "Are You greater than our father Abraham, who is dead?
And the prophets are dead. [a]Who do You make Yourself out
to be?"
54 Jesus answered, [a]"If I honor Myself, My honor is nothing.
[b]It is My Father who honors Me, of whom you say that He is
your[1] God.
55 "Yet [a]you have not known Him, but I know Him. And if
I say, 'I do not know Him,' I shall be a liar like you; but I do
know Him and [b]keep His word.
56 "Your father Abraham [a]rejoiced to see My day, [b]and he
saw *it* and was glad."
57 Then the Jews said to Him, "You are not yet fifty years
old, and have You seen Abraham?"
58 Jesus said to them, "Most assuredly, I say to you, [a]before
Abraham was, [b]I AM."
59 Then [a]they took up stones to throw at Him; but Jesus
hid Himself and went out of the temple,[1] [b]going through the
midst of them, and so passed by.

8:44 [a]Matt. 13:38 [b]1 John 2:16, 17 [c][1 John 3:8–10, 15] [d][Jude 6] 8:47 [a]1 John 4:6
8:48 [a]John 7:20; 10:20 8:49 [a]John 5:41 8:50 [a]John 5:41; 7:18 8:51 [a]John 5:24; 11:26
8:52 [a]John 7:20; 10:20 [b]Zech. 1:5 8:53 [a]John 10:33; 19:7 8:54 [a]John 5:31, 32 [b]Acts
3:13 [1]NU-Text and M-Text read *our.* 8:55 [a]John 7:28, 29 [b][John 15:10] 8:56 [a]Luke
10:24 [b]Heb. 11:13 8:58 [a]Mic. 5:2 [b]Rev. 1:8 8:59 [a]John 10:31; 11:8
[b]Luke 4:30 [1]NU-Text omits the rest of this verse.

JOHN 9

THE MAN BORN BLIND

This beggar did not pray for sight—at least it is not recorded that he did so. Yet Jesus gave him sight. Know you not that glorious declaration of free grace, "I was found by those who did not seek Me" (Is. 65:1)? Is it not a wonderful thing that Jesus does often come to those who did not seek Him? He comes on a sudden to them in the sovereignty of His infinite compassion, and before they have begun to pray for the blessing, He has bestowed it upon them. His free love precedes their desires for it. When they wake up to a consciousness of the value of salvation, they find themselves in possession of it, and so their first prayers are mingled with praises.

I am persuaded that there are some today who are like the man born blind: they do not know what they want, they are not yet aware of the value of the blessing, and consequently they have not sought it. But they are going to receive it.

There was this circumstance in favor of the blind beggar, that he was in the way where Jesus was likely to go, for he was at the temple gate. My friend, you too are on hopeful ground at this time, for you are found in the place where my Lord has often been and where He is very likely to come again. Oh that, as Jesus passes by, He may stand still and look on you with eyes of infinite mercy!

---

1 Now as *Jesus* passed by, He saw a man who was blind from birth.
2 And His disciples asked Him, saying, "Rabbi, [a]who sinned, this man or his parents, that he was born blind?"
3 Jesus answered, "Neither this man nor his parents sinned, [a]but that the works of God should be revealed in him.
4 [a]"I[1] must work the works of Him who sent Me while it is [b]day; *the* night is coming when no one can work.
5 "As long as I am in the world, [a]I am the light of the world."
6 When He had said these things, [a]He spat on the ground and made clay with the saliva; and He anointed the eyes of the blind man with the clay.
7 And He said to him, "Go, wash [a]in the pool of Siloam" (which is translated, Sent). So [b]he went and washed, and came back seeing.
8 Therefore the neighbors and those who previously had seen that he was blind[1] said, "Is not this he who sat and begged?"

9:2 [a]John 9:34 9:3 [a]John 11:4 9:4 [a][John 4:34; 5:19, 36; 17:4] [b]John 11:9, 10; 12:35 [1]NU-Text reads *We*. 9:5 [a][John 1:5, 9; 3:19; 8:12; 12:35, 46] 9:6 [a]Mark 7:33; 8:23 9:7 [a]Neh. 3:15 [b]2 Kin. 5:14 9:8 [1]NU-Text reads *a beggar*.

9 Some said, "This is he." Others *said,* "He is like him."[1] He
said, "I am *he.*"
10 Therefore they said to him, "How were your eyes opened?"
11 He answered and said, [a]"A Man called Jesus made clay
and anointed my eyes and said to me, 'Go to the pool of[1] Si-
loam and wash.' So I went and washed, and I received sight."
12 Then they said to him, "Where is He?" He said, "I do not
know."
13 They brought him who formerly was blind to the Phari-
sees.
14 Now it was a Sabbath when Jesus made the clay and opened
his eyes.
15 Then the Pharisees also asked him again how he had re-
ceived his sight. He said to them, "He put clay on my eyes,
and I washed, and I see."
16 Therefore some of the Pharisees said, "This Man is not
from God, because He does not keep the Sabbath." Others
said, [a]"How can a man who is a sinner do such signs?" And
[b]there was a division among them.
17 They said to the blind man again, "What do you say
about Him because He opened your eyes?" He said, [a]"He is a
prophet."
18 But the Jews did not believe concerning him, that he had
been blind and received his sight, until they called the par-
ents of him who had received his sight.
19 And they asked them, saying, "Is this your son, who you
say was born blind? How then does he now see?"
20 His parents answered them and said, "We know that this
is our son, and that he was born blind;
21 "but by what means he now sees we do not know, or who
opened his eyes we do not know. He is of age; ask him. He
will speak for himself."
22 His parents said these *things* because [a]they feared the
Jews, for the Jews had agreed already that if anyone con-
fessed *that* He *was* Christ, he [b]would be put out of the syna-
gogue.
23 Therefore his parents said, "He is of age; ask him."
24 So they again called the man who was blind, and said to
him, [a]"Give God the glory! [b]We know that this Man is a sin-
ner."
25 He answered and said, "Whether He is a sinner *or not* I
do not know. One thing I know: that though I was blind, now
I see."
26 Then they said to him again, "What did He do to you?
How did He open your eyes?"

9:9[1]NU-Text reads *"No, but he is like him."* 9:11[a]John 9:6, 7 [1]NU-Text omits *the pool of.* 9:16[a]John 3:2; 9:33 [b]John 7:12, 43; 10:19 9:17[a][John 4:19; 6:14] 9:22[a]Acts 5:13 [b]John 16:2 9:24[a]Josh. 7:19 [b]John 9:16

27 He answered them, "I told you already, and you did not
listen. Why do you want to hear *it* again? Do you also want
to become His disciples?"
28 Then they reviled him and said, "You are His disciple, but
we are Moses' disciples.
29 "We know that God [a]spoke to [b]Moses; *as for* this *fellow,*
[c]we do not know where He is from."
30 The man answered and said to them, [a]"Why, this is a mar-
velous thing, that you do not know where He is from; yet He
has opened my eyes!
31 "Now we know that [a]God does not hear sinners; but if any-
one is a worshiper of God and does His will, He hears him.
32 "Since the world began it has been unheard of that any-
one opened the eyes of one who was born blind.
33 [a]"If this Man were not from God, He could do nothing."
34 They answered and said to him, [a]"You were completely
born in sins, and are you teaching us?" And they cast him out.
35 Jesus heard that they had cast him out; and when He had
[a]found him, He said to him, "Do you [b]believe in [c]the Son of
God?"[1]
36 He answered and said, "Who is He, Lord, that I may be-
lieve in Him?"
37 And Jesus said to him, "You have both seen Him and [a]it
is He who is talking with you."
38 Then he said, "Lord, I believe!" And he [a]worshiped Him.
39 And Jesus said, [a]"For judgment I have come into this
world, [b]that those who do not see may see, and that those
who see may be made blind."
40 Then *some* of the Pharisees who were with Him heard
these words, [a]and said to Him, "Are we blind also?"
41 Jesus said to them, [a]"If you were blind, you would have
no sin; but now you say, 'We see.' Therefore your sin remains.

9:29 [a]Num. 12:6–8 [b][John 5:45–47] [c]John 7:27, 28; 8:14 9:30 [a]John 3:10 9:31 [a]Zech. 7:13 9:33 [a]John 3:2; 9:16 9:34 [a]John 9:2 9:35 [a]John 5:14 [b]John 1:7; 16:31 [c]Matt. 14:33; 16:16 [1]NU-Text reads *Son of Man.* 9:37 [a]John 4:26 9:38 [a]Matt. 8:2 9:39 [a][John 3:17; 5:22, 27; 12:47] [b]Matt. 13:13; 15:14 9:40 [a][Rom. 2:19] 9:41 [a]John 15:22, 24

JOHN 10

JESUS THE GOOD SHEPHERD

We hear the Master say, "I lay down My life for the sheep." The Lord Jesus has by His death proved His love to His people, and His determination to save them is made clear by His laying down His life for them; therefore doubt and fear should be banished. Now also are we absolutely certain that Christ's purpose is perpetual: it cannot alter, for the price is paid and the deed is done by which the purpose is to be effected.

But as if the people of God would at times fancy that the purpose of Christ would not be achieved, behold another sentence: "I lay down My life that I may take it again." He who died and so redeemed His people by price lives that He may Himself personally see that they are also redeemed by power. If a Man dies to achieve a purpose, His very soul must have been in it. If He rose with greater power, clothed with higher rank, and elevated to a more eminent position, you would then be more than certain of His never-ending determination to perform His design. In the risen life of Jesus assurance is made doubly sure.

If Jesus died for a purpose, He will accomplish it; if Jesus rose for a purpose, He will accomplish it; if Jesus lives forever for a purpose, He will accomplish it. To me this conclusion seems to be past question: and if it be so, it puts the destiny of the sheep beyond all hazard.

---

1 "Most assuredly, I say to you, he who does not enter the sheepfold by the door, but climbs up some other way, the same is a thief and a robber.
2 "But he who enters by the door is the shepherd of the sheep.
3 "To him the doorkeeper opens, and the sheep hear his voice; and he calls his own sheep by [a]name and leads them out.
4 "And when he brings out his own sheep, he goes before them; and the sheep follow him, for they know his voice.
5 "Yet they will by no means follow a [a]stranger, but will flee from him, for they do not know the voice of strangers."
6 Jesus used this illustration, but they did not understand the things which He spoke to them.
7 Then Jesus said to them again, "Most assuredly, I say to you, I am the door of the sheep.
8 "All who *ever* came before Me[1] are thieves and robbers, but the sheep did not hear them.
9 [a]"I am the door. If anyone enters by Me, he will be saved, and will go in and out and find pasture.

10:3[a] John 20:16 10:5[a] [2 Cor. 11:13–15] 10:8[1] M-Text omits *before Me.* 10:9[a] [Eph. 2:18]

10 "The thief does not come except to steal, and to kill, and
to destroy. I have come that they may have life, and that they
may have *it* more abundantly.
11 [a]"I am the good shepherd. The good shepherd gives His
life for the sheep.
12 "But a hireling, *he who is* not the shepherd, one who does
not own the sheep, sees the wolf coming and [a]leaves the sheep
and flees; and the wolf catches the sheep and scatters them.
13 "The hireling flees because he is a hireling and does not
care about the sheep.
14 "I am the good shepherd; and [a]I know My *sheep,* and [b]am
known by My own.
15 [a]"As the Father knows Me, even so I know the Father; [b]and
I lay down My life for the sheep.
16 "And [a]other sheep I have which are not of this fold; them
also I must bring, and they will hear My voice; [b]and there will
be one flock *and* one shepherd.
17 "Therefore My Father [a]loves Me, [b]because I lay down My
life that I may take it again.
18 "No one takes it from Me, but I lay it down of Myself. I
[a]have power to lay it down, and I have power to take it again.
[b]This command I have received from My Father."
19 Therefore [a]there was a division again among the Jews
because of these sayings.
20 And many of them said, [a]"He has a demon and is mad.
Why do you listen to Him?"
21 Others said, "These are not the words of one who has a
demon. [a]Can a demon [b]open the eyes of the blind?"
22 Now it was the Feast of Dedication in Jerusalem, and it
was winter.
23 And Jesus walked in the temple, [a]in Solomon's porch.
24 Then the Jews surrounded Him and said to Him, "How
long do You keep us in doubt? If You are the Christ, tell us
plainly."
25 Jesus answered them, "I told you, and you do not believe.
[a]The works that I do in My Father's name, they [b]bear witness
of Me.
26 "But [a]you do not believe, because you are not of My sheep,
as I said to you.[1]
27 [a]"My sheep hear My voice, and I know them, and they
follow Me.
28 "And I give them eternal life, and they shall never perish;
neither shall anyone snatch them out of My hand.

10:11[a]Is. 40:11 10:12[a]Zech. 11:16, 17 10:14[a]2 Tim. 2:19 [b]2 Tim. 1:12 10:15[a]Matt. 11:27 [b][John 15:13; 19:30] 10:16[a]Is. 42:6; 56:8 [b]Eph. 2:13–18 10:17[a]John 5:20 [b][Heb. 2:9] 10:18[a][John 2:19; 5:26] [b][John 6:38; 14:31; 17:4; Acts 2:24, 32] 10:19[a]John 7:43; 9:16 10:20[a]John 7:20 10:21[a][Ex. 4:11] [b]John 9:6, 7, 32, 33 10:23[a]Acts 3:11; 5:12 10:25[a]John 5:36; 10:38 [b]Matt. 11:4 10:26[a][John 8:47] [1]NU-Text omits *as I said to you.* 10:27[a]John 10:4, 14

29 [a]"My Father, [b]who has given *them* to Me, is greater than
all; and no one is able to snatch *them* out of My Father's hand.
30 [a]"I and *My* Father are one."
31 Then [a]the Jews took up stones again to stone Him.
32 Jesus answered them, "Many good works I have shown you
from My Father. For which of those works do you stone Me?"
33 The Jews answered Him, saying, "For a good work we do
not stone You, but for [a]blasphemy, and because You, being
a Man, [b]make Yourself God."
34 Jesus answered them, "Is it not written in your law, [a]'I
said, "You are gods"'?[1]
35 "If He called them gods, [a]to whom the word of God came
(and the Scripture [b]cannot be broken),
36 "do you say of Him [a]whom the Father sanctified and [b]sent
into the world, 'You are blaspheming,' [c]because I said, 'I am
[d]the Son of God'?
37 [a]"If I do not do the works of My Father, do not believe Me;
38 "but if I do, though you do not believe Me, [a]believe the
works, that you may know and believe[1] [b]that the Father *is* in
Me, and I in Him."
39 [a]Therefore they sought again to seize Him, but He es-
caped out of their hand.
40 And He went away again beyond the Jordan to the place
[a]where John was baptizing at first, and there He stayed.
41 Then many came to Him and said, "John performed no
sign, [a]but all the things that John spoke about this Man were
true."
42 And many believed in Him there.

10:29[a]John 14:28 [b][John 17:2, 6, 12, 24] 10:30[a]John 17:11, 21–24 10:31[a]John 8:59 10:33[a]Matt. 9:3 [b]John 5:18 10:34[a]Ps. 82:6 [1]Psalm 82:6 10:35[a]Matt. 5:17, 18 [b]1 Pet. 1:25 10:36[a]John 6:27 [b]John 3:17 [c]John 5:17, 18 [d]Luke 1:35 10:37[a]John 10:25; 15:24 10:38[a]John 5:36 [b]John 14:10, 11 [1]NU-Text reads *understand.* 10:39[a]John 7:30, 44 10:40[a]John 1:28 10:41[a][John 1:29, 36; 3:28–36; 5:33]

JOHN 11

JESUS RAISES LAZARUS

"Jesus wept." This is a diamond, and it cannot have another gem set with it, for it is unique. Shortest of verses in words, but where is there a longer one in sense? Add a word to the verse, and it would be out of place. No, let it stand in solitary sublimity and simplicity.

We read of others that they wept. Abraham, when he buried Sarah, wept; Jacob wept and prevailed with the angel; David often wept. His friend Jonathan and he once wept together. We read that Hezekiah wept sore and that Josiah poured forth tears over Judah's sins. Jeremiah was a weeping prophet, and I might continue the list, but if I did, it would not be at all remarkable. With all the sin and sorrow that surrounds us, it is no marvel that it should be said of anyone that he or she wept.

The earth brings forth thorns and thistles, and the heart brings forth sorrow and sighing. Have we not all sometimes felt a sweet relief in tears? The marvel is that the sinless Son of God should, in the days of His flesh, know the meaning of strong crying and tears. The fact worthy to be noticed and recorded is that "Jesus wept."

---

1 Now a certain *man* was sick, Lazarus of Bethany, the town of [a]Mary and her sister Martha.

2 [a]It was *that* Mary who anointed the Lord with fragrant oil and wiped His feet with her hair, whose brother Lazarus was sick.

3 Therefore the sisters sent to Him, saying, "Lord, behold, he whom You love is sick."

4 When Jesus heard *that,* He said, "This sickness is not unto death, but for the glory of God, that the Son of God may be glorified through it."

5 Now Jesus loved Martha and her sister and Lazarus.

6 So, when He heard that he was sick, [a]He stayed two more days in the place where He was.

7 Then after this He said to *the* disciples, "Let us go to Judea again."

8 *The* disciples said to Him, "Rabbi, lately the Jews sought to [a]stone You, and are You going there again?"

9 Jesus answered, "Are there not twelve hours in the day? [a]If anyone walks in the day, he does not stumble, because he sees the [b]light of this world.

10 "But [a]if one walks in the night, he stumbles, because the light is not in him."

11:1 [a]Luke 10:38, 39 11:2 [a]Matt. 26:7 11:6 [a]John 10:40 11:8 [a]John 8:59; 10:31 11:9 [a]John 9:4; 12:35 [b]Is. 9:2 11:10 [a]John 12:35

11 These things He said, and after that He said to them, "Our
friend Lazarus [a]sleeps, but I go that I may wake him up."
12 Then His disciples said, "Lord, if he sleeps he will get well."
13 However, Jesus spoke of his death, but they thought that
He was speaking about taking rest in sleep.
14 Then Jesus said to them plainly, "Lazarus is dead.
15 "And I am glad for your sakes that I was not there, that
you may believe. Nevertheless let us go to him."
16 Then [a]Thomas, who is called the Twin, said to his fellow
disciples, "Let us also go, that we may die with Him."
17 So when Jesus came, He found that he had already been
in the tomb four days.
18 Now Bethany was near Jerusalem, about two miles[1] away.
19 And many of the Jews had joined the women around Mar-
tha and Mary, to comfort them concerning their brother.
20 Then Martha, as soon as she heard that Jesus was com-
ing, went and met Him, but Mary was sitting in the house.
21 Now Martha said to Jesus, "Lord, if You had been here,
my brother would not have died.
22 "But even now I know that [a]whatever You ask of God, God
will give You."
23 Jesus said to her, "Your brother will rise again."
24 Martha said to Him, [a]"I know that he will rise again in the
resurrection at the last day."
25 Jesus said to her, "I am [a]the resurrection and the life. [b]He
who believes in Me, though he may [c]die, he shall live.
26 "And whoever lives and believes in Me shall never die. Do
you believe this?"
27 She said to Him, "Yes, Lord, [a]I believe that You are the
Christ, the Son of God, who is to come into the world."
28 And when she had said these things, she went her way
and secretly called Mary her sister, saying, "The Teacher has
come and is calling for you."
29 As soon as she heard *that,* she arose quickly and came
to Him.
30 Now Jesus had not yet come into the town, but was[1] in
the place where Martha met Him.
31 [a]Then the Jews who were with her in the house, and com-
forting her, when they saw that Mary rose up quickly and
went out, followed her, saying, "She is going to the tomb to
weep there."[1]
32 Then, when Mary came where Jesus was, and saw Him,
she [a]fell down at His feet, saying to Him, [b]"Lord, if You had
been here, my brother would not have died."

11:11[a] Matt. 9:24 11:16[a] John 14:5; 20:26–28 11:18[1] Literally *fifteen stadia* 11:22[a] [John 9:31; 11:41] 11:24[a] [John 5:29] 11:25[a] John 5:21; 6:39, 40, 44 [b]1 John 5:10 [c]1 Cor. 15:22 11:27[a] Matt. 16:16 11:30[1] NU-Text adds *still.* 11:31[a] John 11:19, 33 [1]NU-Text reads *supposing that she was going to the tomb to weep there.* 11:32[a] Rev. 1:17 [b]John 11:21

33 Therefore, when Jesus saw her weeping, and the Jews
who came with her weeping, He groaned in the spirit and
was troubled.
34 And He said, "Where have you laid him?" They said to
Him, "Lord, come and see."
35 [a]Jesus wept.
36 Then the Jews said, "See how He loved him!"
37 And some of them said, "Could not this Man, [a]who opened
the eyes of the blind, also have kept this man from dying?"
38 Then Jesus, again groaning in Himself, came to the tomb.
It was a cave, and a [a]stone lay against it.
39 Jesus said, "Take away the stone." Martha, the sister of
him who was dead, said to Him, "Lord, by this time there is
a stench, for he has been *dead* four days."
40 Jesus said to her, "Did I not say to you that if you would
believe you would [a]see the glory of God?"
41 Then they took away the stone *from the place* where the
dead man was lying.[1] And Jesus lifted up *His* eyes and said,
"Father, I thank You that You have heard Me.
42 "And I know that You always hear Me, but [a]because of the
people who are standing by I said *this,* that they may believe
that You sent Me."
43 Now when He had said these things, He cried with a loud
voice, "Lazarus, come forth!"
44 And he who had died came out bound hand and foot with
[a]graveclothes, and [b]his face was wrapped with a cloth. Jesus
said to them, "Loose him, and let him go."
45 Then many of the Jews who had come to Mary, [a]and had
seen the things Jesus did, believed in Him.
46 But some of them went away to the Pharisees and [a]told
them the things Jesus did.
47 [a]Then the chief priests and the Pharisees gathered a council
and said, [b]"What shall we do? For this Man works many signs.
48 "If we let Him alone like this, everyone will believe in Him,
and the Romans will come and take away both our place and
nation."
49 And one of them, [a]Caiaphas, being high priest that year,
said to them, "You know nothing at all,
50 [a]"nor do you consider that it is expedient for us[1] that one
man should die for the people, and not that the whole nation
should perish."
51 Now this he did not say on his own *authority;* but being
high priest that year he prophesied that Jesus would die for
the nation,

11:35 [a]Luke 19:41 11:37 [a]John 9:6, 7 11:38 [a]Matt. 27:60, 66 11:40 [a][John 11:4, 23] 11:41 [1]NU-Text omits *from the place where the dead man was lying.* 11:42 [a]John 12:30; 17:21 11:44 [a]John 19:40 [b]John 20:7 11:45 [a]John 2:23; 10:42; 12:11, 18 11:46 [a]John 5:15 11:47 [a]Ps. 2:2 [b]Acts 4:16 11:49 [a]Luke 3:2 11:50 [a]John 18:14 [1]NU-Text reads *you.*

52 and [a]not for that nation only, but [b]also that He would
gather together in one the children of God who were scat-
tered abroad.
53 Then, from that day on, they plotted to [a]put Him to death.
54 [a]Therefore Jesus no longer walked openly among the
Jews, but went from there into the country near the wilder-
ness, to a city called [b]Ephraim, and there remained with His
disciples.
55 [a]And the Passover of the Jews was near, and many went
from the country up to Jerusalem before the Passover, to
[b]purify themselves.
56 [a]Then they sought Jesus, and spoke among themselves
as they stood in the temple, "What do you think—that He will
not come to the feast?"
57 Now both the chief priests and the Pharisees had given
a command, that if anyone knew where He was, he should
report *it,* that they might [a]seize Him.

11:52[a]Is. 49:6 [b][Eph. 2:14–17] 11:53[a]Matt. 26:4 11:54[a]John 4:1, 3; 7:1 [b]2 Chr. 13:19 11:55[a]John 2:13; 5:1; 6:4 [b]Num. 9:10, 13; 31:19, 20 11:56[a]John 7:11 11:57[a]Matt. 26:14–16

JOHN 12

JESUS RIDES INTO JERUSALEM

Our Lord passed through His Passion in a kind of rehearsal before it came. His approaching decease was very near; only a few days would elapse, and then He would die upon the cross. In anticipation of Calvary, His soul was full of trouble: not that He feared death, but His death was to be a very peculiar one. He was to die the Just for the unjust; He was to bear our sins in His own body on the tree. To stand in the sinner's place, to bear His Father's wrath, this bewildered Him.

He was very faint of heart, and He cried, "What shall I say? 'Father, save Me from this hour'? But for this purpose I came to this hour. Father, glorify Your name." Without any wicked weakness, He proved how truly human He was; without any sinful repining at His Father's will, He saw how terrible that will was, and He shuddered at what it included.

Again, this was a kind of rehearsal for Gethsemane; it was a sipping of that cup whereof He was to drink until His sweat was great drops of blood falling down to the ground. Then His whole soul would pour out the agonized petition—as He again submitted to God's will—"O My Father, if it is possible, let this cup pass from Me; nevertheless, not as I will, but as You will" (Matt. 26:39).

---

1 Then, six days before the Passover, Jesus came to Betha-
ny, [a]where Lazarus was who had been dead,[1] whom He had
raised from the dead.
2 [a]There they made Him a supper; and Martha served, but
Lazarus was one of those who sat at the table with Him.
3 Then [a]Mary took a pound of very costly oil of [b]spikenard,
anointed the feet of Jesus, and wiped His feet with her hair.
And the house was filled with the fragrance of the oil.
4 But one of His disciples, [a]Judas Iscariot, Simon's *son,* who
would betray Him, said,
5 "Why was this fragrant oil not sold for three hundred de-
narii[1] and given to the poor?"
6 This he said, not that he cared for the poor, but because
he was a thief, and [a]had the money box; and he used to take
what was put in it.
7 But Jesus said, "Let her alone; she has kept[1] this for the
day of My burial.

12:1 [a]John 11:1, 43 [1]NU-Text omits *who had been dead.* 12:2 [a]Mark 14:3; Luke 10:38–41 12:3 [a]John 11:2 [b]Song 1:12 12:4 [a]John 13:26 12:5 [1]About one year's wages for a worker 12:6 [a]John 13:29 12:7 [1]NU-Text reads *that she may keep.*

8 "For [a]the poor you have with you always, but Me you do
not have always."
9 Now a great many of the Jews knew that He was there; and
they came, not for Jesus' sake only, but that they might also
see Lazarus, [a]whom He had raised from the dead.
10 [a]But the chief priests plotted to put Lazarus to death also,
11 [a]because on account of him many of the Jews went away
and believed in Jesus.
12 [a]The next day a great multitude that had come to the feast,
when they heard that Jesus was coming to Jerusalem,
13 took branches of palm trees and went out to meet Him,
and cried out:

> "Hosanna!
> [a]'Blessed *is* He who comes in the name of the LORD!'[1]
> The King of Israel!"

14 [a]Then Jesus, when He had found a young donkey, sat on
it; as it is written:

> 15 "Fear[a] not, daughter of Zion;
> Behold, your King is coming,
> Sitting on a donkey's colt."[1]

16 [a]His disciples did not understand these things at first;
[b]but when Jesus was glorified, [c]then they remembered that
these things were written about Him and *that* they had done
these things to Him.
17 Therefore the people, who were with Him when He called
Lazarus out of his tomb and raised him from the dead, bore
witness.
18 [a]For this reason the people also met Him, because they
heard that He had done this sign.
19 The Pharisees therefore said among themselves, [a]"You
see that you are accomplishing nothing. Look, the world has
gone after Him!"
20 Now there [a]were certain Greeks among those [b]who came
up to worship at the feast.
21 Then they came to Philip, [a]who was from Bethsaida of
Galilee, and asked him, saying, "Sir, we wish to see Jesus."
22 Philip came and told Andrew, and in turn Andrew and
Philip told Jesus.
23 But Jesus answered them, saying, [a]"The hour has come
that the Son of Man should be glorified.

12:8 [a]Mark 14:7 12:9 [a]John 11:43, 44 12:10 [a]Luke 16:31 12:11 [a]John 11:45; 12:18 12:12 [a]Matt. 21:4–9 12:13 [a]Ps. 118:25, 26 [1]Psalm 118:26 12:14 [a]Matt. 21:7 12:15 [a]Is. 40:9; Zech. 9:9 [1]Zechariah 9:9 12:16 [a]Luke 18:34 [b]John 7:39; 12:23 [c][John 14:26] 12:18 [a]John 12:11 12:19 [a]John 11:47, 48 12:20 [a]Acts 17:4 [b]1 Kin. 8:41, 42 12:21 [a]John 1:43, 44; 14:8–11 12:23 [a]John 13:32

24 "Most assuredly, I say to you, [a]unless a grain of wheat falls
into the ground and dies, it remains alone; but if it dies, it
produces much grain.
25 [a]"He who loves his life will lose it, and he who hates his
life in this world will keep it for eternal life.
26 "If anyone serves Me, let him [a]follow Me; and [b]where I
am, there My servant will be also. If anyone serves Me, him
My Father will honor.
27 [a]"Now My soul is troubled, and what shall I say? 'Father,
save Me from this hour'? [b]But for this purpose I came to this
hour.
28 "Father, glorify Your name." [a]Then a voice came from
heaven, *saying,* "I have both glorified *it* and will glorify *it*
again."
29 Therefore the people who stood by and heard *it* said that
it had thundered. Others said, "An angel has spoken to Him."
30 Jesus answered and said, [a]"This voice did not come be-
cause of Me, but for your sake.
31 "Now is the judgment of this world; now [a]the ruler of this
world will be cast out.
32 "And I, [a]if I am lifted up from the earth, will draw [b]all *peo-
ples* to Myself."
33 [a]This He said, signifying by what death He would die.
34 The people answered Him, [a]"We have heard from the law
that the Christ remains forever; and how *can* You say, 'The
Son of Man must be lifted up'? Who is this Son of Man?"
35 Then Jesus said to them, "A little while longer [a]the light is
with you. [b]Walk while you have the light, lest darkness over-
take you; [c]he who walks in darkness does not know where he
is going.
36 "While you have the light, believe in the light, that you
may become [a]sons of light." These things Jesus spoke, and
departed, and [b]was hidden from them.
37 But although He had done so many [a]signs before them,
they did not believe in Him,
38 that the word of Isaiah the prophet might be fulfilled,
which he spoke:

> [a]"Lord, who has believed our report?
> And to whom has the arm of the
> LORD been revealed?"[1]

39 Therefore they could not believe, because Isaiah said
again:

12:24[a]1 Cor. 15:36 12:25[a]Mark 8:35 12:26[a][Matt. 16:24] [b]John 14:3; 17:24 12:27[a][Matt. 26:38, 39] [b]Luke 22:53 12:28[a]Matt. 3:17; 17:5 12:30[a]John 11:42 12:31[a][2 Cor. 4:4] 12:32[a]John 3:14; 8:28 [b][Rom. 5:18] 12:33[a]John 18:32; 21:19 12:34[a]Mic. 4:7 12:35[a][John 1:9; 7:33; 8:12] [b]Eph. 5:8 [c][1 John 2:9–11] 12:36[a]Luke 16:8 [b]John 8:59 12:37[a]John 11:47 12:38[a]Is. 53:1 [1]Isaiah 53:1

40 "He[a] has blinded their eyes and
hardened their hearts,
[b]Lest they should see with *their* eyes,
Lest they should understand with
their hearts and turn,
So that I should heal them."[1]

41 [a]These things Isaiah said when[1] he saw His glory and
spoke of Him.
42 Nevertheless even among the rulers many believed in
Him, but [a]because of the Pharisees they did not confess *Him,*
lest they should be put out of the synagogue;
43 [a]for they loved the praise of men more than the praise
of God.
44 Then Jesus cried out and said, [a]"He who believes in Me,
[b]believes not in Me [c]but in Him who sent Me.
45 "And [a]he who sees Me sees Him who sent Me.
46 [a]"I have come *as* a light into the world, that whoever be-
lieves in Me should not abide in darkness.
47 "And if anyone hears My words and does not believe,[1] [a]I
do not judge him; for [b]I did not come to judge the world but
to save the world.
48 [a]"He who rejects Me, and does not receive My words, has
that which judges him—[b]the word that I have spoken will
judge him in the last day.
49 "For [a]I have not spoken on My own *authority;* but the Fa-
ther who sent Me gave Me a command, [b]what I should say
and what I should speak.
50 "And I know that His command is everlasting life. There-
fore, whatever I speak, just as the Father has told Me, so I
[a]speak."

12:40 [a]Is. 6:9, 10 [b]Matt. 13:14 [1]Isaiah 6:10 12:41 [a]Is. 6:1 [1]NU-Text reads *because.* 12:42 [a]John 7:13; 9:22 12:43 [a]John 5:41, 44 12:44 [a]Mark 9:37 [b][John 3:16, 18, 36; 11:25, 26] [c][John 5:24] 12:45 [a][John 14:9] 12:46 [a]John 1:4, 5; 8:12; 12:35, 36 12:47 [a]John 5:45 [b]John 3:17 [1]NU-Text reads *keep them.* 12:48 [a][Luke 10:16] [b]Deut. 18:18, 19 12:49 [a]John 8:38 [b]Deut. 18:18 12:50 [a]John 5:19; 8:28

JOHN 13

DISCIPLES MUST BE SERVANTS

"Lord, are You washing my feet?" It is perfectly wonderful that He should, for we have scarcely desired the mercy. If you look the chapter through, you do not find that Peter asked Christ to do it. Peter was lying down: he had just been eating at the supper, and he had no thought of Christ's washing his feet; not one of the twelve ever dreamed of such a thing. And when the Lord began to wash the feet of one, the others did not say, "Lord, come and do the same to me." No, it was unsolicited, unexpected; He comes, without any prayers or supplications on their part, and He begins to wash their feet.

It is great goodness on Christ's part to do what we ask Him to do—to bear our prayers when we really feel our need—but does He perform for us such menial, such generous acts as to wash our feet without being asked? Oh! Beloved, if Christ did no more for us than we ask Him to do, we should perish forever; for nine out of ten of the things He gives us we never asked for, and what if I were to say that three out of four of them we scarcely know that we want? We do not know our own needs. We have a general view of our necessities, wholesale, as it were, but our daily needs, our daily wants, who among us can tell them? We should bless God not only for the mercies we have known but for those we have not known—for probably those make up the larger proportion.

---

1 Now [a]before the Feast of the Passover, when Jesus knew
that [b]His hour had come that He should depart from this
world to the Father, having loved His own who were in the
world, He [c]loved them to the end.
2 And supper being ended,[1] [a]the devil having already put it
into the heart of Judas Iscariot, Simon's *son,* to betray Him,
3 Jesus, knowing [a]that the Father had given all things into
His hands, and that He [b]had come from God and [c]was going
to God,
4 [a]rose from supper and laid aside His garments, took a
towel and girded Himself.
5 After that, He poured water into a basin and began to wash
the disciples' feet, and to wipe *them* with the towel with which
He was girded.
6 Then He came to Simon Peter. And *Peter* said to Him,
[a]"Lord, are You washing my feet?"

13:1[a]Matt. 26:2 [b]John 12:23; 17:1 [c]John 15:9 13:2[a]Luke 22:3 [1]NU-Text reads *And during supper.* 13:3[a]Acts 2:36 [b]John 8:42; 16:28 [c]John 17:11; 20:17 13:4[a][Luke 22:27] 13:6[a]Matt. 3:14

7 Jesus answered and said to him, "What I am doing you [a]do
not understand now, [b]but you will know after this."
8 Peter said to Him, "You shall never wash my feet!" Jesus an-
swered him, [a]"If I do not wash you, you have no part with Me."
9 Simon Peter said to Him, "Lord, not my feet only, but also
my hands and *my* head!"
10 Jesus said to him, "He who is bathed needs only to wash
his feet, but is completely clean; and [a]you are clean, but not
all of you."
11 For [a]He knew who would betray Him; therefore He said,
"You are not all clean."
12 So when He had washed their feet, taken His garments,
and sat down again, He said to them, "Do you know what I
have done to you?
13 [a]"You call Me Teacher and Lord, and you say well, for *so*
I am.
14 [a]"If I then, *your* Lord and Teacher, have washed your feet,
[b]you also ought to wash one another's feet.
15 "For [a]I have given you an example, that you should do as
I have done to you.
16 [a]"Most assuredly, I say to you, a servant is not greater
than his master; nor is he who is sent greater than he who
sent him.
17 [a]"If you know these things, blessed are you if you do them.
18 "I do not speak concerning all of you. I know whom I have
chosen; but that the [a]Scripture may be fulfilled, [b]'He who eats
bread with Me[1] has lifted up his heel against Me.'[2]
19 [a]"Now I tell you before it comes, that when it does come
to pass, you may believe that I am *He*.
20 [a]"Most assuredly, I say to you, he who receives whomev-
er I send receives Me; and he who receives Me receives Him
who sent Me."
21 [a]When Jesus had said these things, [b]He was troubled in
spirit, and testified and said, "Most assuredly, I say to you,
[c]one of you will betray Me."
22 Then the disciples looked at one another, perplexed about
whom He spoke.
23 Now [a]there was leaning on Jesus' bosom one of His dis-
ciples, whom Jesus loved.
24 Simon Peter therefore motioned to him to ask who it was
of whom He spoke.
25 Then, leaning back[1] on Jesus' breast, he said to Him, "Lord,
who is it?"

13:7[a]John 12:16; 16:12 [b]John 13:19 13:8[a][1 Cor. 6:11] 13:10[a][John 15:3] 13:11[a]John 6:64; 18:4 13:13[a]Matt. 23:8, 10 13:14[a]Luke 22:27 [b][Rom. 12:10] 13:15[a][1 Pet. 2:21–24] 13:16[a]Matt. 10:24 13:17[a][James 1:25] 13:18[a]John 15:25; 17:12 [b]Ps. 41:9 [1]NU-Text reads *My bread.* [2]Psalm 41:9 13:19[a]John 14:29; 16:4 13:20[a]Matt. 10:40 13:21[a]Luke 22:21 [b]John 12:27 [c]1 John 2:19 13:23[a]John 19:26; 20:2; 21:7, 20 13:25[1]NU-Text and M-Text add *thus.*

26 Jesus answered, "It is he to whom I shall give a piece of
bread when I have dipped *it*." And having dipped the bread,
He gave *it* to [a]Judas Iscariot, *the son* of Simon.
27 [a]Now after the piece of bread, Satan entered him. Then
Jesus said to him, "What you do, do quickly."
28 But no one at the table knew for what reason He said this
to him.
29 For some thought, because [a]Judas had the money box,
that Jesus had said to him, "Buy *those things* we need for the
feast," or that he should give something to the poor.
30 Having received the piece of bread, he then went out im-
mediately. And it was night.
31 So, when he had gone out, Jesus said, [a]"Now the Son of
Man is glorified, and [b]God is glorified in Him.
32 "If God is glorified in Him, God will also glorify Him in
Himself, and [a]glorify Him immediately.
33 "Little children, I shall be with you a [a]little while longer.
You will seek Me; [b]and as I said to the Jews, 'Where I am go-
ing, you cannot come,' so now I say to you.
34 [a]"A new commandment I give to you, that you love one
another; as I have loved you, that you also love one another.
35 [a]"By this all will know that you are My disciples, if you
have love for one another."
36 Simon Peter said to Him, "Lord, where are You going?"
Jesus answered him, "Where I [a]am going you cannot follow
Me now, but [b]you shall follow Me afterward."
37 Peter said to Him, "Lord, why can I not follow You now?
I will [a]lay down my life for Your sake."
38 Jesus answered him, "Will you lay down your life for My
sake? Most assuredly, I say to you, the rooster shall not [a]crow
till you have denied Me three times.

13:26 [a]John 6:70, 71; 12:4 13:27 [a]Luke 22:3 13:29 [a]John 12:6 13:31 [a]John 12:23 [b][1 Pet. 4:11] 13:32 [a]John 12:23 13:33 [a]John 12:35; 14:19; 16:16–19 [b][John 7:34; 8:21] 13:34 [a]1 Thess. 4:9 13:35 [a]1 John 2:5 13:36 [a]John 13:33; 14:2; 16:5 [b]2 Pet. 1:14 13:37 [a]Mark 14:29–31 13:38 [a]John 18:25–27

JOHN 14

JESUS IS THE WAY, THE TRUTH, AND THE LIFE

There are many choice gifts comprehended in the covenant of grace, but the first and richest of them are these twain—the gift of Jesus Christ for us and the gift of the Holy Ghost to us. The first of these I trust we are not likely to undervalue. But the second great gift, by no means inferior to the first—the gift of the Holy Spirit to us—is so spiritual and we are so carnal, is so mysterious and we are so material, that we are very apt to forget its value and even to forget the gift altogether.

And yet, my brethren, let us ever remember that Christ on the cross is of no value to us apart from the Holy Spirit in us. In vain that blood is flowing unless the finger of the Spirit applies the blood to our conscience; in vain is that garment of righteousness wrought out, a garment without seam, woven from the top throughout, unless the Holy Spirit wraps it around us and arrays us in its costly folds. The river of the water of life cannot quench our thirst till the Spirit presents the goblet and lifts it to our lip.

We do not hesitate to say that we owe as much to God the Holy Ghost as we do to God the Son. Magnify, then, the Spirit, you who are partakers of it: "Praise, laud, and love His name always, for it is seemly so to do."

---

1 "Let [a]not your heart be troubled; you believe in God, be-
lieve also in Me.
2 "In My Father's house are many mansions;[1] if *it were* not
so, I would have told you. [a]I go to prepare a place for you.[2]
3 "And if I go and prepare a place for you, [a]I will come again
and receive you to Myself; that [b]where I am, *there* you may
be also.
4 "And where I go you know, and the way you know."
5 [a]Thomas said to Him, "Lord, we do not know where You
are going, and how can we know the way?"
6 Jesus said to him, "I am [a]the way, [b]the truth, and [c]the life.
[d]No one comes to the Father [e]except through Me.
7 [a]"If you had known Me, you would have known My Father
also; and from now on you know Him and have seen Him."
8 Philip said to Him, "Lord, show us the Father, and it is suf-
ficient for us."
9 Jesus said to him, "Have I been with you so long, and yet

14:1[a][John 14:27; 16:22, 24] 14:2[a]John 13:33, 36 [1]Literally *dwellings* [2]NU-Text adds a word which would cause the text to read either *if it were not so, would I have told you that I go to prepare a place for you?* or *if it were not so I would have told you; for I go to prepare a place for you.* 14:3[a][Acts 1:11] [b][John 12:26] 14:5[a]Matt. 10:3 14:6[a][Heb. 9:8; 10:19, 20] [b][John 1:14, 17; 8:32; 18:37] [c][John 11:25] [d]1 Tim. 2:5 [e][John 10:7–9] 14:7[a]John 8:19

you have not known Me, Philip? [a]He who has seen Me has
seen the Father; so how can you say, 'Show us the Father'?
10 "Do you not believe that [a]I am in the Father, and the Father
in Me? The words that I speak to you [b]I do not speak on My own
authority; but the Father who dwells in Me does the works.
11 "Believe Me that I *am* in the Father and the Father in Me,
[a]or else believe Me for the sake of the works themselves.
12 [a]"Most assuredly, I say to you, he who believes in Me, the
works that I do he will do also; and greater *works* than these
he will do, because I go to My Father.
13 [a]"And whatever you ask in My name, that I will do, that
the Father may be [b]glorified in the Son.
14 "If you ask[1] anything in My name, I will do *it.*
15 [a]"If you love Me, keep[1] My commandments.
16 "And I will pray the Father, and [a]He will give you another
Helper, that He may abide with you forever—
17 [a]"the Spirit of truth, [b]whom the world cannot receive,
because it neither sees Him nor knows Him; but you know
Him, for He dwells with you [c]and will be in you.
18 [a]"I will not leave you orphans; [b]I will come to you.
19 "A little while longer and the world will see Me no more,
but [a]you will see Me. [b]Because I live, you will live also.
20 "At that day you will know that [a]I *am* in My Father, and
you in Me, and I in you.
21 [a]"He who has My commandments and keeps them, it is
he who loves Me. And he who loves Me will be loved by My
Father, and I will love him and manifest Myself to him."
22 [a]Judas (not Iscariot) said to Him, "Lord, how is it that You
will manifest Yourself to us, and not to the world?"
23 Jesus answered and said to him, "If anyone loves Me, he
will keep My word; and My Father will love him, [a]and We will
come to him and make Our home with him.
24 "He who does not love Me does not keep My words; and
[a]the word which you hear is not Mine but the Father's who
sent Me.
25 "These things I have spoken to you while being present
with you.
26 "But [a]the Helper, the Holy Spirit, whom the Father will
[b]send in My name, [c]He will teach you all things, and bring to
your [d]remembrance all things that I said to you.
27 [a]"Peace I leave with you, My peace I give to you; not as
the world gives do I give to you. Let not your heart be trou-
bled, neither let it be afraid.

14:9[a]Col. 1:15 14:10[a]John 10:38; 14:11, 20 [b]John 5:19; 14:24 14:11[a]John 5:36; 10:38 14:12[a]Luke 10:17 14:13[a]Matt. 7:7 [b]John 13:31 14:14[1]NU-Text adds *Me*. 14:15[a]1 John 5:3 [1]NU-Text reads *you will keep*. 14:16[a]Rom. 8:15 14:17[a][1 John 4:6; 5:7] [b][1 Cor. 2:14] [c][1 John 2:27] 14:18[a][Matt. 28:20] [b][John 14:3, 28] 14:19[a]John 16:16, 22 [b][1 Cor. 15:20] 14:20[a]John 10:38; 14:11 14:21[a]1 John 2:5 14:22[a]Luke 6:16 14:23[a]Rev. 3:20; 21:3 14:24[a]John 5:19 14:26[a]Luke 24:49 [b]John 15:26 [c]1 Cor. 2:13 [d]John 2:22; 12:16 14:27[a][Phil. 4:7]

28 "You have heard Me [a]say to you, 'I am going away and
coming *back* to you.' If you loved Me, you would rejoice be-
cause I said,[1] [b]'I am going to the Father,' for [c]My Father is
greater than I.
29 "And [a]now I have told you before it comes, that when it
does come to pass, you may believe.
30 "I will no longer talk much with you, [a]for the ruler of this
world is coming, and he has [b]nothing in Me.
31 "But that the world may know that I love the Father, and
[a]as the Father gave Me commandment, so I do. Arise, let us
go from here.

14:28 [a]John 14:3, 18 [b]John 16:16 [c][Phil. 2:6] [1]NU-Text omits *I said.* 14:29 [a]John 13:19 14:30 [a][John 12:31] [b][Heb. 4:15] 14:31 [a]Is. 50:5; John 10:18

JOHN 15

CHRIST THE TRUE VINE

This is not the language of a man of ordinary mold. No saint, no prophet, no apostle would ever have addressed a company of faithful men and said to them, "Without Me you can do nothing." Had Jesus Christ been, as some say, a good man and nothing more, such language as this would have been unseemly and inconsistent. Among the virtues of a perfect man we must certainly reckon modesty, but this from a mere man would have been shamelessly immodest. It is impossible to conceive that Jesus of Nazareth, had He not been more than man, could ever have uttered the sentence "Without Me you can do nothing."

My brethren, I hear in this sentence the voice of that divine Person without whom was not anything made that was made (John 1:3). The majesty of the words reveals the Godhead of Him who uttered them. The claim of all power unveils the Omnipotent. The spirit in which we listen to this language is that of adoration. Let us bow our heads in solemn worship and so unite with the multitude before the throne who ascribe power and dominion and might to Him who sits upon the throne and to the Lamb.

---

1 "I am the true vine, and My Father is the vinedresser.
2 [a]"Every branch in Me that does not bear fruit He takes
away;[1] and every *branch* that bears fruit He prunes, that it
may bear [b]more fruit.
3 [a]"You are already clean because of the word which I have
spoken to you.
4 [a]"Abide in Me, and I in you. As the branch cannot bear fruit
of itself, unless it abides in the vine, neither can you, unless
you abide in Me.
5 "I am the vine, you *are* the branches. He who abides in Me,
and I in him, bears much [a]fruit; for without Me you can do
[b]nothing.
6 "If anyone does not abide in Me, [a]he is cast out as a branch
and is withered; and they gather them and throw *them* into
the fire, and they are burned.
7 "If you abide in Me, and My words [a]abide in you, [b]you will[1]
ask what you desire, and it shall be done for you.
8 [a]"By this My Father is glorified, that you bear much fruit;
[b]so you will be My disciples.
9 "As the Father [a]loved Me, I also have loved you; abide in
My love.

15:2 [a]Matt. 15:13 [b][Matt. 13:12] [1]Or *lifts up* 15:3 [a][John 13:10; 17:17] 15:4 [a][Col. 1:23] 15:5 [a]Hos. 14:8 [b]2 Cor. 3:5 15:6 [a]Matt. 3:10 15:7 [a]1 John 2:14 [b]John 14:13; 16:23 [1]NU-Text omits *you will.* 15:8 [a][Matt. 5:16] [b]John 8:31 15:9 [a]John 5:20; 17:26

10 [a]"If you keep My commandments, you will abide in My
love, just as I have kept My Father's commandments and
abide in His love.
11 "These things I have spoken to you, that My joy may re-
main in you, and [a]*that* your joy may be full.
12 [a]"This is My [b]commandment, that you love one another
as I have loved you.
13 [a]"Greater love has no one than this, than to lay down one's
life for his friends.
14 [a]"You are My friends if you do whatever I command you.
15 "No longer do I call you servants, for a servant does not
know what his master is doing; but I have called you friends,
[a]for all things that I heard from My Father I have made known
to you.
16 [a]"You did not choose Me, but I chose you and [b]appoint-
ed you that you should go and bear fruit, and *that* your fruit
should remain, that whatever you ask the Father [c]in My name
He may give you.
17 "These things I command you, that you love one another.
18 [a]"If the world hates you, you know that it hated Me before
it hated you.
19 [a]"If you were of the world, the world would love its own.
Yet [b]because you are not of the world, but I chose you out of
the world, therefore the world hates you.
20 "Remember the word that I said to you, [a]'A servant is not
greater than his master.' If they persecuted Me, they will also
persecute you. [b]If they kept My word, they will keep yours
also.
21 "But [a]all these things they will do to you for My name's
sake, because they do not know Him who sent Me.
22 [a]"If I had not come and spoken to them, they would have
no sin, [b]but now they have no excuse for their sin.
23 [a]"He who hates Me hates My Father also.
24 "If I had not done among them [a]the works which no one
else did, they would have no sin; but now they have [b]seen and
also hated both Me and My Father.
25 "But *this happened* that the word might be fulfilled which
is written in their law, [a]'They hated Me without a cause.'[1]
26 [a]"But when the Helper comes, whom I shall send to you
from the Father, the Spirit of truth who proceeds from the
Father, [b]He will testify of Me.
27 "And [a]you also will bear witness, because [b]you have been
with Me from the beginning.

15:10[a]John 14:15 15:11[a]1 John 1:4 15:12[a]1 John 3:11 [b]Rom. 12:9 15:13[a]1 John 3:16 15:14[a][Matt. 12:50; 28:20] 15:15[a]Gen. 18:17 15:16[a]John 6:70; 13:18; 15:19 [b][Col. 1:6] [c]John 14:13; 16:23, 24 15:18[a]1 John 3:13 15:19[a]1 John 4:5 [b]John 17:14 15:20[a]John 13:16 [b]Ezek. 3:7 15:21[a]Matt. 10:22; 24:9 15:22[a]John 9:41; 15:24 [b][James 4:17] 15:23[a]1 John 2:23 15:24[a]John 3:2 [b]John 14:9 15:25[a]Ps. 35:19; 69:4; 109:3–5 [1]Psalm 69:4 15:26[a]Luke 24:49 [b]1 John 5:6 15:27[a]Luke 24:48 [b]Luke 1:2

JOHN 16

JESUS WARNS AND COMFORTS HIS DISCIPLES

"Your sorrow will be turned into joy." Not exchanged for joy but actually transmuted so that the grief becomes joy, the cause of sorrow becomes the source of rejoicing.

That Jesus Christ died for our sins is a sharp sorrow: we lament that our crimes became the nails and our unbelief the spear. And yet, my brethren, this is the greatest joy of all. If each one of us can say, "He loved me and gave Himself for me," we are truly happy. If you know by personal faith that Jesus took your sin and suffered for it on the tree, so that now your debt is paid and your transgression is blotted out forever by His precious blood, that which was the center of your grief is also the essence of your joy. What were it to us if He had saved all the rest of mankind if He had not redeemed us unto God by His blood? We might have been glad from sheer humanity that others should be benefited, but what would have been our deep regret to be ourselves excluded from the grace?

'Tis a sad thought that we committed the sin that burdened our Lord, but it is a joy to think that He has taken on Himself our personal sin and carried it right away.

---

1 "These things I have spoken to you, that you [a]should not
be made to stumble.
2 [a]"They will put you out of the synagogues; yes, the time is
coming [b]that whoever kills you will think that he offers God
service.
3 "And [a]these things they will do to you[1] because they have
not known the Father nor Me.
4 "But these things I have told you, that when the[1] time comes,
you may remember that I told you of them. And these things
I did not say to you at the beginning, because I was with you.
5 "But now I [a]go away to Him who sent Me, and none of you
asks Me, 'Where are You going?'
6 "But because I have said these things to you, [a]sorrow has
filled your heart.
7 "Nevertheless I tell you the truth. It is to your advantage
that I go away; for if I do not go away, the Helper will not
come to you; but [a]if I depart, I will send Him to you.
8 "And when He has [a]come, He will convict the world of sin,
and of righteousness, and of judgment:
9 [a]"of sin, because they do not believe in Me;

16:1 [a]Matt. 11:6 16:2 [a]John 9:22 [b]Acts 8:1 16:3 [a]John 8:19; 15:21 [1]NU-Text and M-Text omit *to you.* 16:4 [1]NU-Text reads *their.* 16:5 [a]John 7:33; 13:33; 14:28; 17:11 16:6 [a][John 16:20, 22] 16:7 [a]Acts 2:33 16:8 [a]Acts 1:8; 2:1–4, 37 16:9 [a]Acts 2:22

10 [a]"of righteousness, [b]because I go to My Father and you
see Me no more;
11 [a]"of judgment, because [b]the ruler of this world is judged.
12 "I still have many things to say to you, [a]but you cannot
bear *them* now.
13 "However, when He, [a]the Spirit of truth, has come, [b]He
will guide you into all truth; for He will not speak on His own
authority, but whatever He hears He will speak; and He will
tell you things to come.
14 [a]"He will glorify Me, for He will take of what is Mine and
declare *it* to you.
15 [a]"All things that the Father has are Mine. Therefore I said
that He will take of Mine and declare *it* to you.[1]
16 "A [a]little while, and you will not see Me; and again a little
while, and you will see Me, [b]because I go to the Father."
17 Then *some* of His disciples said among themselves, "What
is this that He says to us, 'A little while, and you will not see
Me; and again a little while, and you will see Me'; and, 'be-
cause I go to the Father'?"
18 They said therefore, "What is this that He says, 'A little
while'? We do not know what He is saying."
19 Now Jesus knew that they desired to ask Him, and He said
to them, "Are you inquiring among yourselves about what I
said, 'A little while, and you will not see Me; and again a little
while, and you will see Me'?
20 "Most assuredly, I say to you that you will weep and
[a]lament, but the world will rejoice; and you will be sorrow-
ful, but your sorrow will be turned into [b]joy.
21 [a]"A woman, when she is in labor, has sorrow because her
hour has come; but as soon as she has given birth to the child,
she no longer remembers the anguish, for joy that a human
being has been born into the world.
22 "Therefore you now have sorrow; but I will see you again
and [a]your heart will rejoice, and your joy no one will take
from you.
23 "And in that day you will ask Me nothing. [a]Most assured-
ly, I say to you, whatever you ask the Father in My name He
will give you.
24 "Until now you have asked nothing in My name. Ask, and
you will receive, [a]that your joy may be [b]full.
25 "These things I have spoken to you in figurative language;
but the time is coming when I will no longer speak to you in
figurative language, but I will tell you [a]plainly about the Father.

16:10[a]Acts 2:32 [b]John 5:32 16:11[a]Acts 26:18 [b][Luke 10:18] 16:12[a]Mark 4:33 16:13[a][John 14:17] [b]John 14:26 16:14[a]John 15:26 16:15[a]Matt. 11:27 [1]NU-Text and M-Text read *He takes of Mine and will declare it to you.* 16:16[a]John 7:33; 12:35; 13:33; 14:19; 19:40–42; 20:19 [b]John 13:3 16:20[a]Mark 16:10 [b]Luke 24:32, 41 16:21[a]Is. 13:8; 26:17; 42:14 16:22[a]1 Pet. 1:8 16:23[a]Matt. 7:7 16:24[a]John 17:13 [b]John 15:11 16:25[a]John 7:13

26 "In that day you will ask in My name, and I do not say to
you that I shall pray the Father for you;
27 [a]"for the Father Himself loves you, because you have
loved Me, and [b]have believed that I came forth from God.
28 [a]"I came forth from the Father and have come into the
world. Again, I leave the world and go to the Father."
29 His disciples said to Him, "See, now You are speaking
plainly, and using no figure of speech!
30 "Now we are sure that [a]You know all things, and have no
need that anyone should question You. By this [b]we believe
that You came forth from God."
31 Jesus answered them, "Do you now believe?
32 [a]"Indeed the hour is coming, yes, has now come, that you
will be scattered, [b]each to his own, and will leave Me alone.
And [c]yet I am not alone, because the Father is with Me.
33 "These things I have spoken to you, that [a]in Me you may
have peace. [b]In the world you will[1] have tribulation; but be
of good cheer, [c]I have overcome the world."

16:27 [a][John 14:21, 23] [b]John 3:13 16:28 [a]John 13:1, 3; 16:5, 10, 17 16:30 [a]John 21:17 [b]John 17:8 16:32 [a]Matt. 26:31, 56 [b]John 20:10 [c]John 8:29 16:33 [a][Eph. 2:14] [b]2 Tim. 3:12 [c]Rom. 8:37 [1]NU-Text and M-Text omit *will*.

JOHN 17

JESUS PRAYS TO GOD FOR HIS DISCIPLES

Our Lord Jesus prayed much for His people while He was here on earth. In this wonderful prayer, our Lord, as our Great High Priest, appears to enter upon that perpetual office of intercession that He is now exercising at the right hand of the Father. Our Lord ever seemed, in the eagerness of His love, to be anticipating His future work.

Here we are admitted to that secret place where the Son of God speaks with the Father in closest fellowship of love. Here we look into the heart of Jesus as He sets out in order His desires and requests before His Father on our behalf. Here inspiration lifts her veil, and we behold truth face-to-face.

Our Lord's desire for the sanctification of His people pervades the whole prayer, but it is gathered up, declared, and intensified in one sentence: "Sanctify them by Your truth. Your word is truth." How invaluable must the blessing of sanctification be when our Lord, in the highest reach of His intercession, cries, "Sanctify them"!

In sight of His Passion, on the night before His death, our Savior lifts His eyes to the great Father and cries in His most plaintive tones, "Sanctify them." The place whereon we stand is holy ground, and the subject whereof we speak demands our solemn thought. Come, Holy Spirit, and teach us the full meaning of this prayer for holiness!

---

1 Jesus spoke these words, lifted up His eyes to heaven, and
said: "Father, [a]the hour has come. Glorify Your Son, that Your
Son also may glorify You,
2 [a]"as You have given Him authority over all flesh, that He
should[1] give eternal life to as many [b]as You have given Him.
3 "And [a]this is eternal life, that they may know You, [b]the only
true God, and Jesus Christ [c]whom You have sent.
4 [a]"I have glorified You on the earth. [b]I have finished the
work [c]which You have given Me to do.
5 "And now, O Father, glorify Me together with Yourself, with
the glory [a]which I had with You before the world was.
6 [a]"I have manifested Your name to the men [b]whom You
have given Me out of the world. [c]They were Yours, You gave
them to Me, and they have kept Your word.
7 "Now they have known that all things which You have given
Me are from You.

17:1 [a]John 12:23 17:2 [a]John 3:35 [b]John 6:37, 39; 17:6, 9, 24 [1]M-Text reads *shall.* 17:3 [a]Jer. 9:23, 24 [b]1 Cor. 8:4 [c]John 3:34 17:4 [a]John 13:31 [b]John 4:34; 19:30 [c]John 14:31 17:5 [a]Phil. 2:6 17:6 [a]Ps. 22:22 [b]John 6:37 [c]Ezek. 18:4

8 "For I have given to them the words [a]which You have given Me; and they have received *them,* [b]and have known surely that I came forth from You; and they have believed that [c]You sent Me.

9 "I pray for them. [a]I do not pray for the world but for those whom You have given Me, for they are Yours.

10 "And all Mine are Yours, and [a]Yours are Mine, and I am glorified in them.

11 [a]"Now I am no longer in the world, but these are in the world, and I come to You. Holy Father, [b]keep through Your name those whom You have given Me,[1] that they may be one [c]as We *are.*

12 "While I was with them in the world,[1] [a]I kept them in Your name. Those whom You gave Me I have kept;[2] and [b]none of them is lost [c]except the son of perdition, [d]that the Scripture might be fulfilled.

13 "But now I come to You, and these things I speak in the world, that they may have My joy fulfilled in themselves.

14 "I have given them Your word; [a]and the world has hated them because they are not of the world, [b]just as I am not of the world.

15 "I do not pray that You should take them out of the world, but [a]that You should keep them from the evil one.

16 "They are not of the world, just as I am not of the world.

17 [a]"Sanctify them by Your truth. [b]Your word is truth.

18 [a]"As You sent Me into the world, I also have sent them into the world.

19 "And [a]for their sakes I sanctify Myself, that they also may be sanctified by the truth.

20 "I do not pray for these alone, but also for those who will[1] believe in Me through their word;

21 [a]"that they all may be one, as [b]You, Father, *are* in Me, and I in You; that they also may be one in Us, that the world may believe that You sent Me.

22 "And the [a]glory which You gave Me I have given them, [b]that they may be one just as We are one:

23 "I in them, and You in Me; [a]that they may be made perfect in one, and that the world may know that You have sent Me, and have loved them as You have loved Me.

24 [a]"Father, I desire that they also whom You gave Me may be with Me where I am, that they may behold My glory which

17:8[a]John 8:28 [b]John 8:42; 16:27, 30 [c]Deut. 18:15, 18 17:9[a][1 John 5:19] 17:10[a]John 16:15 17:11[a]John 13:1 [b][1 Pet. 1:5] [c]John 10:30 [1]NU-Text and M-Text read *keep them through Your name which You have given Me.* 17:12[a]Heb. 2:13 [b]1 John 2:19 [c]John 6:70 [d]Ps. 41:9; 109:8 [1]NU-Text omits *in the world.* [2]NU-Text reads *in Your name which You gave Me. And I guarded them;* (or *it;*). 17:14[a]John 15:19 [b]John 8:23 17:15[a]1 John 5:18 17:17[a][Eph. 5:26] [b]Ps. 119:9, 142, 151 17:18[a]John 4:38; 20:21 17:19[a][Heb. 10:10] 17:20[1]NU-Text and M-Text omit *will.* 17:21[a][Gal. 3:28] [b]John 10:38; 17:11, 23 17:22[a]1 John 1:3 [b][2 Cor. 3:18] 17:23[a][Col. 3:14] 17:24[a][1 Thess. 4:17]

You have given Me; [b]for You loved Me before the foundation
of the world.
25 "O righteous Father! [a]The world has not known You, but
[b]I have known You; and [c]these have known that You sent Me.
26 [a]"And I have declared to them Your name, and will de-
clare *it,* that the love [b]with which You loved Me may be in
them, and I in them."

17:24[b] John 17:5 17:25[a] John 15:21 [b] John 7:29; 8:55; 10:15 [c] John 3:17; 17:3, 8, 18, 21, 23 17:26[a] John 17:6 [b] John 15:9

JOHN 18

THE BETRAYAL, ARREST, AND TRIAL OF JESUS

The voluntary character of Christ's suffering makes it beam with a matchless splendor of love. He needed not to have died. If it had been His good pleasure, He might have tarried gloriously among the songs of angels. He came not to earth to win a crown, for all honor and glory are His by right. When He descended from the skies, He had nothing to gain—rather He had everything to lose; and yet let me say to correct myself by that losing He did gain, for now as our Mediator He is clothed with a special glory of unrivaled grace, unequaled by any other manifestation of the divine perfections.

The willingness of Jesus! Let us see it clearly, and let us reverently adore Him for it. Blessed Master! You came to die for us through no compulsion but that of Your own heart! Nothing brought You to the tomb but Your almighty love for us.

Let us take care that our service of Christ shall ever be most manifestly a cheerful and a willing one. Let us never enter upon Christian exercises as a slave would enter upon his labor, but let love put wings to our feet and inspire our souls with a sacred alacrity, that as the seraphs fly upon the high behests of heaven, we may run upon our Savior's commands with as much swiftness as mortals can command. Let our duty be our delight. Let the service of Christ be a kingdom to us.

---

1 When Jesus had spoken these words, [a]He went out with His disciples over [b]the Brook Kidron, where there was a garden, which He and His disciples entered.
2 And Judas, who betrayed Him, also knew the place; [a]for Jesus often met there with His disciples.
3 [a]Then Judas, having received a detachment *of troops,* and officers from the chief priests and Pharisees, came there with lanterns, torches, and weapons.
4 Jesus therefore, [a]knowing all things that would come upon Him, went forward and said to them, "Whom are you seeking?"
5 They answered Him, [a]"Jesus of Nazareth." Jesus said to them, "I am *He.*" And Judas, who [b]betrayed Him, also stood with them.
6 Now when He said to them, "I am *He,*" they drew back and fell to the ground.
7 Then He asked them again, "Whom are you seeking?" And they said, "Jesus of Nazareth."

18:1[a]Mark 14:26, 32 [b]2 Sam. 15:23 18:2[a]Luke 21:37; 22:39 18:3[a]Luke 22:47–53 18:4[a]John 6:64; 13:1, 3; 19:28 18:5[a]Matt. 21:11 [b]Ps. 41:9

8 Jesus answered, "I have told you that I am *He*. Therefore,
if you seek Me, let these go their way,"
9 that the saying might be fulfilled which He spoke, [a]"Of
those whom You gave Me I have lost none."
10 [a]Then Simon Peter, having a sword, drew it and struck the
high priest's servant, and cut off his right ear. The servant's
name was Malchus.
11 So Jesus said to Peter, "Put your sword into the sheath.
Shall I not drink [a]the cup which My Father has given Me?"
12 Then the detachment *of troops* and the captain and the
officers of the Jews arrested Jesus and bound Him.
13 And [a]they led Him away to [b]Annas first, for he was the
father-in-law of [c]Caiaphas who was high priest that year.
14 [a]Now it was Caiaphas who advised the Jews that it was ex-
pedient that one man should die for the people.
15 [a]And Simon Peter followed Jesus, and so *did* [b]another[1]
disciple. Now that disciple was known to the high priest, and
went with Jesus into the courtyard of the high priest.
16 [a]But Peter stood at the door outside. Then the other dis-
ciple, who was known to the high priest, went out and spoke
to her who kept the door, and brought Peter in.
17 Then the servant girl who kept the door said to Peter, "You
are not also *one* of this Man's disciples, are you?" He said, "I
am [a]not."
18 Now the servants and officers who had made a fire of coals
stood there, for it was cold, and they warmed themselves.
And Peter stood with them and warmed himself.
19 The high priest then asked Jesus about His disciples and
His doctrine.
20 Jesus answered him, [a]"I spoke openly to the world. I al-
ways taught [b]in synagogues and [c]in the temple, where the
Jews always meet,[1] and in secret I have said nothing.
21 "Why do you ask Me? Ask [a]those who have heard Me what
I said to them. Indeed they know what I said."
22 And when He had said these things, one of the officers
who stood by [a]struck Jesus with the palm of his hand, say-
ing, "Do You answer the high priest like that?"
23 Jesus answered him, "If I have spoken evil, bear witness
of the evil; but if well, why do you strike Me?"
24 [a]Then Annas sent Him bound to [b]Caiaphas the high priest.
25 Now Simon Peter stood and warmed himself. [a]Therefore
they said to him, "You are not also *one* of His disciples, are
you?" He denied *it* and said, "I am not!"
26 One of the servants of the high priest, a relative *of him*

18:9 [a][John 6:39; 17:12] 18:10 [a]Matt. 26:51 18:11 [a]Matt. 20:22; 26:39 18:13 [a]Matt. 26:57 [b]Luke 3:2 [c]Matt. 26:3 18:14 [a]John 11:50 18:15 [a]Mark 14:54 [b]John 20:2–5 [1]M-Text reads *the other*. 18:16 [a]Matt. 26:69 18:17 [a]Matt. 26:34 18:20 [a]Luke 4:15 [b]John 6:59 [c]Mark 14:49 [1]NU-Text reads *where all the Jews meet*. 18:21 [a]Mark 12:37 18:22 [a]Jer. 20:2 18:24 [a]Matt. 26:57 [b]John 11:49 18:25 [a]Luke 22:58–62

whose ear Peter cut off, said, "Did I not see you in the garden
with Him?"
27 Peter then denied again; and [a]immediately a rooster
crowed.
28 [a]Then they led Jesus from Caiaphas to the Praetorium,
and it was early morning. [b]But they themselves did not go
into the Praetorium, lest they should be defiled, but that they
might eat the Passover.
29 [a]Pilate then went out to them and said, "What accusation
do you bring against this Man?"
30 They answered and said to him, "If He were not an evil-
doer, we would not have delivered Him up to you."
31 Then Pilate said to them, "You take Him and judge Him
according to your law." Therefore the Jews said to him, "It is
not lawful for us to put anyone to death,"
32 [a]that the saying of Jesus might be fulfilled which He
spoke, [b]signifying by what death He would die.
33 [a]Then Pilate entered the Praetorium again, called Jesus,
and said to Him, "Are You the King of the Jews?"
34 Jesus answered him, "Are you speaking for yourself about
this, or did others tell you this concerning Me?"
35 Pilate answered, "Am I a Jew? Your own nation and the
chief priests have delivered You to me. What have You done?"
36 [a]Jesus answered, [b]"My kingdom is not of this world. If My
kingdom were of this world, My servants would fight, so that
I should not be delivered to the Jews; but now My kingdom
is not from here."
37 Pilate therefore said to Him, "Are You a king then?" Jesus
answered, "You say *rightly* that I am a king. For this cause I
was born, and for this cause I have come into the world, [a]that
I should bear [b]witness to the truth. Everyone who [c]is of the
truth [d]hears My voice."
38 Pilate said to Him, "What is truth?" And when he had said
this, he went out again to the Jews, and said to them, [a]"I find
no fault in Him at all.
39 [a]"But you have a custom that I should release someone
to you at the Passover. Do you therefore want me to release
to you the King of the Jews?"
40 [a]Then they all cried again, saying, "Not this Man, but Bar-
abbas!" [b]Now Barabbas was a robber.

18:27[a]John 13:38 18:28[a]Mark 15:1 [b]Acts 10:28; 11:3 18:29[a]Matt. 27:11–14
18:32[a]Matt. 20:17–19; 26:2 [b]John 3:14; 8:28; 12:32, 33 18:33[a]Matt. 27:11
18:36[a]1 Tim. 6:13 [b][Dan. 2:44; 7:14] 18:37[a][Matt. 5:17; 20:28] [b]Is. 55:4 [c][John 14:6]
[d]John 8:47; 10:27 18:38[a]John 19:4, 6 18:39[a]Luke 23:17–25
18:40[a]Acts 3:14 [b]Luke 23:19

JOHN 19

THE CRUCIFIXION AND BURIAL OF JESUS

Dear friend, take comfort from this "It is finished," for the redemption of Christ's church is perfected! There is not another penny to be paid for her full release. There is no mortgage upon Christ's inheritance. Those whom He bought with blood are forever clear of all charges, paid for to the utmost. There was a handwriting of ordinances against us; all those overwhelming debts, which would have sunk us to the lowest hell, have been discharged. And they who believe in Christ may appear with boldness even before the throne of God itself. "It is finished!" What comfort there is in this glorious truth!

By that one word He declared that He had broken the head of the old dragon. By His death, Jesus has routed the hosts of darkness and crushed the rising hopes of hell. We have a stern battle yet to fight; it looks as if there are to be sterner times and darker days than we have ever yet known. But what of that? Our Lord has defeated the foe, and we have to fight with one who is already vanquished. The old serpent has been crushed, his head is bruised, and we have now to trample on him.

Let every Christian here, let the whole church of God, as one mighty army, take comfort from this dying word of the now risen and ever-living Savior, "It is finished!"

---

1 So then [a]Pilate took Jesus and scourged *Him.*
2 And the soldiers twisted a crown of thorns and put *it* on
His head, and they put on Him a purple robe.
3 Then they said,[1] "Hail, King of the Jews!" And they [a]struck
Him with their hands.
4 Pilate then went out again, and said to them, "Behold, I
am bringing Him out to you, [a]that you may know that I find
no fault in Him."
5 Then Jesus came out, wearing the crown of thorns and the
purple robe. And *Pilate* said to them, "Behold the Man!"
6 [a]Therefore, when the chief priests and officers saw Him,
they cried out, saying, "Crucify *Him,* crucify *Him!*" Pilate said
to them, "You take Him and crucify *Him,* for I find no fault
in Him."
7 The Jews answered him, [a]"We have a law, and according
to our[1] law He ought to die, because [b]He made Himself the
Son of God."

19:1[a]Matt. 20:19; 27:26 19:3[a]Is. 50:6 [1]NU-Text reads *And they came up to Him and said.* 19:4[a]John 18:33, 38 19:6[a]Acts 3:13 19:7[a]Lev. 24:16 [b]Matt. 26:63–66 [1]NU-Text reads *the law.*

8 Therefore, when Pilate heard that saying, he was the more
afraid,
9 and went again into the Praetorium, and said to Jesus,
"Where are You from?" [a]But Jesus gave him no answer.
10 Then Pilate said to Him, "Are You not speaking to me? Do
You not know that I have power to crucify You, and power to
release You?"
11 Jesus answered, [a]"You could have no power at all against
Me unless it had been given you from above. Therefore [b]the
one who delivered Me to you has the greater sin."
12 From then on Pilate sought to release Him, but the Jews
cried out, saying, "If you let this Man go, you are not Caesar's
friend. [a]Whoever makes himself a king speaks against Cae-
sar."
13 [a]When Pilate therefore heard that saying, he brought
Jesus out and sat down in the judgment seat in a place that
is called *The* Pavement, but in Hebrew, Gabbatha.
14 Now [a]it was the Preparation Day of the Passover, and about
the sixth hour. And he said to the Jews, "Behold your King!"
15 But they cried out, "Away with *Him,* away with *Him!* Cru-
cify Him!" Pilate said to them, "Shall I crucify your King?"
The chief priests answered, [a]"We have no king but Caesar!"
16 [a]Then he delivered Him to them to be crucified. Then they
took Jesus and led *Him* away.[1]
17 [a]And He, bearing His cross, [b]went out to a place called *the
Place* of a Skull, which is called in Hebrew, Golgotha,
18 where they crucified Him, and [a]two others with Him, one
on either side, and Jesus in the center.
19 [a]Now Pilate wrote a title and put *it* on the cross. And the
writing was:

JESUS OF NAZARETH, THE KING OF THE JEWS.

20 Then many of the Jews read this title, for the place where
Jesus was crucified was near the city; and it was written in
Hebrew, Greek, *and* Latin.
21 Therefore the chief priests of the Jews said to Pilate, "Do
not write, 'The King of the Jews,' but, 'He said, "I am the King
of the Jews."'"
22 Pilate answered, "What I have written, I have written."
23 [a]Then the soldiers, when they had crucified Jesus, took
His garments and made four parts, to each soldier a part,
and also the tunic. Now the tunic was without seam, woven
from the top in one piece.
24 They said therefore among themselves, "Let us not tear

19:9 [a]Is. 53:7 19:11 [a][Luke 22:53] [b]Rom. 13:1 19:12 [a]Luke 23:2 19:13 [a]1 Sam. 15:24 19:14 [a]Matt. 27:62 19:15 [a][Gen. 49:10] 19:16 [a]Luke 23:24 [1]NU-Text omits *and led Him away.* 19:17 [a]Mark 15:21, 22 [b]Num. 15:36 19:18 [a]Is. 53:12 19:19 [a]Matt. 27:37 19:23 [a]Luke 23:34

it, but cast lots for it, whose it shall be," that the Scripture
might be fulfilled which says:

> [a]"They divided My garments among them,
> And for My clothing they cast lots."[1]

Therefore the soldiers did these things.
25 [a]Now there stood by the cross of Jesus His mother, and
His mother's sister, Mary the *wife* of [b]Clopas, and Mary Mag-
dalene.
26 When Jesus therefore saw His mother, and [a]the disciple
whom He loved standing by, He said to His mother, [b]"Woman,
behold your son!"
27 Then He said to the disciple, "Behold your mother!" And
from that hour that disciple took her [a]to his own *home*.
28 After this, Jesus, knowing[1] that all things were now ac-
complished, [a]that the Scripture might be fulfilled, said, "I
thirst!"
29 Now a vessel full of sour wine was sitting there; and [a]they
filled a sponge with sour wine, put *it* on hyssop, and put *it* to
His mouth.
30 So when Jesus had received the sour wine, He said, [a]"It
is finished!" And bowing His head, He gave up His spirit.
31 [a]Therefore, because it was the Preparation *Day*, [b]that
the bodies should not remain on the cross on the Sabbath
(for that Sabbath was a [c]high day), the Jews asked Pilate that
their legs might be broken, and *that* they might be taken
away.
32 Then the soldiers came and broke the legs of the first and
of the other who was crucified with Him.
33 But when they came to Jesus and saw that He was already
dead, they did not break His legs.
34 But one of the soldiers pierced His side with a spear, and
immediately [a]blood and water came out.
35 And he who has seen has testified, and his testimony is
[a]true; and he knows that he is telling the truth, so that you
may [b]believe.
36 For these things were done that the Scripture should be
fulfilled, [a]"Not *one* of His bones shall be broken."[1]
37 And again another Scripture says, [a]"They shall look on
Him whom they pierced."[1]
38 [a]After this, Joseph of Arimathea, being a disciple of Jesus,
but secretly, [b]for fear of the Jews, asked Pilate that he might

19:24 [a]Ps. 22:18 [1]Psalm 22:18 19:25 [a]Mark 15:40 [b]Luke 24:18 19:26 [a]John 13:23; 20:2; 21:7, 20, 24 [b]John 2:4 19:27 [a]John 1:11; 16:32 19:28 [a]Ps. 22:15 [1]M-Text reads *seeing.* 19:29 [a]Ps. 69:21; Matt. 27:48, 50 19:30 [a]John 17:4 19:31 [a]Mark 15:42 [b]Deut. 21:23 [c]Ex. 12:16; [Ex. 12:46; Num. 9:12]; Ps. 34:20 19:34 [a][1 John 5:6, 8] 19:35 [a]John 21:24 [b][John 20:31] 19:36 [a][Ex. 12:46; Num. 9:12]; Ps. 34:20 [1]Exodus 12:46; Numbers 9:12; Psalm 34:20 19:37 [a]Ps. 22:16, 17; Zech. 12:10; 13:6 [1]Zechariah 12:10 19:38 [a]Luke 23:50–56 [b][John 7:13; 9:22; 12:42]

take away the body of Jesus; and Pilate gave *him* permission.
So he came and took the body of Jesus.
39 And [a]Nicodemus, who at first came to Jesus by night,
also came, bringing a mixture of [b]myrrh and aloes, about a
hundred pounds.
40 Then they took the body of Jesus, and [a]bound it in strips
of linen with the spices, as the custom of the Jews is to bury.
41 Now in the place where He was crucified there was a gar-
den, and in the garden a new tomb in which no one had yet
been laid.
42 So [a]there they laid Jesus, [b]because of the Jews' Prepara-
tion *Day,* for the tomb was nearby.

19:39 [a]John 3:1, 2; 7:50 [b]Matt. 2:11 19:40 [a]John 20:5, 7
19:42 [a]Is. 53:9 [b]John 19:14, 31

JOHN 20

THE RISEN CHRIST

Among us at this day we have many persons who are like Thomas—dubious, demanding signs and tokens, suspicious, and ofttimes sad. There is a slight touch of Thomas in most of us. Notice, Thomas asked of our Lord what he ought not to have asked. He wanted to put our risen Lord to tests that were scarcely reverent to His sacred Person.

Admire his Master's patience with him. He fixes His eye upon the doubter and addresses Himself specially to him, yet not in words of reproach or anger. Jesus could bear with Thomas. To put his finger into the print of the nails and thrust his hand into His side was much more than any disciple had a right to ask of his divine Master—and yet see the condescension of Jesus! Our Lord always acts toward us not according to His own dignity but according to our necessity. Observe that Thomas was at once convinced. He said, "My Lord and my God!" This shows our Master's wisdom, that He indulged Thomas with such familiarity because He knew that though the demand was presumptuous, yet the act would work for his good.

---

1 Now the [a]first *day* of the week Mary Magdalene went to the
tomb early, while it was still dark, and saw *that* the [b]stone had
been taken away from the tomb.
2 Then she ran and came to Simon Peter, and to the [a]other
disciple, [b]whom Jesus loved, and said to them, "They have
taken away the Lord out of the tomb, and we do not know
where they have laid Him."
3 [a]Peter therefore went out, and the other disciple, and were
going to the tomb.
4 So they both ran together, and the other disciple outran
Peter and came to the tomb first.
5 And he, stooping down and looking in, saw [a]the linen cloths
lying *there;* yet he did not go in.
6 Then Simon Peter came, following him, and went into the
tomb; and he saw the linen cloths lying *there,*
7 and [a]the handkerchief that had been around His head, not
lying with the linen cloths, but folded together in a place by
itself.
8 Then the [a]other disciple, who came to the tomb first, went
in also; and he saw and believed.

20:1 [a]Matt. 28:1–8 [b]Matt. 27:60, 66; 28:2 20:2 [a]John 21:23, 24 [b]John 13:23; 19:26; 21:7, 20, 24 20:3 [a]Luke 24:12 20:5 [a]John 19:40 20:7 [a]John 11:44 20:8 [a]John 21:23, 24

9 For as yet they did not know the [a]Scripture, that He must
rise again from the dead.
10 Then the disciples went away again to their own homes.
11 [a]But Mary stood outside by the tomb weeping, and as she
wept she stooped down *and looked* into the tomb.
12 And she saw two angels in white sitting, one at the head
and the other at the feet, where the body of Jesus had lain.
13 Then they said to her, "Woman, why are you weeping?"
She said to them, "Because they have taken away my Lord,
and I do not know where they have laid Him."
14 [a]Now when she had said this, she turned around and saw
Jesus standing *there,* and [b]did not know that it was Jesus.
15 Jesus said to her, "Woman, why are you weeping? Whom
are you seeking?" She, supposing Him to be the gardener,
said to Him, "Sir, if You have carried Him away, tell me where
You have laid Him, and I will take Him away."
16 Jesus said to her, [a]"Mary!" She turned and said to Him,[1]
"Rabboni!" (which is to say, Teacher).
17 Jesus said to her, "Do not cling to Me, for I have not yet
[a]ascended to My Father; but go to [b]My brethren and say to
them, [c]'I am ascending to My Father and your Father, and *to*
[d]My God and your God.'"
18 [a]Mary Magdalene came and told the disciples that she had
seen the Lord,[1] and *that* He had spoken these things to her.
19 [a]Then, the same day at evening, being the first *day* of the
week, when the doors were shut where the disciples were as-
sembled,[1] for [b]fear of the Jews, Jesus came and stood in the
midst, and said to them, [c]"Peace *be* with you."
20 When He had said this, He [a]showed them *His* hands and
His side. [b]Then the disciples were glad when they saw the
Lord.
21 So Jesus said to them again, "Peace to you! [a]As the Father
has sent Me, I also send you."
22 And when He had said this, He breathed on *them,* and
said to them, "Receive the Holy Spirit.
23 [a]"If you forgive the sins of any, they are forgiven them;
if you retain the *sins* of any, they are retained."
24 Now Thomas, [a]called the Twin, one of the twelve, was not
with them when Jesus came.
25 The other disciples therefore said to him, "We have seen
the Lord." So he said to them, "Unless I see in His hands the
print of the nails, and put my finger into the print of the nails,
and put my hand into His side, I will not believe."

20:9[a]Ps. 16:10 20:11[a]Mark 16:5 20:14[a]Matt. 28:9 [b]John 21:4 20:16[a]John 10:3 [1]NU-Text adds *in Hebrew.* 20:17[a]Heb. 4:14 [b]Heb. 2:11 [c]John 16:28; 17:11 [d]Eph. 1:17 20:18[a]Luke 24:10, 23 [1]NU-Text reads *disciples, "I have seen the Lord,"* .... 20:19[a]Luke 24:36 [b]John 9:22; 19:38 [c]John 14:27; 16:33 [1]NU-Text omits *assembled.* 20:20[a]Acts 1:3 [b]John 16:20, 22 20:21[a]John 17:18, 19 20:23[a]Matt. 16:19; 18:18 20:24[a]John 11:16

26 And after eight days His disciples were again inside, and
Thomas with them. Jesus came, the doors being shut, and
stood in the midst, and said, "Peace to you!"
27 Then He said to Thomas, "Reach your finger here, and
look at My hands; and [a]reach your hand *here,* and put *it* into
My side. Do not be [b]unbelieving, but believing."
28 And Thomas answered and said to Him, "My Lord and
my God!"
29 Jesus said to him, "Thomas,[1] because you have seen Me,
you have believed. [a]Blessed *are* those who have not seen and
yet have believed."
30 And [a]truly Jesus did many other signs in the presence of
His disciples, which are not written in this book;
31 [a]but these are written that [b]you may believe that Jesus
[c]is the Christ, the Son of God, [d]and that believing you may
have life in His name.

20:27 [a]1 John 1:1 [b]Mark 16:14 20:29 [a]1 Pet. 1:8 [1]NU-Text and M-Text omit *Thomas.* 20:30 [a]John 21:25 20:31 [a]Luke 1:4 [b]1 John 5:13 [c]Luke 2:11 [d]John 3:15, 16; 5:24

JOHN 21

A BREAKFAST BY THE SEA

From this answer of Christ in verse 22, we learn that we are not to be curious as to what God is going to do with other people. One may think, *I am a poor, humble believer in Jesus. I have to struggle yet God graciously helps me, and I can tell of many instances of His delivering mercy.* Well, dear friend, God is greatly glorified by this testimony. But don't go on to ask about others who seem to have an easier time in life, *What is God going to do with them?* I can only reply, What is that to you? Follow Christ, and be not curious about others.

God has all sorts of stones in His temple, and some of them are of such a queer shape that I am glad the placing of them is not left to me, for I could not do it. I am thankful that God never sent me into the world to make people perfect but to use them as I find them; and I believe that He also uses them as He finds them and gradually prepares them for higher uses and for the place which He means them to occupy in His temple above. So do not wonder what this man will do, what that man will do, and what others around you will do, but do what you can for Christ yourself; and as for others, leave them to the Master.

---

1 After these things Jesus showed Himself again to the dis-
ciples at the [a]Sea of Tiberias, and in this way He showed *Him-
self*:
2 Simon Peter, [a]Thomas called the Twin, [b]Nathanael of [c]Cana
in Galilee, [d]the *sons* of Zebedee, and two others of His disci-
ples were together.
3 Simon Peter said to them, "I am going fishing." They said to
him, "We are going with you also." They went out and imme-
diately[1] got into the boat, and that night they caught nothing.
4 But when the morning had now come, Jesus stood on the
shore; yet the disciples [a]did not know that it was Jesus.
5 Then [a]Jesus said to them, "Children, have you any food?"
They answered Him, "No."
6 And He said to them, [a]"Cast the net on the right side of
the boat, and you will find *some*." So they cast, and now they
were not able to draw it in because of the multitude of fish.
7 Therefore [a]that disciple whom Jesus loved said to Peter,
"It is the Lord!" Now when Simon Peter heard that it was the
Lord, he put on *his* outer garment (for he had removed it),
and plunged into the sea.

21:1[a]John 6:1 21:2[a]John 20:24 [b]John 1:45–51 [c]John 2:1 [d]Matt. 4:21 21:3[1]NU-Text omits *immediately*. 21:4[a]John 20:14 21:5[a]Luke 24:41 21:6[a]Luke 5:4, 6, 7 21:7[a]John 13:23; 20:2

8 But the other disciples came in the little boat (for they were
not far from land, but about two hundred cubits), dragging
the net with fish.
9 Then, as soon as they had come to land, they saw a fire of
coals there, and fish laid on it, and bread.
10 Jesus said to them, "Bring some of the fish which you
have just caught."
11 Simon Peter went up and dragged the net to land, full of
large fish, one hundred and fifty-three; and although there
were so many, the net was not broken.
12 Jesus said to them, [a]"Come *and* eat breakfast." Yet none
of the disciples dared ask Him, "Who are You?"—knowing
that it was the Lord.
13 Jesus then came and took the bread and gave it to them,
and likewise the fish.
14 This *is* now [a]the third time Jesus showed Himself to His
disciples after He was raised from the dead.
15 So when they had eaten breakfast, Jesus said to Simon
Peter, "Simon, *son* of Jonah,[1] do you love Me more than these?"
He said to Him, "Yes, Lord; You know that I love You." He said
to him, [a]"Feed My lambs."
16 He said to him again a second time, "Simon, *son* of Jonah,[1]
do you love Me?" He said to Him, "Yes, Lord; You know that
I love You." [a]He said to him, "Tend My [b]sheep."
17 He said to him the third time, "Simon, *son* of Jonah,[1] do
you love Me?" Peter was grieved because He said to him the
third time, "Do you love Me?" And he said to Him, "Lord, [a]You
know all things; You know that I love You." Jesus said to him,
"Feed My sheep.
18 [a]"Most assuredly, I say to you, when you were younger,
you girded yourself and walked where you wished; but when
you are old, you will stretch out your hands, and another will
gird you and carry *you* where you do not wish."
19 This He spoke, signifying [a]by what death he would glori-
fy God. And when He had spoken this, He said to him, [b]"Fol-
low Me."
20 Then Peter, turning around, saw the disciple [a]whom Jesus
loved following, [b]who also had leaned on His breast at the
supper, and said, "Lord, who is the one who betrays You?"
21 Peter, seeing him, said to Jesus, "But Lord, what *about*
this man?"
22 Jesus said to him, "If I will that he remain [a]till I come,
what *is that* to you? You follow Me."
23 Then this saying went out among the brethren that this
disciple would not die. Yet Jesus did not say to him that he

21:12[a]Acts 10:41 21:14[a]John 20:19, 26 21:15[a]Acts 20:28 [1]NU-Text reads *John.* 21:16[a]Heb. 13:20 [b]Ps. 79:13 [1]NU-Text reads *John.* 21:17[a]John 2:24, 25; 16:30 [1]NU-Text reads *John.* 21:18[a]Acts 12:3, 4 21:19[a]2 Pet. 1:13, 14 [b][Matt. 4:19; 16:24] 21:20[a]John 13:23; 20:2 [b]John 13:25 21:22[a][Rev. 2:25; 3:11; 22:7, 20]

would not die, but, "If I will that he remain till I come, what
is that to you?"
24 This is the disciple who [a]testifies of these things, and
wrote these things; and we know that his testimony is true.
25 [a]And there are also many other things that Jesus did,
which if they were written one by one, [b]I suppose that even
the world itself could not contain the books that would be
written. Amen.

21:24[a] John 19:35 21:25[a] John 20:30 [b] Amos 7:10

BIBLIOGRAPHY

GOK Spurgeon, C.H., *The Gospel of the Kingdom: A Commentary on the Book of Matthew* (London: Passmore and Alabaster, 1893).

MTP Spurgeon, C.H., *The Metropolitan Tabernacle Pulpit Sermons vols. 7–63* (London: Passmore and Alabaster, 1861–1917).

NPSP Spurgeon, C.H., *The New Park Street Pulpit Sermons vols. 1–6* (London: Passmore and Alabaster, 1855–1860).

INDEX BY BOOK AND CHAPTER

Introduction

MTP, 596; *GOK*, v.

The Gospel According to Matthew

1. *GOK*, 1; *MTP*, 21:710.
2. *MTP*, 16:710.
3. *GOK*, 10.
4. *GOK*, 19.
5. *MTP*, 55:373–374.
6. *GOK*, 35.
7. *GOK*, 40–41.
8. *MTP*, 36:481.
9. *MTP*, 42:566.
10. *MTP*, 60:218.
11. *MTP*, 59:205, 207.
12. *MTP*, 25:628–629.
13. *MTP*, 60:77–78.
14. *MTP*, 51:111.
15. *MTP*, 44:556.
16. *GOK*, 131.
17. *MTP*, 61:2.
18. *GOK*, 153.
19. *NPSP*, 3:302.
20. *NPSP*, 2:185.
21. *GOK*, 183.
22. *MTP*, 17:93.
23. *MTP*, 45:326.
24. *MTP*, 58:224.
25. *NPSP*, 4:81.
26. *MTP*, 47:90.
27. *MTP*, 55:160.
28. *GOK*, 255–256.

The Gospel According to Mark

1. *MTP*, 30:86.
2. *MTP*, 23:170.
3. *MTP*, 26:181.
4. *MTP*, 27:330.
5. *MTP*, 43:113.
6. *MTP*, 16:326.
7. *MTP*, 22:458.
8. *MTP*, 22:458.
9. *MTP*, 37:506.
10. *NPSP*, 5:329–330.
11. *MTP*, 10:98.
12. *MTP*, 33:135.
13. *NPSP*, 6:301.
14. *MTP*, 28:74.
15. *MTP*, 41:590.
16. *MTP*, 61:147–148.

The Gospel According to Luke

1. *MTP*, 51:301–302.
2. *MTP*, 24:314.
3. *MTP*, 56:4.
4. *MTP*, 13:306.
5. *MTP*, 52:577–578.
6. *MTP*, 29:55.
7. *MTP*, 48:98.
8. *MTP*, 53:1.
9. *MTP*, 38:433–434.
10. *MTP*, 23:350.
11. *MTP*, 16:615.
12. *MTP*, 26:230.
13. *MTP*, 35:567.
14. *MTP*, 23:283.
15. *MTP*, 37:649–650.
16. *NPSP*, 3:285.
17. *MTP*, 51:531.
18. *MTP*, 15:99.
19. *MTP*, 58:314.
20. *MTP*, 31:542.
21. *MTP*, 42:602.
22. *MTP*, 54:411.
23. *MTP*, 63:157.
24. *MTP*, 28:217.

The Gospel According to John

1. *MTP*, 7:537–538.
2. *MTP*, 26:494.
3. *MTP*, 31:387.
4. *MTP*, 28:495.
5. *MTP*, 15:577.
6. *MTP*, 10:633.
7. *MTP*, 28:301–302.
8. *MTP*, 62:494.
9. *MTP*, 33:446.
10. *MTP*, 29:181.
11. *MTP*, 35:338.
12. *MTP*, 39:589.
13. *MTP*, 11:62.
14. *NPSP*, 6:229.
15. *MTP*, 27:593–594.
16. *MTP*, 24:614.
17. *MTP*, 32:148.
18. *MTP*, 12:650–651.
19. *MTP*, 40:26.
20. *MTP*, 34:713–714.
21. *MTP*, 53:445–446.

A Note Regarding the Type

This Bible was set in the Thomas Nelson NKJV Typeface, commissioned by Thomas Nelson Publishers and designed in Aarhus by Klaus Krogh and Heidi Rand Sørensen of 2K/DENMARK. The letterforms take inspiration from a distinctive typeface found in an early Thomas Nelson *Novum Testamentum*, printed in 1844 in Edinburgh—which in turn reflects the Scotch Roman typefaces created by the celebrated English punchcutter Richard Austin for the type foundry of William Miller, circa 1808–1813.

Just as the NKJV translation inherits the tradition and literary beauty of the King James Bible while updating the language for today's readers, so Thomas Nelson's custom NKJV font family builds on classic letterforms of the past while reflecting cutting-edge typographical design. The result is a type design that is at once beautiful and efficient, traditional and modern—ideal for presenting the sacred words of ancient Scripture to readers today.